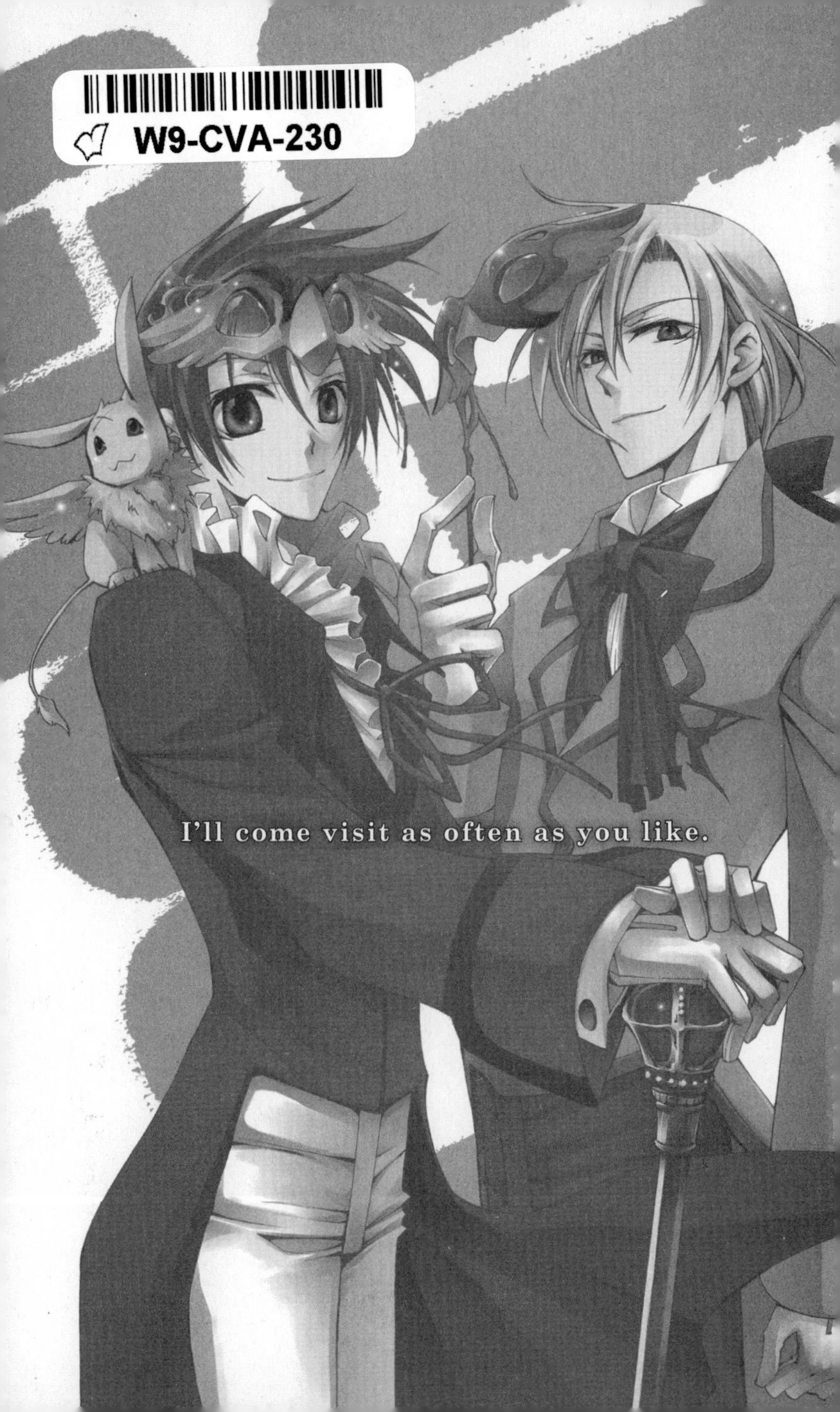
I'll come visit as often as you like.

CONTENTS

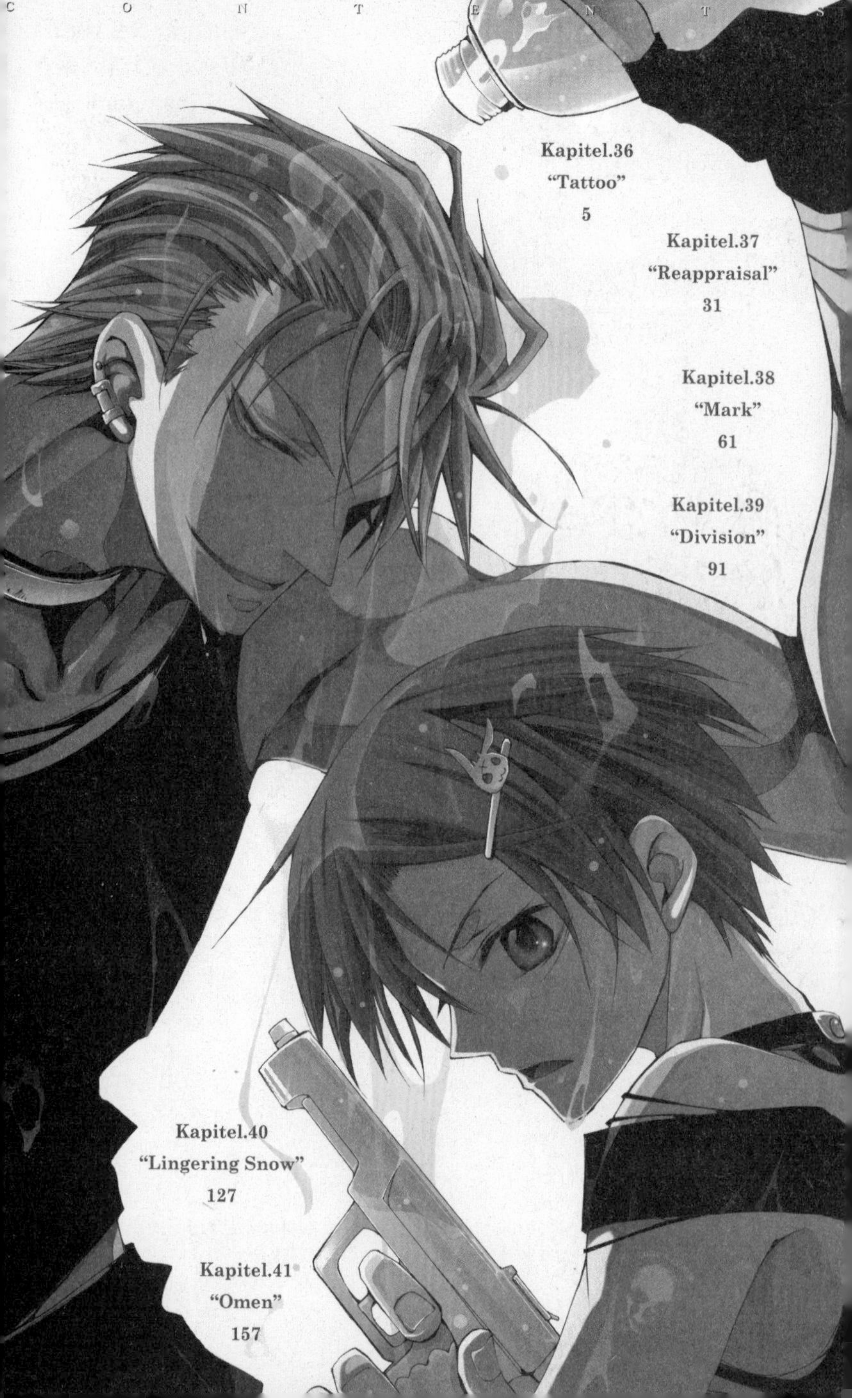

07-GHOST

Yuki Amemiya
Yukino Ichihara

7

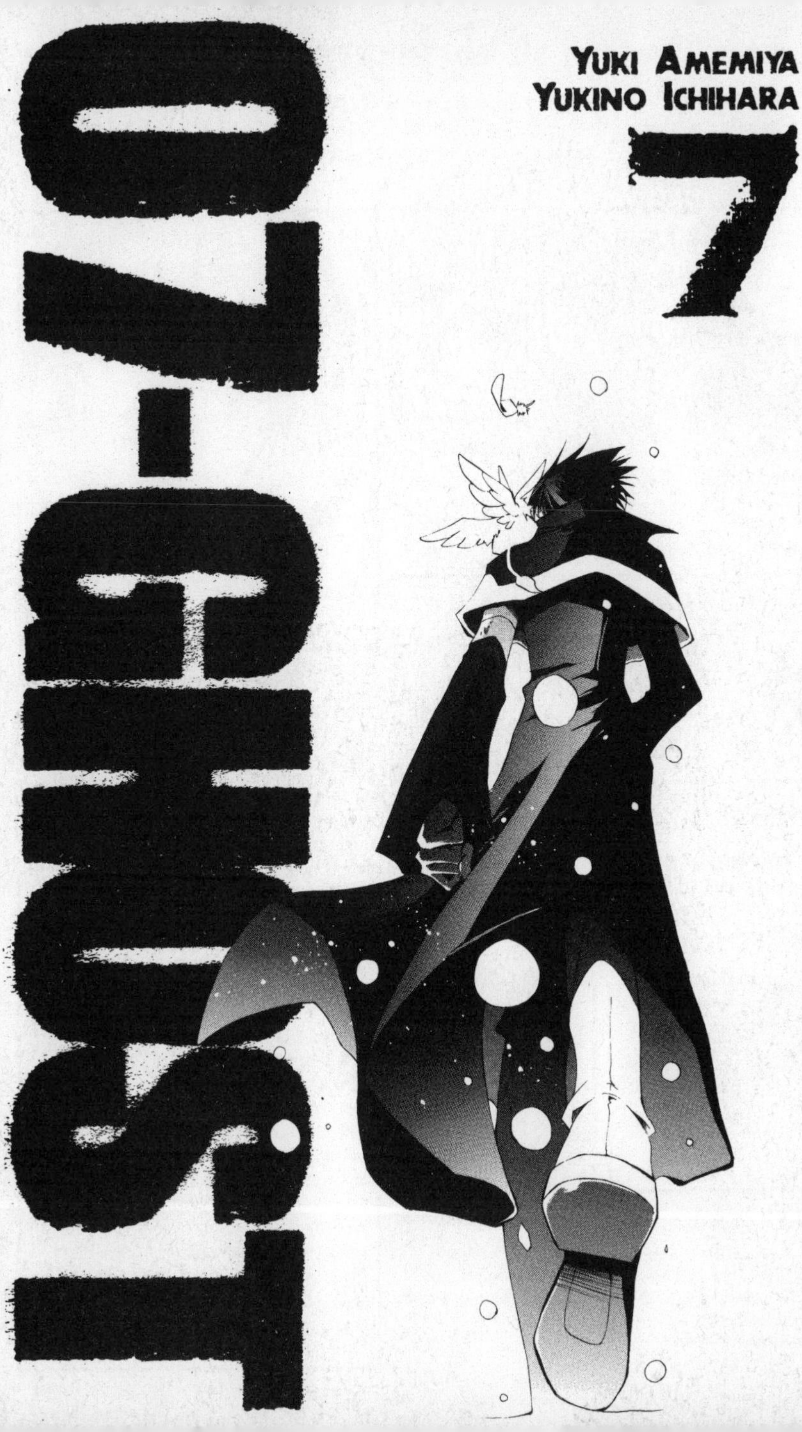

07 GHOST

Characters

One thousand years ago, two equally powerful nations coexisted. One was the Barsburg Empire, protected by the Eye of Rafael. The other was the Raggs Kingdom, protected by the Eye of Mikael. Now that the Raggs Kingdom has been destroyed, things have changed...

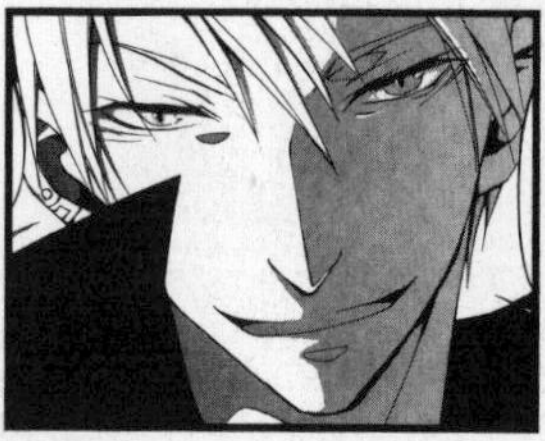

Frau

Bishop who saved Teito when he was fleeing from the academy and now watches over him. He is Zehel of the Seven Ghosts.

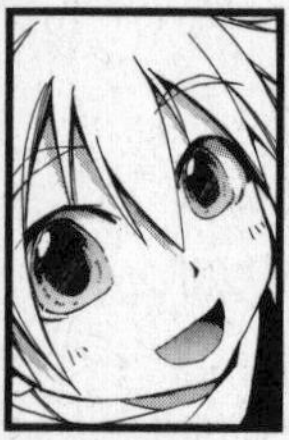

Capella

Child Teito saved from a slave trader.

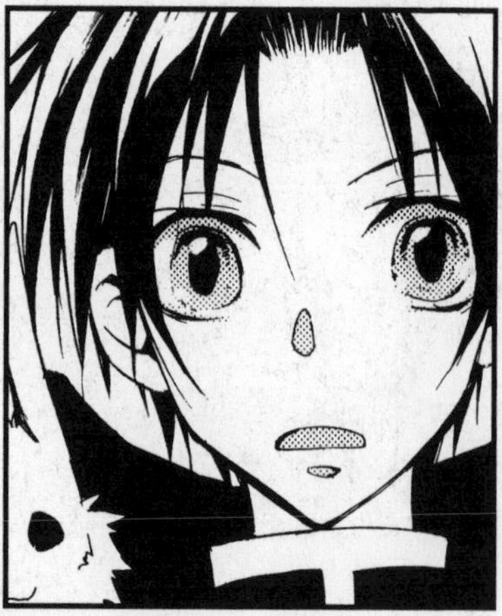

Teito Klein

Born a prince of Raggs, Teito was stripped of his memories and raised as a soldier by the military academy's chairman. He harbored the Eye of Mikael (an artifact said to bring either the world's salvation or destruction) in his right hand until the Black Hawks stole it. Currently Frau's apprentice.

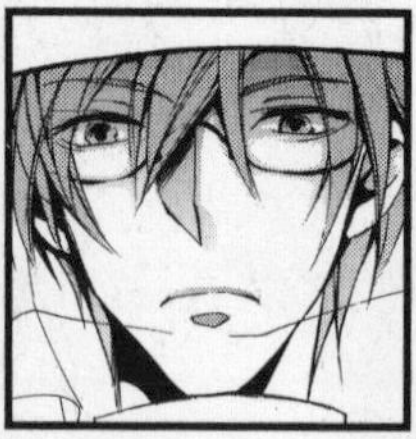

Castor

Bishop who can manipulate puppets. He watches over Teito and is Fest of the Seven Ghosts.

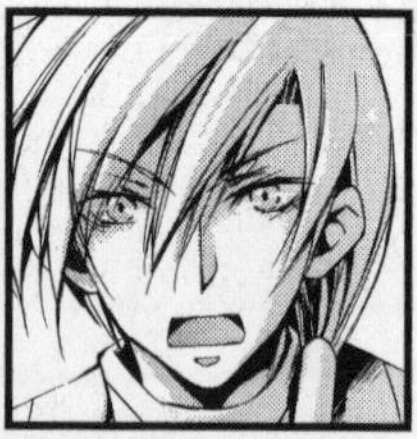

Hakuren

An apprentice bishop from the prestigious Oak family. He's Teito's friend, Castor's apprentice and an ardent admirer of Frau.

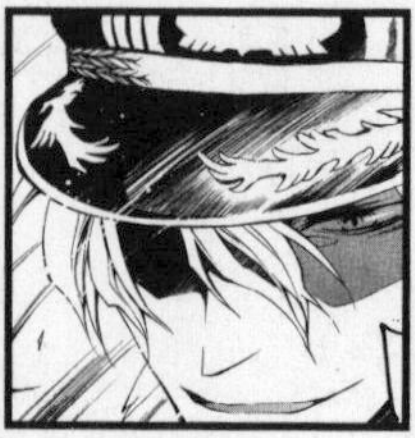

Ayanami

Imperial Army's Chief of Staff. Thief of the Eye of Mikael, and possibly responsible for the king of Raggs' death.

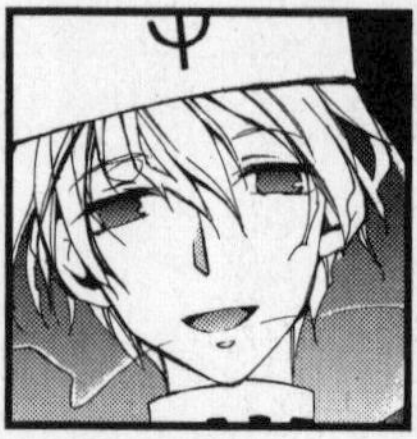

Labrador

Flower-loving bishop with the power of prophecy. One of the Seven Ghosts.

Story

Teito is a student at the Barsburg Empire's military academy until the day he discovers that his father was the king of Raggs, the ruler of a kingdom the Barsburg Empire destroyed. Teito receives sanctuary from the Barsburg Church, but loses his best friend Mikage, who Ayanami controls like a puppet to get at Teito. As a first step in avenging Mikage's death, Teito becomes an apprentice bishop to obtain special privileges. He then embarks on a journey to the "Land of Seele," which holds the key to his past and the truth about the fall of Raggs. In order to gain his first Cursed Ticket to Seele, he exposes the corruption of District 6's God House. Now it's on to District 5!

Kapitel.36 “Tattoo”

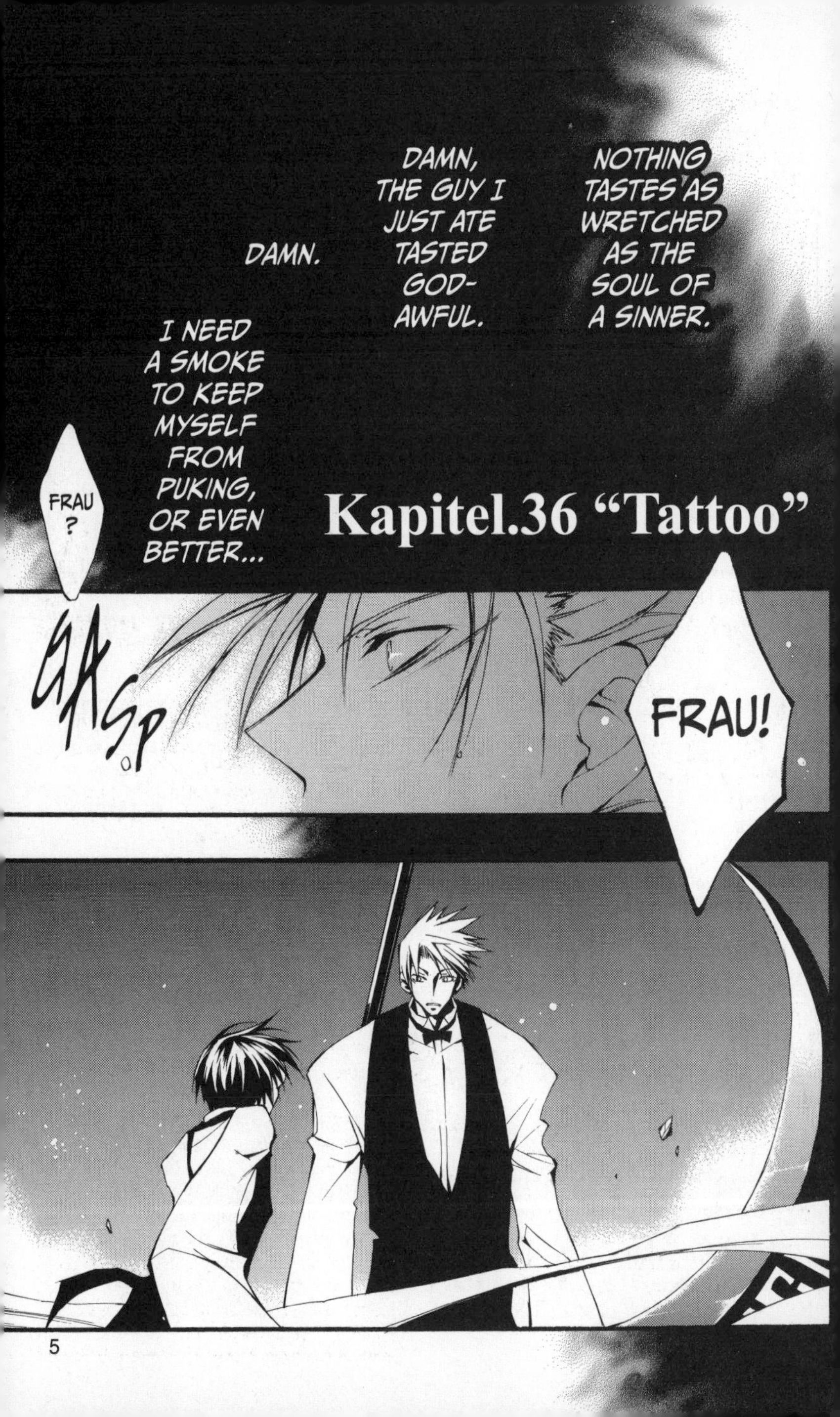

NOTHING TASTES AS WRETCHED AS THE SOUL OF A SINNER.
DAMN, THE GUY I JUST ATE TASTED GOD-AWFUL.
DAMN.
I NEED A SMOKE TO KEEP MYSELF FROM PUKING, OR EVEN BETTER...
FRAU?
FRAU!
GASP

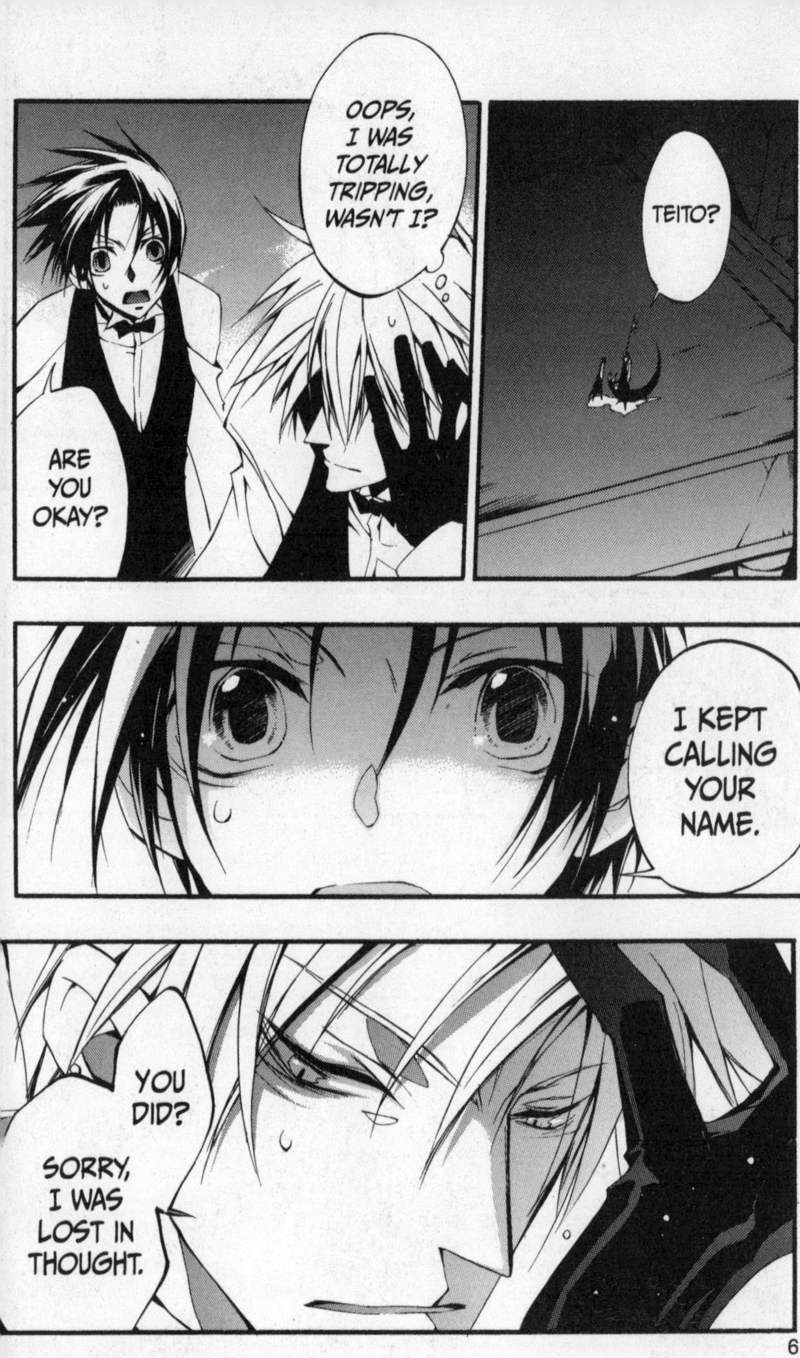
TEITO?
OOPS, I WAS TOTALLY TRIPPING, WASN'T I?
ARE YOU OKAY?
I KEPT CALLING YOUR NAME.
YOU DID?
SORRY, I WAS LOST IN THOUGHT.

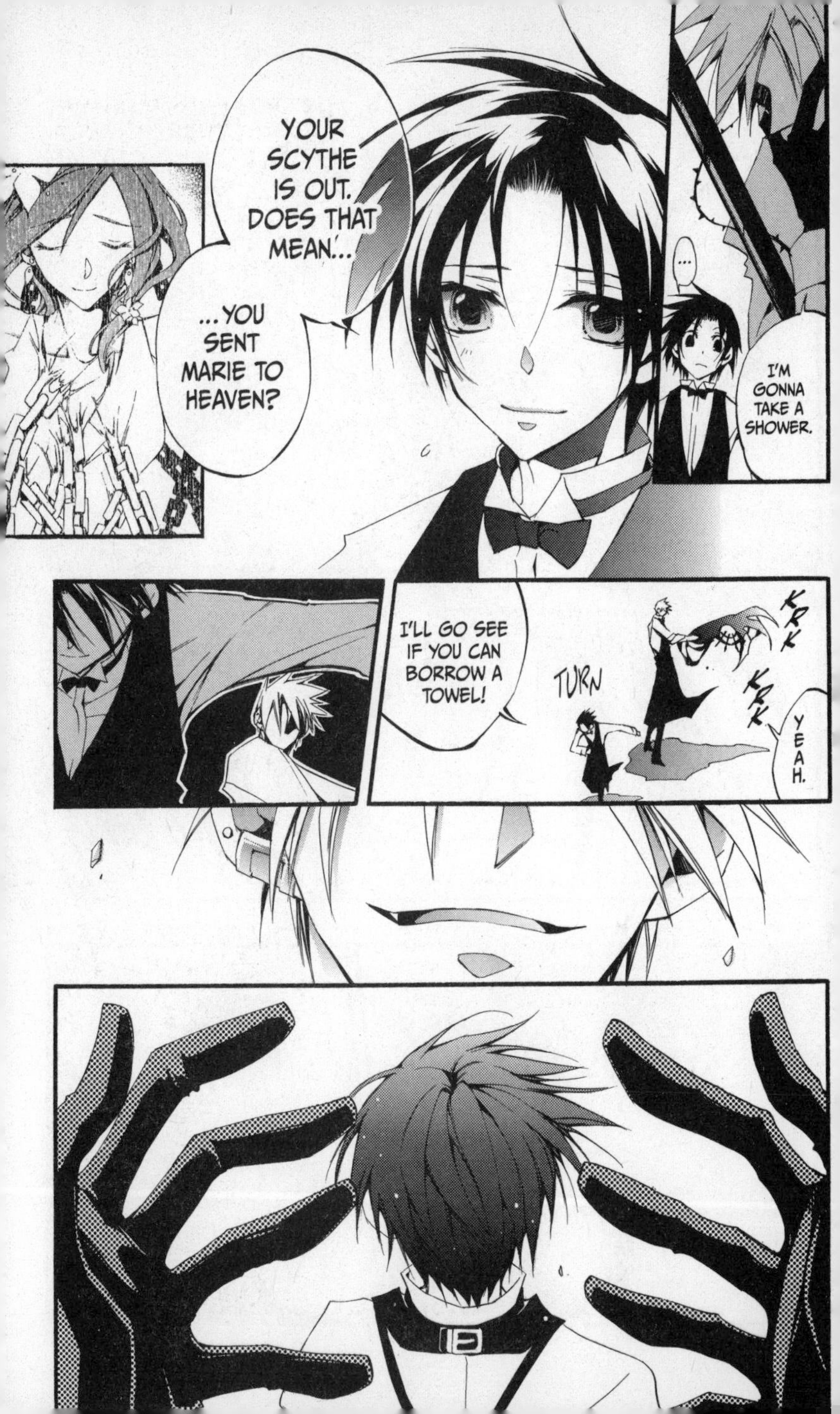
...
I'M GONNA TAKE A SHOWER.
YOUR SCYTHE IS OUT. DOES THAT MEAN...
...YOU SENT MARIE TO HEAVEN?
KRK
KRK
I'LL GO SEE IF YOU CAN BORROW A TOWEL!
YEAH.
TURN

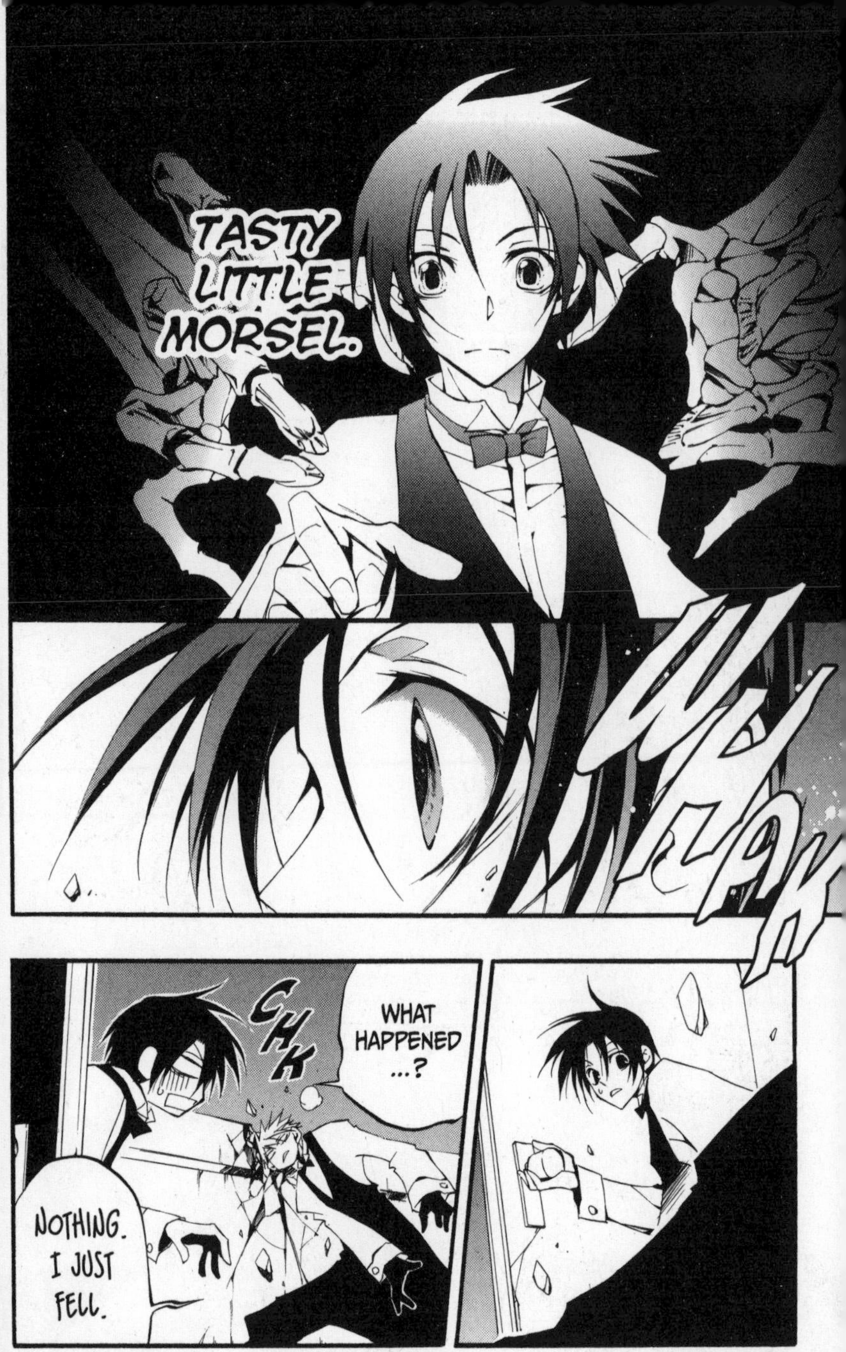
TASTY LITTLE MORSEL.
WHAT HAPPENED ...?
CHK
NOTHING. I JUST FELL.

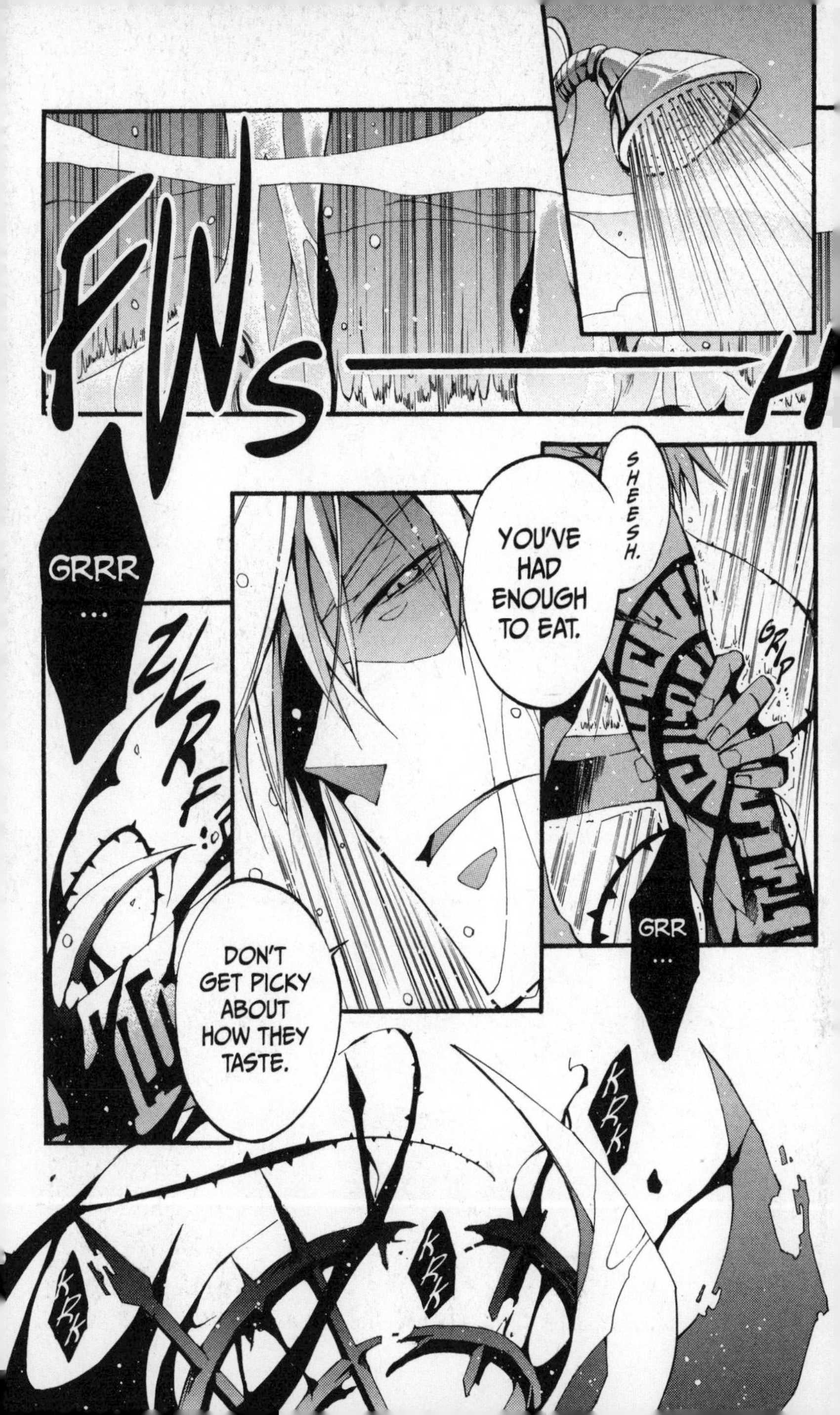
FWSH
SHEEESH.
YOU'VE HAD ENOUGH TO EAT.
GRIP
GRR...
DON'T GET PICKY ABOUT HOW THEY TASTE.
GRRR...
ZLRF
KRK
KRK
KRK

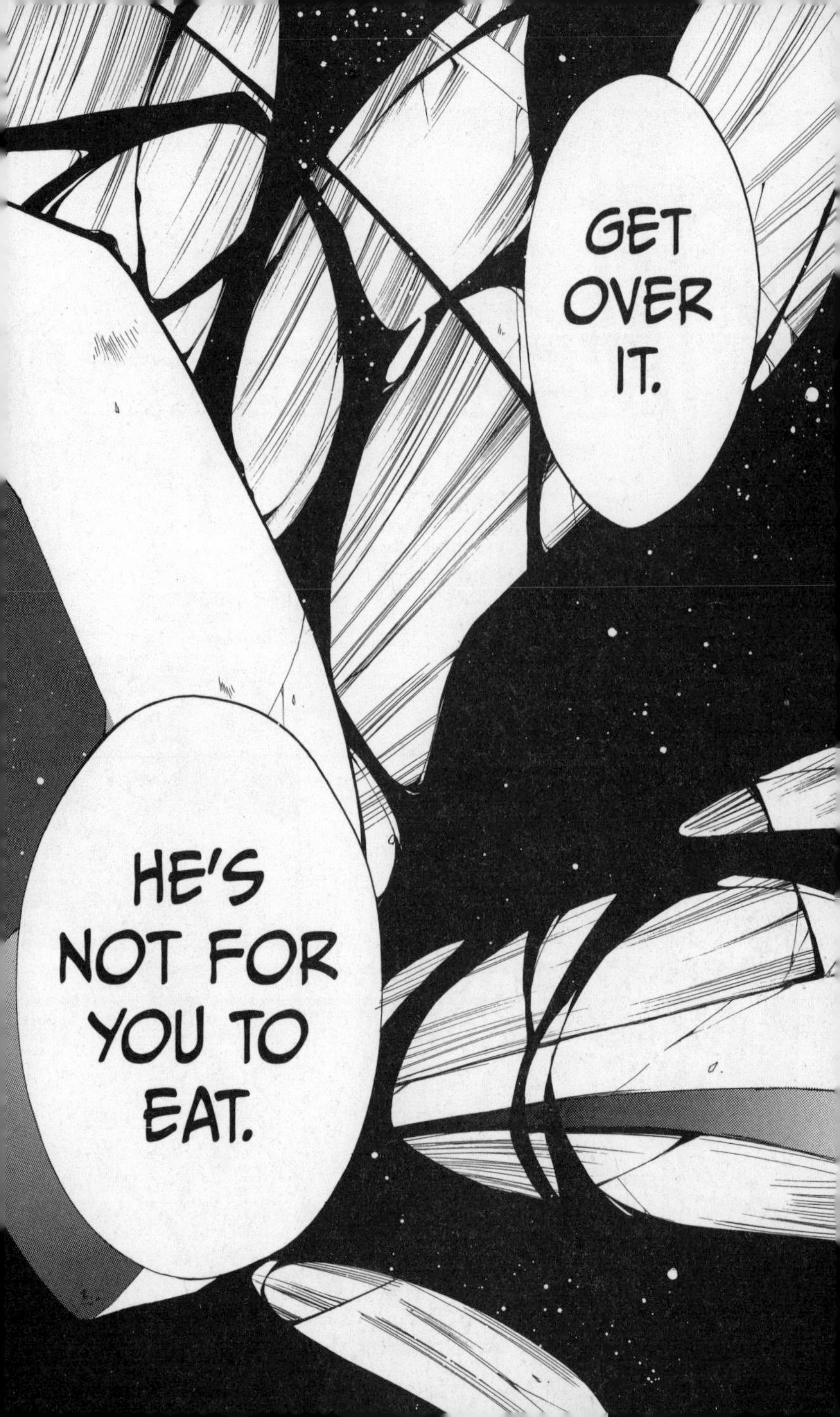
GET OVER IT.
HE'S NOT FOR YOU TO EAT.

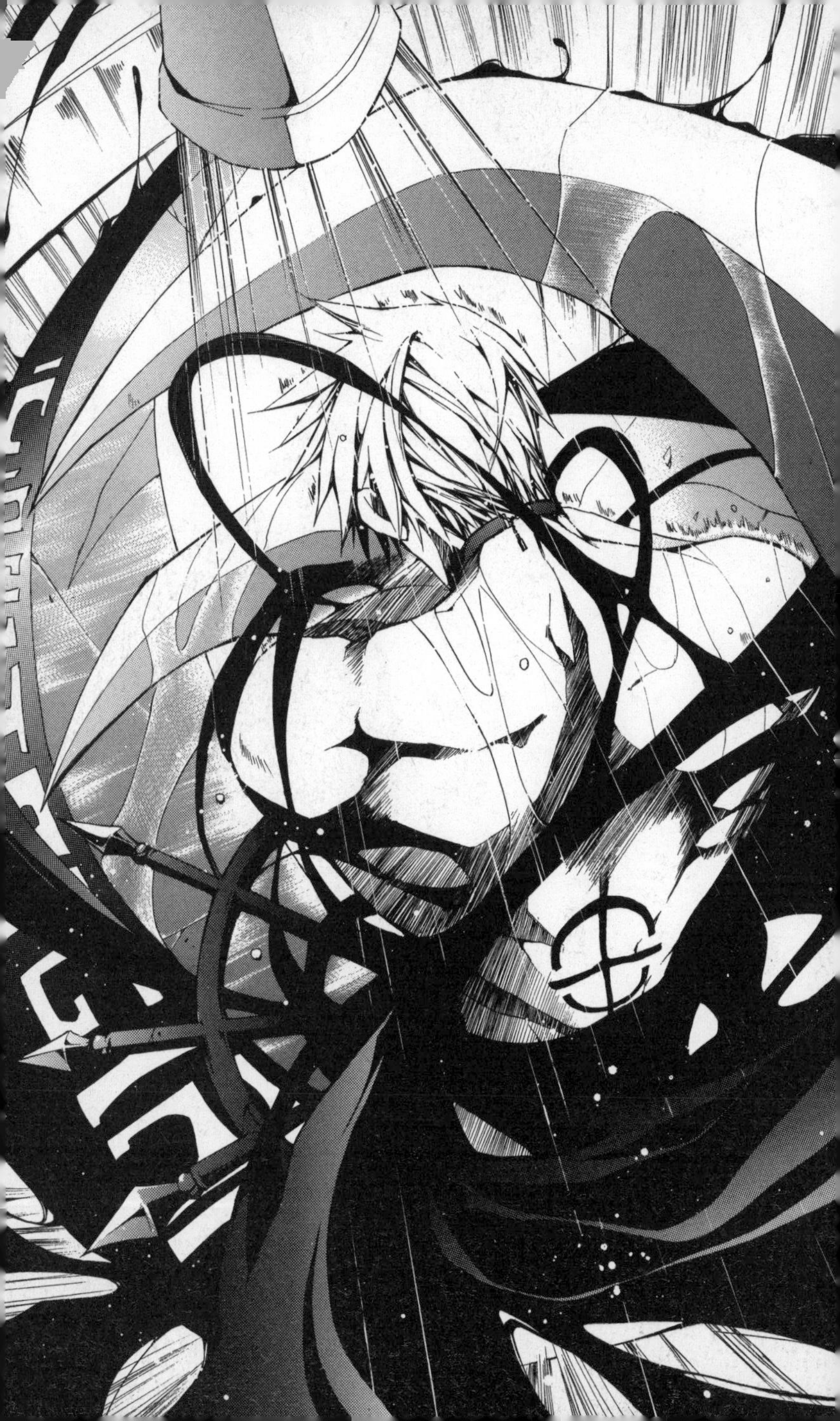

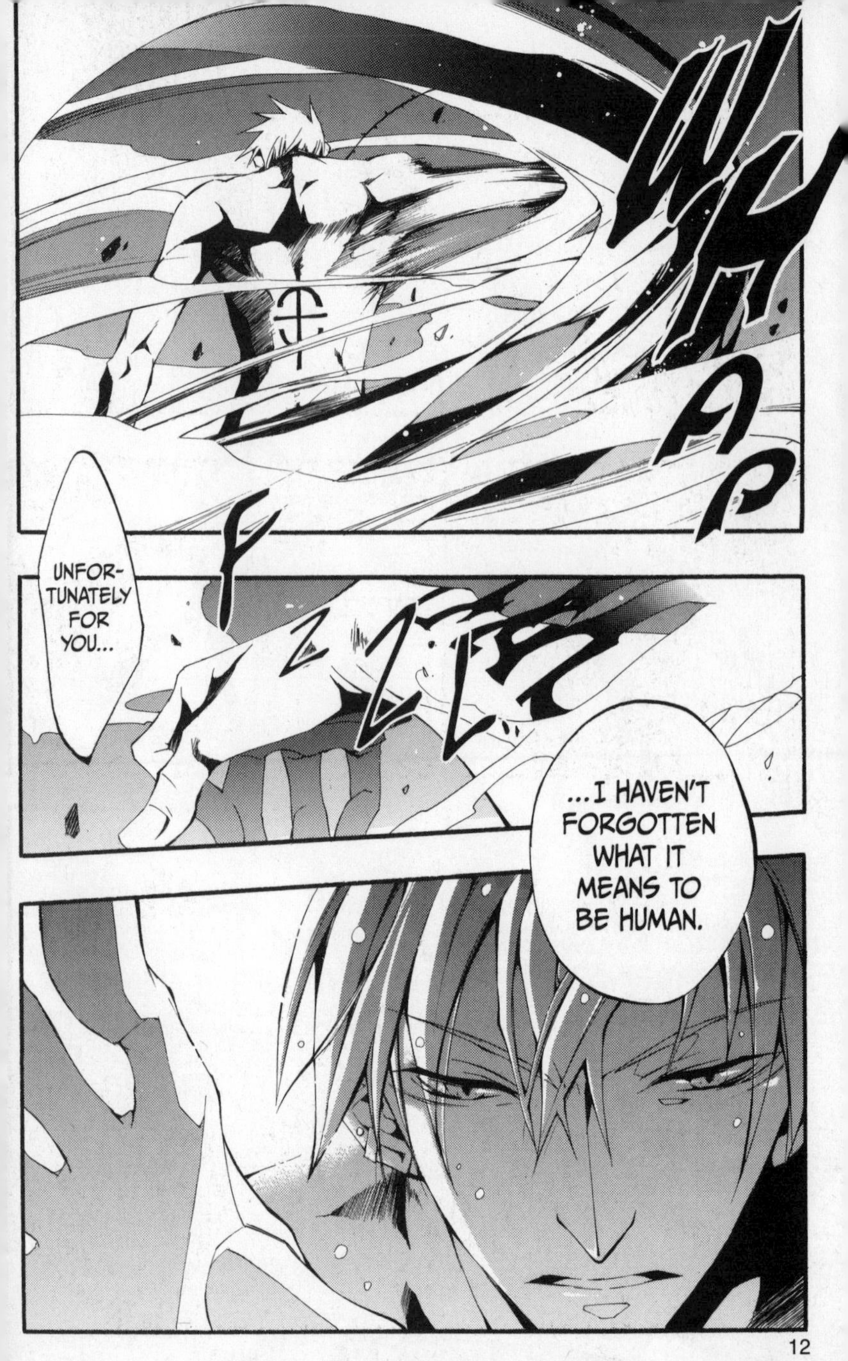
UNFOR-TUNATELY FOR YOU...
...I HAVEN'T FORGOTTEN WHAT IT MEANS TO BE HUMAN.

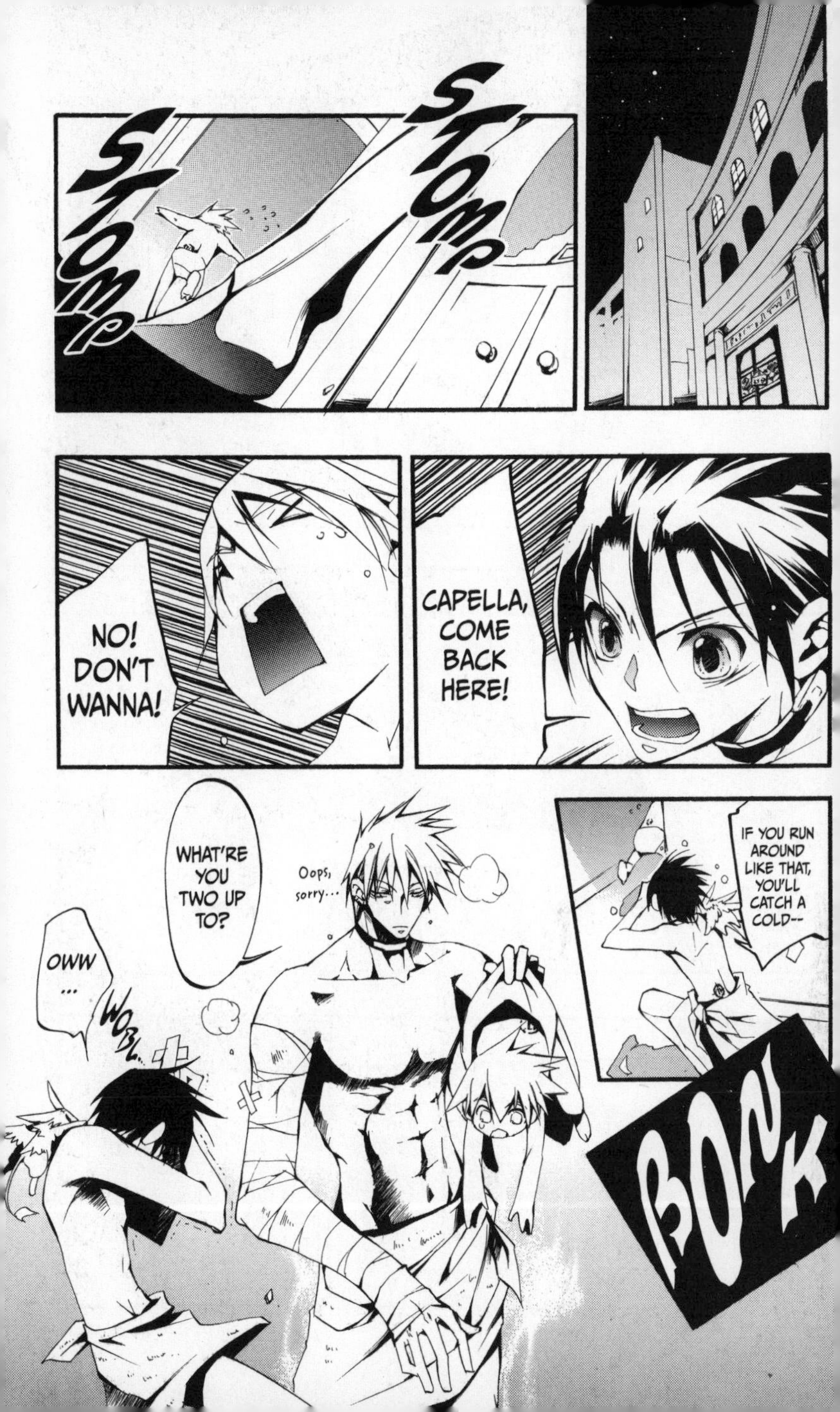
STOMP STOMP
CAPELLA, COME BACK HERE!
NO! DON'T WANNA!
IF YOU RUN AROUND LIKE THAT, YOU'LL CATCH A COLD--
BONK
WHAT'RE YOU TWO UP TO?
Oops, sorry...
OWW ...
WOBBL...

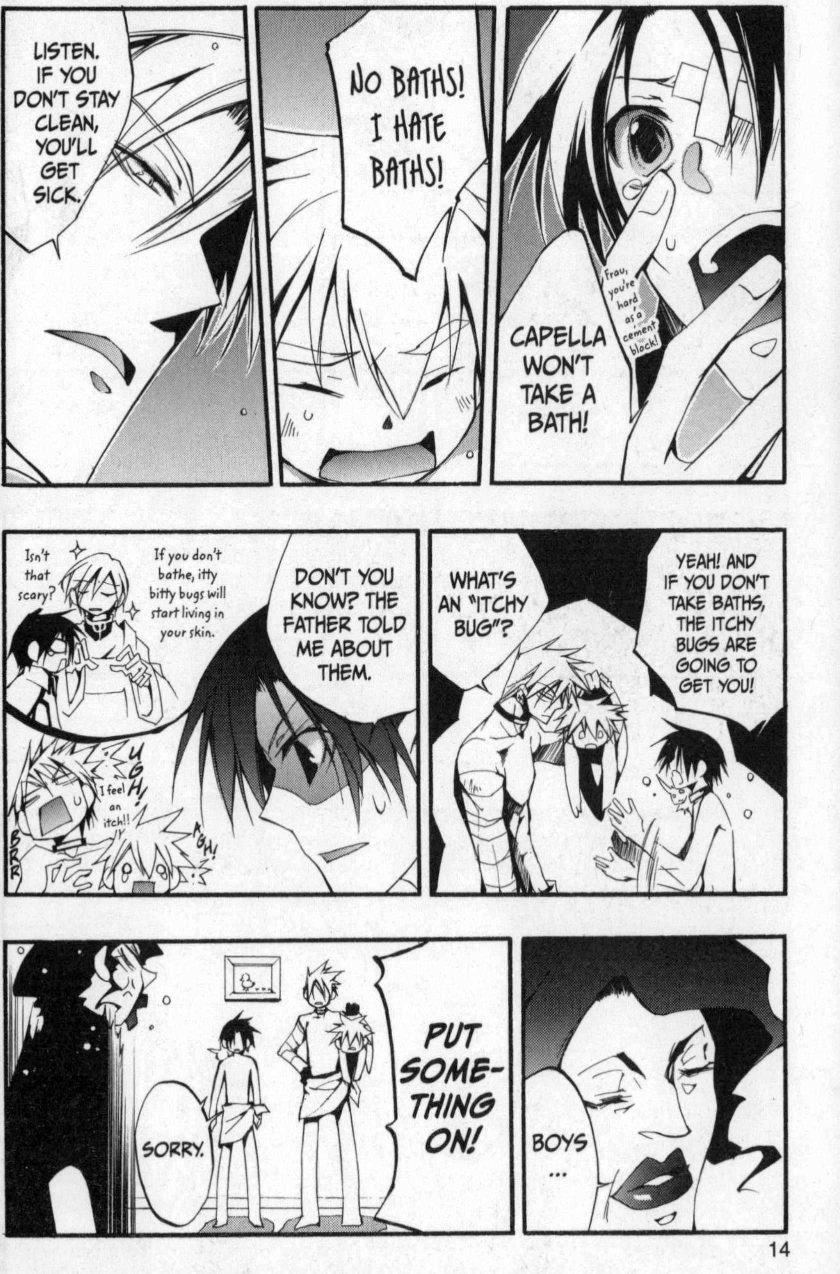
Frau, you're hard as a cement block!
CAPELLA WON'T TAKE A BATH!
NO BATHS! I HATE BATHS!
LISTEN. IF YOU DON'T STAY CLEAN, YOU'LL GET SICK.
YEAH! AND IF YOU DON'T TAKE BATHS, THE ITCHY BUGS ARE GOING TO GET YOU!
WHAT'S AN "ITCHY BUG"?
DON'T YOU KNOW? THE FATHER TOLD ME ABOUT THEM.
If you don't bathe, itty bitty bugs will start living in your skin.
Isn't that scary?
UGH!
I feel an itch!!
AGH!
BRR
BOYS ...
PUT SOME-THING ON!
SORRY.

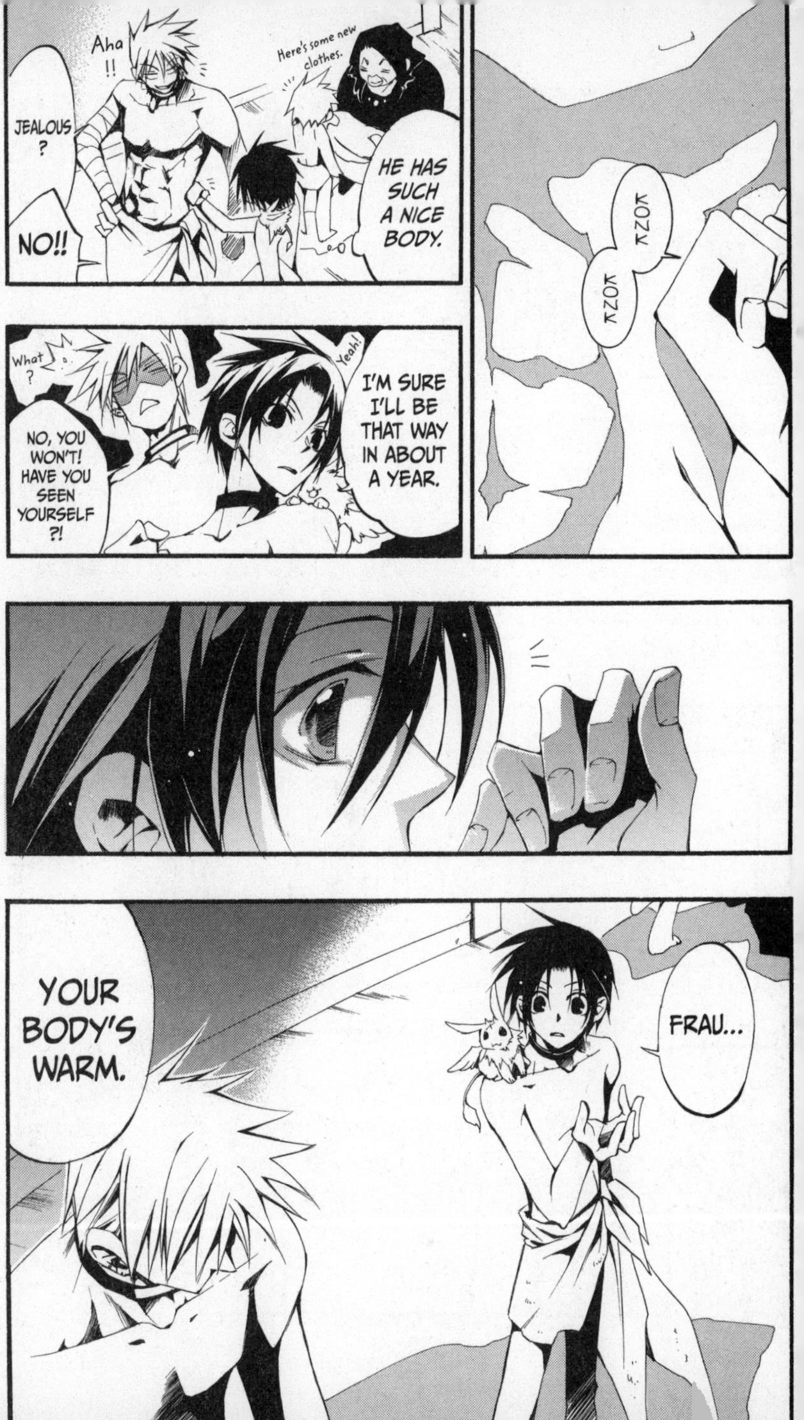
KONK
KONK
Here's some new clothes.
HE HAS SUCH A NICE BODY.
Aha !!
JEALOUS ?
NO!!
Yeah!
I'M SURE I'LL BE THAT WAY IN ABOUT A YEAR.
What ?
NO, YOU WON'T! HAVE YOU SEEN YOURSELF ?!
FRAU...
YOUR BODY'S WARM.

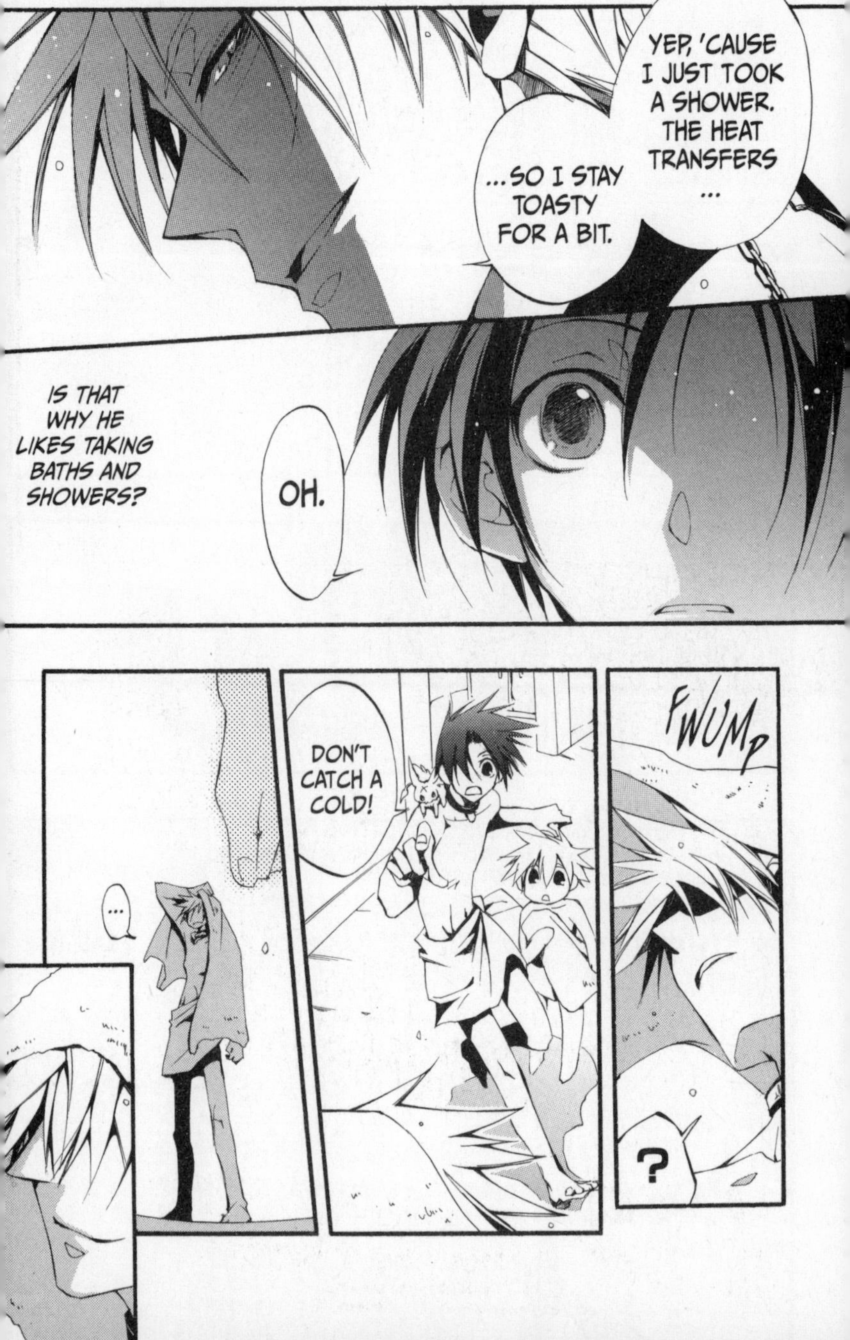
YEP, 'CAUSE I JUST TOOK A SHOWER. THE HEAT TRANSFERS ...
...SO I STAY TOASTY FOR A BIT.
OH.
IS THAT WHY HE LIKES TAKING BATHS AND SHOWERS?
FWUMP
?
DON'T CATCH A COLD!
...

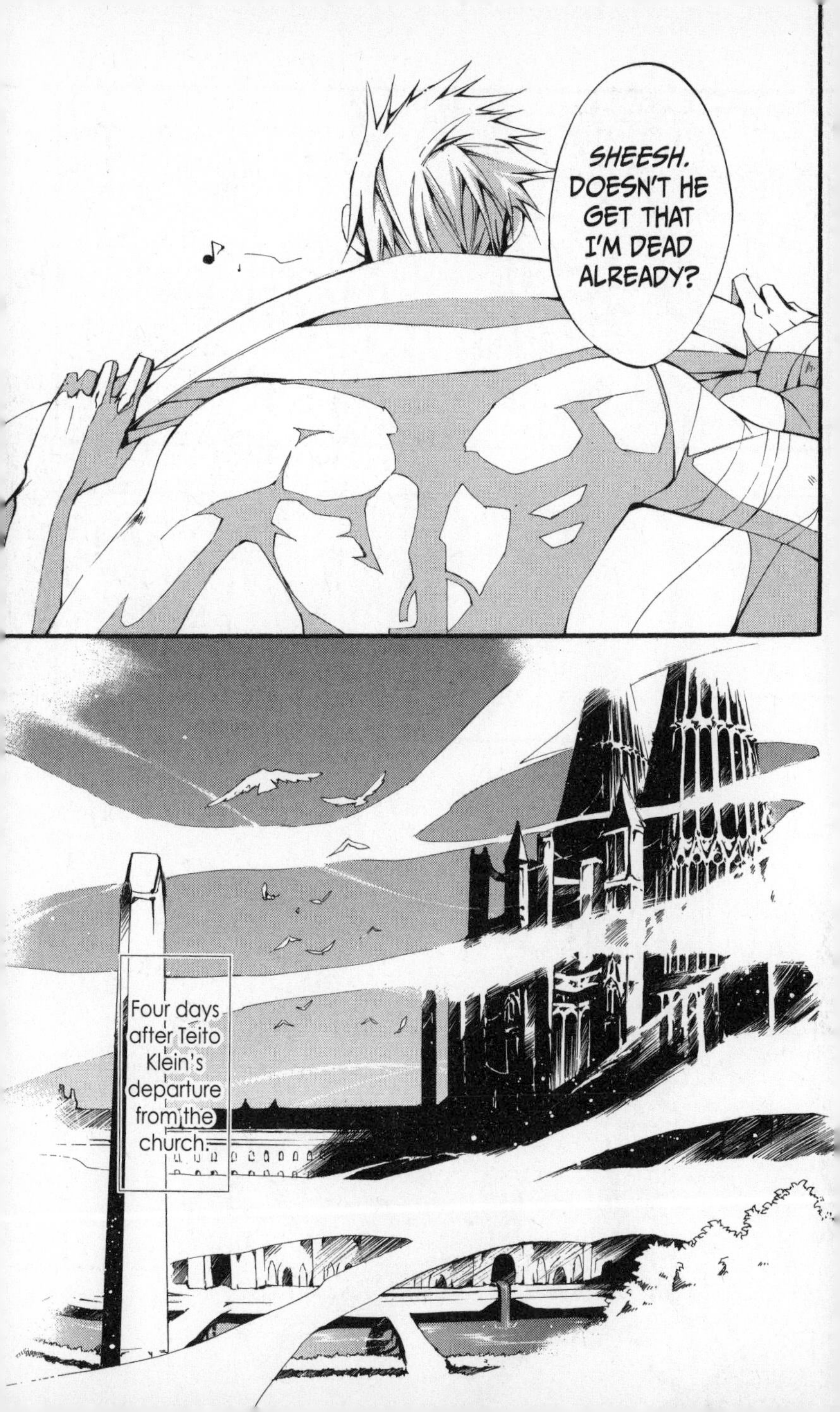
SHEESH. DOESN'T HE GET THAT I'M DEAD ALREADY?
Four days after Teito Klein's departure from the church.

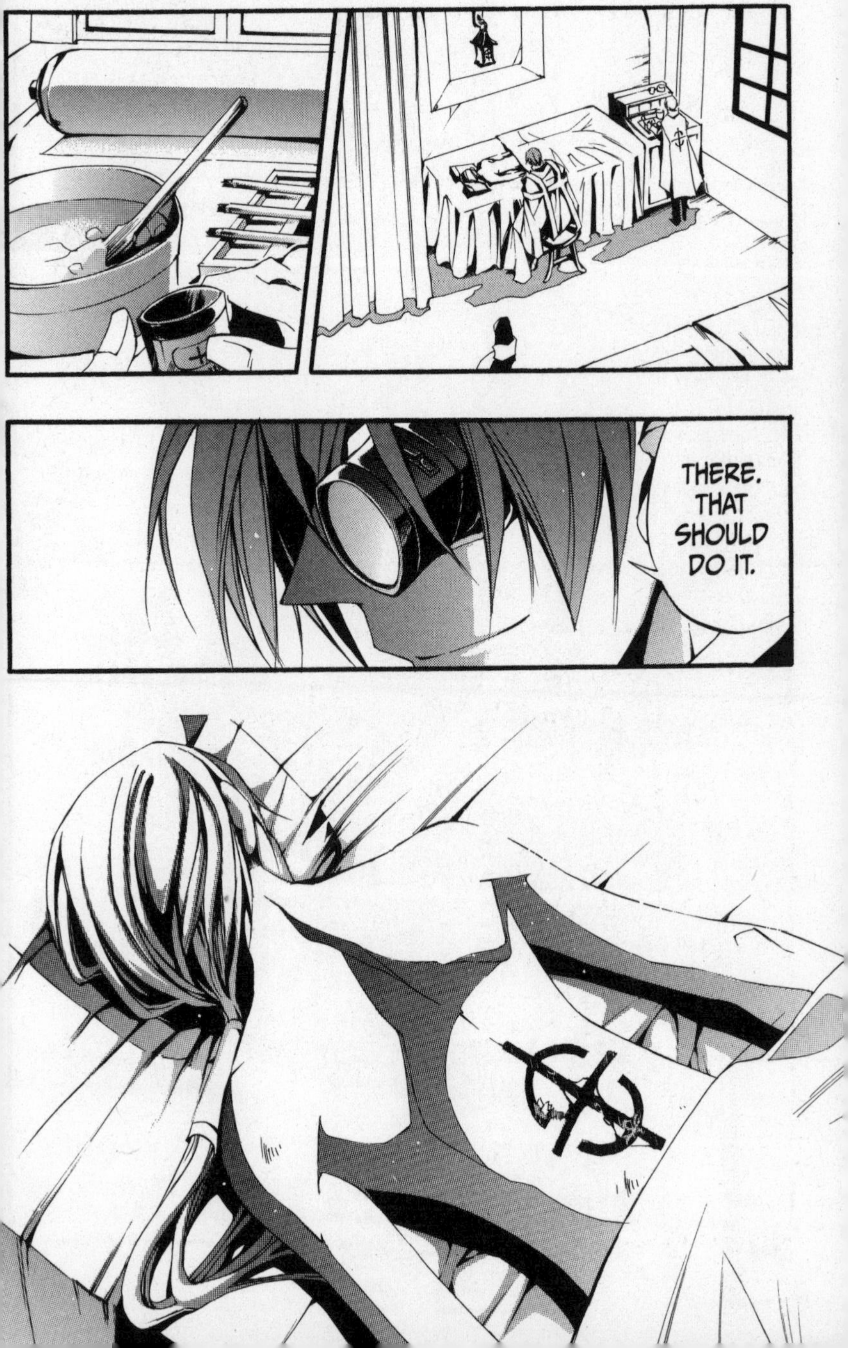
THERE. THAT SHOULD DO IT.

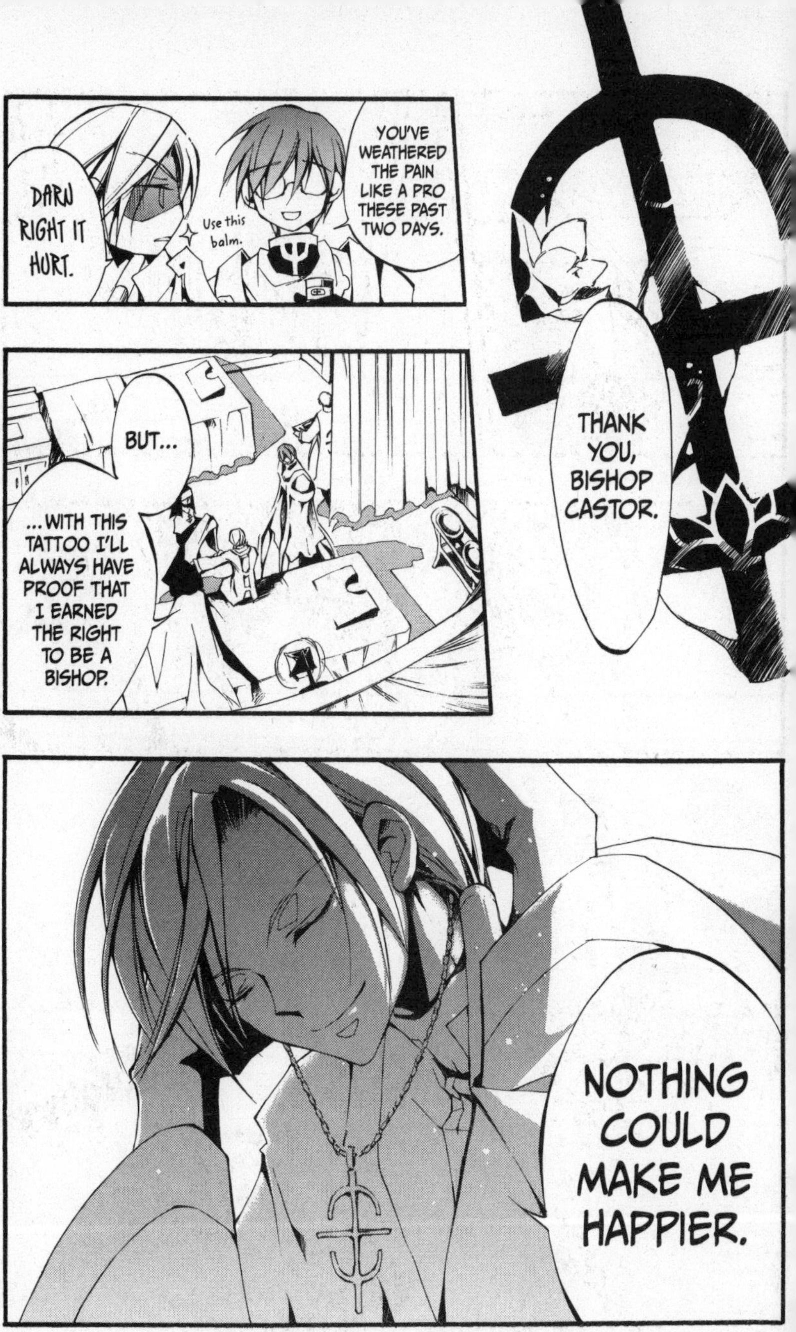
THANK YOU, BISHOP CASTOR.
YOU'VE WEATHERED THE PAIN LIKE A PRO THESE PAST TWO DAYS.
Use this balm.
DARN RIGHT IT HURT.
BUT...
...WITH THIS TATTOO I'LL ALWAYS HAVE PROOF THAT I EARNED THE RIGHT TO BE A BISHOP.
NOTHING COULD MAKE ME HAPPIER.

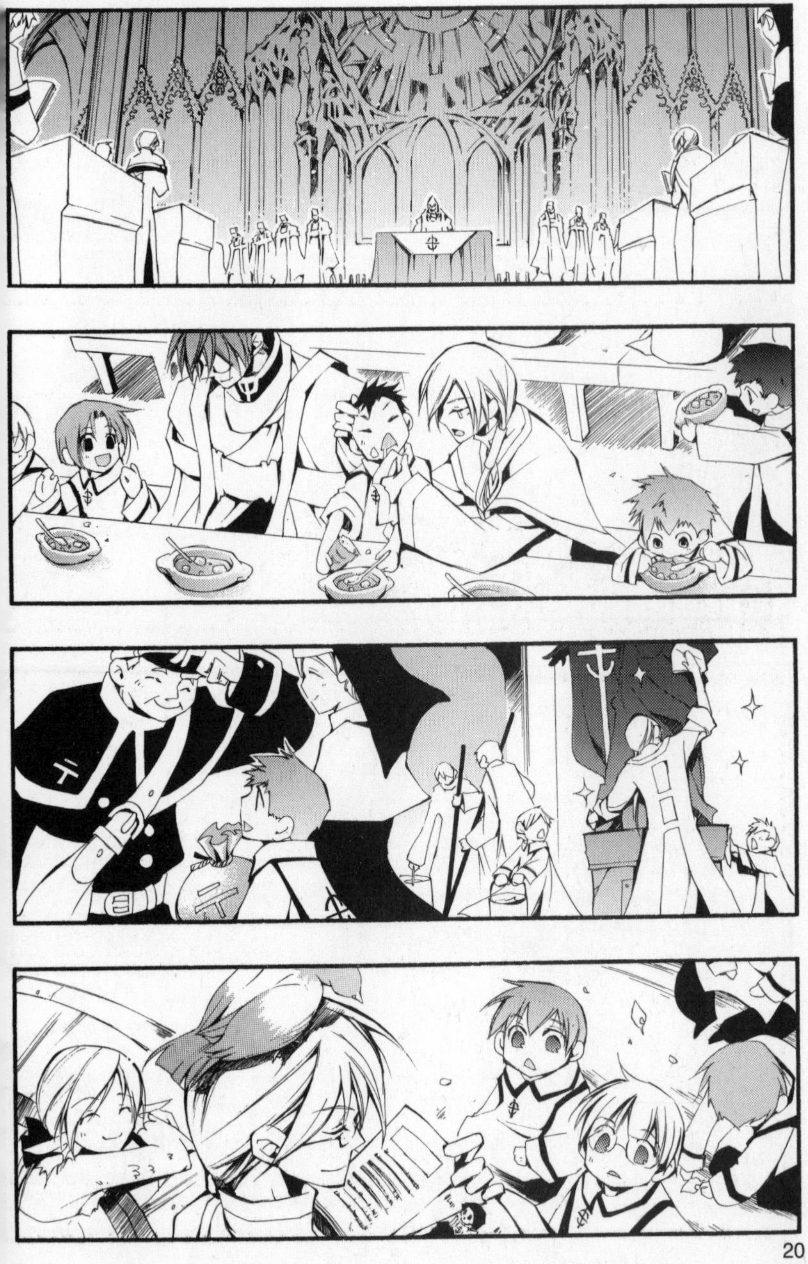

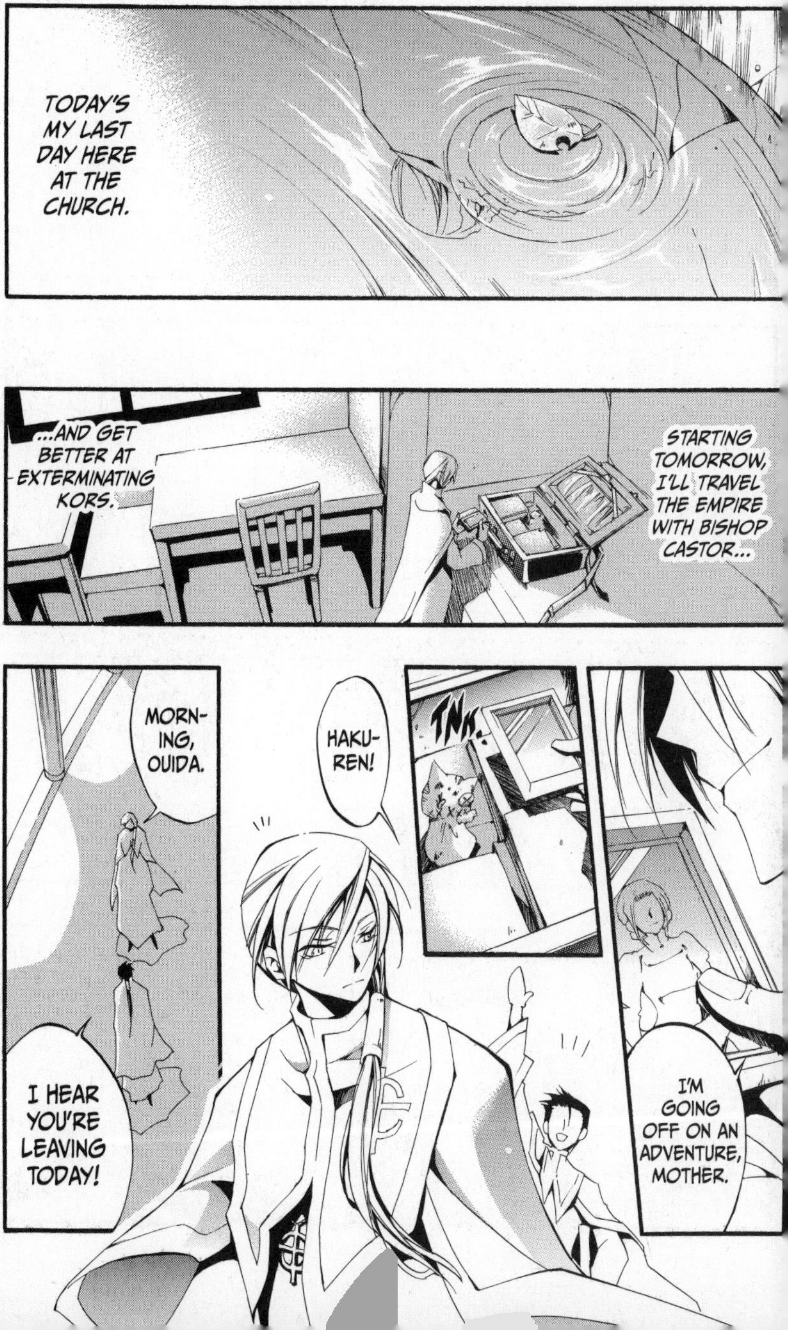
TODAY'S MY LAST DAY HERE AT THE CHURCH.
STARTING TOMORROW, I'LL TRAVEL THE EMPIRE WITH BISHOP CASTOR...
...AND GET BETTER AT EXTERMINATING KORS.
I'M GOING OFF ON AN ADVENTURE, MOTHER.
TNK
HAKU-REN!
MORN-ING, OUIDA.
I HEAR YOU'RE LEAVING TODAY!

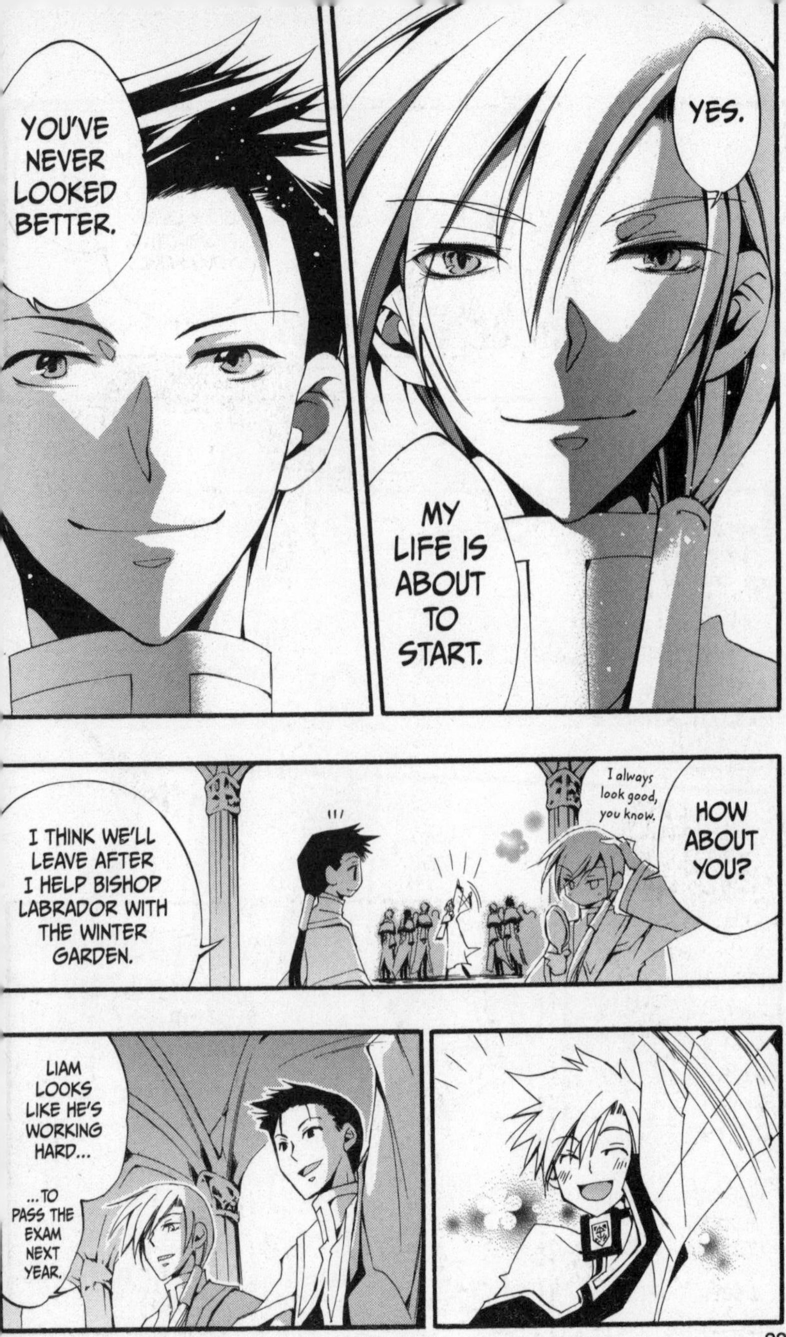
YES.
MY LIFE IS ABOUT TO START.
YOU'VE NEVER LOOKED BETTER.
HOW ABOUT YOU?
I always look good, you know.
I THINK WE'LL LEAVE AFTER I HELP BISHOP LABRADOR WITH THE WINTER GARDEN.
LIAM LOOKS LIKE HE'S WORKING HARD...
...TO PASS THE EXAM NEXT YEAR.

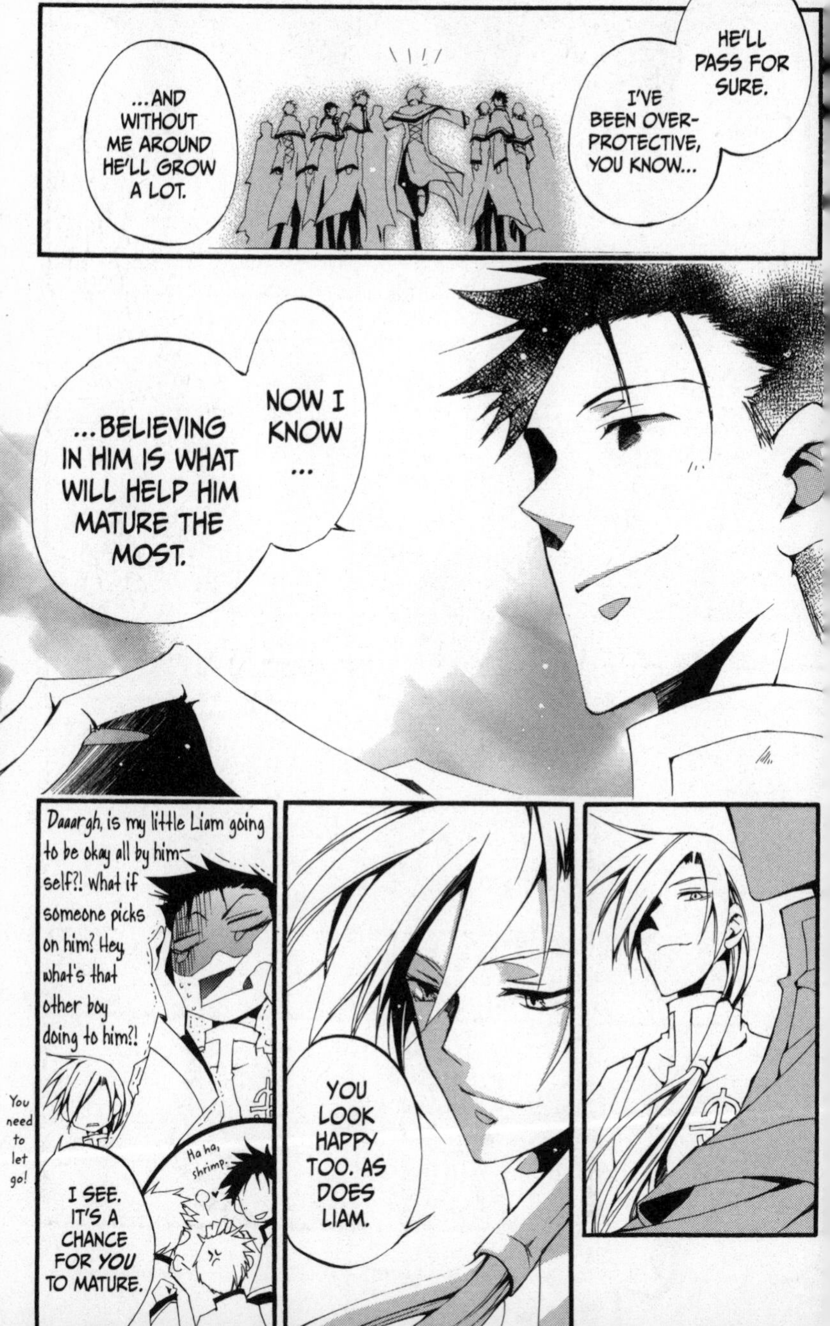
HE'LL PASS FOR SURE.
I'VE BEEN OVER-PROTECTIVE, YOU KNOW...
...AND WITHOUT ME AROUND HE'LL GROW A LOT.
NOW I KNOW...
...BELIEVING IN HIM IS WHAT WILL HELP HIM MATURE THE MOST.
YOU LOOK HAPPY TOO. AS DOES LIAM.
Daaargh, is my little Liam going to be okay all by him-self?! What if someone picks on him? Hey, what's that other boy doing to him?!
You need to let go!
Ha ha, shrimp.
I SEE. IT'S A CHANCE FOR YOU TO MATURE.

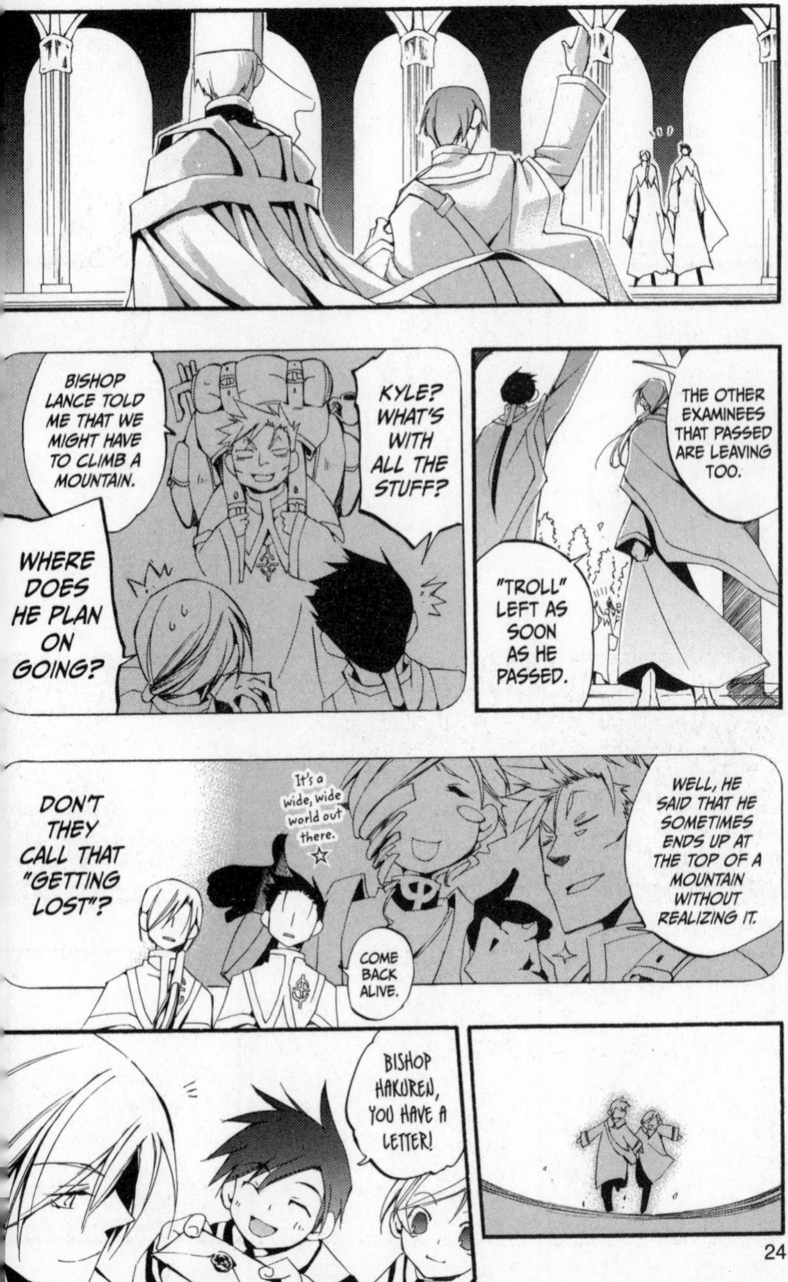

THE OTHER EXAMINEES THAT PASSED ARE LEAVING TOO.
"TROLL" LEFT AS SOON AS HE PASSED.
KYLE? WHAT'S WITH ALL THE STUFF?
BISHOP LANCE TOLD ME THAT WE MIGHT HAVE TO CLIMB A MOUNTAIN.
WHERE DOES HE PLAN ON GOING?
WELL, HE SAID THAT HE SOMETIMES ENDS UP AT THE TOP OF A MOUNTAIN WITHOUT REALIZING IT.
It's a wide, wide world out there. ☆
COME BACK ALIVE.
DON'T THEY CALL THAT "GETTING LOST"?
BISHOP HAKUREN, YOU HAVE A LETTER!

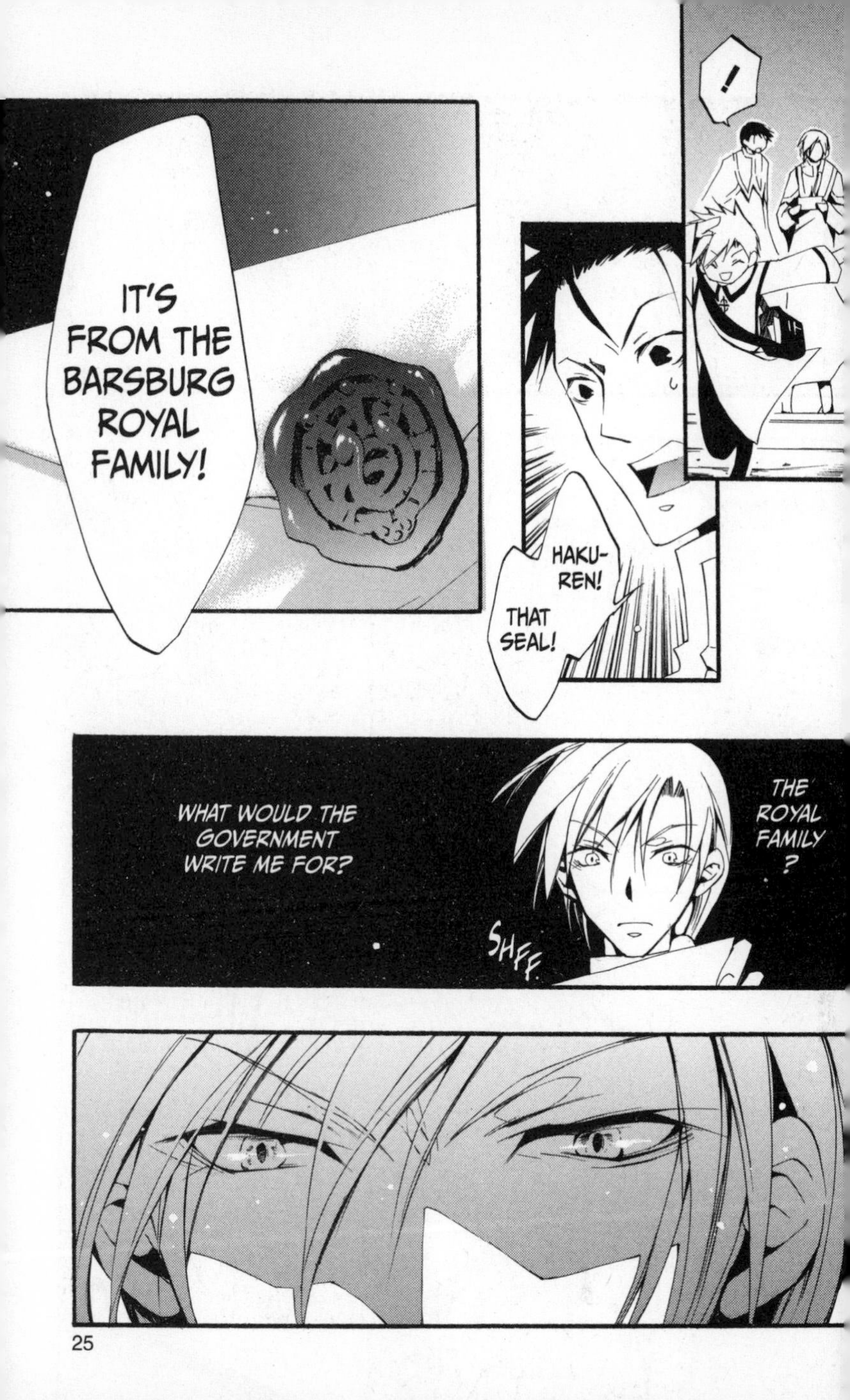
!
HAKU-REN!
THAT SEAL!
IT'S FROM THE BARSBURG ROYAL FAMILY!
THE ROYAL FAMILY?
SHFF.
WHAT WOULD THE GOVERNMENT WRITE ME FOR?

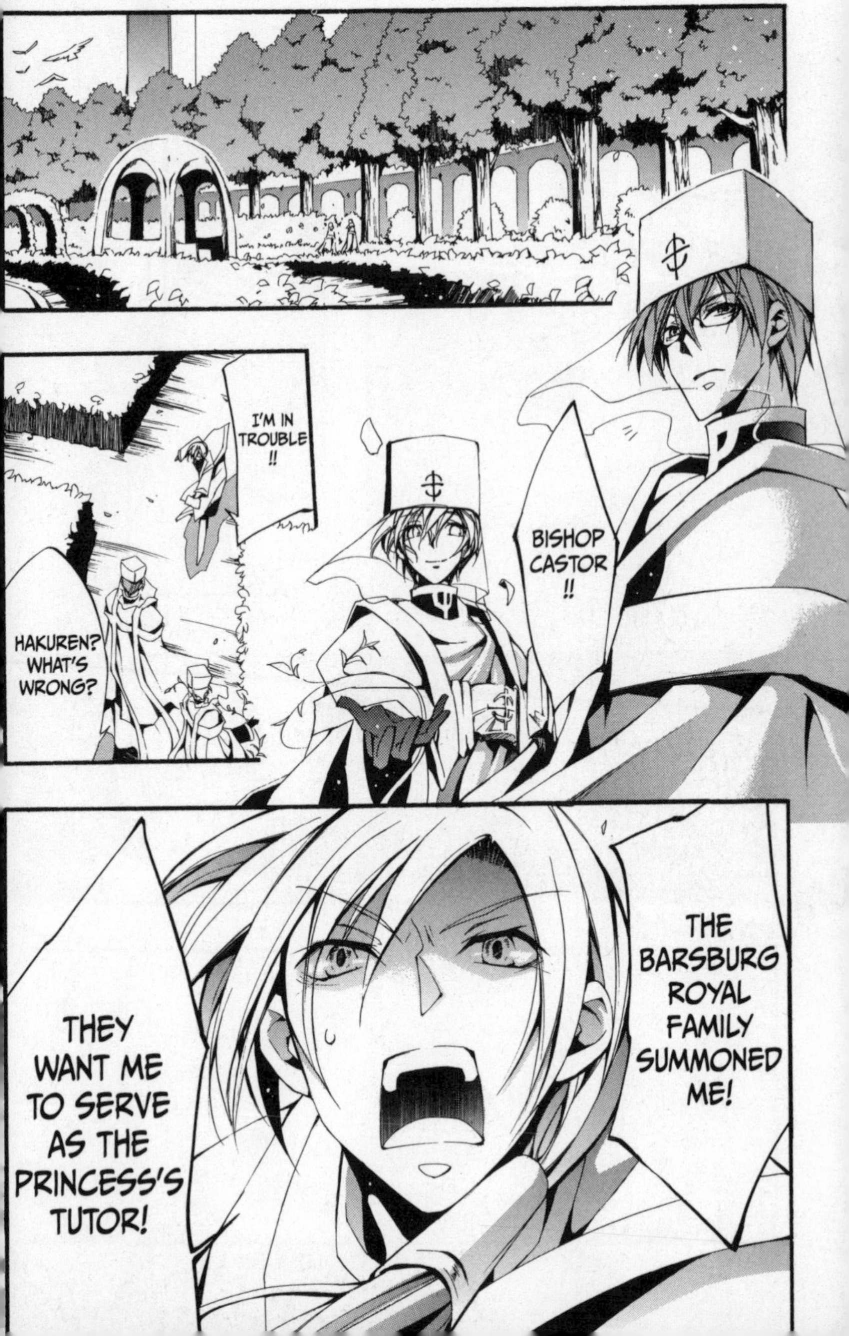
BISHOP CASTOR!!
I'M IN TROUBLE!!
HAKUREN? WHAT'S WRONG?
THE BARSBURG ROYAL FAMILY SUMMONED ME!
THEY WANT ME TO SERVE AS THE PRINCESS'S TUTOR!

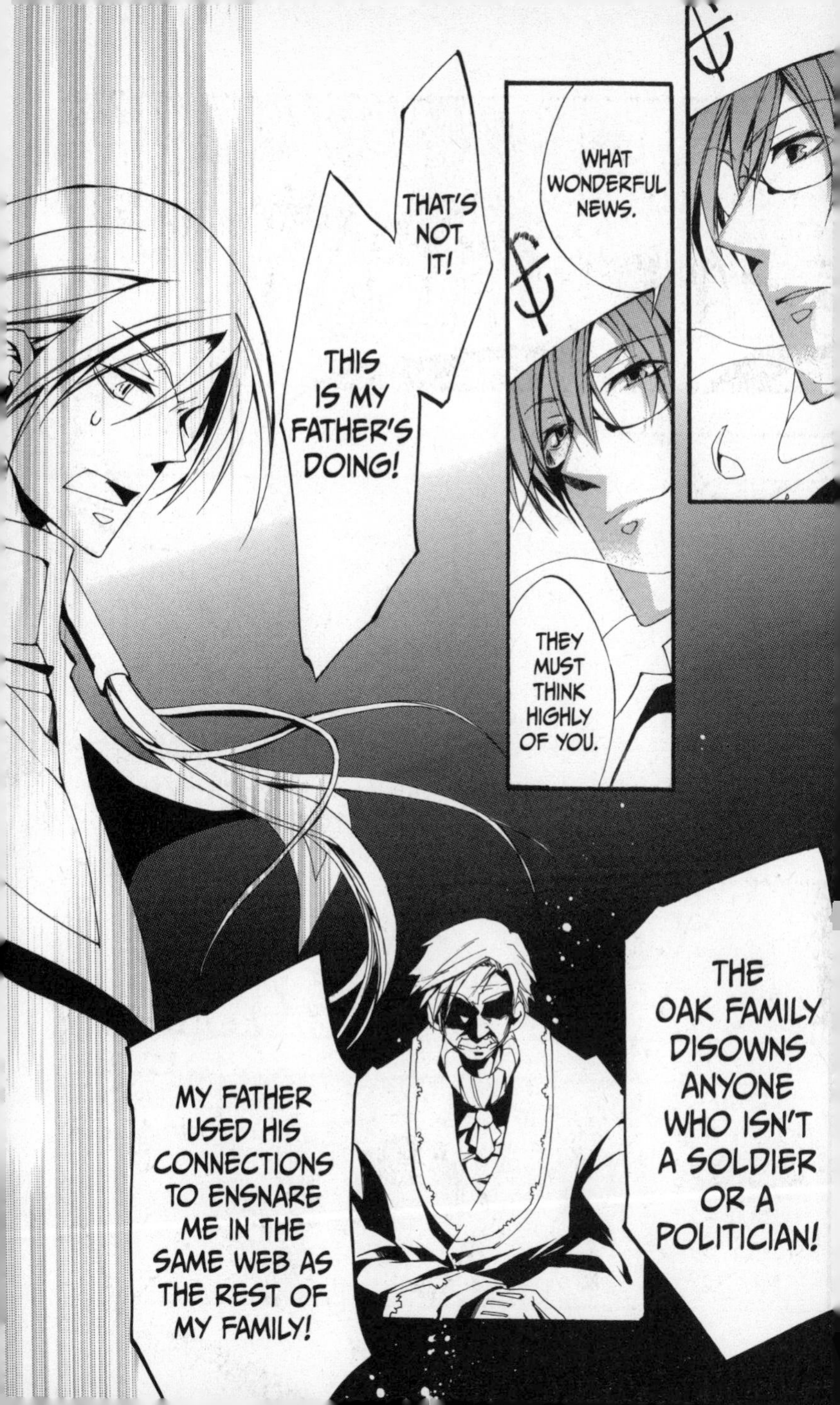
WHAT WONDERFUL NEWS.
THEY MUST THINK HIGHLY OF YOU.
THAT'S NOT IT!
THIS IS MY FATHER'S DOING!
THE OAK FAMILY DISOWNS ANYONE WHO ISN'T A SOLDIER OR A POLITICIAN!
MY FATHER USED HIS CONNECTIONS TO ENSNARE ME IN THE SAME WEB AS THE REST OF MY FAMILY!

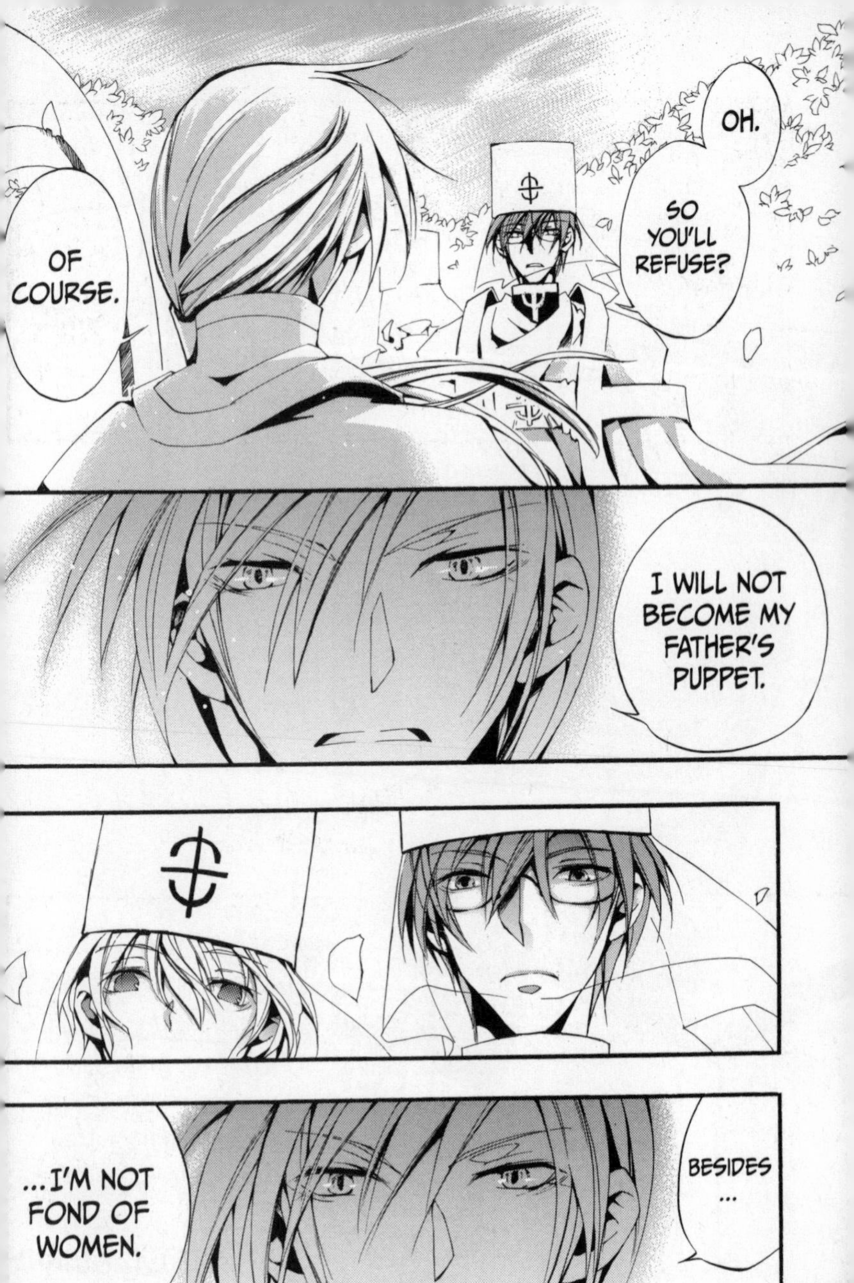
OH.
SO YOU'LL REFUSE?
OF COURSE.
I WILL NOT BECOME MY FATHER'S PUPPET.
BESIDES ...
...I'M NOT FOND OF WOMEN.

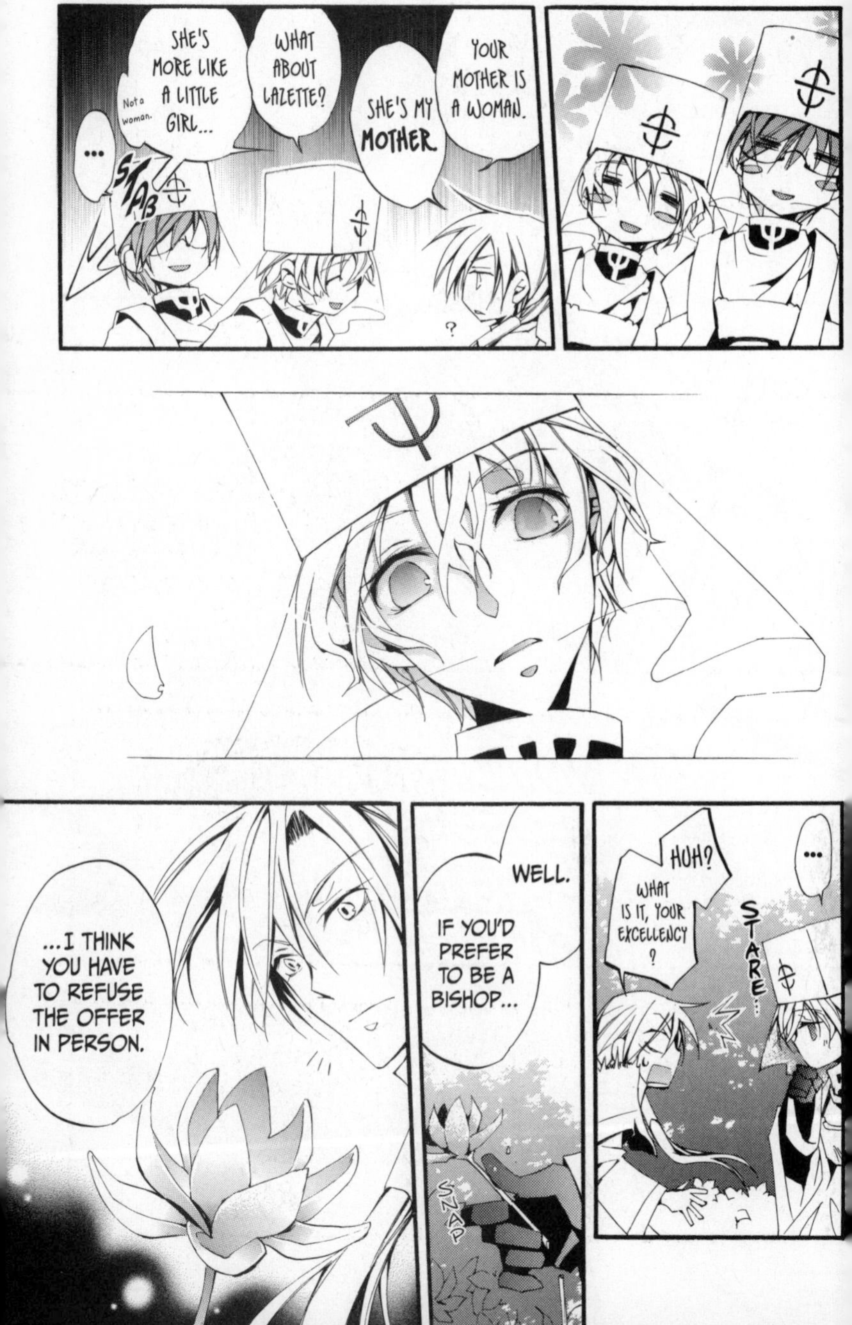
YOUR MOTHER IS A WOMAN.
SHE'S MY MOTHER.
WHAT ABOUT LAZETTE?
SHE'S MORE LIKE A LITTLE GIRL...
Not a woman.
STAB
...
?
...
HUH?
WHAT IS IT, YOUR EXCELLENCY?
STARE...
WELL.
IF YOU'D PREFER TO BE A BISHOP...
SNAP
...I THINK YOU HAVE TO REFUSE THE OFFER IN PERSON.

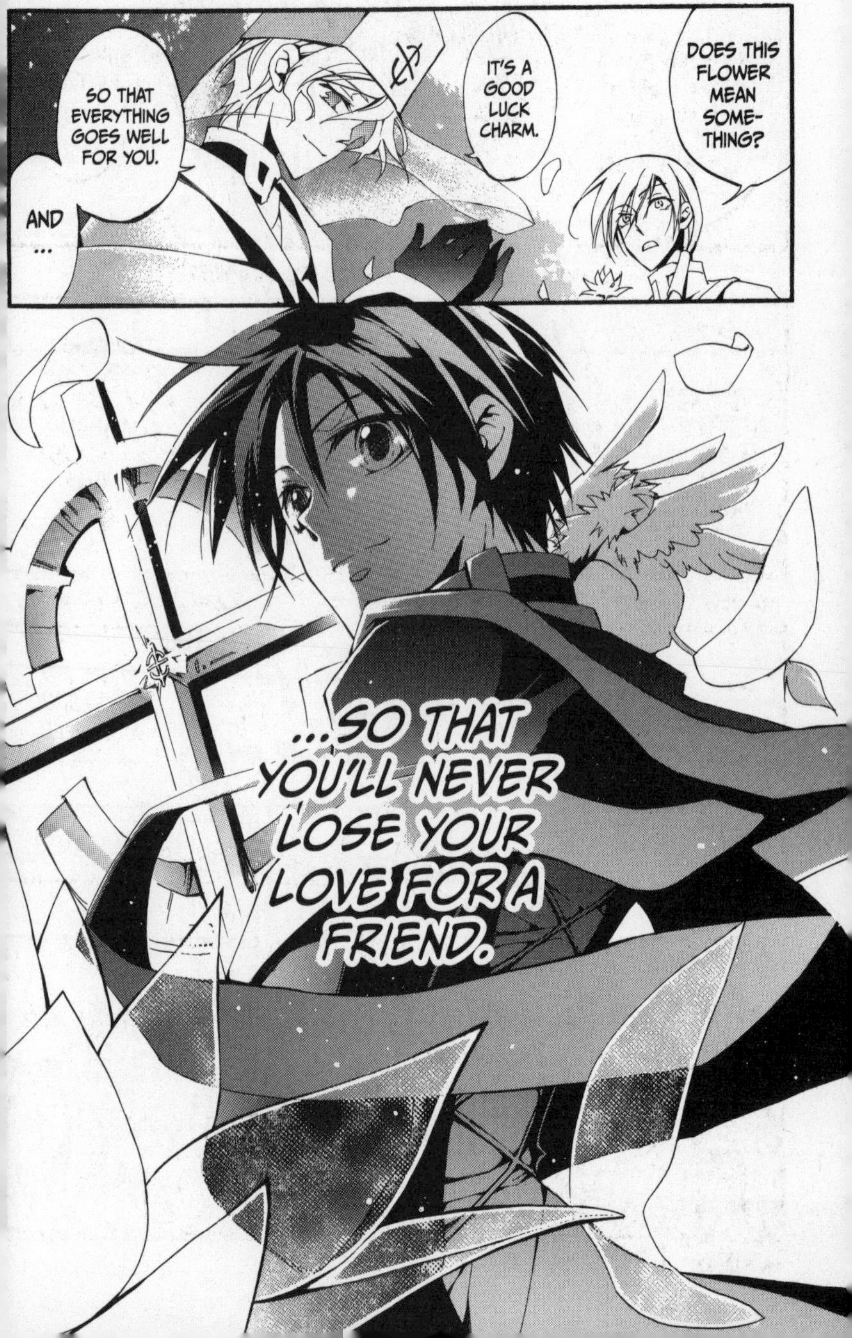
DOES THIS FLOWER MEAN SOME-THING?
IT'S A GOOD LUCK CHARM.
SO THAT EVERYTHING GOES WELL FOR YOU.
AND ...
...SO THAT YOU'LL NEVER LOSE YOUR LOVE FOR A FRIEND.

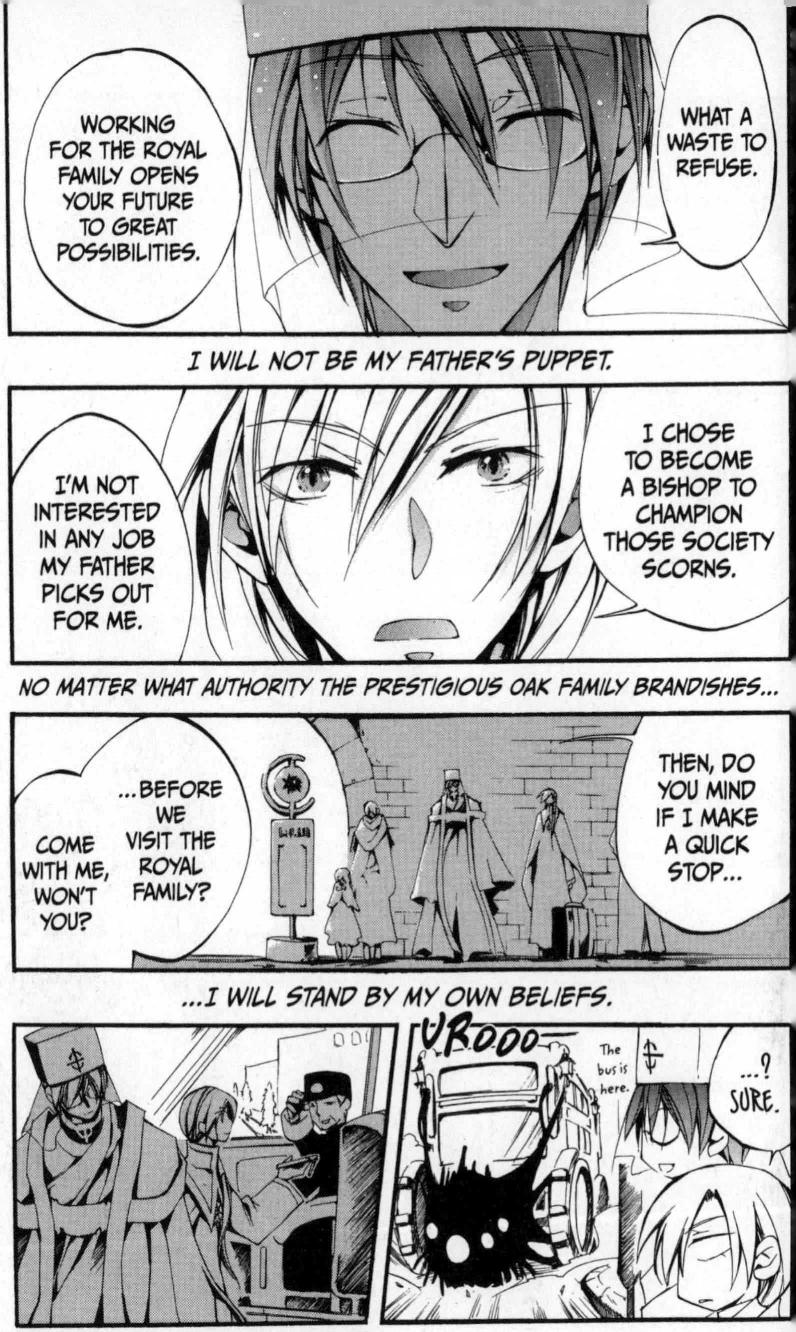
WHAT A WASTE TO REFUSE.
WORKING FOR THE ROYAL FAMILY OPENS YOUR FUTURE TO GREAT POSSIBILITIES.
I WILL NOT BE MY FATHER'S PUPPET.
I CHOSE TO BECOME A BISHOP TO CHAMPION THOSE SOCIETY SCORNS.
I'M NOT INTERESTED IN ANY JOB MY FATHER PICKS OUT FOR ME.
NO MATTER WHAT AUTHORITY THE PRESTIGIOUS OAK FAMILY BRANDISHES...
THEN, DO YOU MIND IF I MAKE A QUICK STOP...
...BEFORE WE VISIT THE ROYAL FAMILY?
COME WITH ME, WON'T YOU?
...I WILL STAND BY MY OWN BELIEFS.
...? SURE.
The bus is here.
VROOOO

Kapitel.37 "Reappraisal"

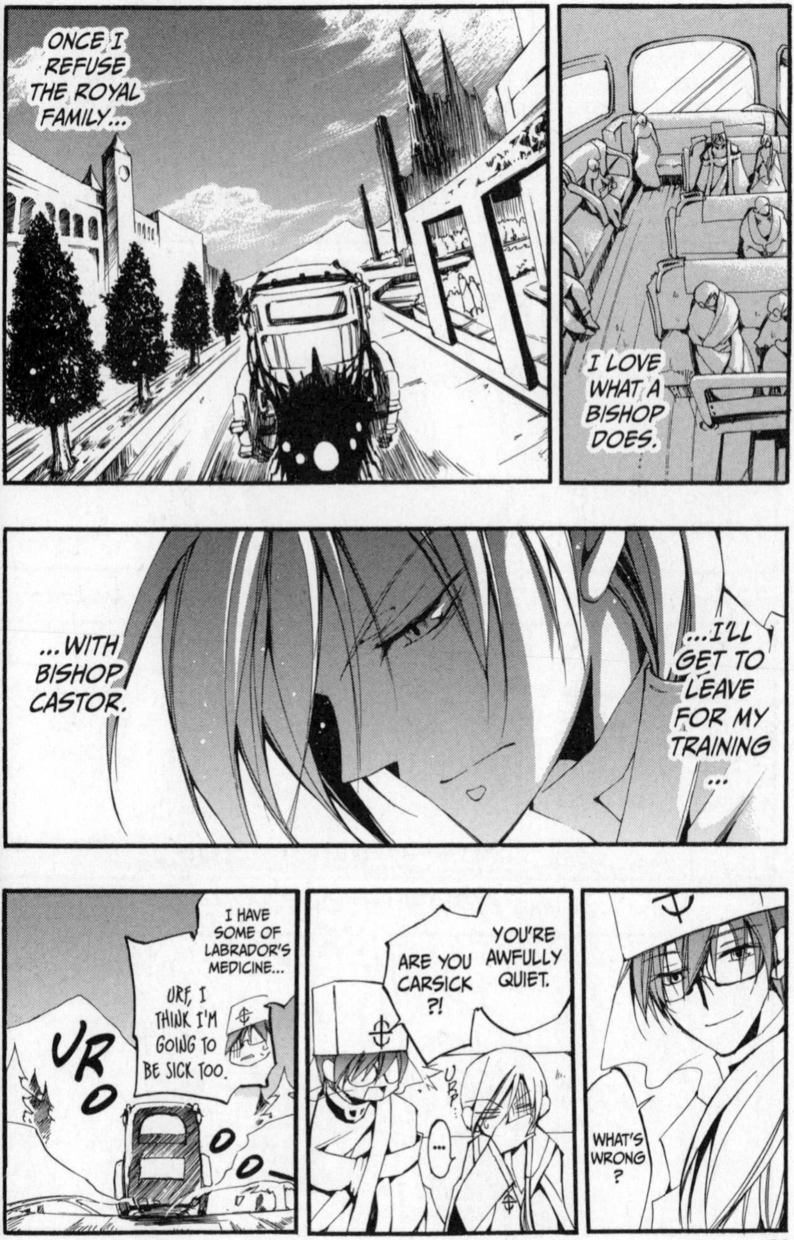

I LOVE WHAT A BISHOP DOES.
ONCE I REFUSE THE ROYAL FAMILY...
...I'LL GET TO LEAVE FOR MY TRAINING ...
...WITH BISHOP CASTOR.
WHAT'S WRONG ?
YOU'RE AWFULLY QUIET.
ARE YOU CARSICK ?!
URP...
...
I HAVE SOME OF LABRADOR'S MEDICINE...
URF, I THINK I'M GOING TO BE SICK TOO.
VROOOO

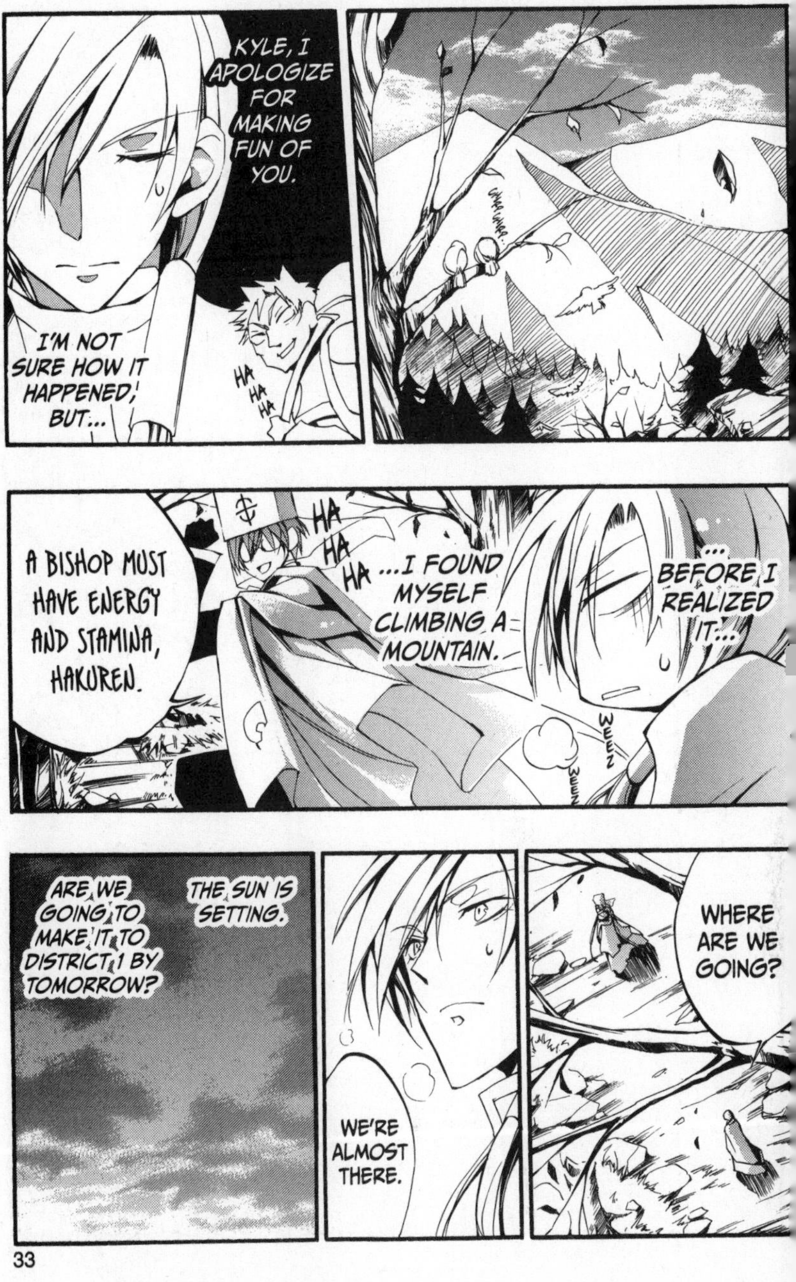
KYLE, I APOLOGIZE FOR MAKING FUN OF YOU.
I'M NOT SURE HOW IT HAPPENED, BUT...
HA HA HA
... BEFORE I REALIZED IT...
WEEZ
WEEZ
...I FOUND MYSELF CLIMBING A MOUNTAIN.
HA HA HA
A BISHOP MUST HAVE ENERGY AND STAMINA, HAKUREN.
WHERE ARE WE GOING?
WE'RE ALMOST THERE.
THE SUN IS SETTING.
ARE WE GOING TO MAKE IT TO DISTRICT 1 BY TOMORROW?

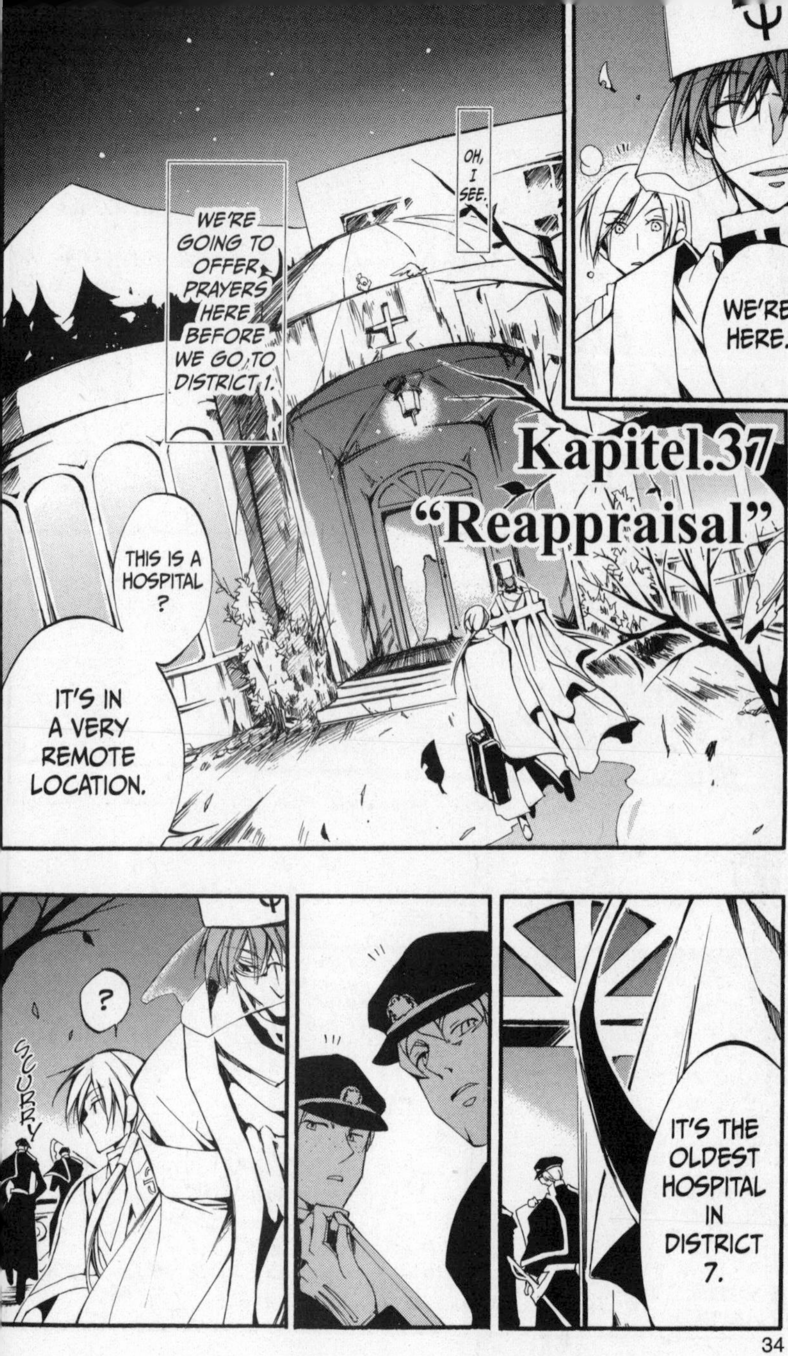
WE'RE HERE.
OH, I SEE.
WE'RE GOING TO OFFER PRAYERS HERE BEFORE WE GO TO DISTRICT 1.
Kapitel.37
"Reappraisal"
THIS IS A HOSPITAL?
IT'S IN A VERY REMOTE LOCATION.
IT'S THE OLDEST HOSPITAL IN DISTRICT 7.
?
SCURRY

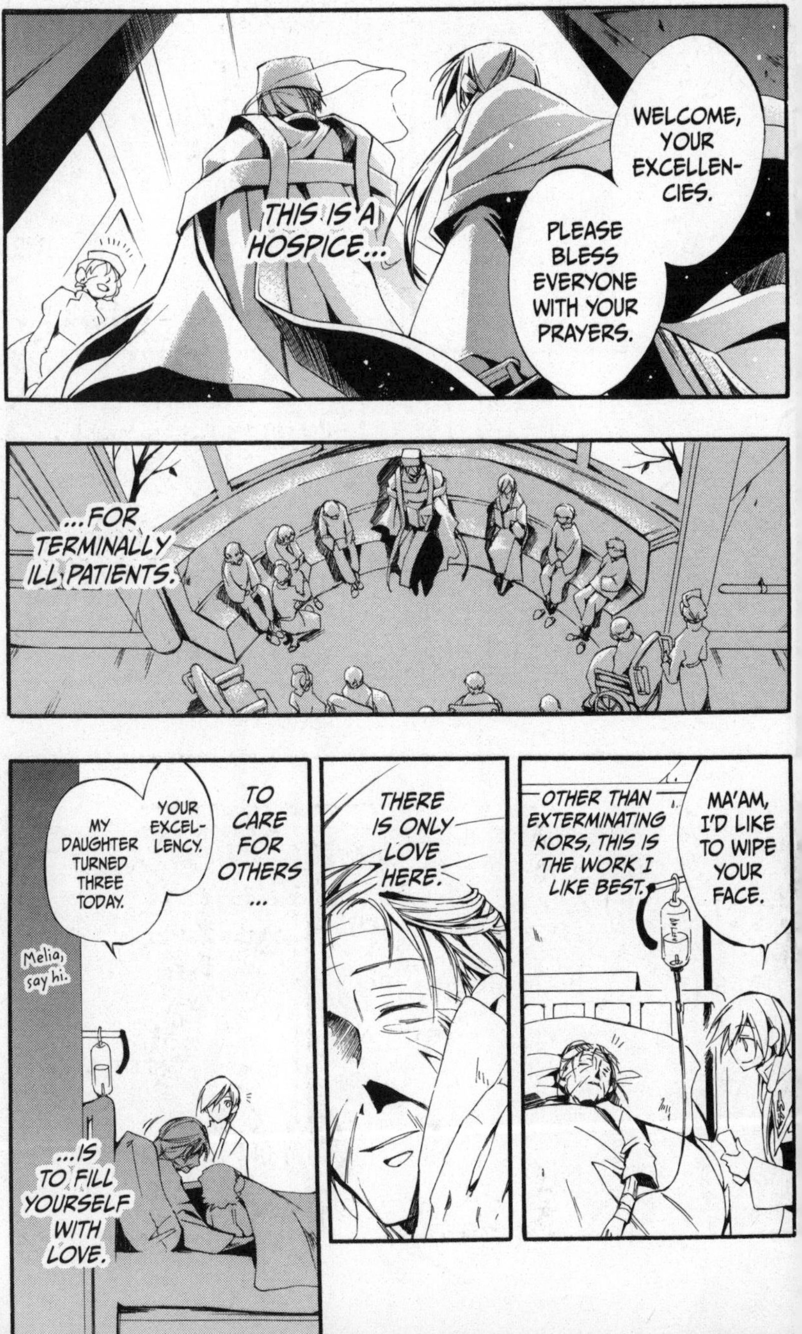
WELCOME, YOUR EXCELLENCIES.
PLEASE BLESS EVERYONE WITH YOUR PRAYERS.
THIS IS A HOSPICE...
...FOR TERMINALLY ILL PATIENTS.
MA'AM, I'D LIKE TO WIPE YOUR FACE.
OTHER THAN EXTERMINATING KORS, THIS IS THE WORK I LIKE BEST.
THERE IS ONLY LOVE HERE.
TO CARE FOR OTHERS ...
YOUR EXCELLENCY.
MY DAUGHTER TURNED THREE TODAY.
Melia, say hi.
...IS TO FILL YOURSELF WITH LOVE.

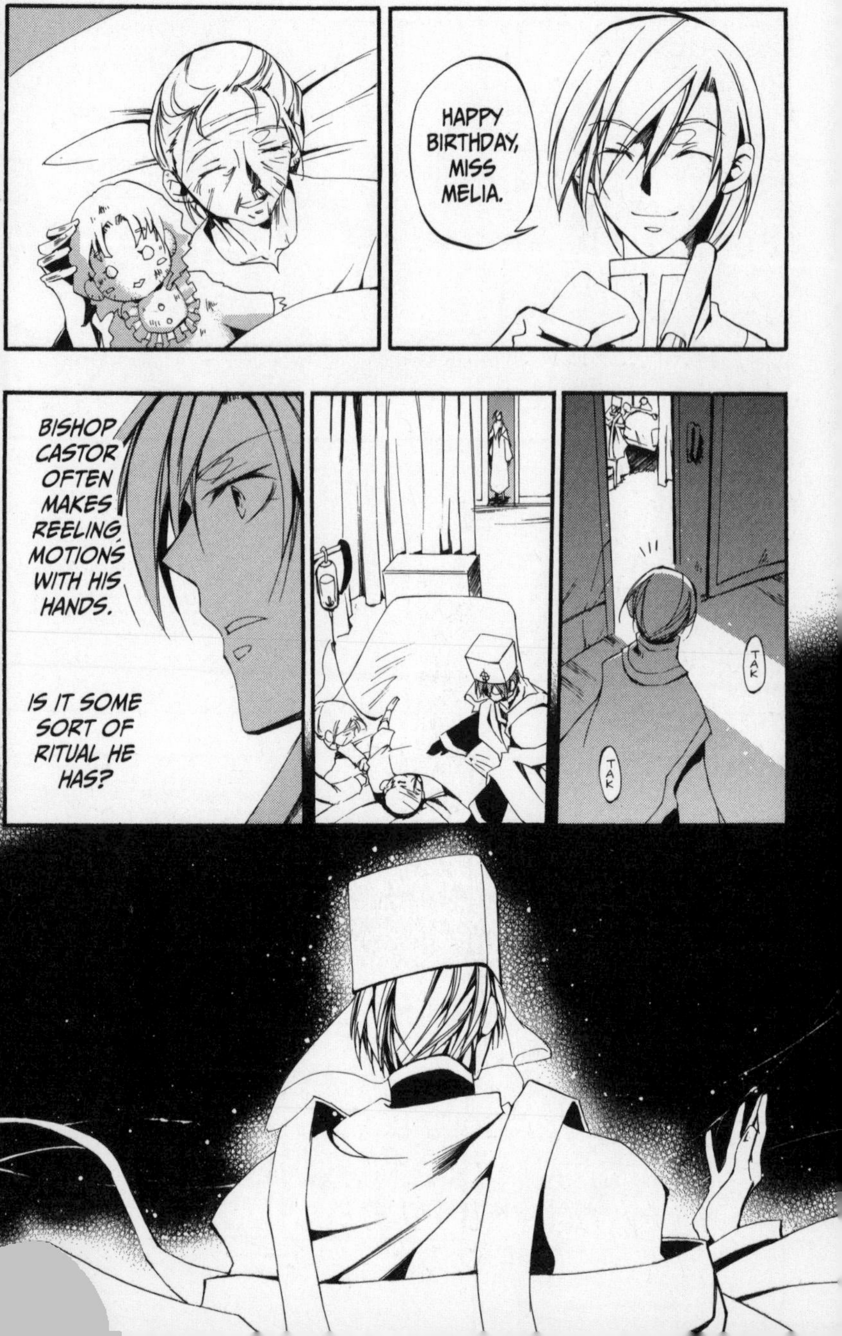
HAPPY BIRTHDAY, MISS MELIA.
TAK
TAK
BISHOP CASTOR OFTEN MAKES REELING MOTIONS WITH HIS HANDS.
IS IT SOME SORT OF RITUAL HE HAS?

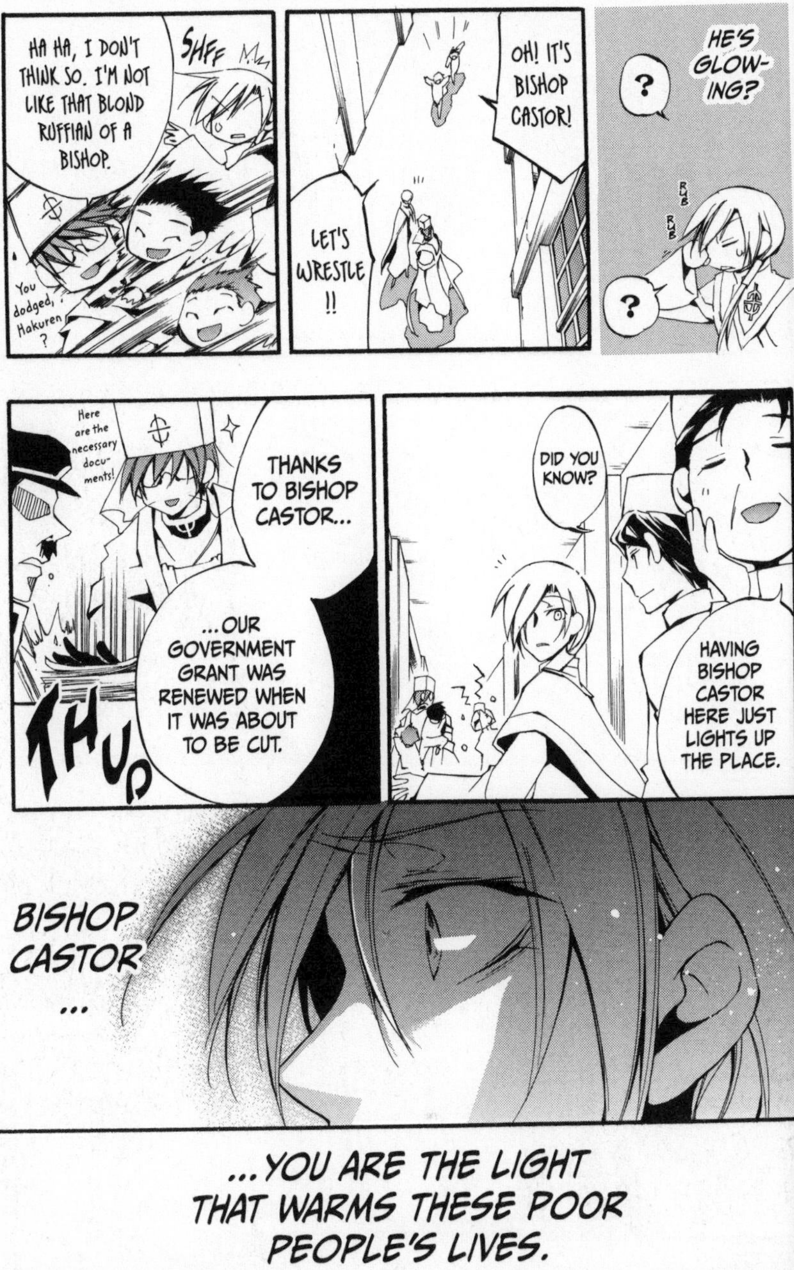
HE'S GLOWING?
?
RUB
RUB
?
OH! IT'S BISHOP CASTOR!
LET'S WRESTLE!!
SHFF
HA HA, I DON'T THINK SO. I'M NOT LIKE THAT BLOND RUFFIAN OF A BISHOP.
You dodged, Hakuren?
DID YOU KNOW?
HAVING BISHOP CASTOR HERE JUST LIGHTS UP THE PLACE.
Here are the necessary docu-ments!
THANKS TO BISHOP CASTOR...
...OUR GOVERNMENT GRANT WAS RENEWED WHEN IT WAS ABOUT TO BE CUT.
THUD
BISHOP CASTOR...
...YOU ARE THE LIGHT THAT WARMS THESE POOR PEOPLE'S LIVES.

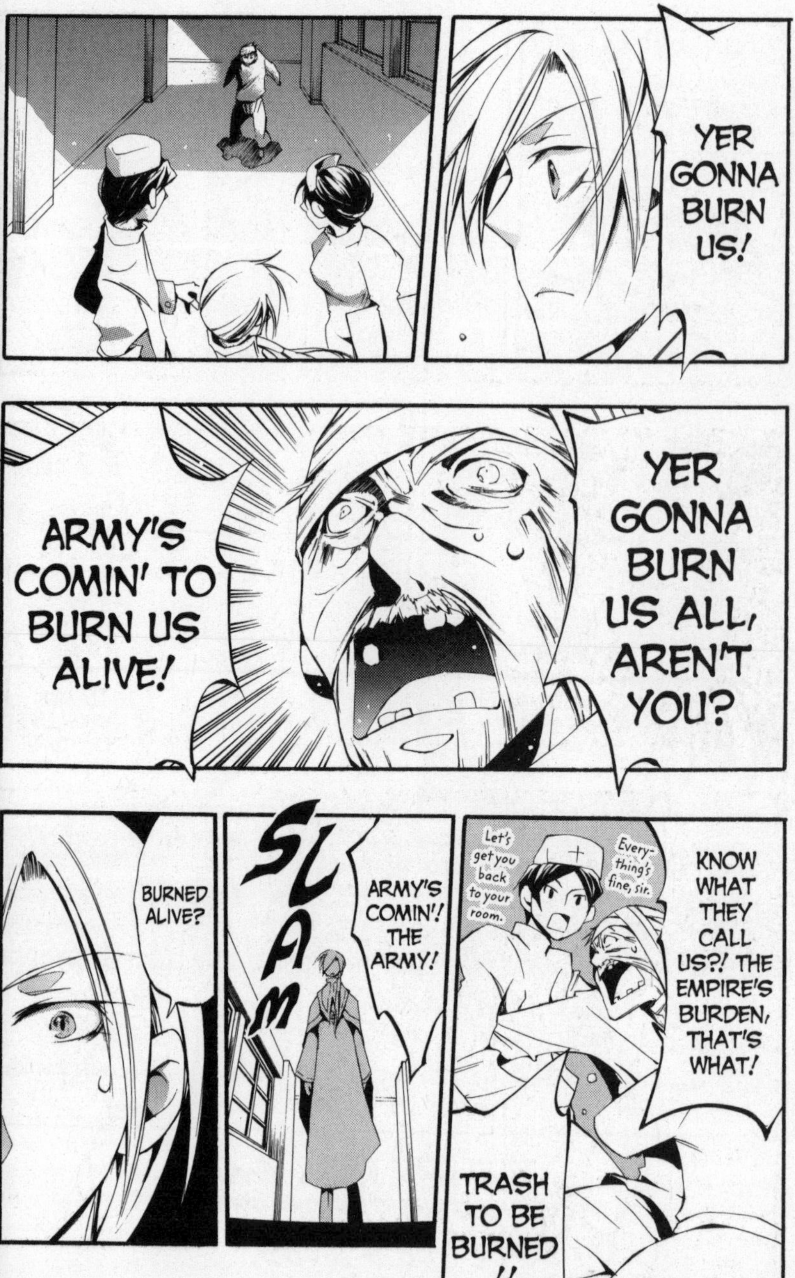
YER GONNA BURN US!
YER GONNA BURN US ALL, AREN'T YOU?
ARMY'S COMIN' TO BURN US ALIVE!
KNOW WHAT THEY CALL US?! THE EMPIRE'S BURDEN, THAT'S WHAT!
Everything's fine, sir.
Let's get you back to your room.
TRASH TO BE BURNED!!
SLAM
ARMY'S COMIN'! THE ARMY!
BURNED ALIVE?

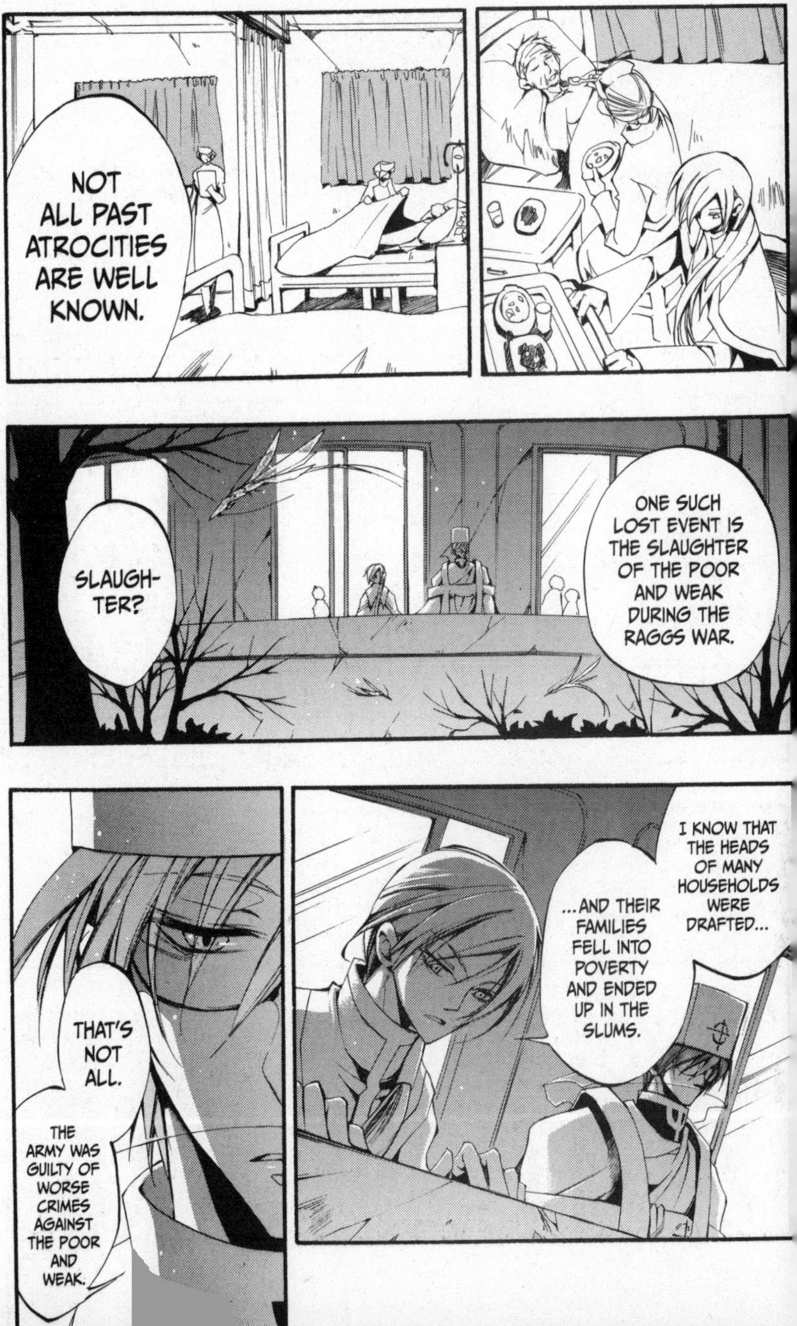
NOT ALL PAST ATROCITIES ARE WELL KNOWN.
ONE SUCH LOST EVENT IS THE SLAUGHTER OF THE POOR AND WEAK DURING THE RAGGS WAR.
SLAUGH-TER?
I KNOW THAT THE HEADS OF MANY HOUSEHOLDS WERE DRAFTED...
...AND THEIR FAMILIES FELL INTO POVERTY AND ENDED UP IN THE SLUMS.
THAT'S NOT ALL.
THE ARMY WAS GUILTY OF WORSE CRIMES AGAINST THE POOR AND WEAK.

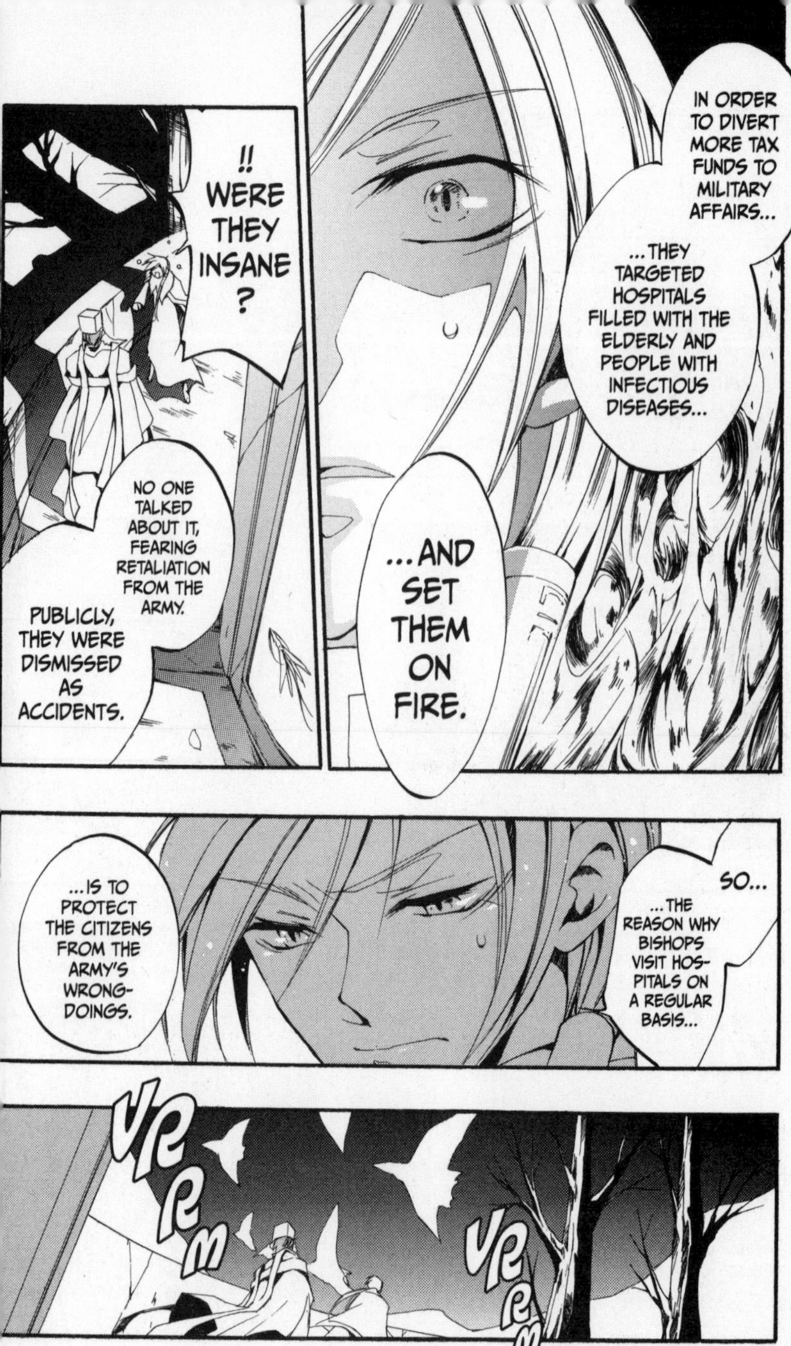
IN ORDER TO DIVERT MORE TAX FUNDS TO MILITARY AFFAIRS...
...THEY TARGETED HOSPITALS FILLED WITH THE ELDERLY AND PEOPLE WITH INFECTIOUS DISEASES...
...AND SET THEM ON FIRE.
!! WERE THEY INSANE?
NO ONE TALKED ABOUT IT, FEARING RETALIATION FROM THE ARMY.
PUBLICLY, THEY WERE DISMISSED AS ACCIDENTS.
SO...
...THE REASON WHY BISHOPS VISIT HOS-PITALS ON A REGULAR BASIS...
...IS TO PROTECT THE CITIZENS FROM THE ARMY'S WRONG-DOINGS.
VREEM
VREEM

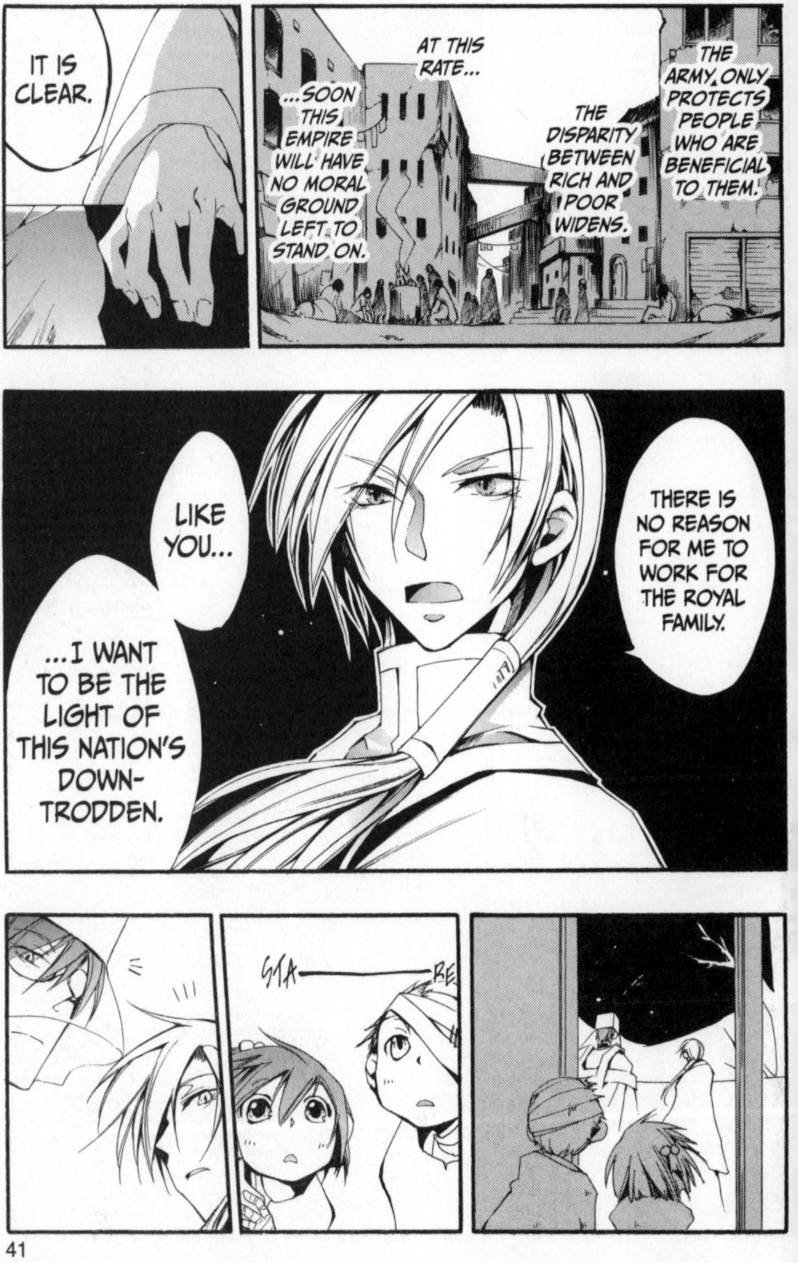
THE ARMY ONLY PROTECTS PEOPLE WHO ARE BENEFICIAL TO THEM.
THE DISPARITY BETWEEN RICH AND POOR WIDENS.
AT THIS RATE...
...SOON THIS EMPIRE WILL HAVE NO MORAL GROUND LEFT TO STAND ON.
IT IS CLEAR.
THERE IS NO REASON FOR ME TO WORK FOR THE ROYAL FAMILY.
LIKE YOU...
...I WANT TO BE THE LIGHT OF THIS NATION'S DOWN-TRODDEN.
STA——RE

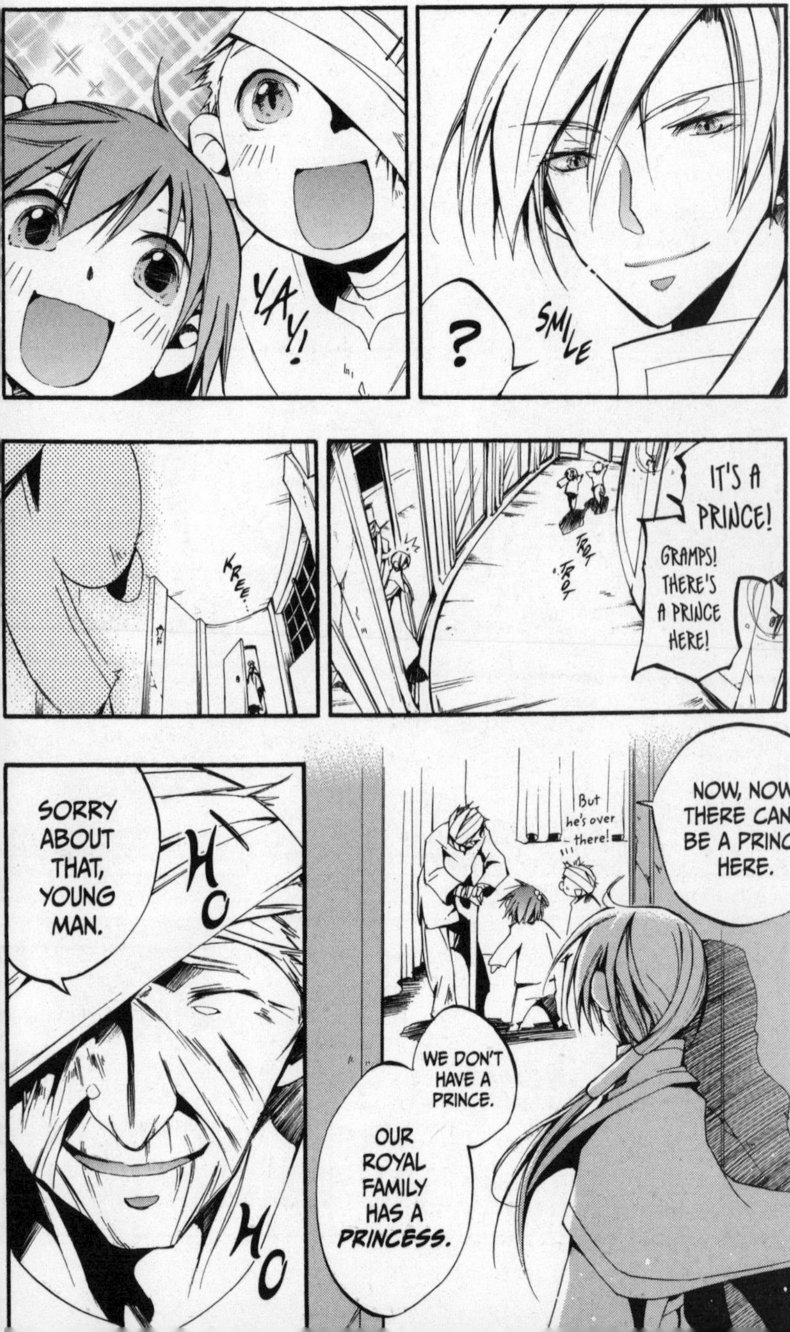
?
SMILE
YAY!!
IT'S A PRINCE!
GRAMPS! THERE'S A PRINCE HERE!
TROT TROT
KREE...
NOW, NOW. THERE CAN'T BE A PRINCE HERE.
But he's over there!
WE DON'T HAVE A PRINCE.
OUR ROYAL FAMILY HAS A PRINCESS.
SORRY ABOUT THAT, YOUNG MAN.
HO HO

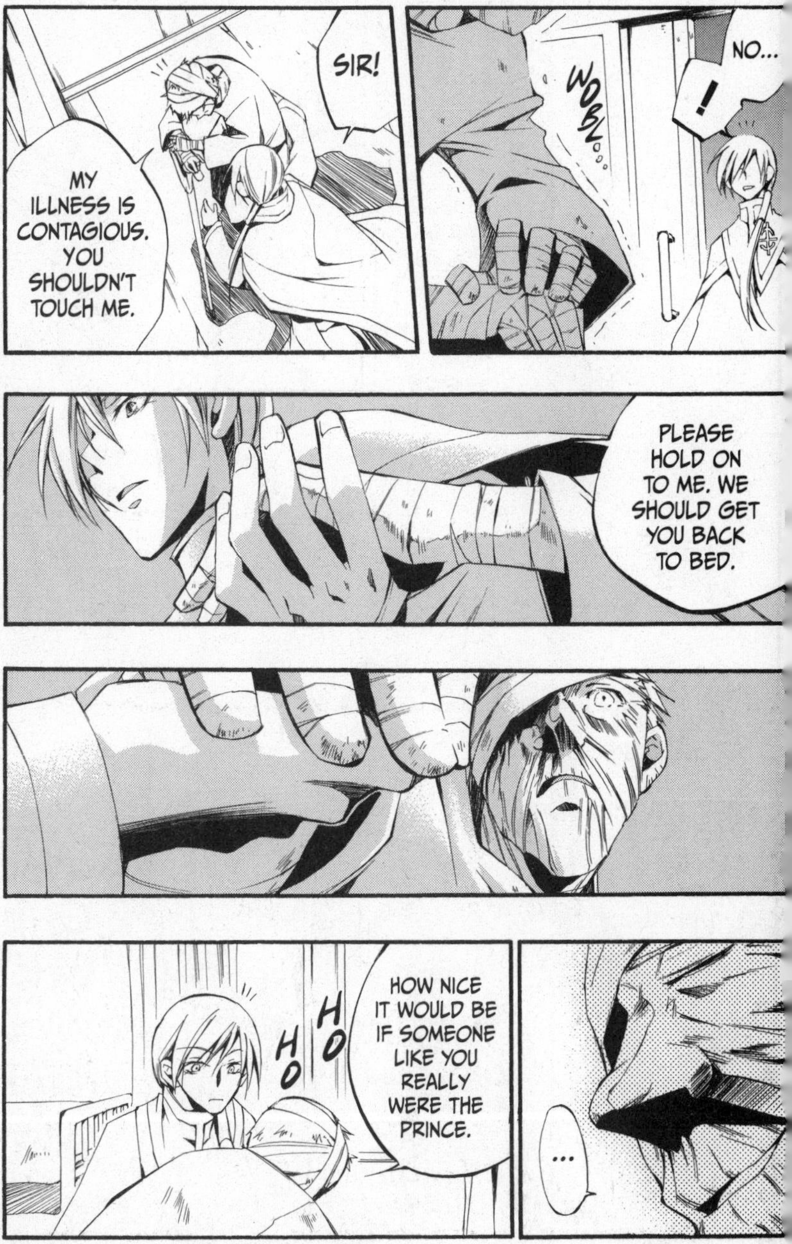
NO...
!
WOBL
SIR!
MY ILLNESS IS CONTAGIOUS. YOU SHOULDN'T TOUCH ME.
PLEASE HOLD ON TO ME. WE SHOULD GET YOU BACK TO BED.
...
HOW NICE IT WOULD BE IF SOMEONE LIKE YOU REALLY WERE THE PRINCE.
HO HO

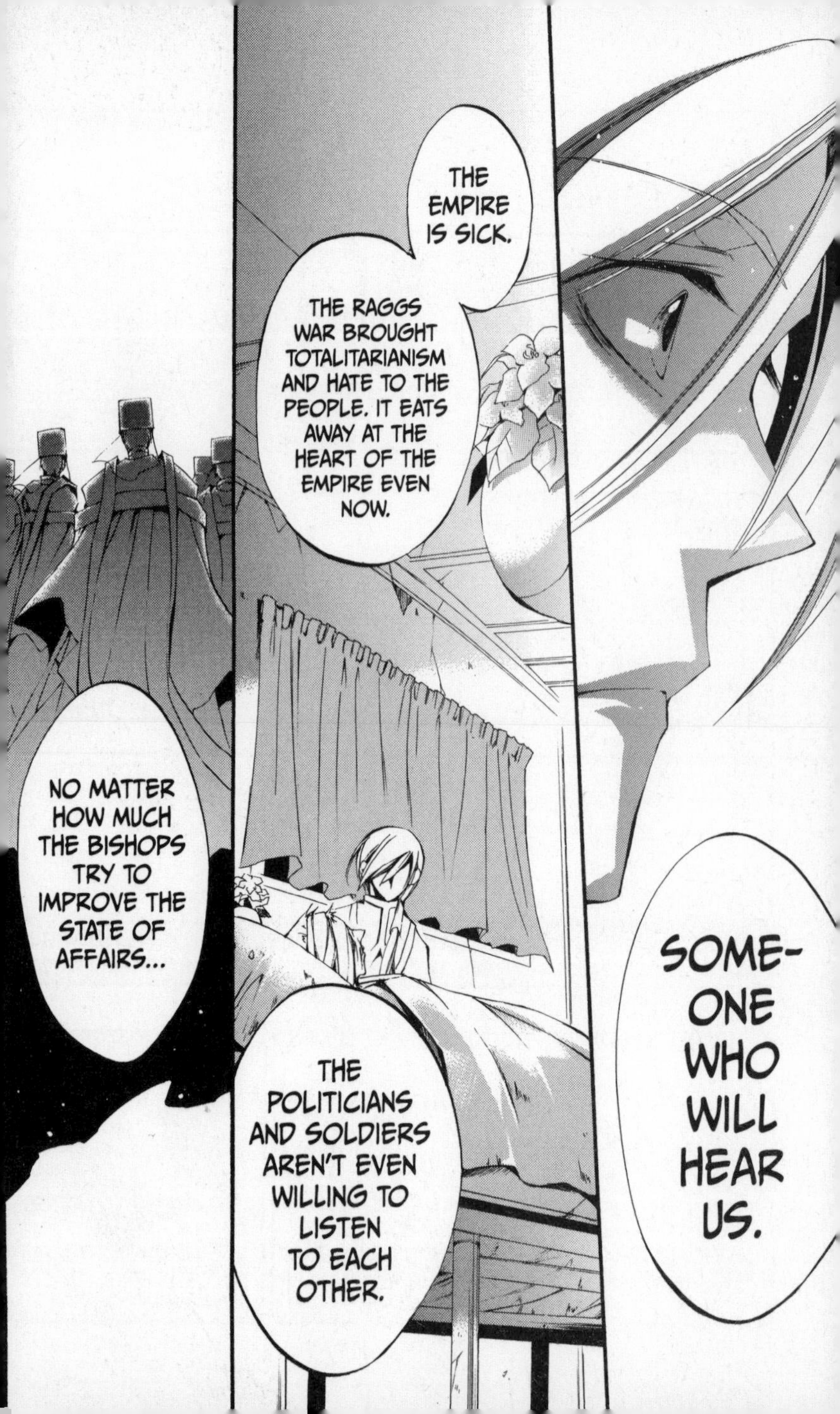
SOME-ONE WHO WILL HEAR US.
THE EMPIRE IS SICK.
THE RAGGS WAR BROUGHT TOTALITARIANISM AND HATE TO THE PEOPLE. IT EATS AWAY AT THE HEART OF THE EMPIRE EVEN NOW.
THE POLITICIANS AND SOLDIERS AREN'T EVEN WILLING TO LISTEN TO EACH OTHER.
NO MATTER HOW MUCH THE BISHOPS TRY TO IMPROVE THE STATE OF AFFAIRS...

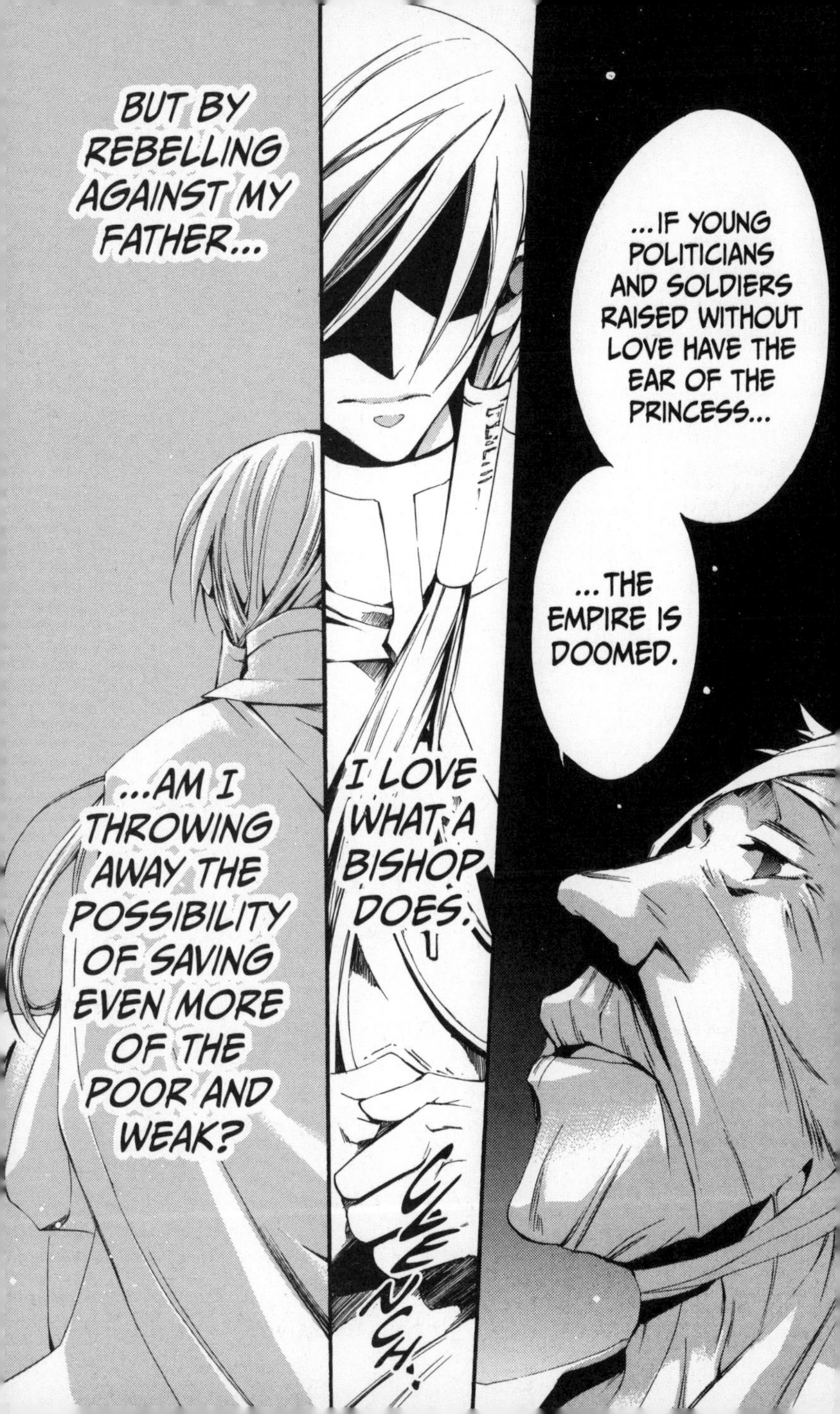
...IF YOUNG POLITICIANS AND SOLDIERS RAISED WITHOUT LOVE HAVE THE EAR OF THE PRINCESS...
...THE EMPIRE IS DOOMED.
I LOVE WHAT A BISHOP DOES.
CLENCH!
BUT BY REBELLING AGAINST MY FATHER...
...AM I THROWING AWAY THE POSSIBILITY OF SAVING EVEN MORE OF THE POOR AND WEAK?

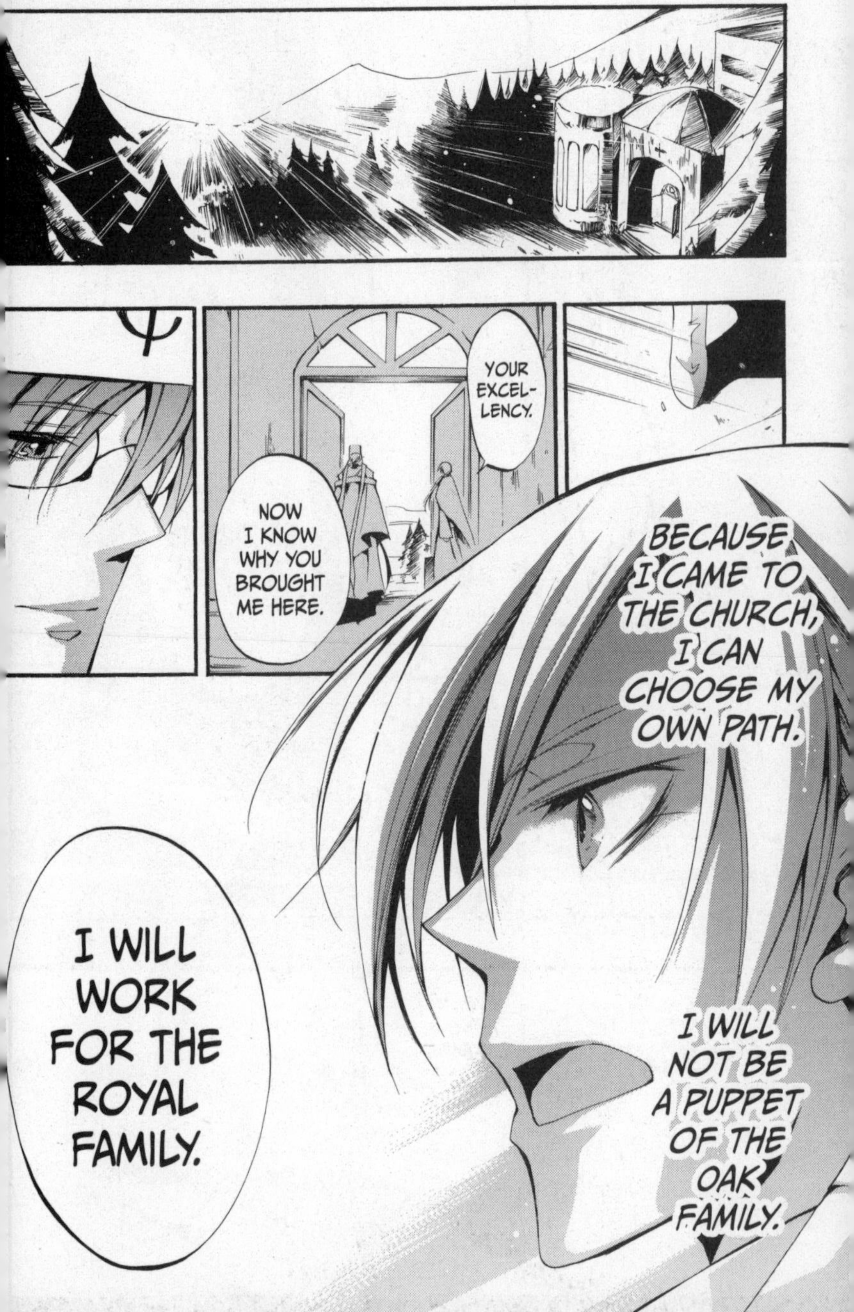
YOUR EXCEL-LENCY.
NOW I KNOW WHY YOU BROUGHT ME HERE.
BECAUSE I CAME TO THE CHURCH, I CAN CHOOSE MY OWN PATH.
I WILL NOT BE A PUPPET OF THE OAK FAMILY.
I WILL WORK FOR THE ROYAL FAMILY.

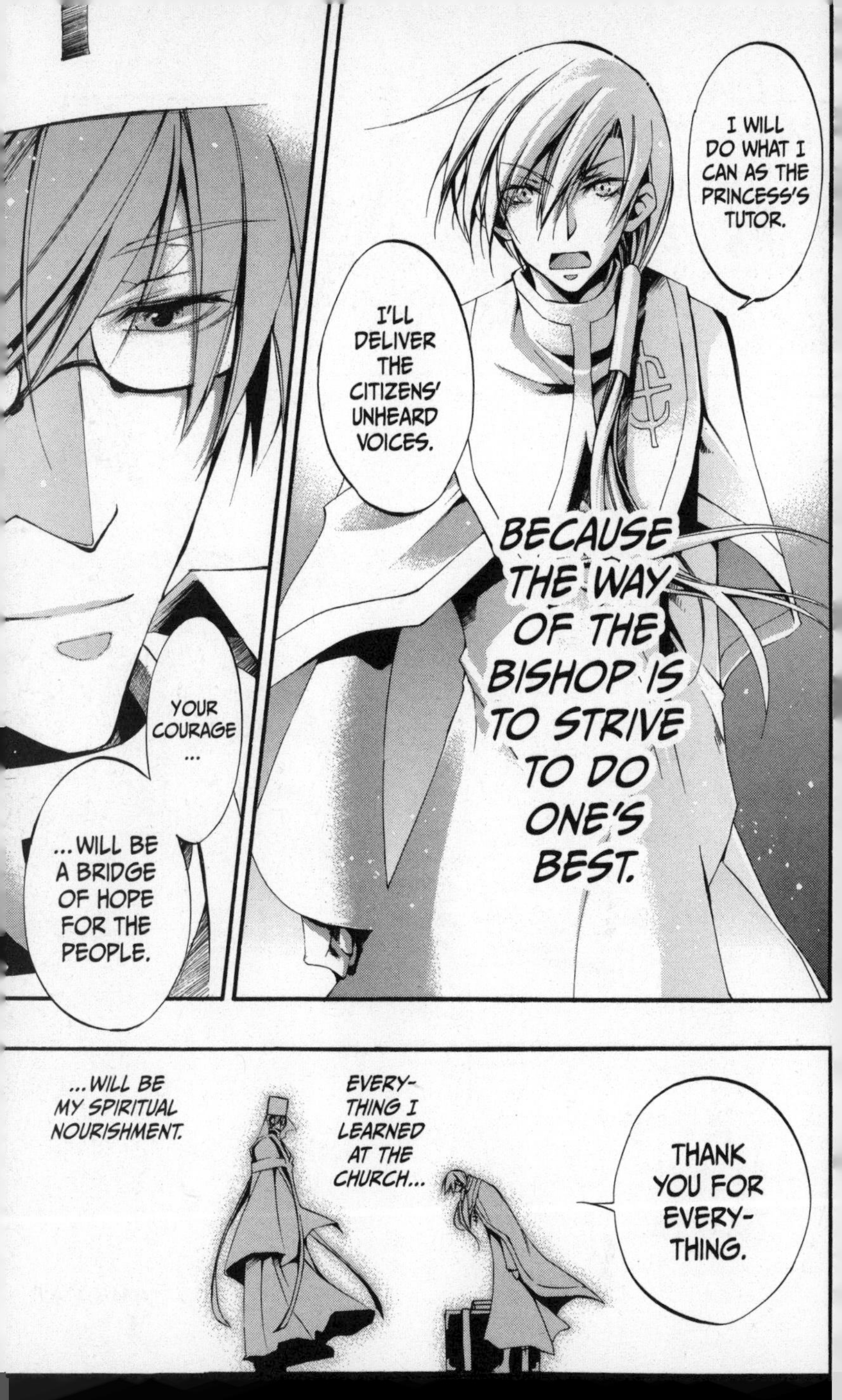
I WILL DO WHAT I CAN AS THE PRINCESS'S TUTOR.
I'LL DELIVER THE CITIZENS' UNHEARD VOICES.
BECAUSE THE WAY OF THE BISHOP IS TO STRIVE TO DO ONE'S BEST.
YOUR COURAGE...
...WILL BE A BRIDGE OF HOPE FOR THE PEOPLE.
THANK YOU FOR EVERY-THING.
EVERY-THING I LEARNED AT THE CHURCH...
...WILL BE MY SPIRITUAL NOURISHMENT.

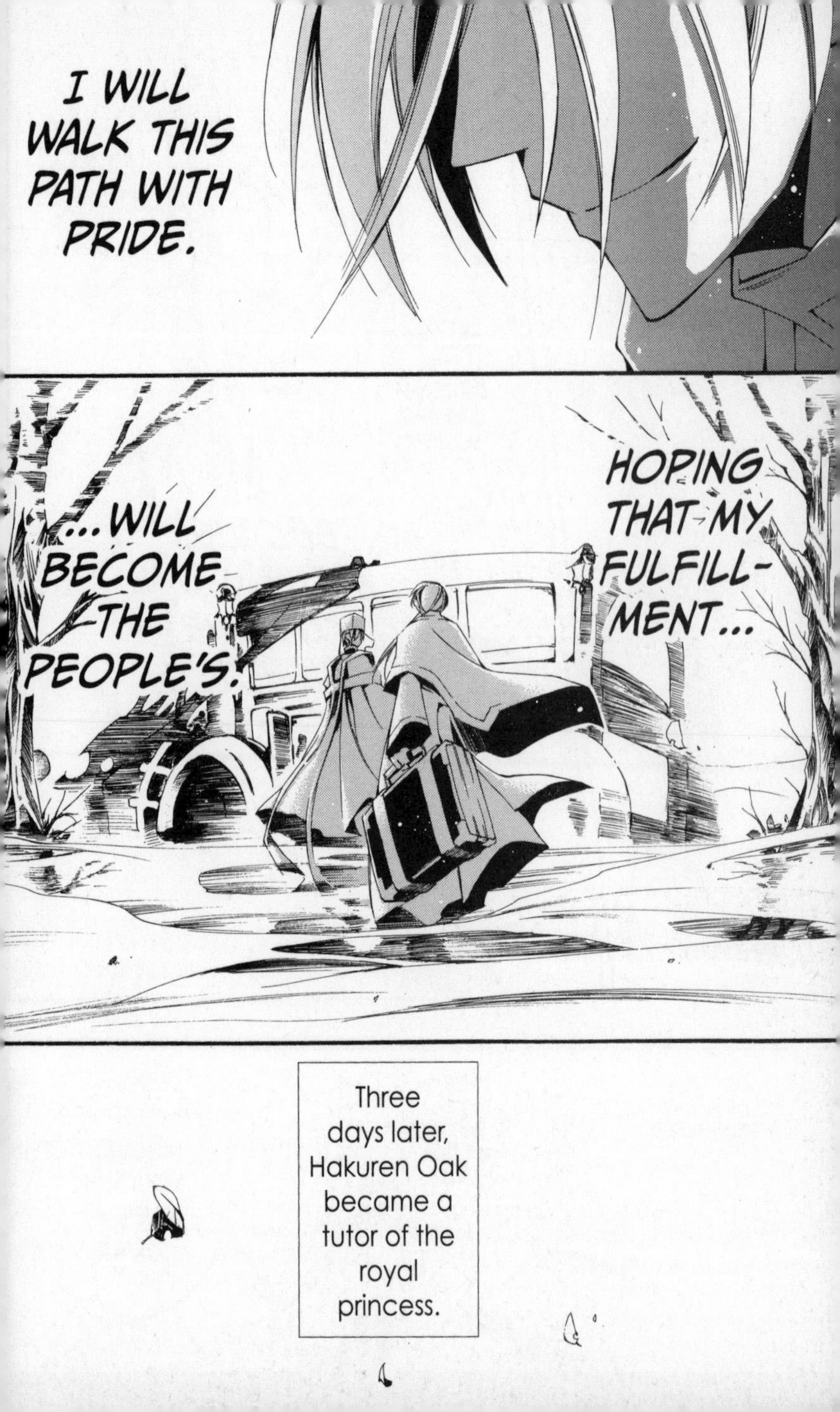
I WILL WALK THIS PATH WITH PRIDE.
HOPING THAT MY FULFILL-MENT...
...WILL BECOME THE PEOPLE'S.
Three days later, Hakuren Oak became a tutor of the royal princess.

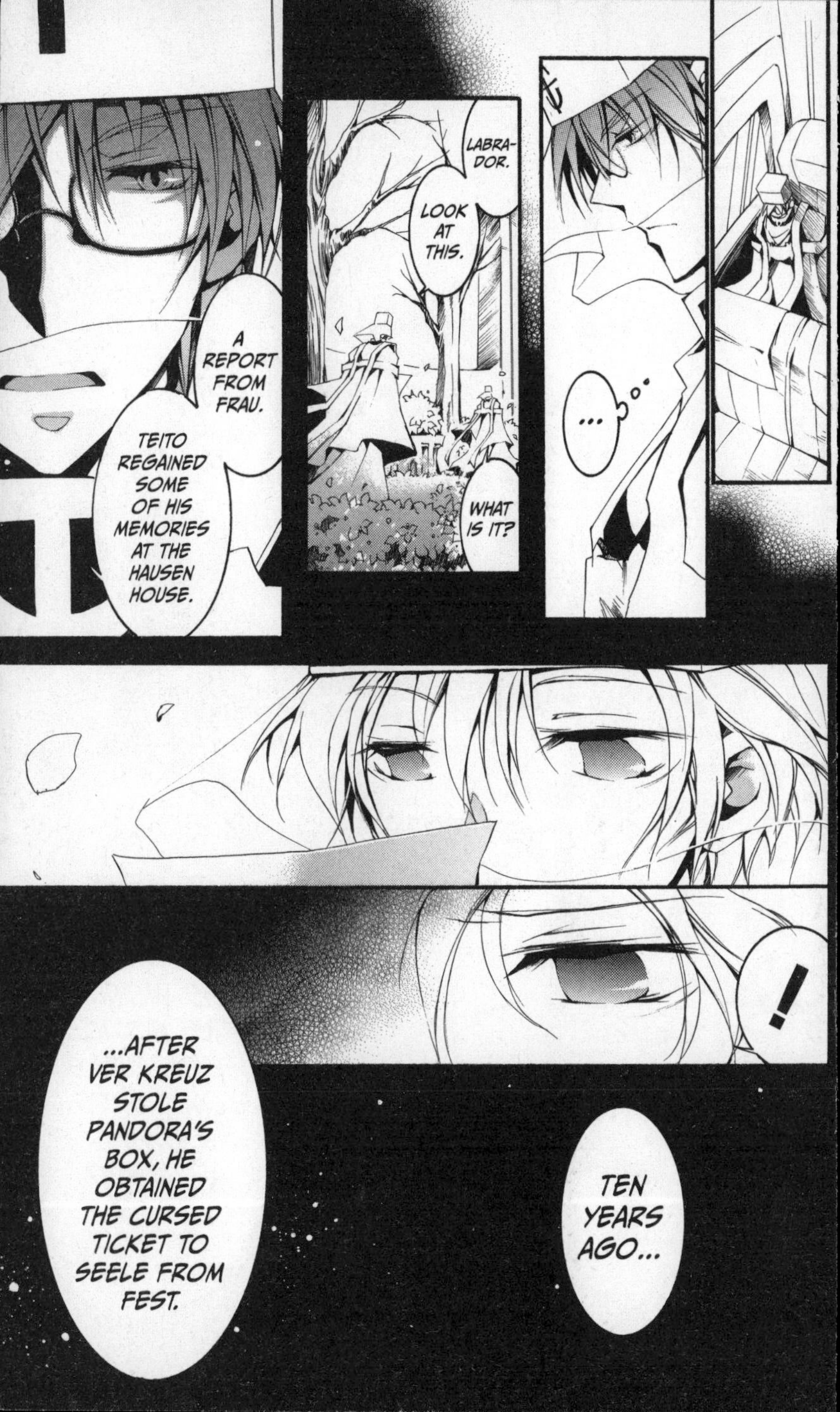
...
LABRA-DOR.
LOOK AT THIS.
WHAT IS IT?
A REPORT FROM FRAU.
TEITO REGAINED SOME OF HIS MEMORIES AT THE HAUSEN HOUSE.
!
TEN YEARS AGO...
...AFTER VER KREUZ STOLE PANDORA'S BOX, HE OBTAINED THE CURSED TICKET TO SEELE FROM FEST.

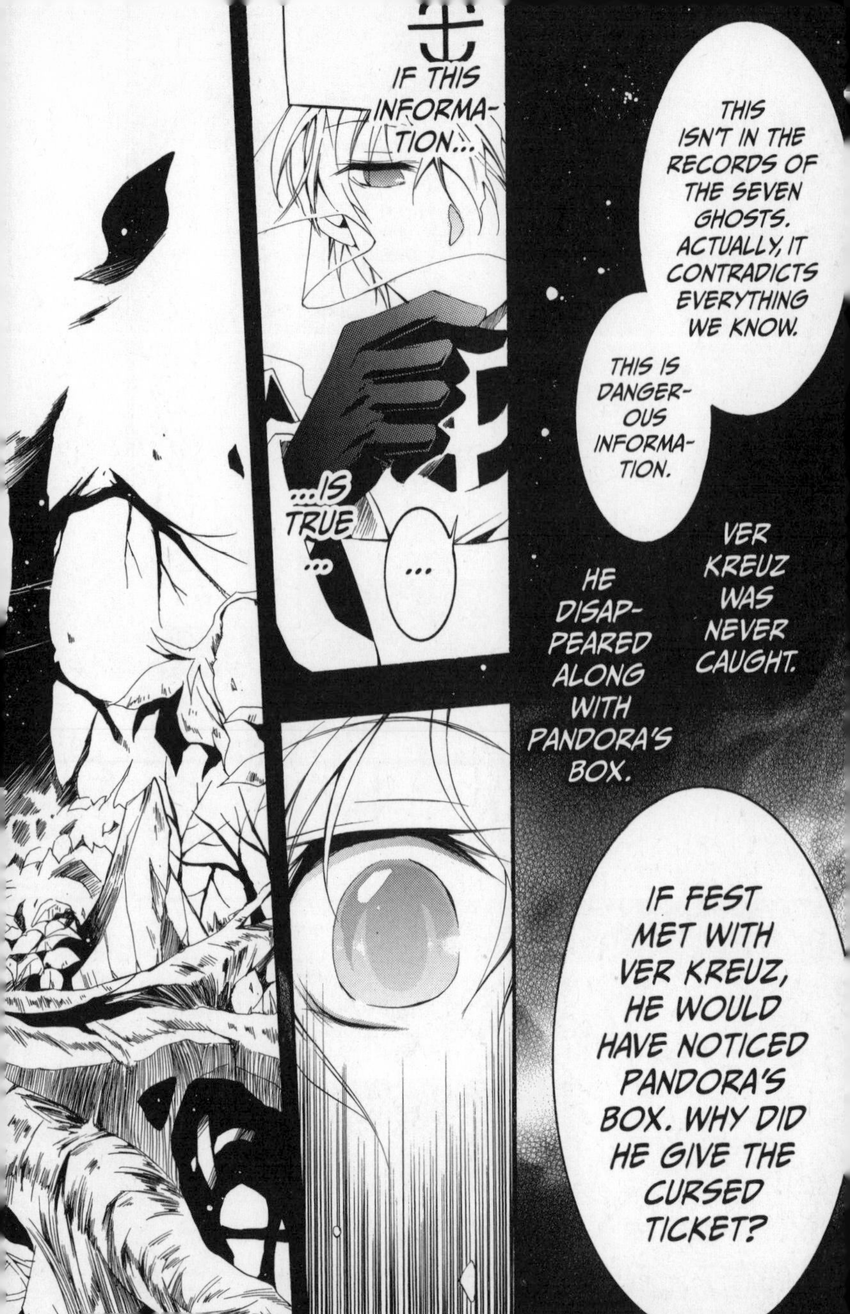
THIS ISN'T IN THE RECORDS OF THE SEVEN GHOSTS. ACTUALLY, IT CONTRADICTS EVERYTHING WE KNOW.
THIS IS DANGEROUS INFORMATION.
VER KREUZ WAS NEVER CAUGHT.
HE DISAPPEARED ALONG WITH PANDORA'S BOX.
IF FEST MET WITH VER KREUZ, HE WOULD HAVE NOTICED PANDORA'S BOX. WHY DID HE GIVE THE CURSED TICKET?
IF THIS INFORMATION...
...IS TRUE...
...

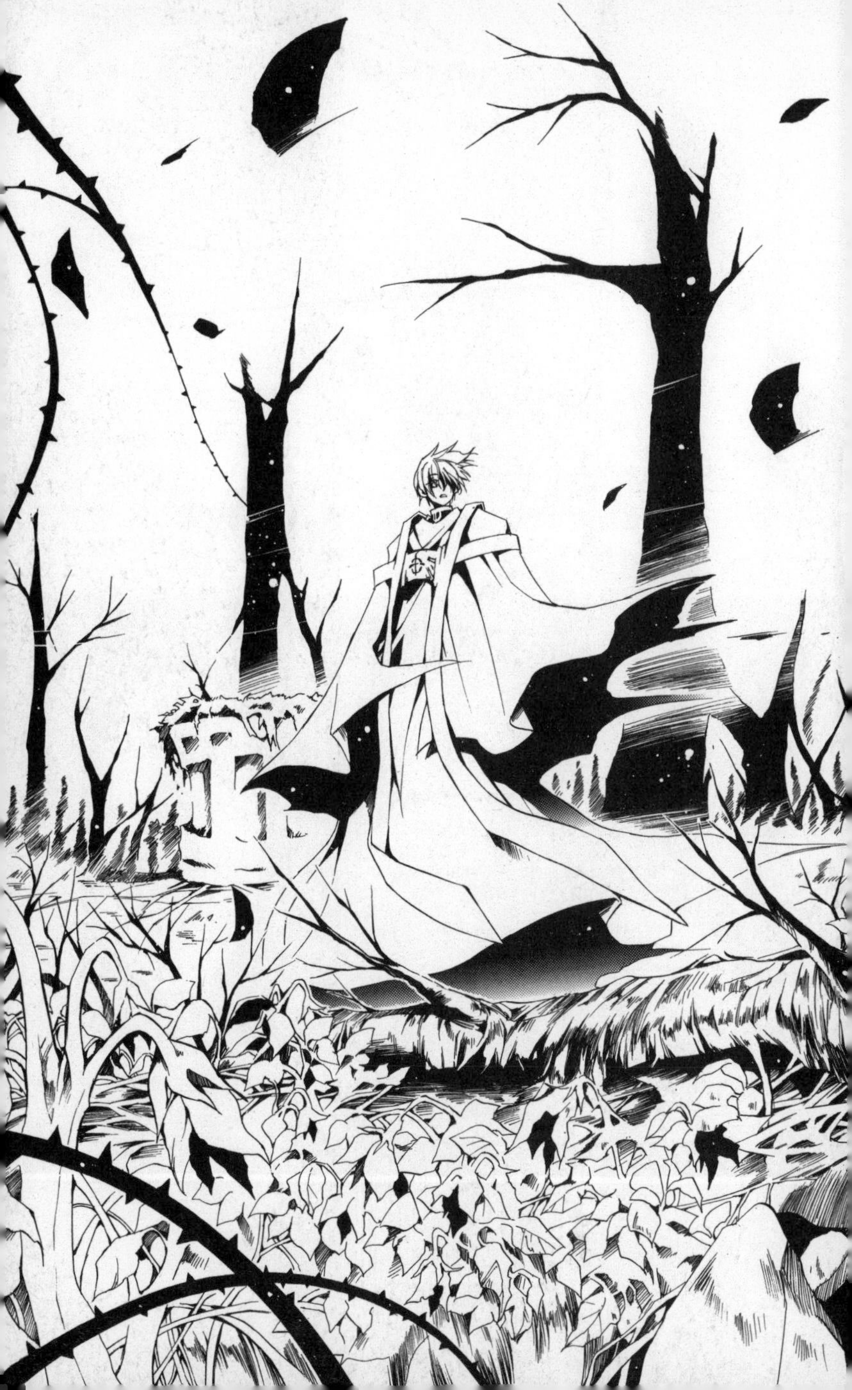

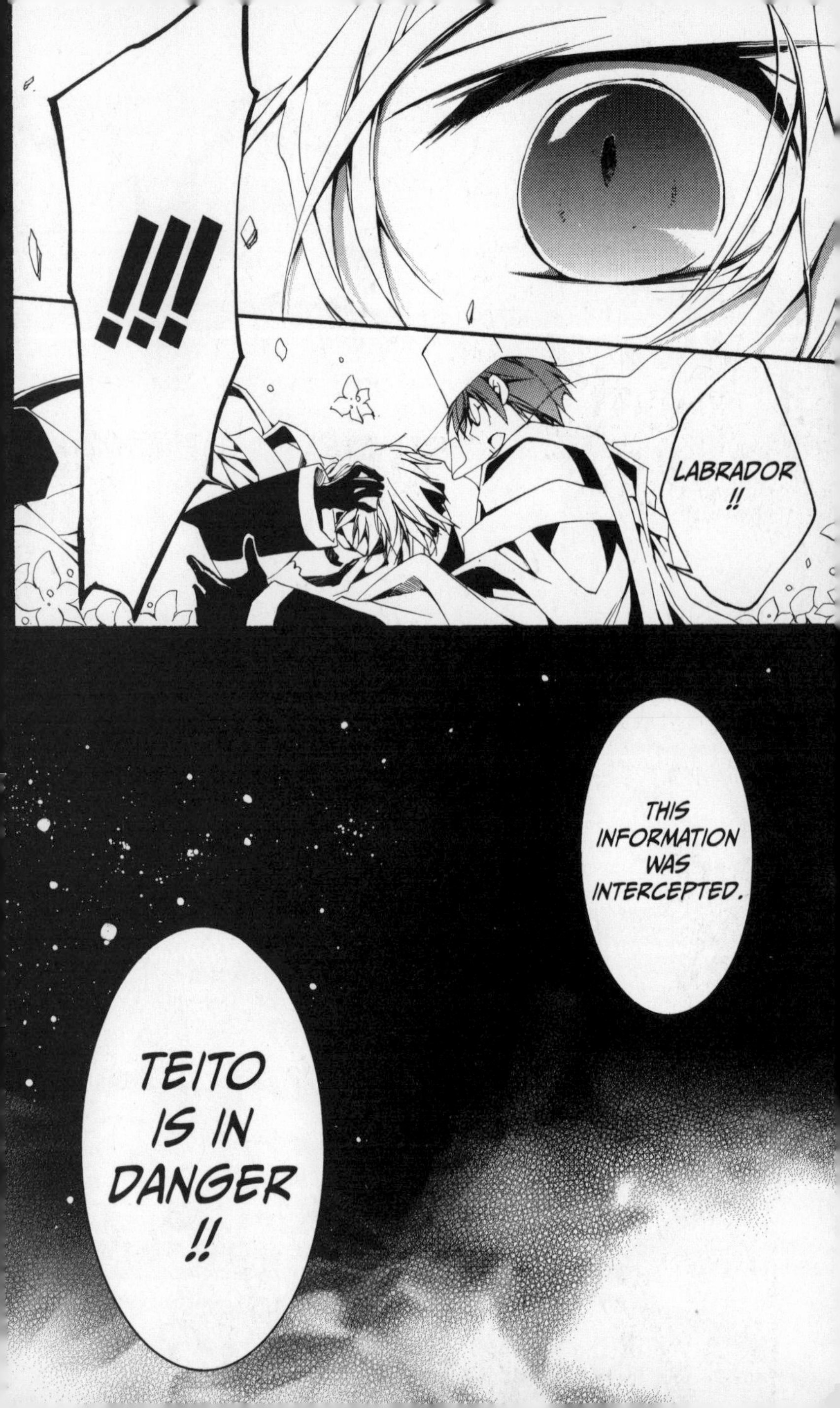
!!!
LABRADOR !!
THIS INFORMATION WAS INTERCEPTED.
TEITO IS IN DANGER !!

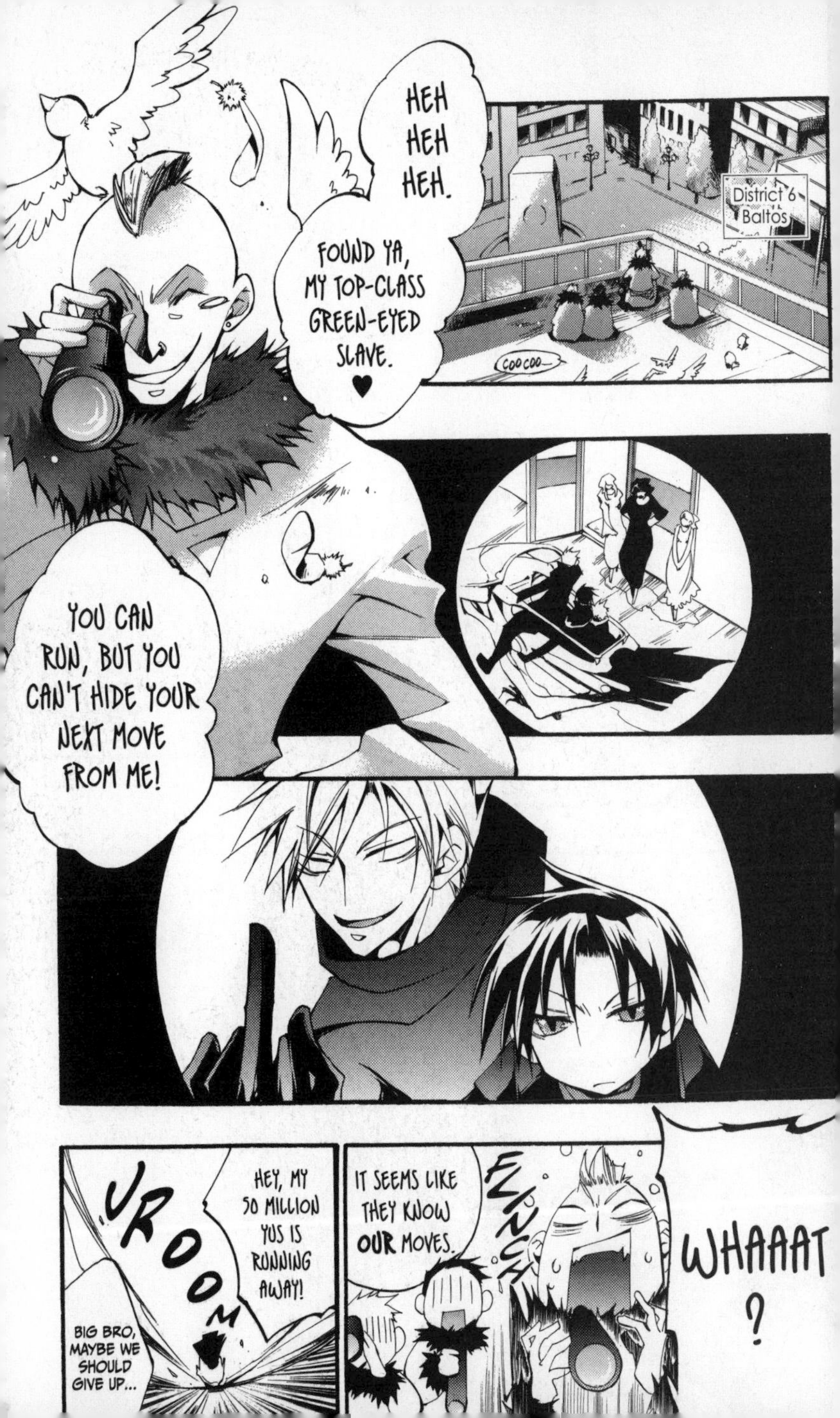
District 6 Baltos
COO COO
HEH HEH HEH.
FOUND YA, MY TOP-CLASS GREEN-EYED SLAVE. ♥
YOU CAN RUN, BUT YOU CAN'T HIDE YOUR NEXT MOVE FROM ME!
WHAAAT?
FLINCH
IT SEEMS LIKE THEY KNOW OUR MOVES.
HEY, MY 50 MILLION YUS IS RUNNING AWAY!
VROOOM
BIG BRO, MAYBE WE SHOULD GIVE UP...

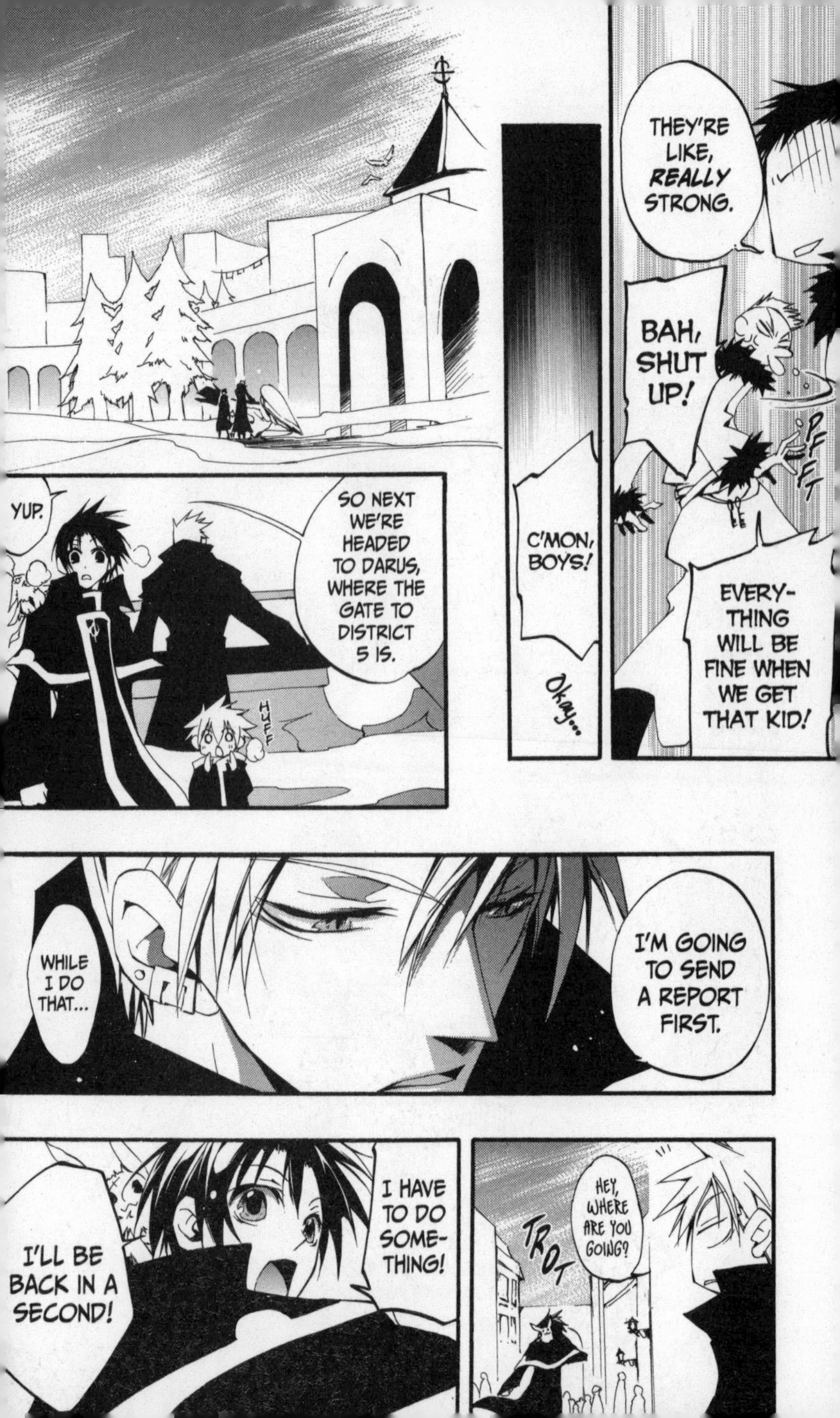
THEY'RE LIKE, REALLY STRONG.
BAH, SHUT UP!
PFFT
EVERYTHING WILL BE FINE WHEN WE GET THAT KID!
C'MON, BOYS!
Okay...
SO NEXT WE'RE HEADED TO DARUS, WHERE THE GATE TO DISTRICT 5 IS.
YUP.
HUFF
I'M GOING TO SEND A REPORT FIRST.
WHILE I DO THAT...
HEY, WHERE ARE YOU GOING?
TROT
I HAVE TO DO SOMETHING!
I'LL BE BACK IN A SECOND!

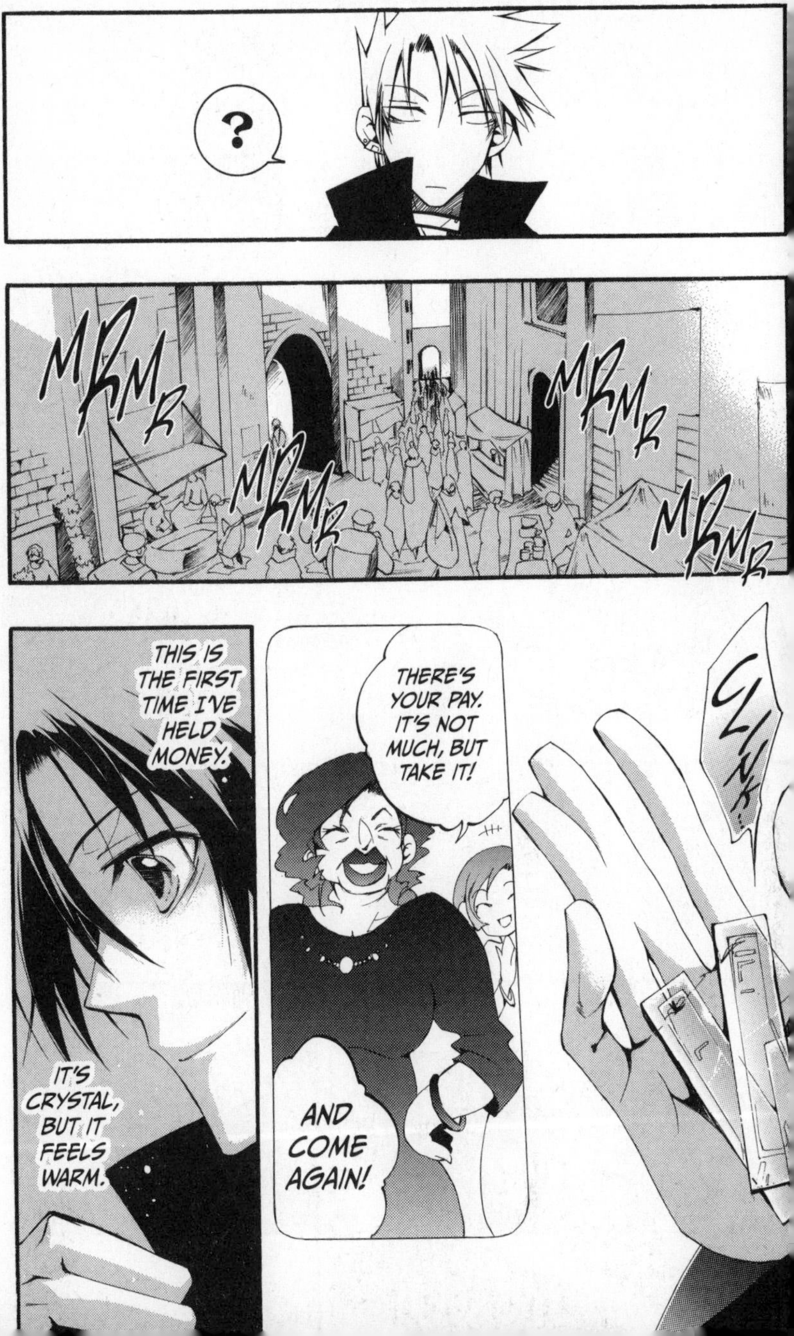
?
MRMR
MRMR
MRMR
MRMR
CLINK...
THERE'S YOUR PAY. IT'S NOT MUCH, BUT TAKE IT!
AND COME AGAIN!
THIS IS THE FIRST TIME I'VE HELD MONEY.
IT'S CRYSTAL, BUT IT FEELS WARM.

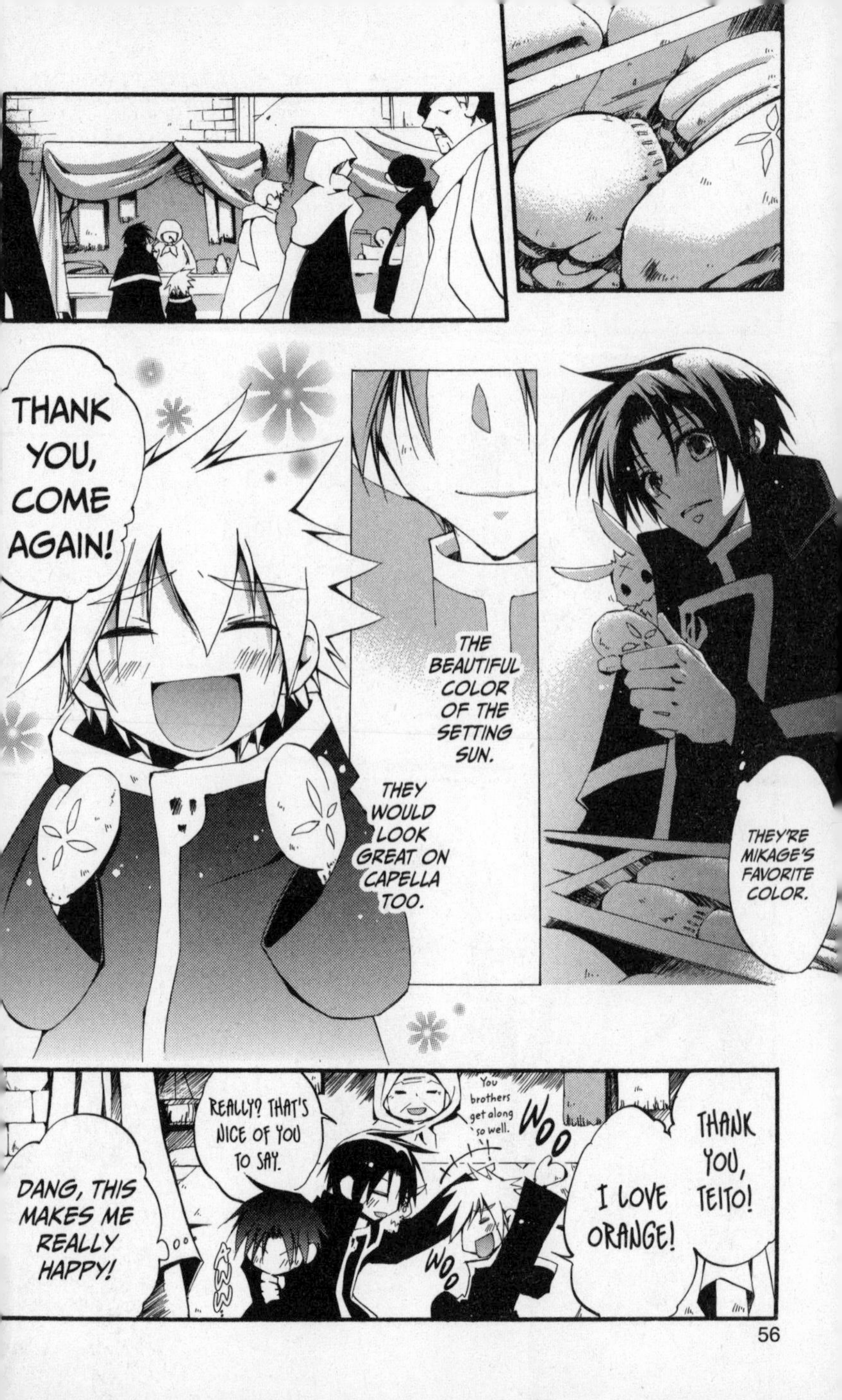
THEY'RE MIKAGE'S FAVORITE COLOR.
THE BEAUTIFUL COLOR OF THE SETTING SUN.
THEY WOULD LOOK GREAT ON CAPELLA TOO.
THANK YOU, COME AGAIN!
THANK YOU, TEITO!
I LOVE ORANGE!
WOO
WOO
You brothers get along so well.
REALLY? THAT'S NICE OF YOU TO SAY.
DANG, THIS MAKES ME REALLY HAPPY!
AWW

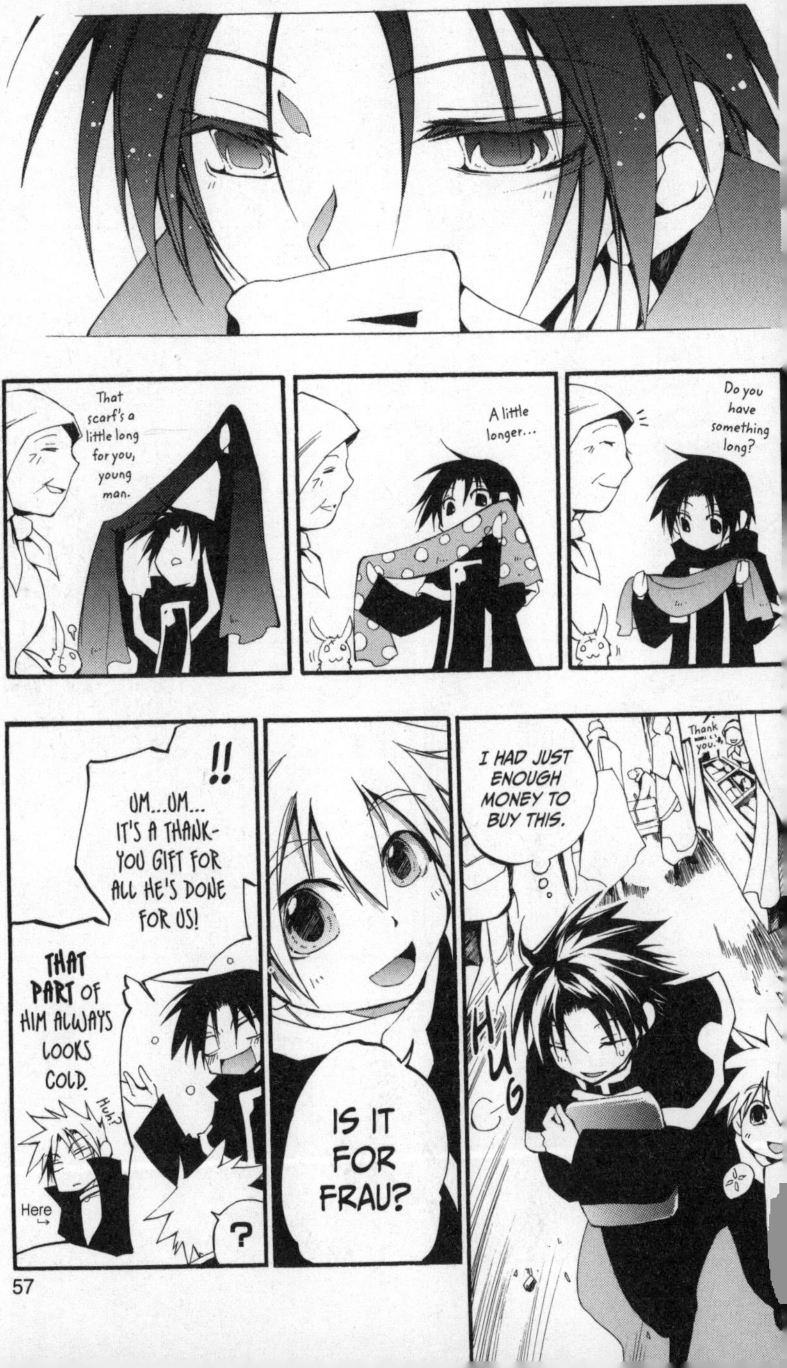
Do you have something long?
A little longer...
That scarf's a little long for you, young man.
Thank you.
I HAD JUST ENOUGH MONEY TO BUY THIS.
HUG
IS IT FOR FRAU?
!!
UM...UM... IT'S A THANK-YOU GIFT FOR ALL HE'S DONE FOR US!
THAT PART OF HIM ALWAYS LOOKS COLD.
Huh?
Here
?

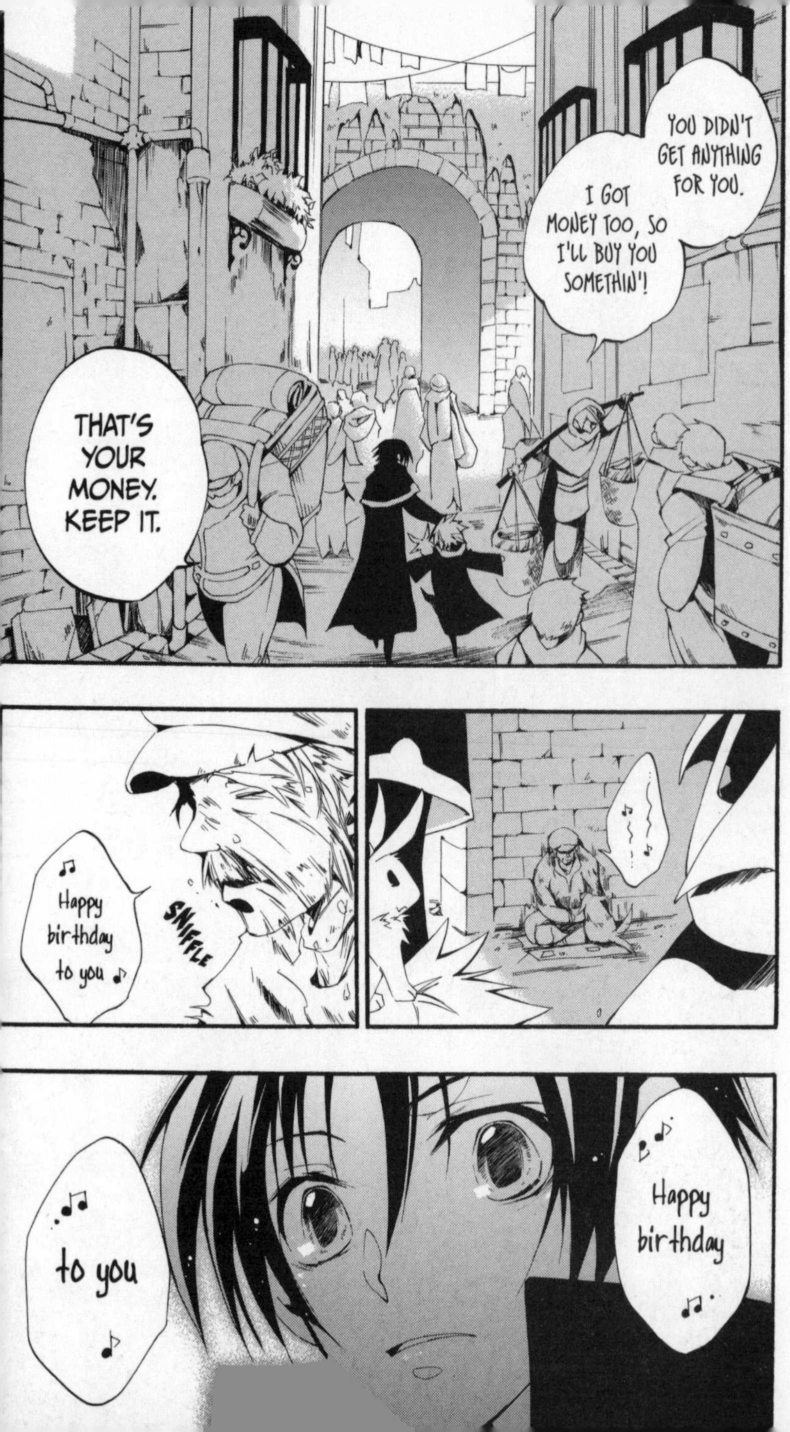
YOU DIDN'T GET ANYTHING FOR YOU.
I GOT MONEY TOO, SO I'LL BUY YOU SOMETHIN'!
THAT'S YOUR MONEY. KEEP IT.
Happy birthday to you
SNIFFLE
Happy birthday
to you

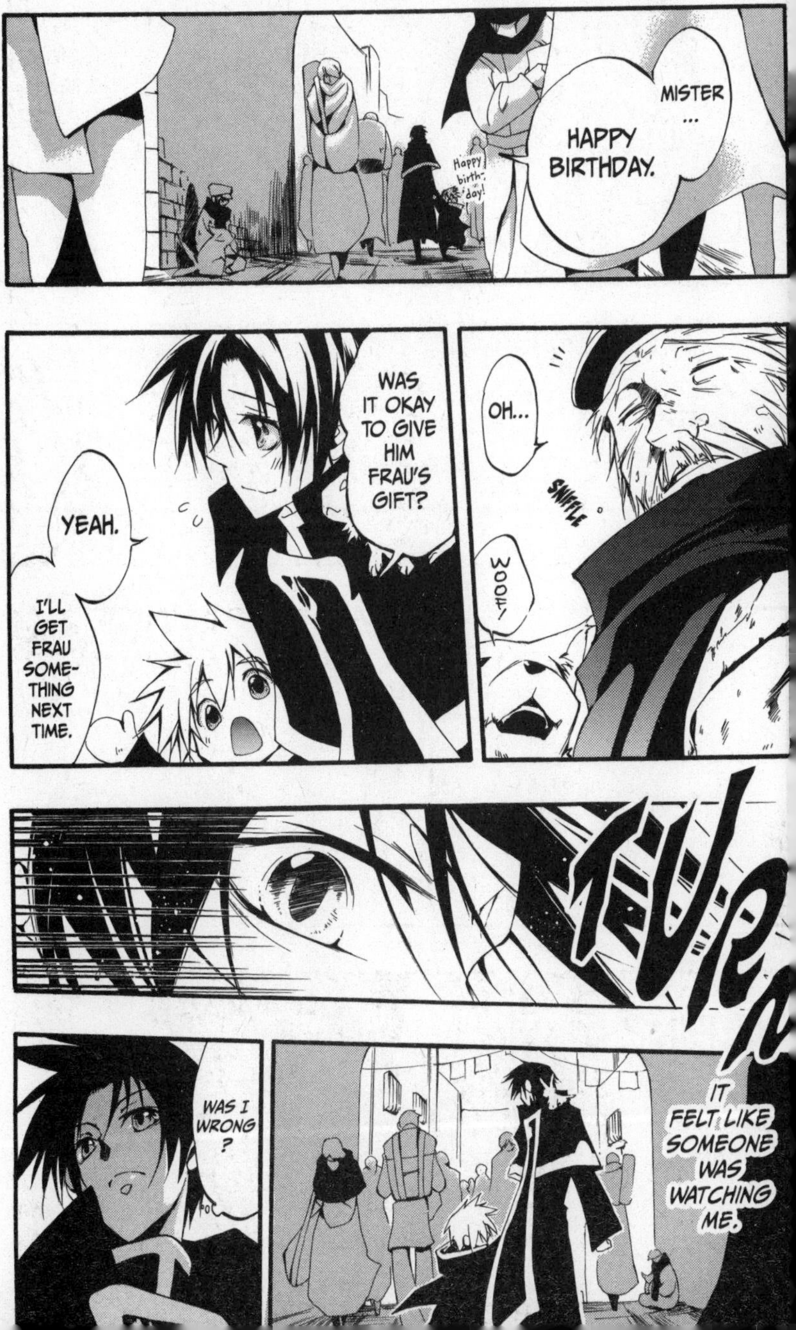
MISTER ...
HAPPY BIRTHDAY.
Happy birth-day!
OH...
SNIFFLE
WOOF!
WAS IT OKAY TO GIVE HIM FRAU'S GIFT?
YEAH.
I'LL GET FRAU SOMETHING NEXT TIME.
TURN
IT FELT LIKE SOMEONE WAS WATCHING ME.
WAS I WRONG?

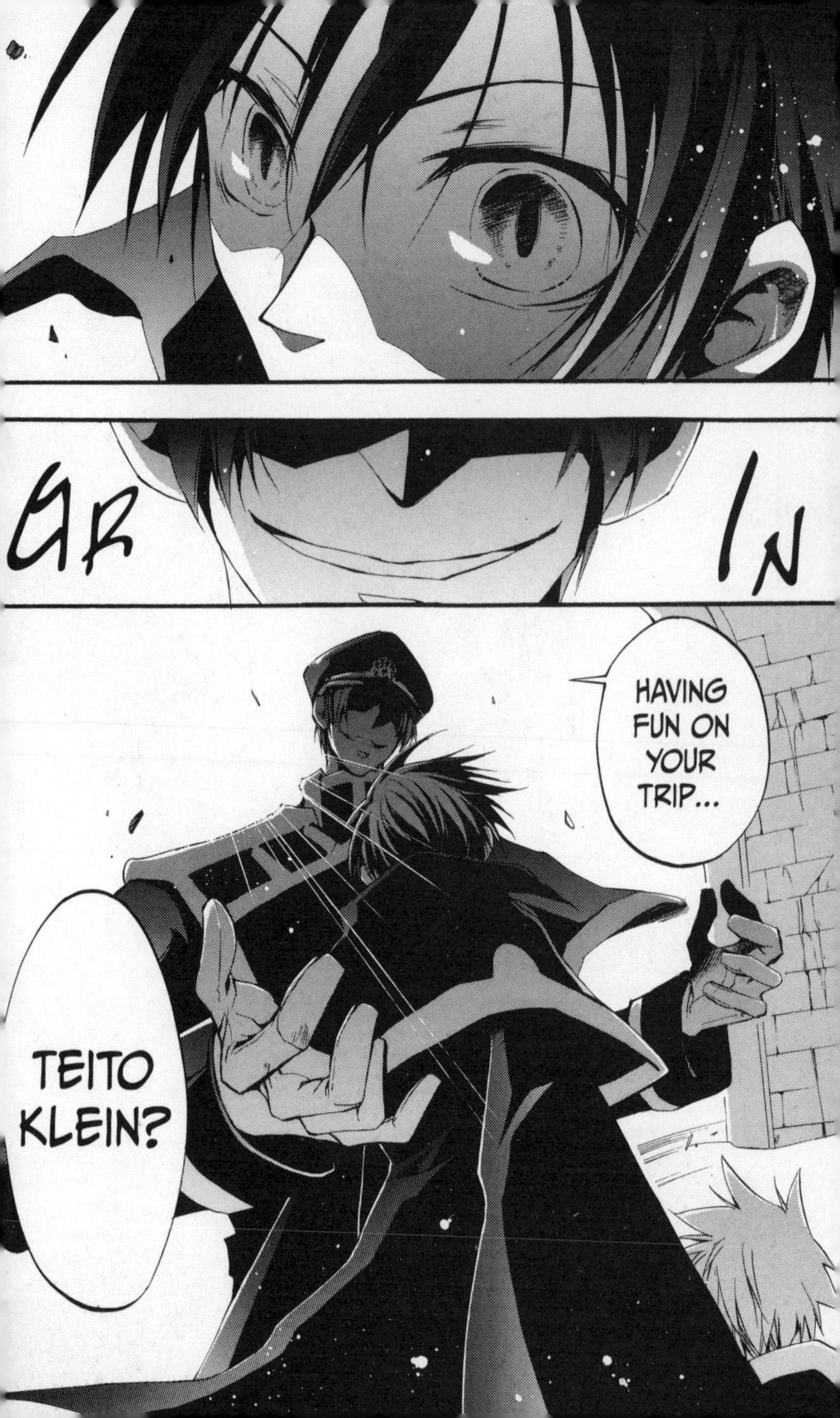
GRIN
HAVING FUN ON YOUR TRIP...
TEITO KLEIN?

Kapitel.38
“Mark”

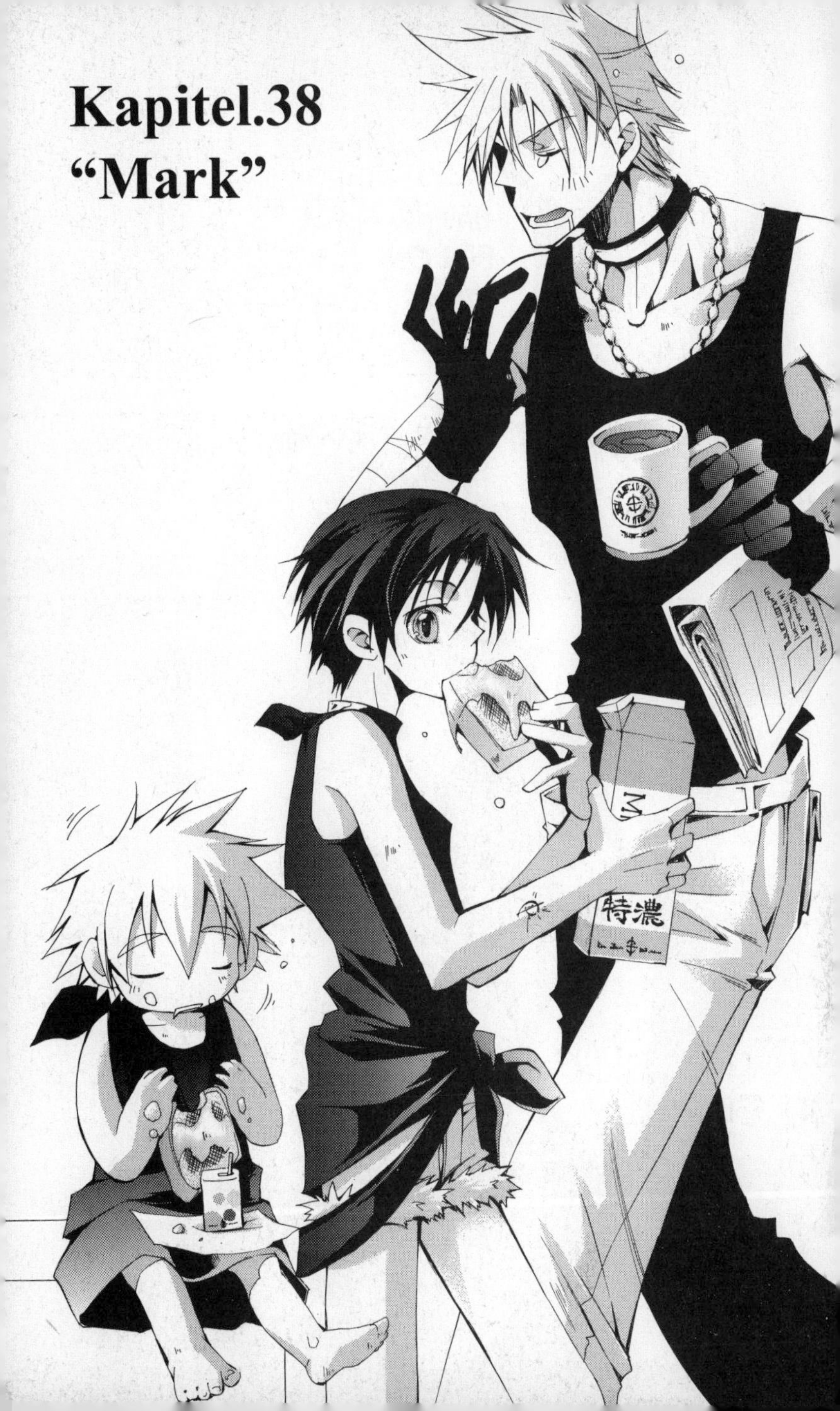
特濃

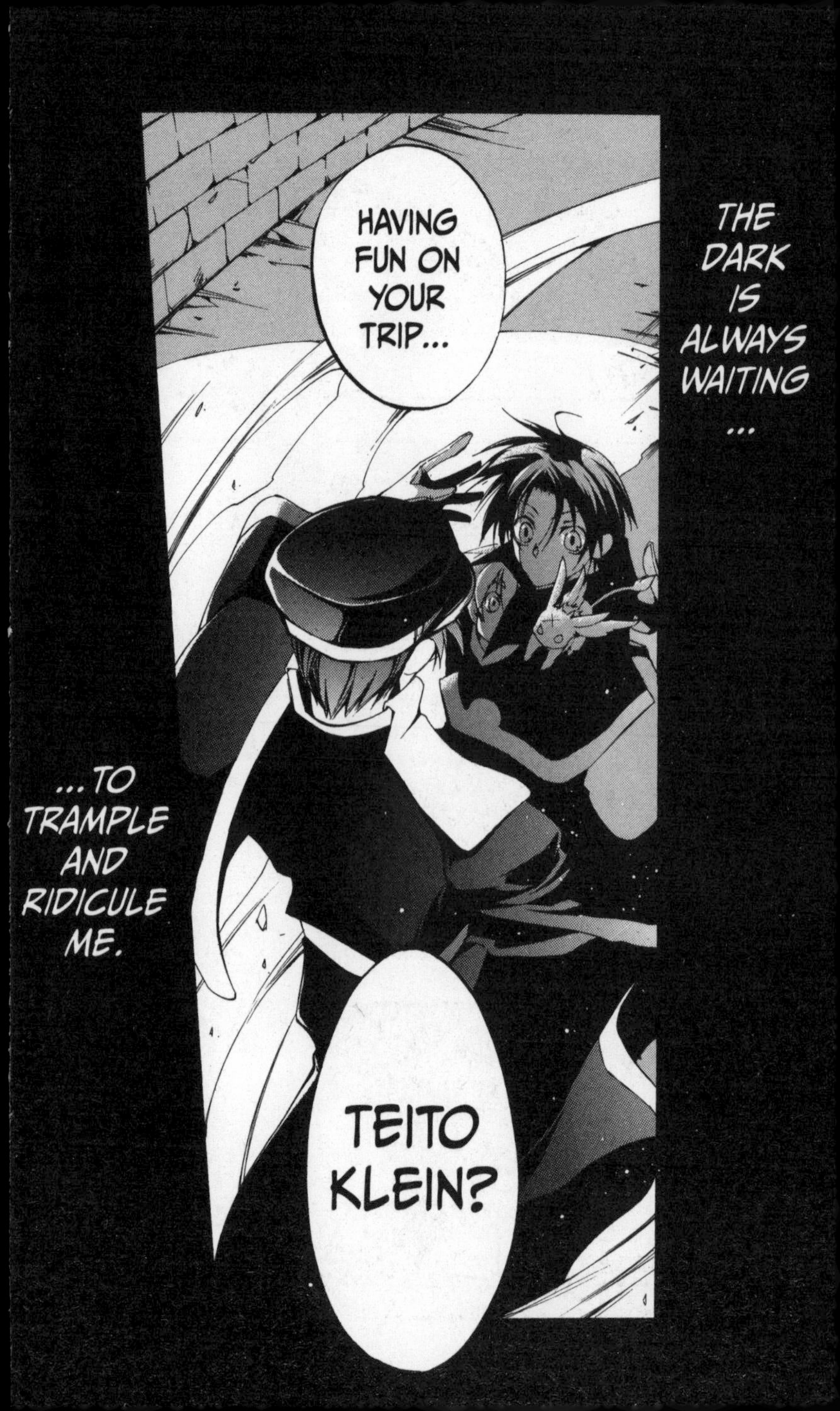
THE DARK IS ALWAYS WAITING ...
HAVING FUN ON YOUR TRIP...
...TO TRAMPLE AND RIDICULE ME.
TEITO KLEIN?

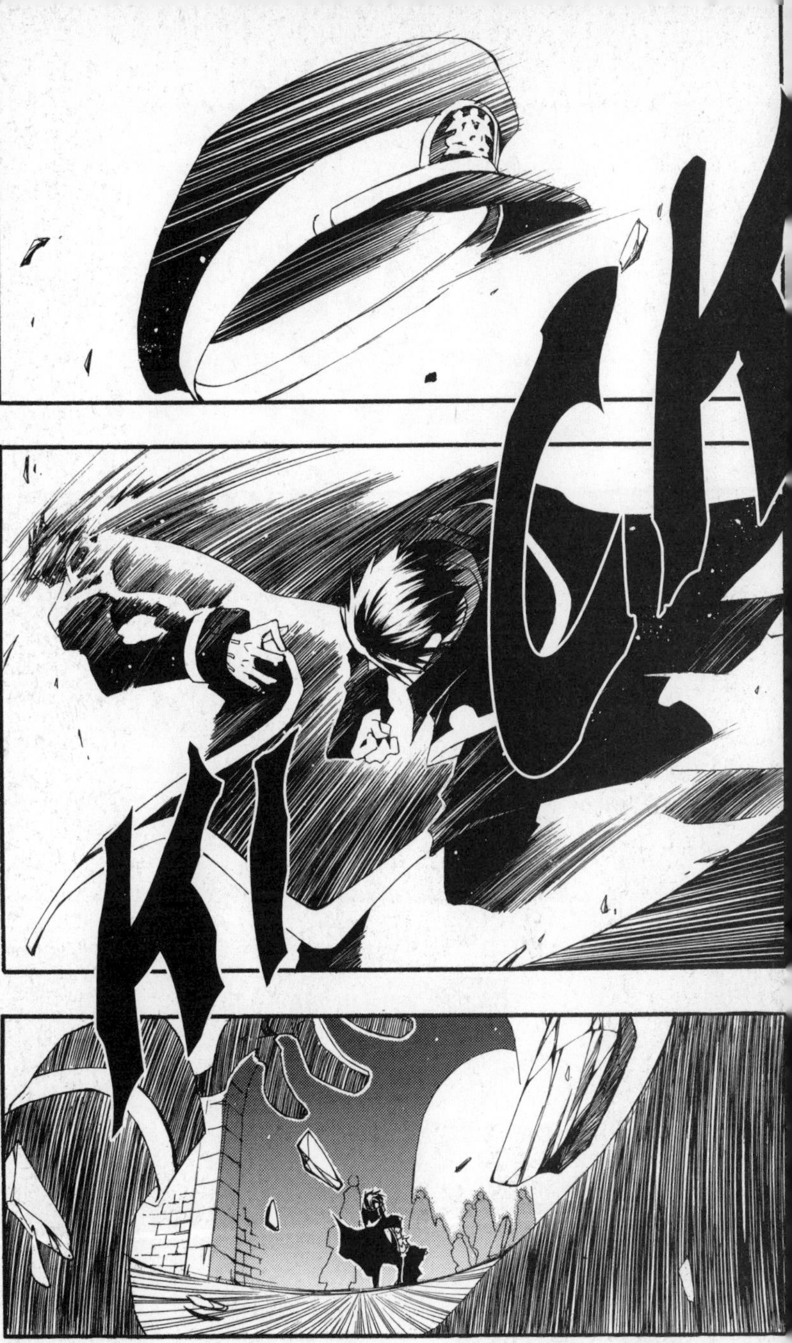

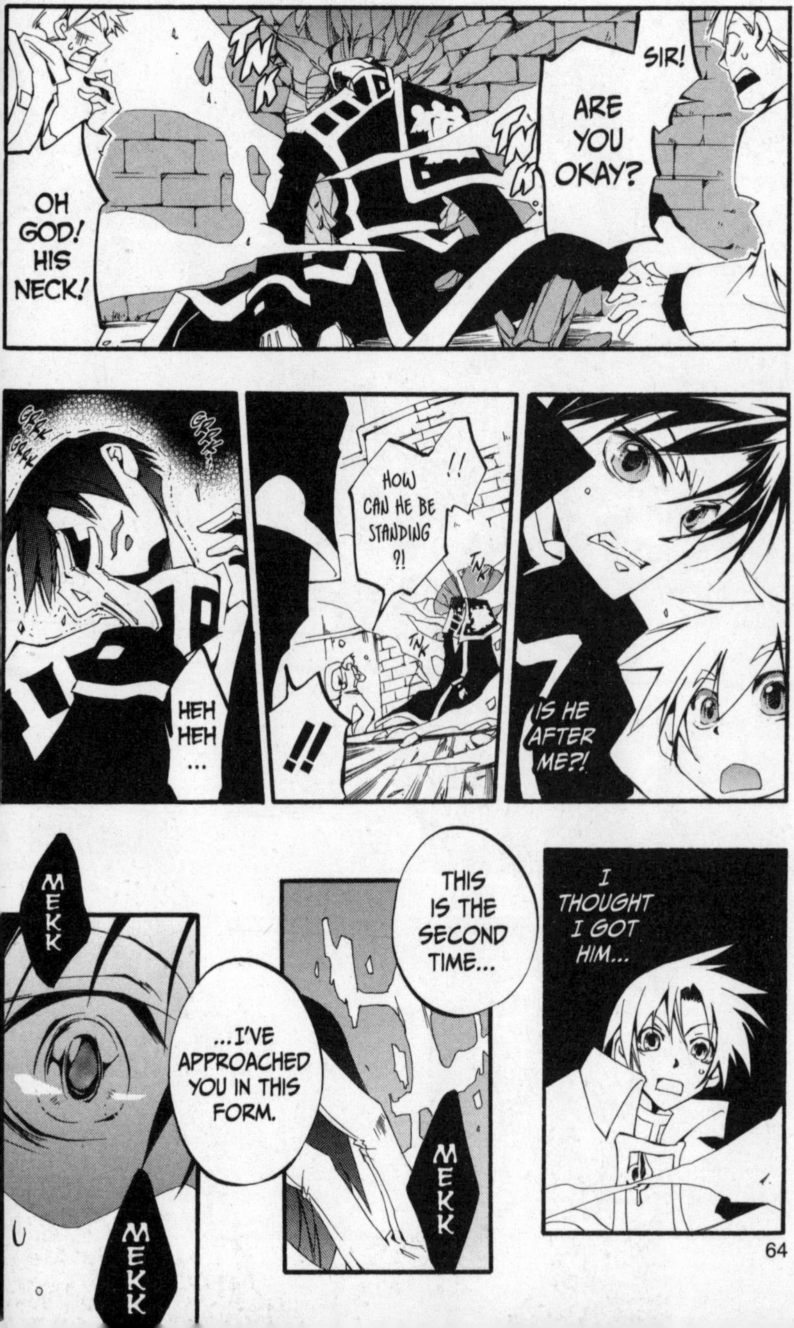
SIR!
ARE YOU OKAY?
TNK
TNK
OH GOD! HIS NECK!
IS HE AFTER ME?!
HOW CAN HE BE STANDING ?!
!!
TNK
TNK
!!
GRAK...
GRAK
GRAK
HEH HEH ...
I THOUGHT I GOT HIM...
THIS IS THE SECOND TIME...
...I'VE APPROACHED YOU IN THIS FORM.
MEKK
MEKK
MEKK

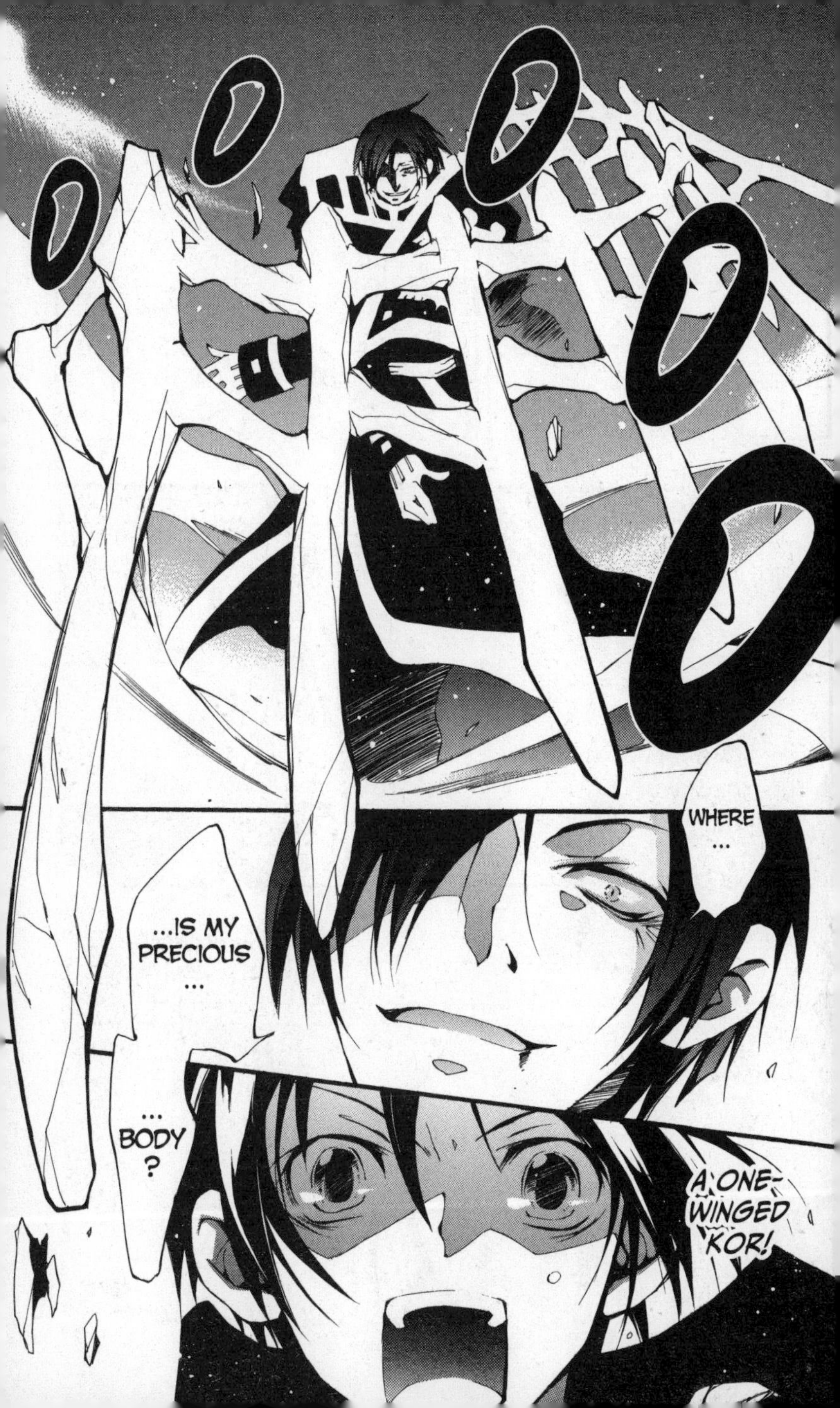
WHERE ...
...IS MY PRECIOUS ...
... BODY ?
A ONE-WINGED KOR!

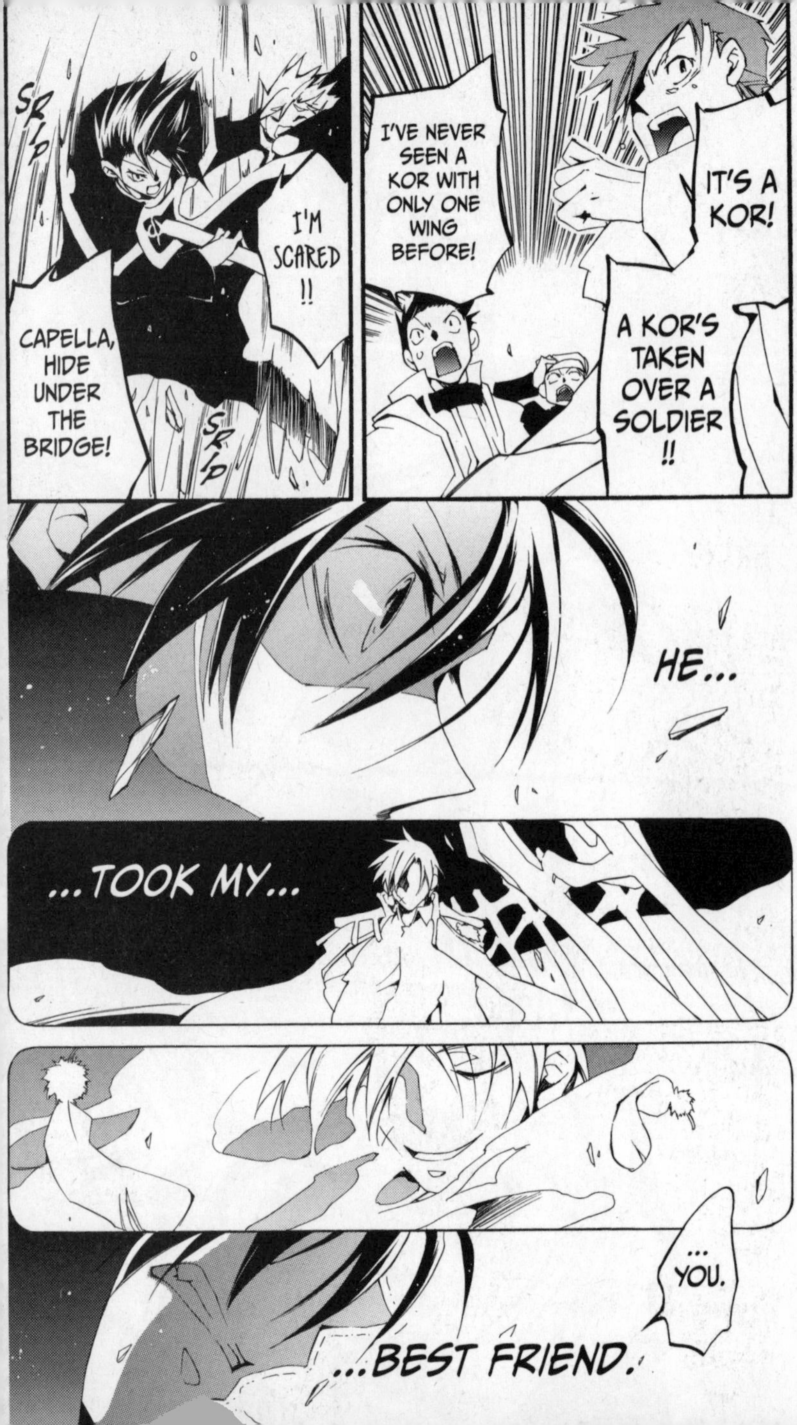
IT'S A KOR!
A KOR'S TAKEN OVER A SOLDIER!!
I'VE NEVER SEEN A KOR WITH ONLY ONE WING BEFORE!
I'M SCARED!!
SRIP
CAPELLA, HIDE UNDER THE BRIDGE!
SRIP
HE...
...TOOK MY...
...YOU.
...BEST FRIEND.

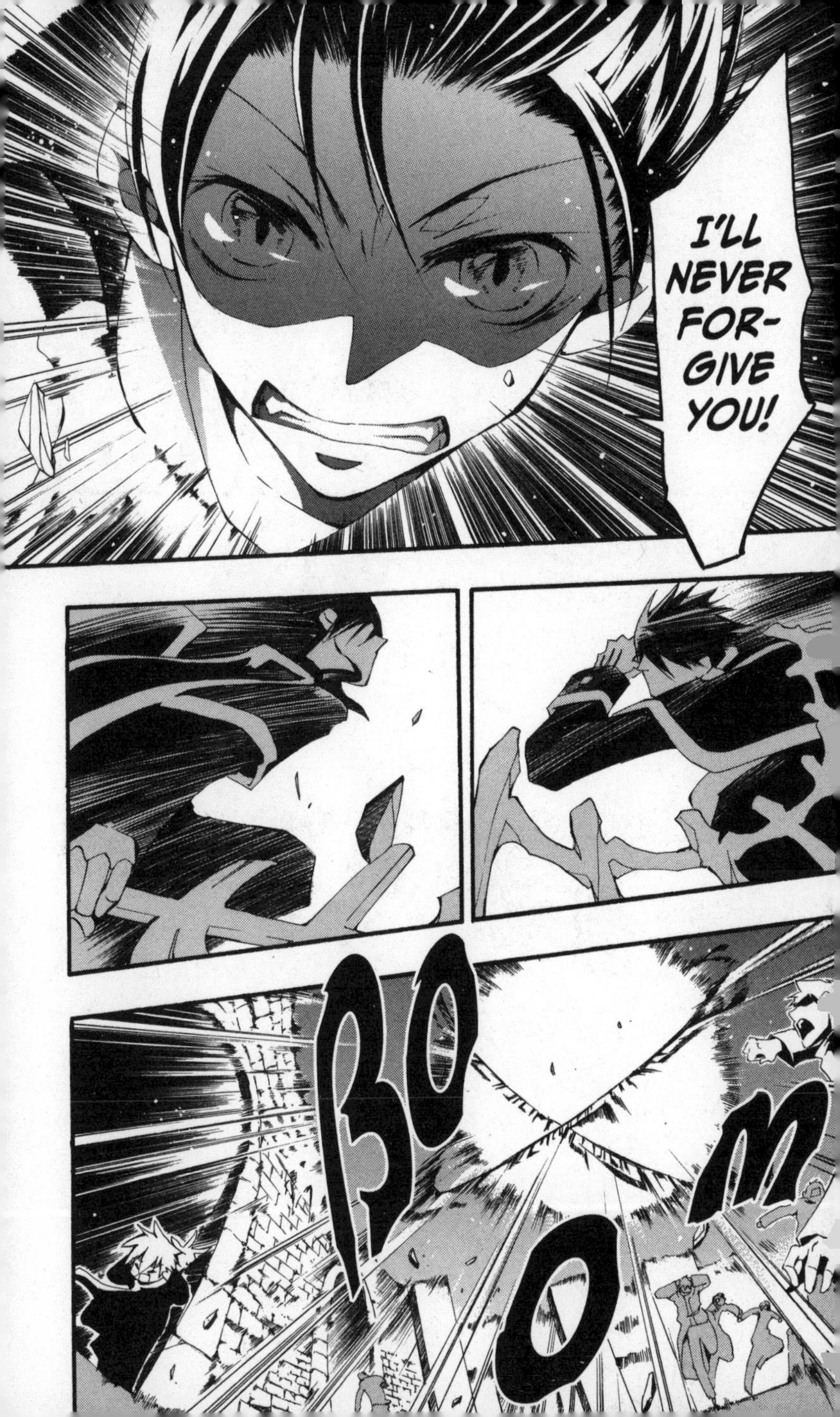
I'LL NEVER FOR-GIVE YOU!
BOOOM

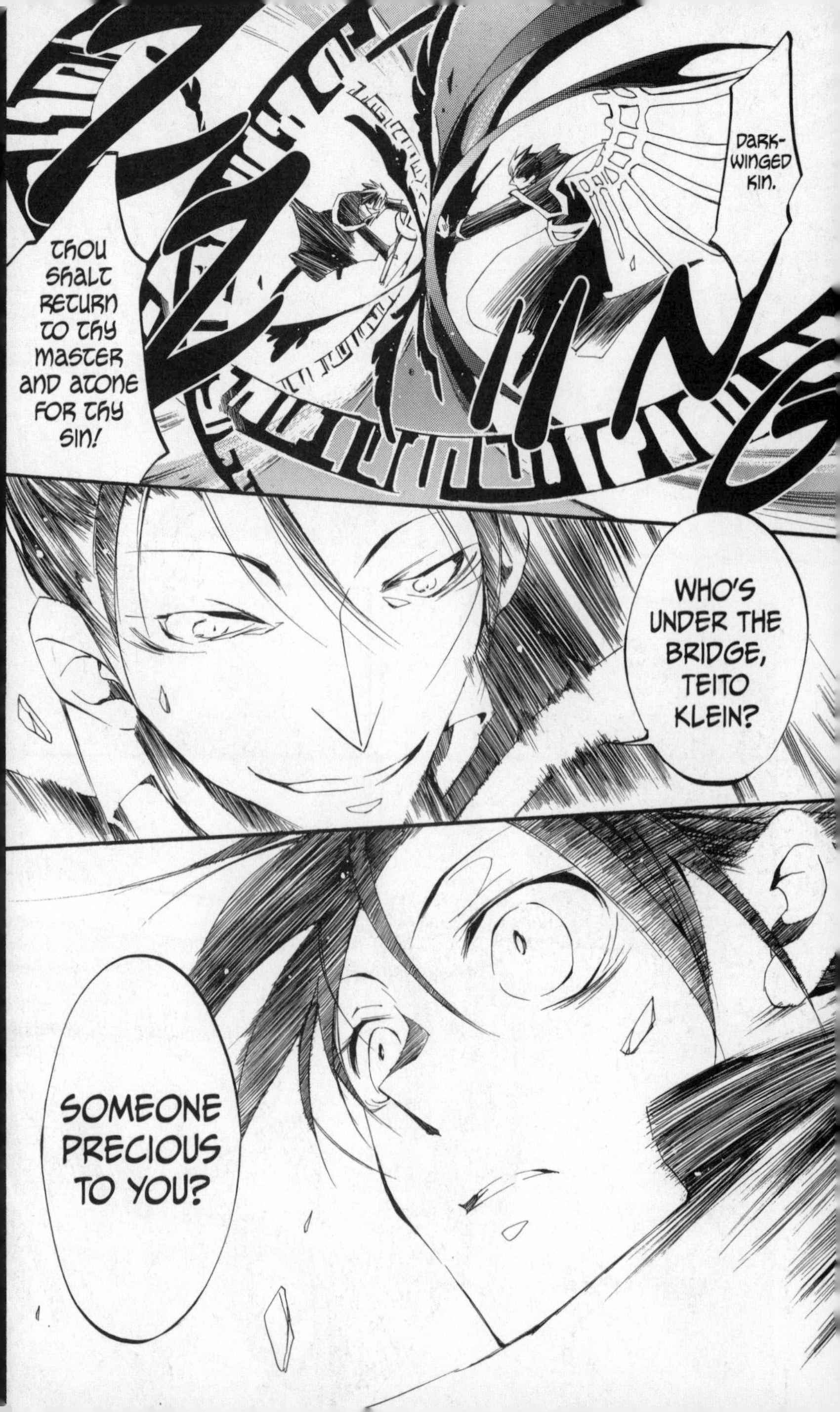
DARK-WINGED KIN.
THOU SHALT RETURN TO THY MASTER AND ATONE FOR THY SIN!
WHO'S UNDER THE BRIDGE, TEITO KLEIN?
SOMEONE PRECIOUS TO YOU?

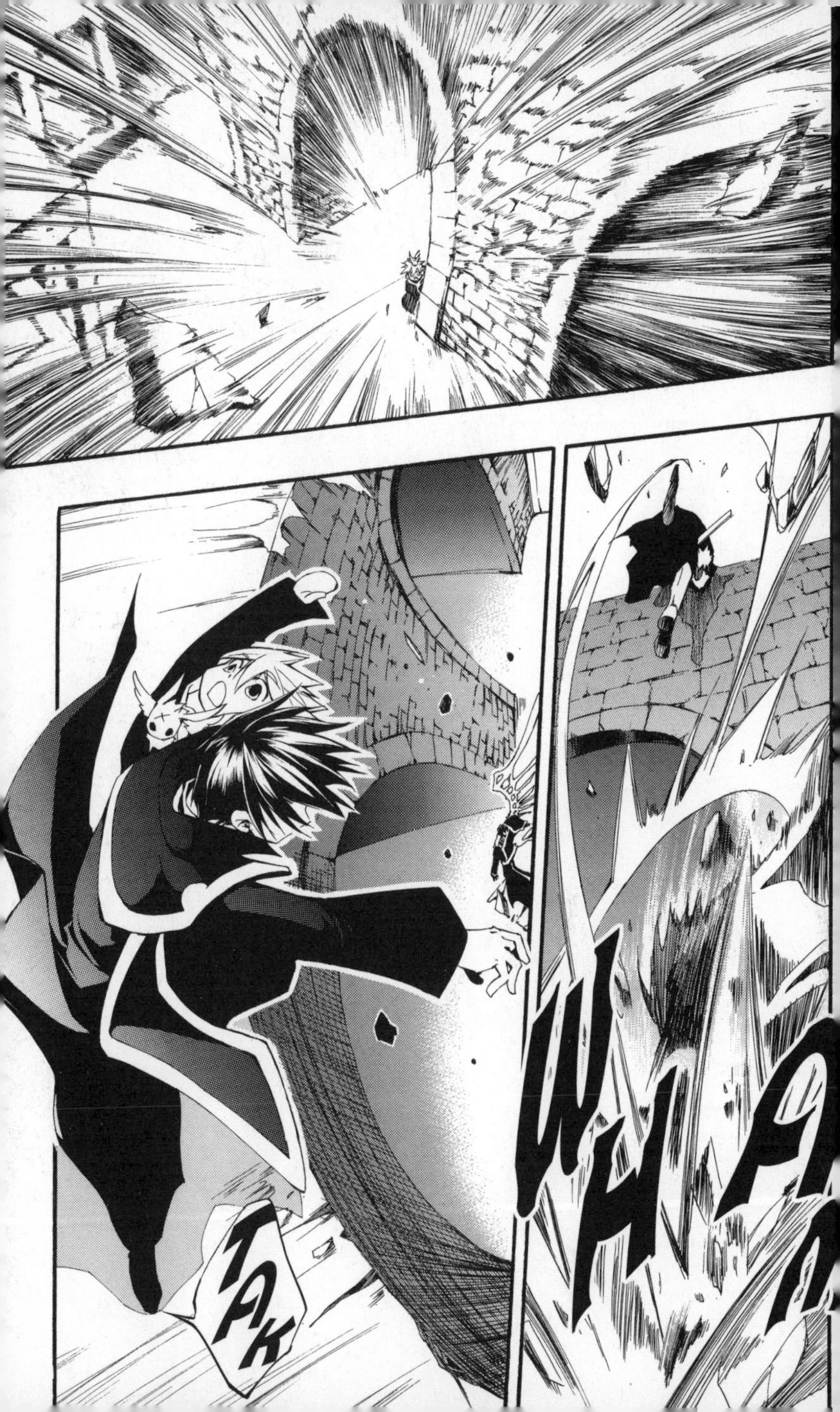
TAK

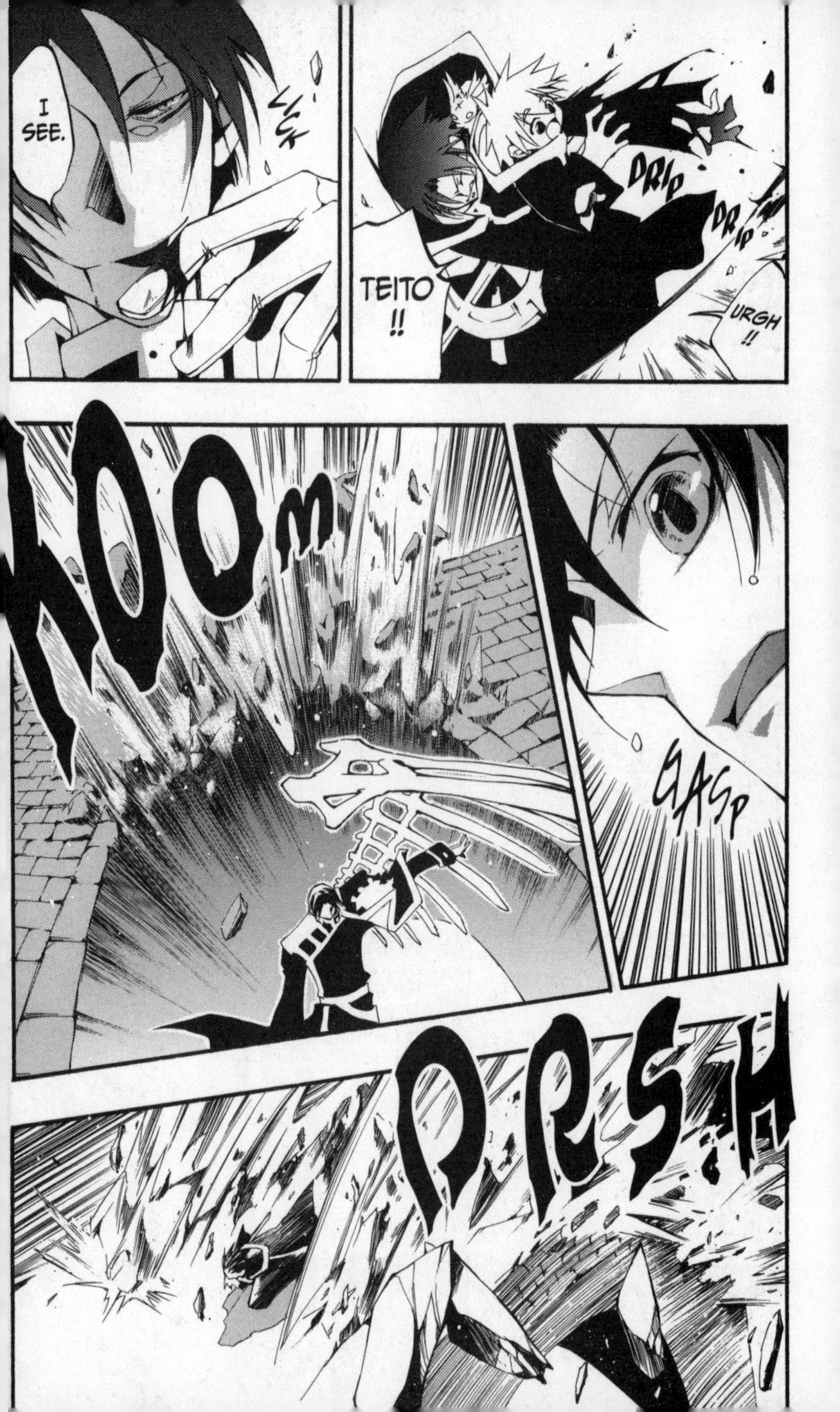
DRIP
DRIP
URGH !!
TEITO !!
LICK
I SEE.
GASP

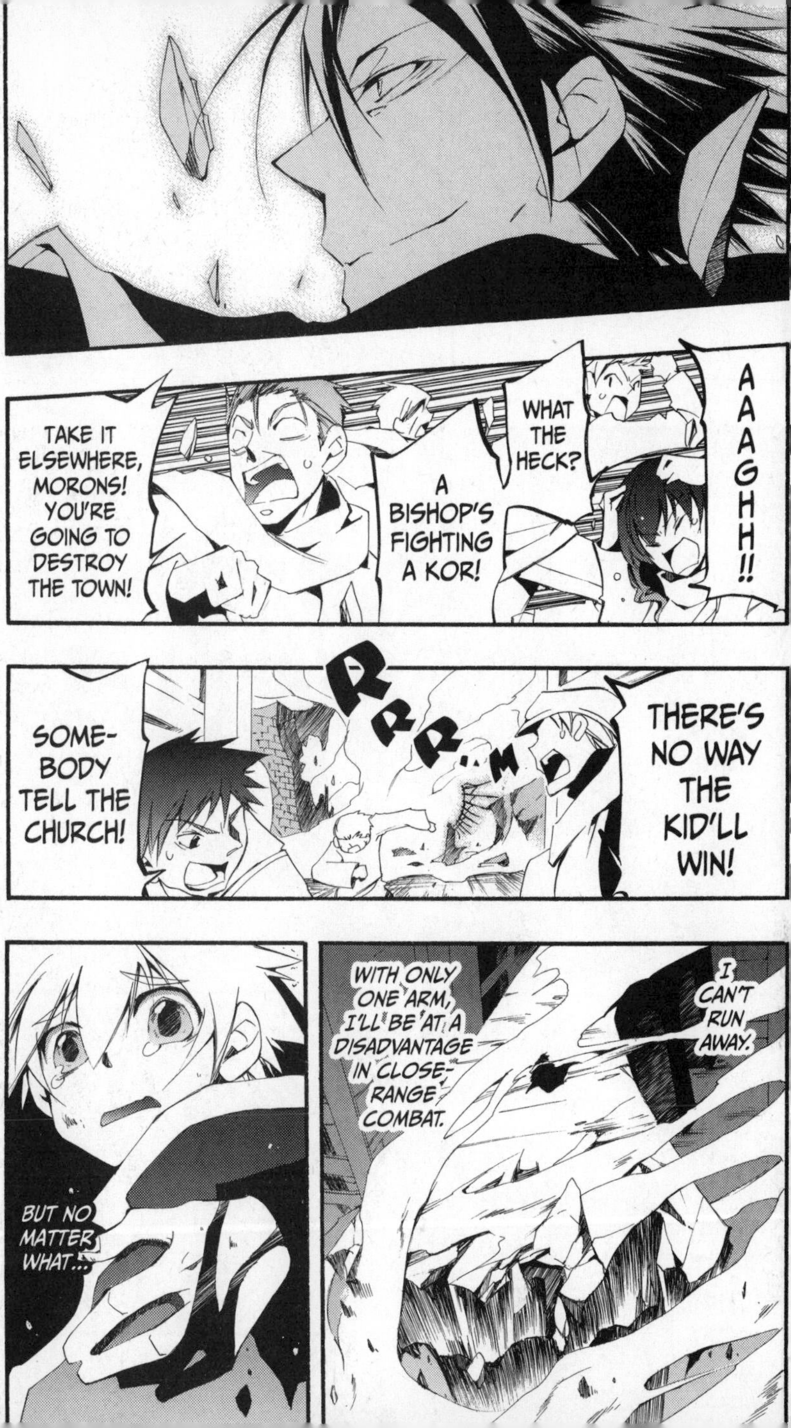
AAAAGHH!!
WHAT THE HECK?
A BISHOP'S FIGHTING A KOR!
TAKE IT ELSEWHERE, MORONS! YOU'RE GOING TO DESTROY THE TOWN!
THERE'S NO WAY THE KID'LL WIN!
RRR..M
SOME-BODY TELL THE CHURCH!
I CAN'T RUN AWAY.
WITH ONLY ONE ARM, I'LL BE AT A DISADVANTAGE IN CLOSE-RANGE COMBAT.
BUT NO MATTER WHAT...

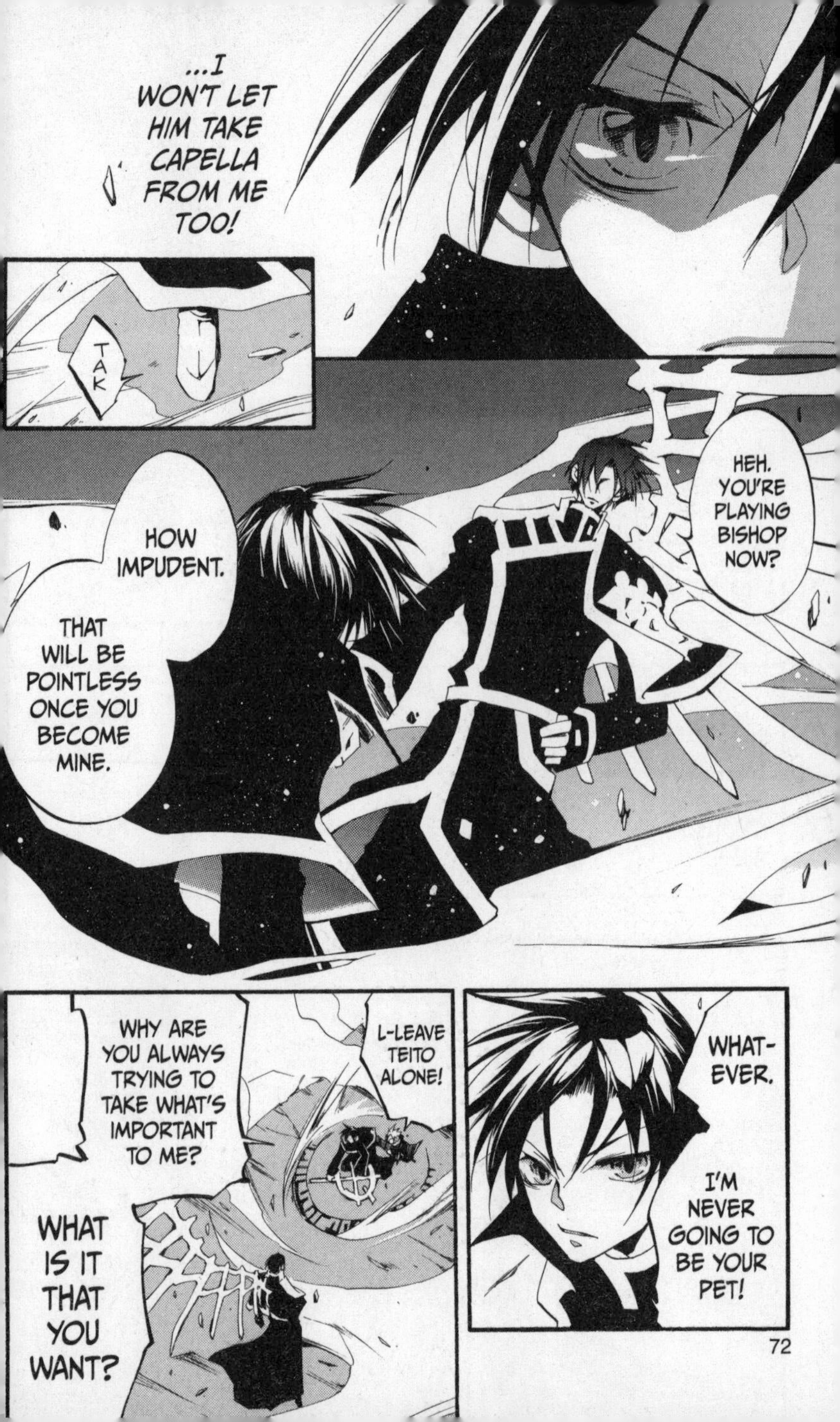
...I WON'T LET HIM TAKE CAPELLA FROM ME TOO!
TAK
HEH. YOU'RE PLAYING BISHOP NOW?
HOW IMPUDENT.
THAT WILL BE POINTLESS ONCE YOU BECOME MINE.
WHAT-EVER.
I'M NEVER GOING TO BE YOUR PET!
L-LEAVE TEITO ALONE!
WHY ARE YOU ALWAYS TRYING TO TAKE WHAT'S IMPORTANT TO ME?
WHAT IS IT THAT YOU WANT?

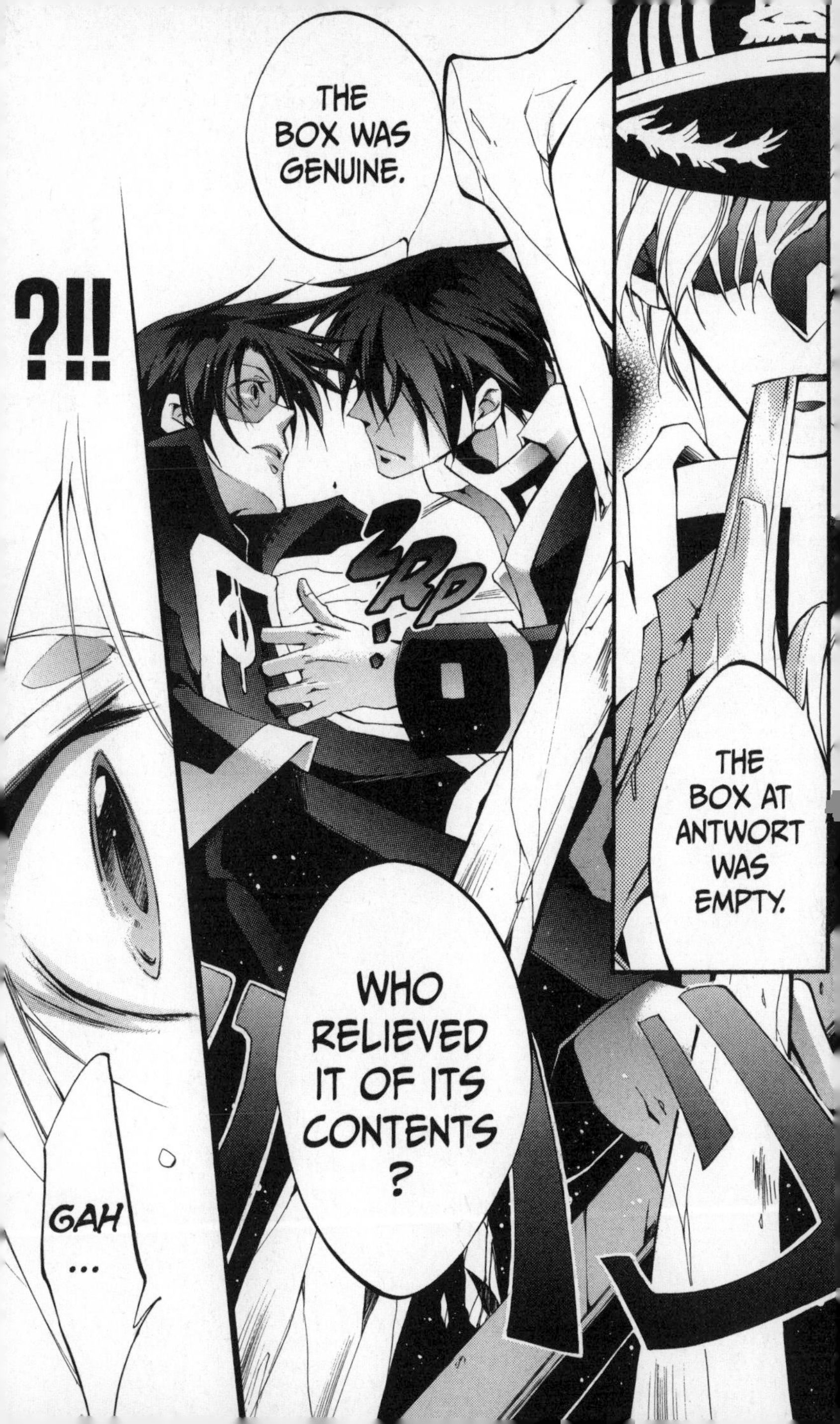
THE BOX AT ANTWORT WAS EMPTY.
THE BOX WAS GENUINE.
ZAP
WHO RELIEVED IT OF ITS CONTENTS ?
?!!
GAH ...

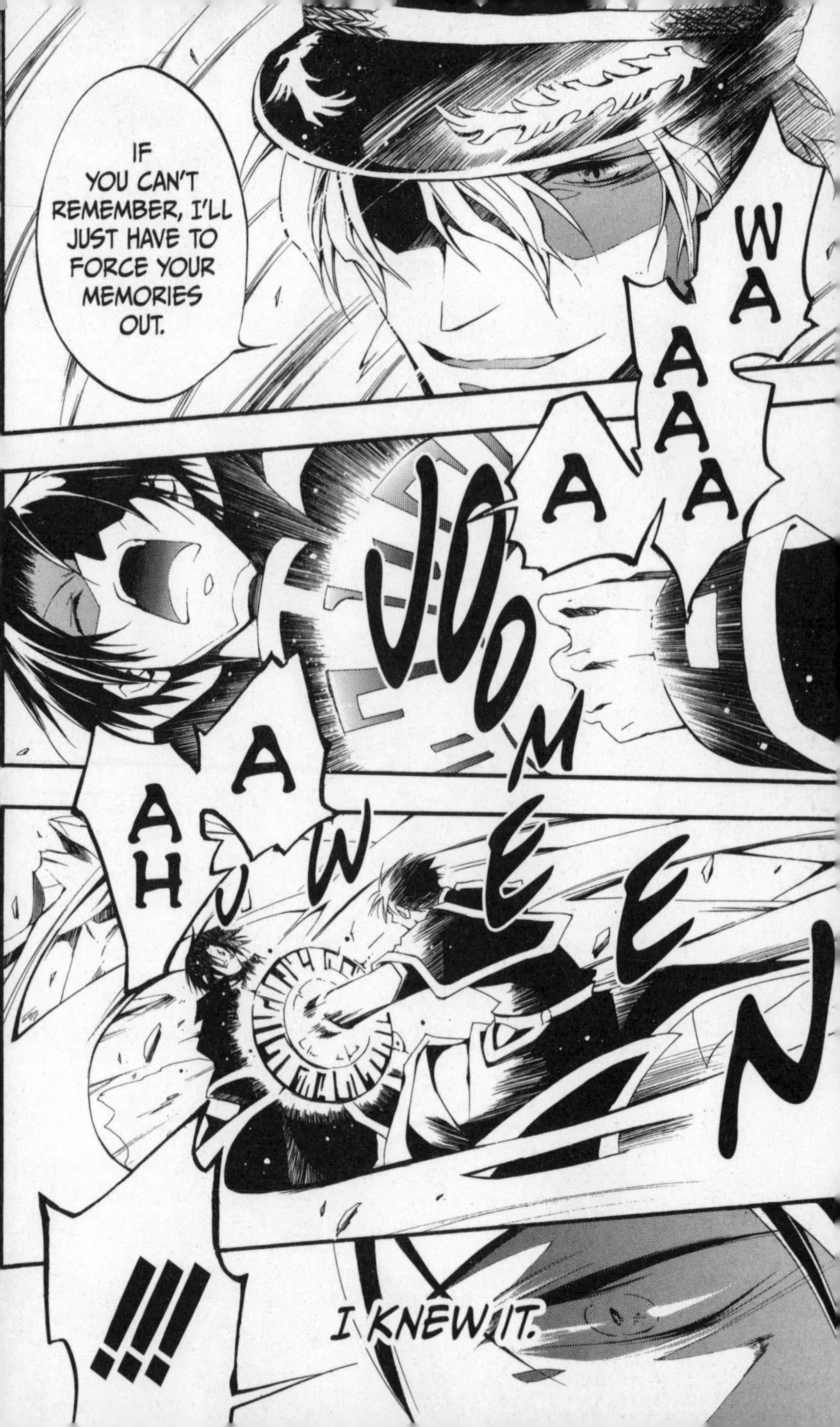
IF YOU CAN'T REMEMBER, I'LL JUST HAVE TO FORCE YOUR MEMORIES OUT.
WAAAAAAAH
!!!
I KNEW IT.

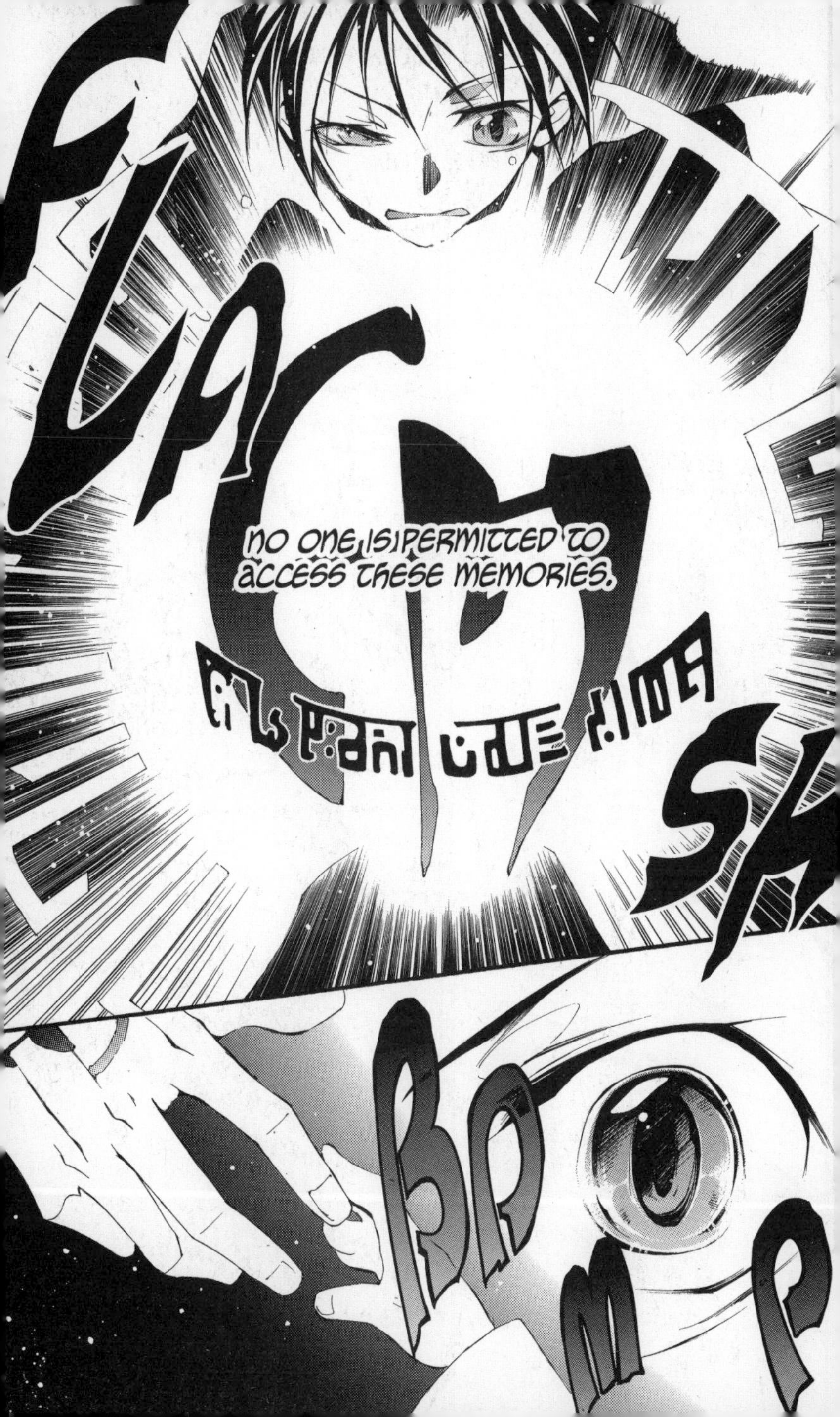
NO ONE IS PERMITTED TO ACCESS THESE MEMORIES.

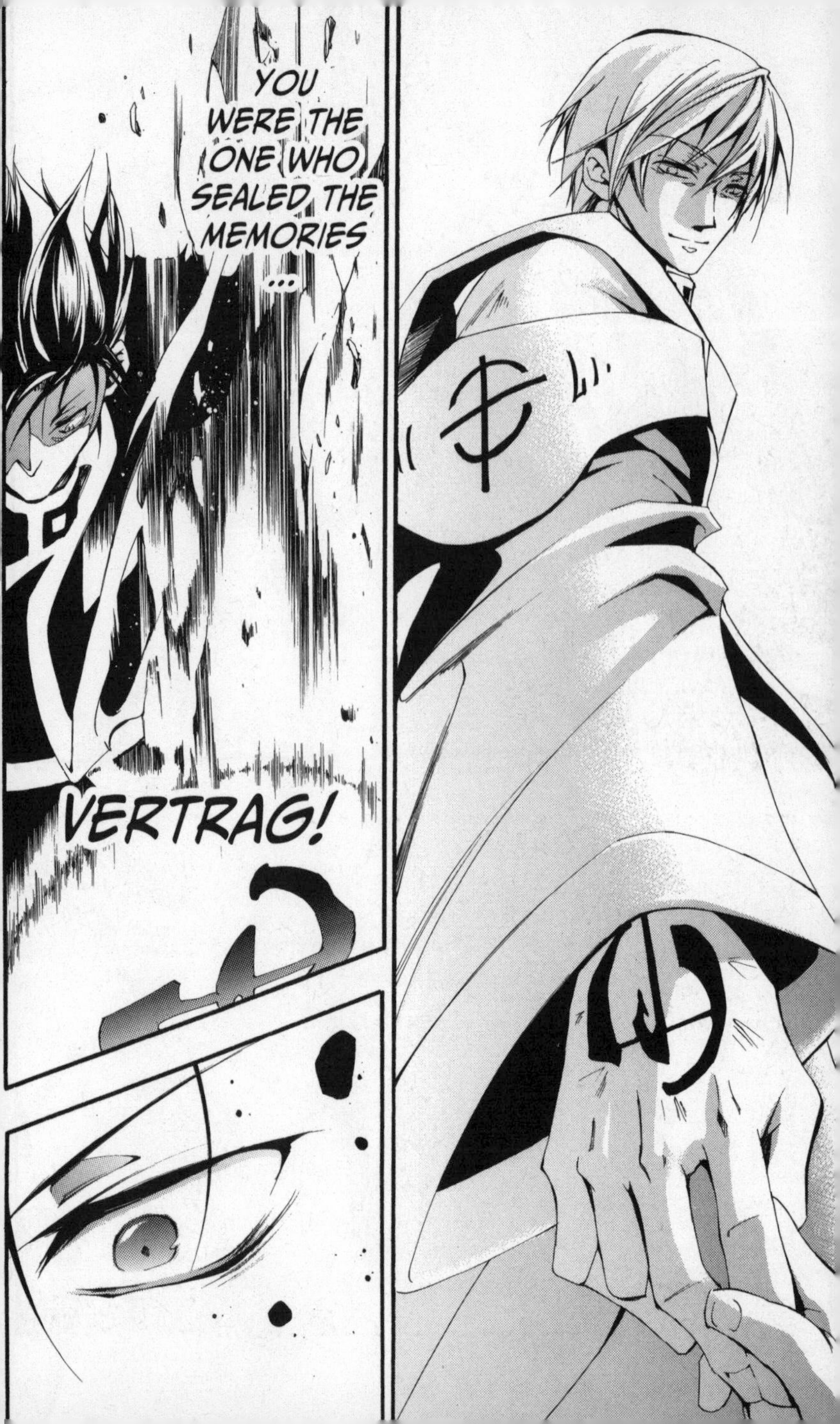
YOU WERE THE ONE WHO SEALED THE MEMORIES ...
VERTRAG!

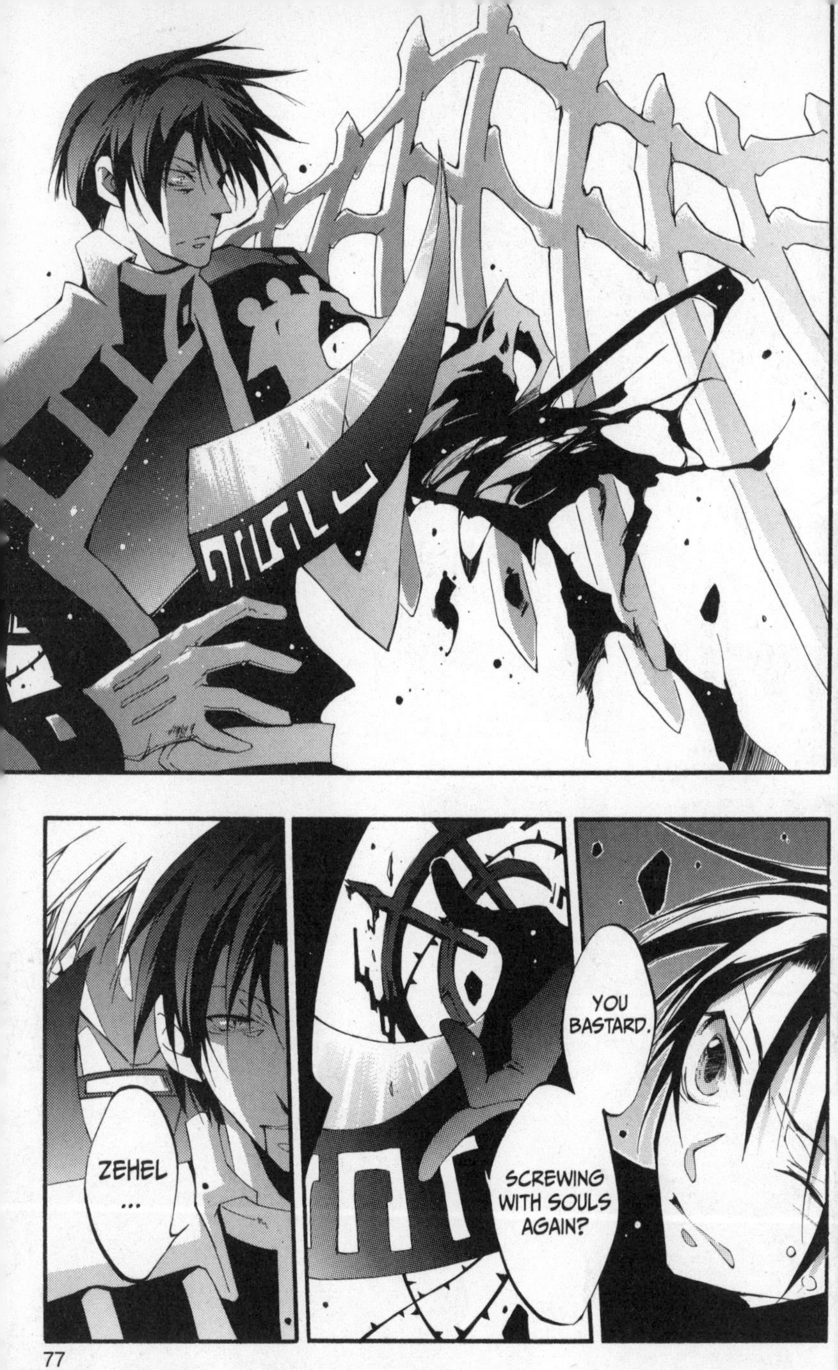
YOU BASTARD.
SCREWING WITH SOULS AGAIN?
ZEHEL ...

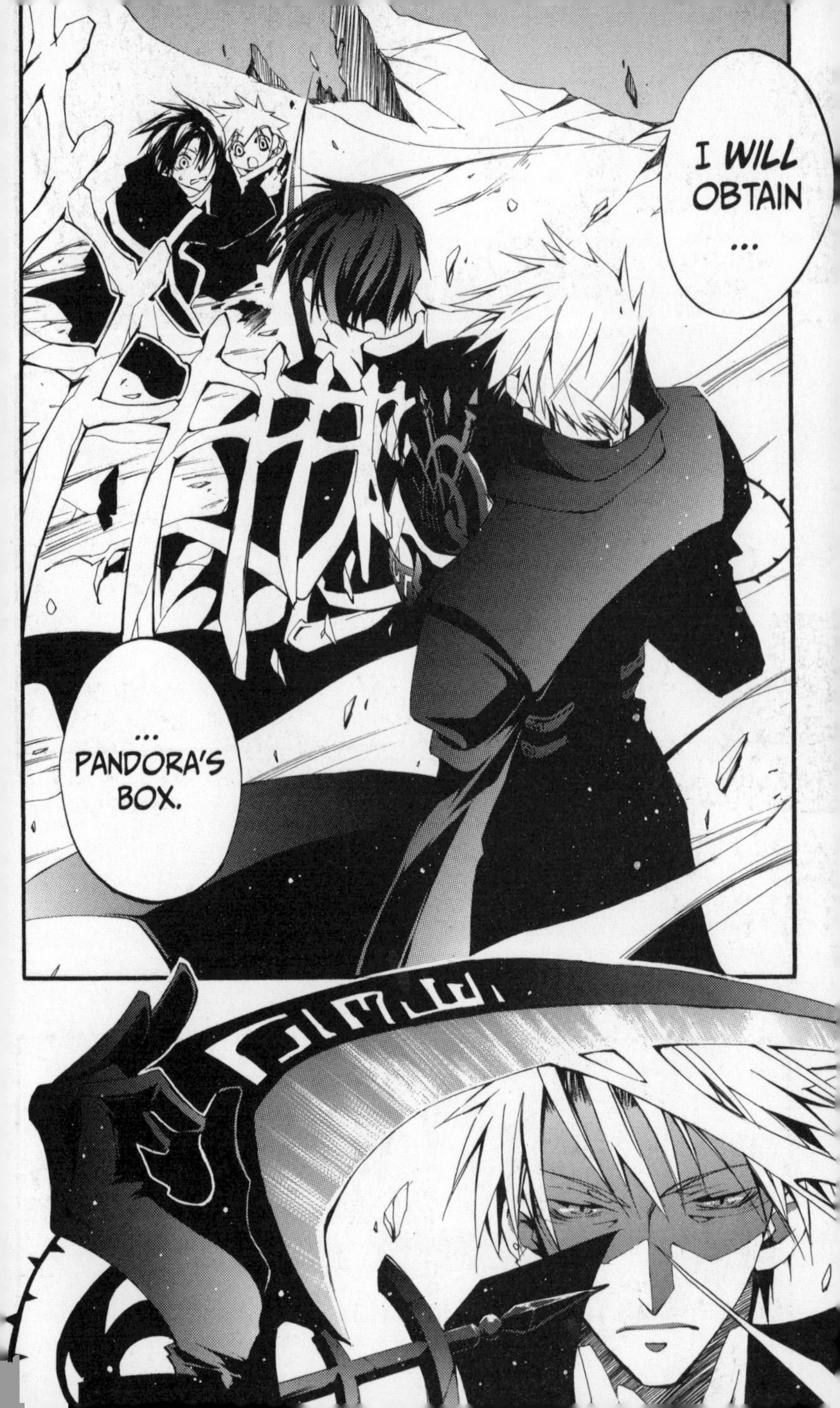
I WILL OBTAIN ...
... PANDORA'S BOX.

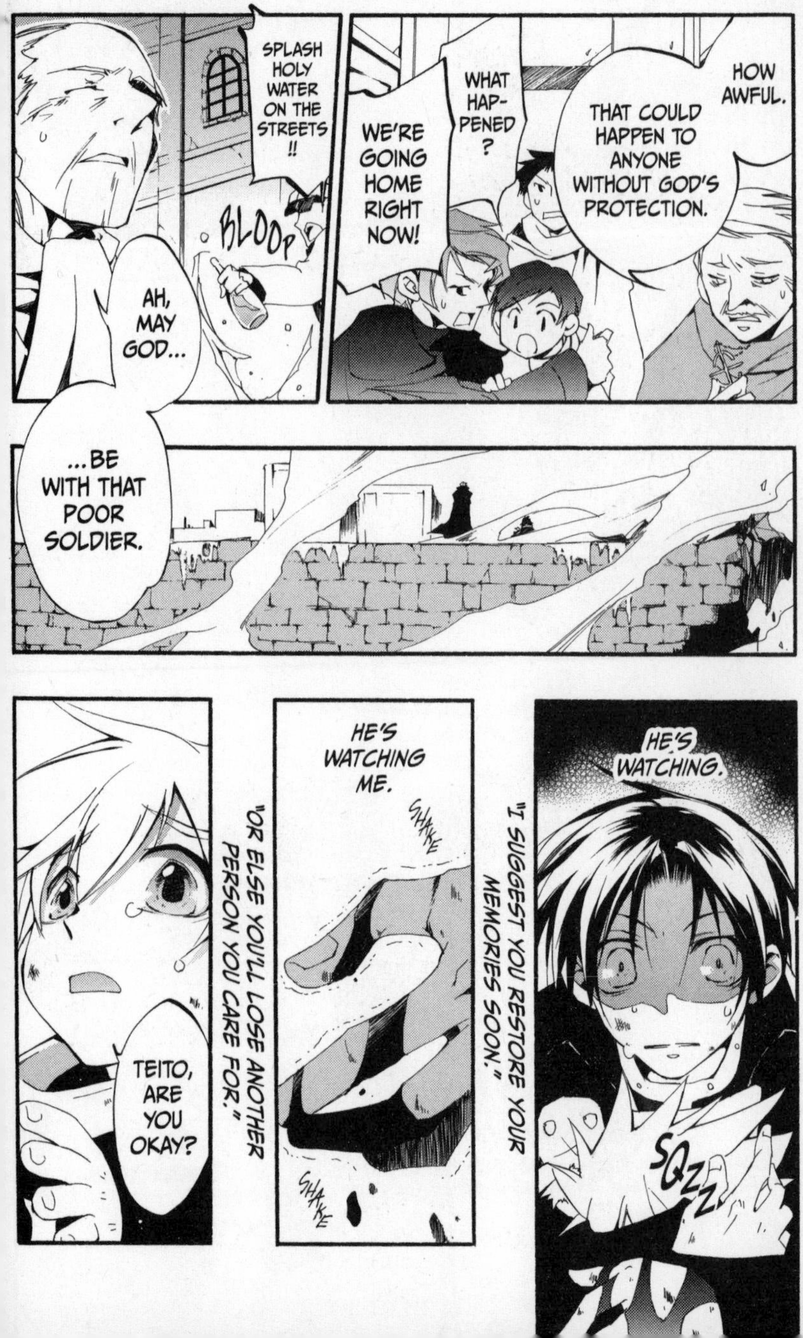
HOW AWFUL.
THAT COULD HAPPEN TO ANYONE WITHOUT GOD'S PROTECTION.
WHAT HAP-PENED?
WE'RE GOING HOME RIGHT NOW!
SPLASH HOLY WATER ON THE STREETS!!
BLOOP
AH, MAY GOD...
...BE WITH THAT POOR SOLDIER.
HE'S WATCHING.
"I SUGGEST YOU RESTORE YOUR MEMORIES SOON."
SQZZ
HE'S WATCHING ME.
SHAKE
"OR ELSE YOU'LL LOSE ANOTHER PERSON YOU CARE FOR."
SHAKE
TEITO, ARE YOU OKAY?

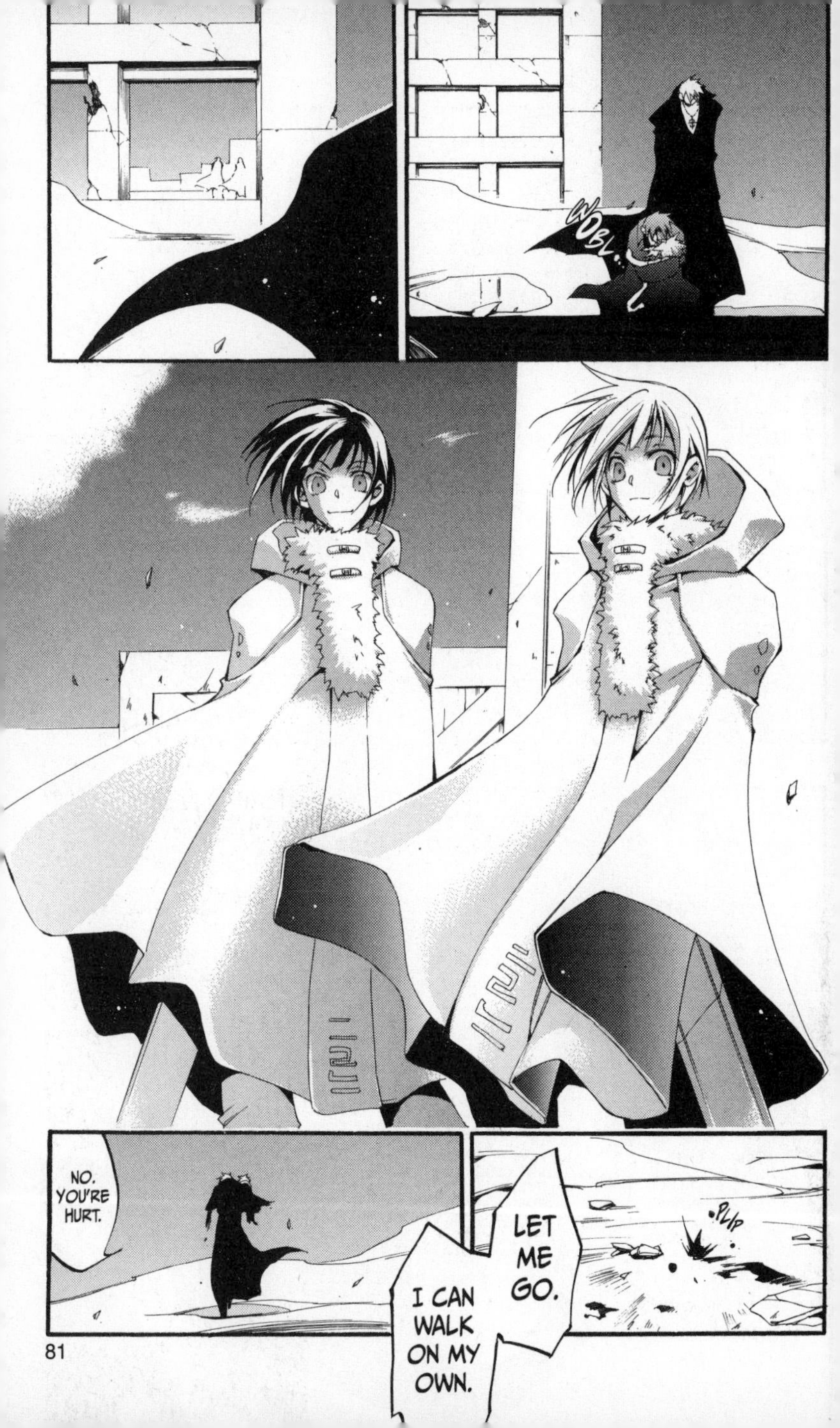
WOBL...
LET ME GO.
I CAN WALK ON MY OWN.
PLIP
NO. YOU'RE HURT.

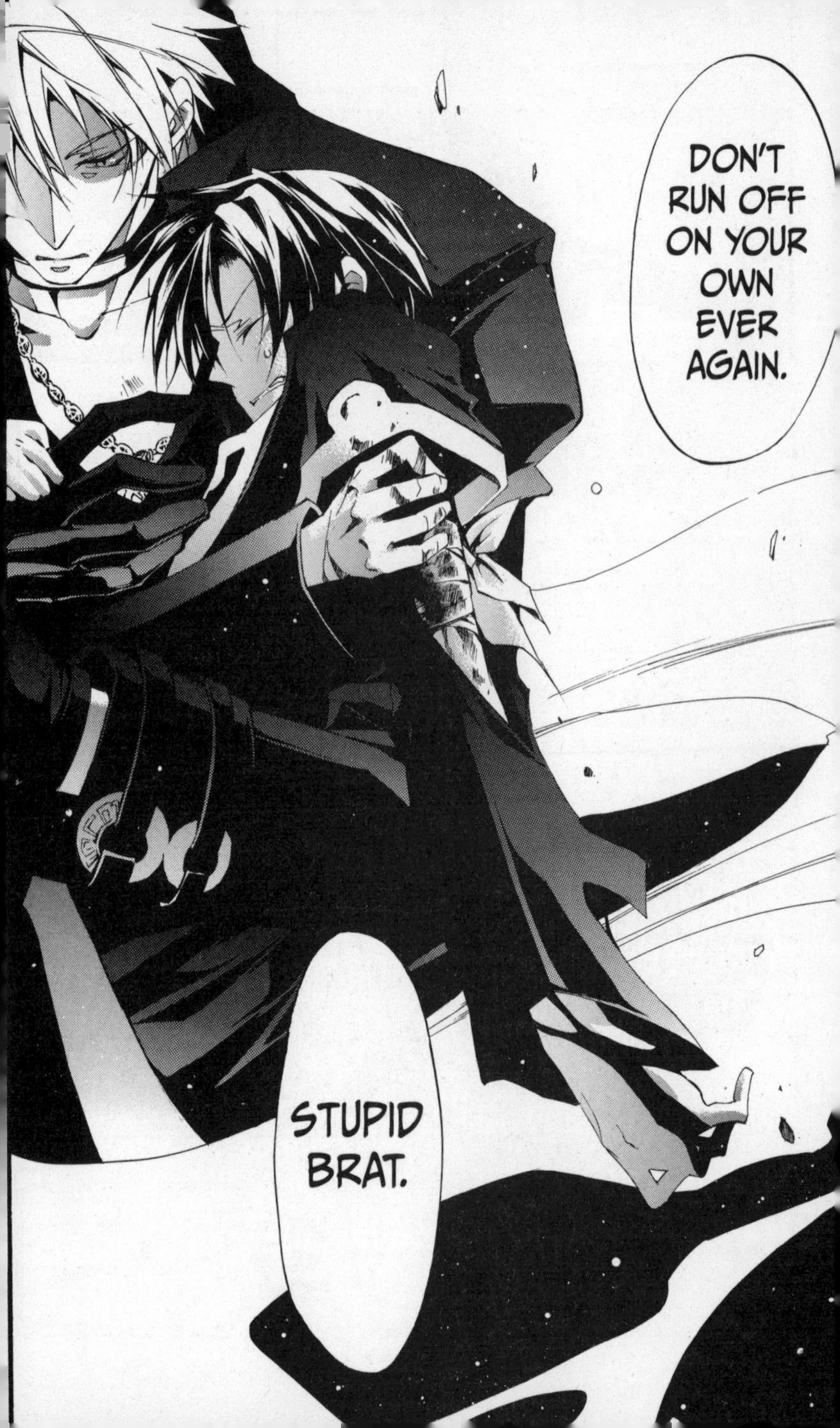
DON'T RUN OFF ON YOUR OWN EVER AGAIN.
STUPID BRAT.

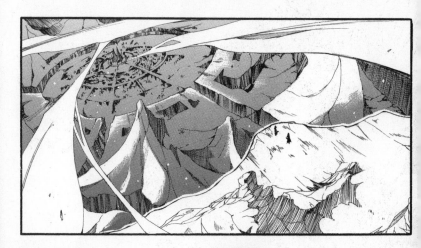

AREN'T YOU, AYA?

YOU'RE A BIG FAN OF TEITO KLEIN.

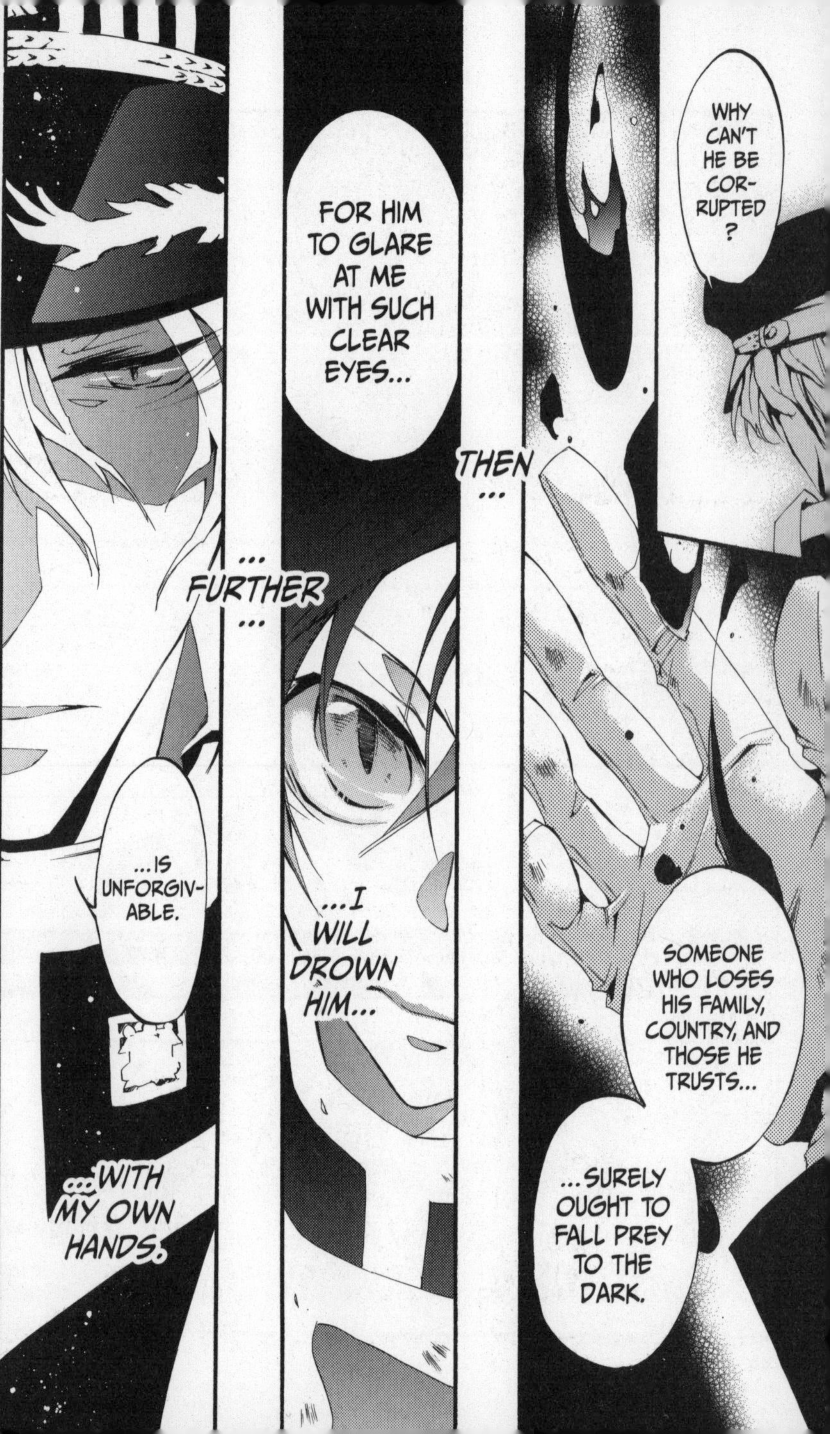
WHY CAN'T HE BE COR-RUPTED?
THEN...
SOMEONE WHO LOSES HIS FAMILY, COUNTRY, AND THOSE HE TRUSTS...
...SURELY OUGHT TO FALL PREY TO THE DARK.
FOR HIM TO GLARE AT ME WITH SUCH CLEAR EYES...
...FURTHER...
...I WILL DROWN HIM...
...IS UNFORGIV-ABLE.
...WITH MY OWN HANDS.

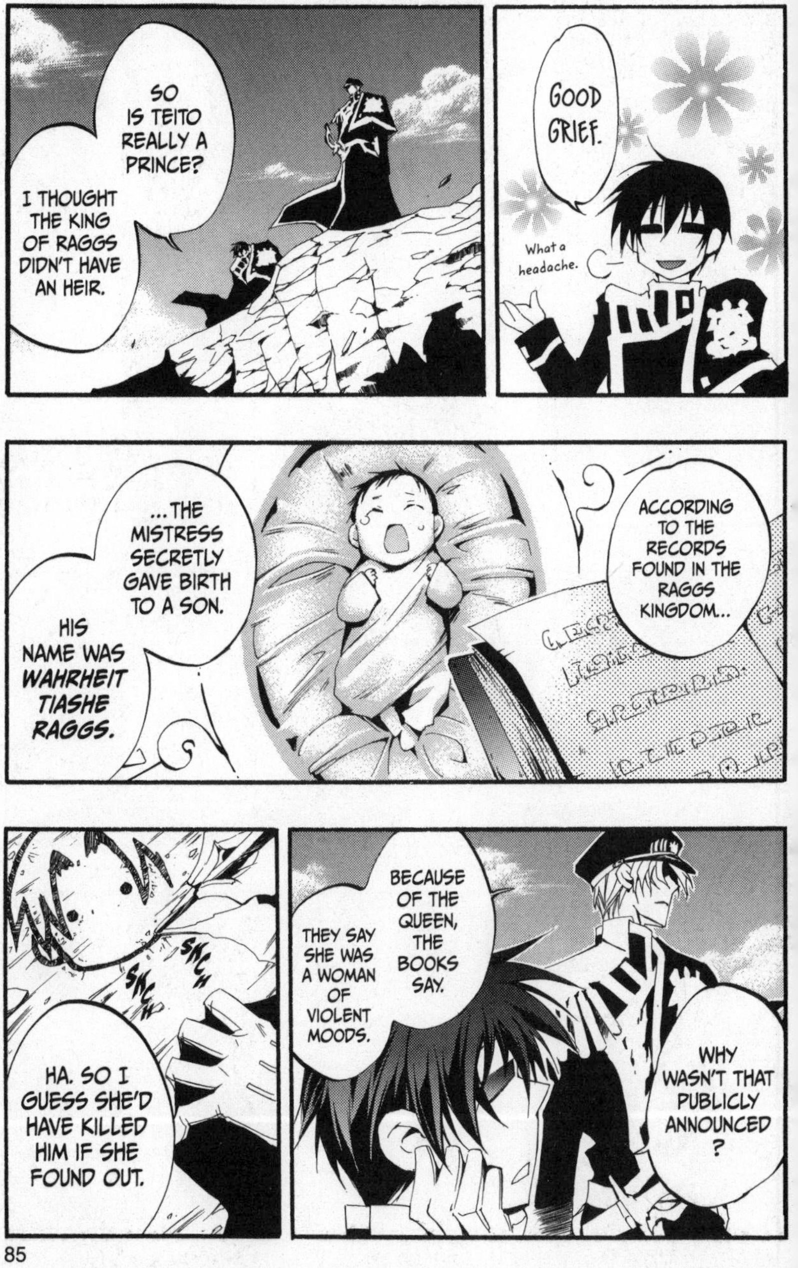

GOOD GRIEF.
What a headache.
SO IS TEITO REALLY A PRINCE?
I THOUGHT THE KING OF RAGGS DIDN'T HAVE AN HEIR.
ACCORDING TO THE RECORDS FOUND IN THE RAGGS KINGDOM...
...THE MISTRESS SECRETLY GAVE BIRTH TO A SON.
HIS NAME WAS *WAHRHEIT TIASHE RAGGS.*
WHY WASN'T THAT PUBLICLY ANNOUNCED?
BECAUSE OF THE QUEEN, THE BOOKS SAY.
THEY SAY SHE WAS A WOMAN OF VIOLENT MOODS.
SKCH
SKCH
HA. SO I GUESS SHE'D HAVE KILLED HIM IF SHE FOUND OUT.

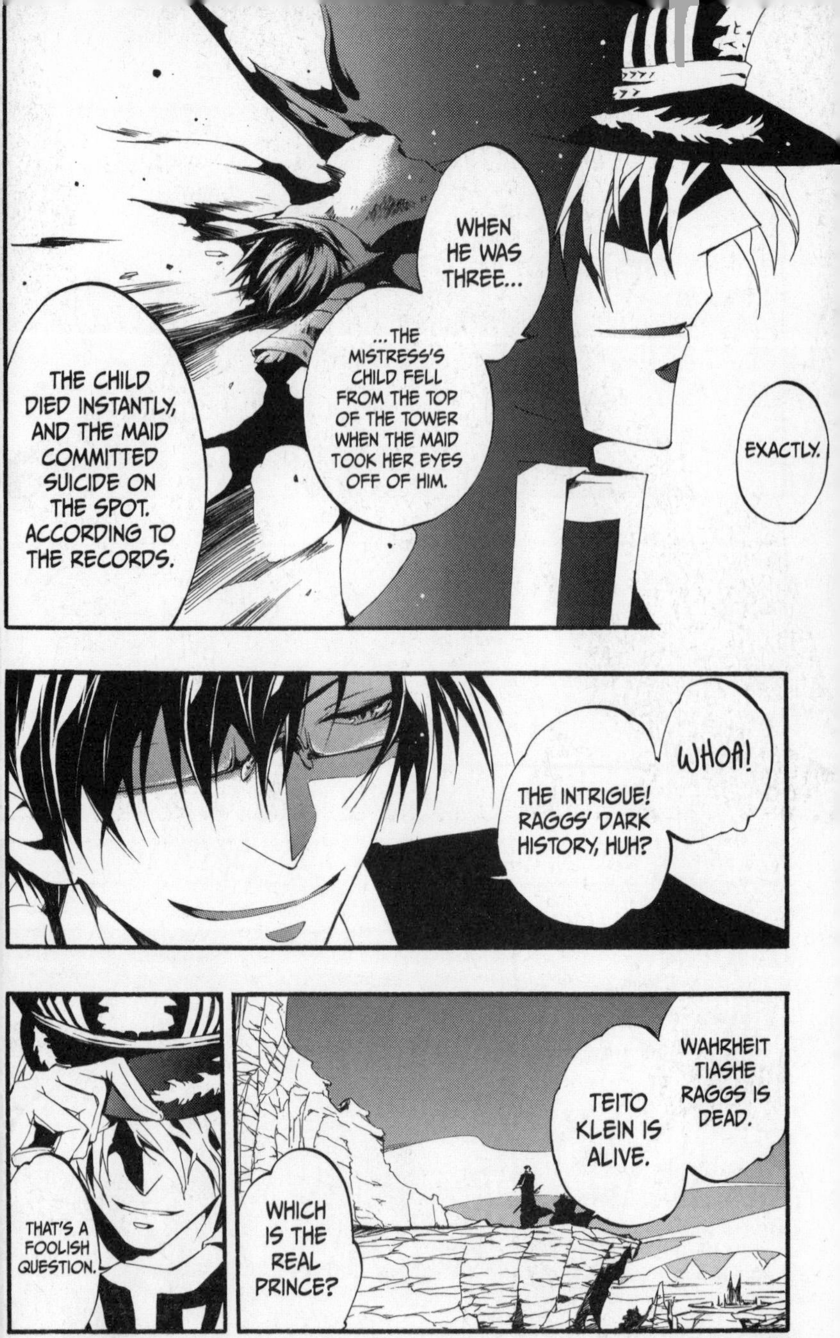
EXACTLY.
WHEN HE WAS THREE...
...THE MISTRESS'S CHILD FELL FROM THE TOP OF THE TOWER WHEN THE MAID TOOK HER EYES OFF OF HIM.
THE CHILD DIED INSTANTLY, AND THE MAID COMMITTED SUICIDE ON THE SPOT. ACCORDING TO THE RECORDS.
WHOA!
THE INTRIGUE! RAGGS' DARK HISTORY, HUH?
WAHRHEIT TIASHE RAGGS IS DEAD.
TEITO KLEIN IS ALIVE.
WHICH IS THE REAL PRINCE?
THAT'S A FOOLISH QUESTION.

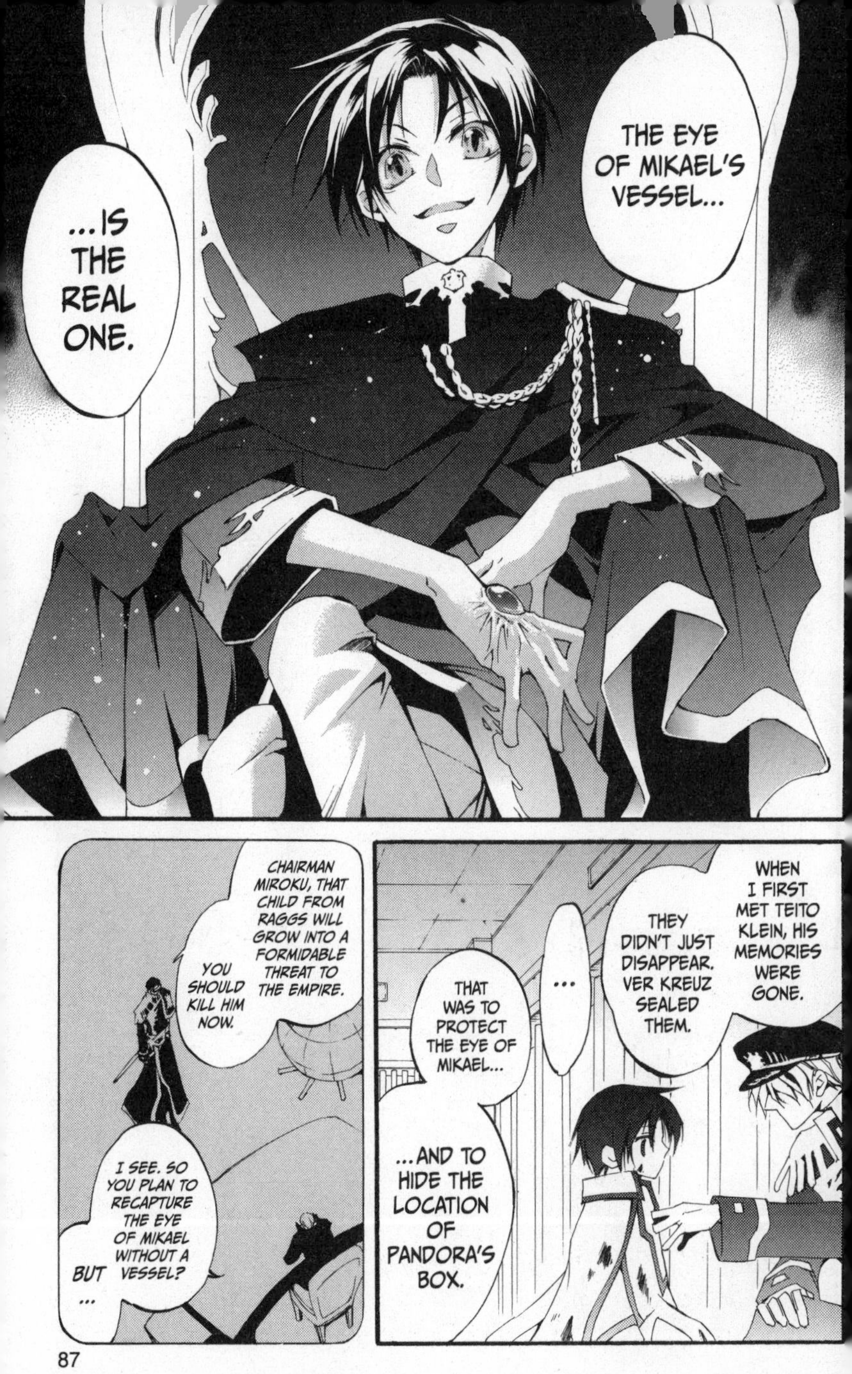
THE EYE OF MIKAEL'S VESSEL...
...IS THE REAL ONE.
WHEN I FIRST MET TEITO KLEIN, HIS MEMORIES WERE GONE.
THEY DIDN'T JUST DISAPPEAR. VER KREUZ SEALED THEM.
...
THAT WAS TO PROTECT THE EYE OF MIKAEL...
...AND TO HIDE THE LOCATION OF PANDORA'S BOX.
CHAIRMAN MIROKU, THAT CHILD FROM RAGGS WILL GROW INTO A FORMIDABLE THREAT TO THE EMPIRE.
YOU SHOULD KILL HIM NOW.
I SEE. SO YOU PLAN TO RECAPTURE THE EYE OF MIKAEL WITHOUT A VESSEL?
BUT ...

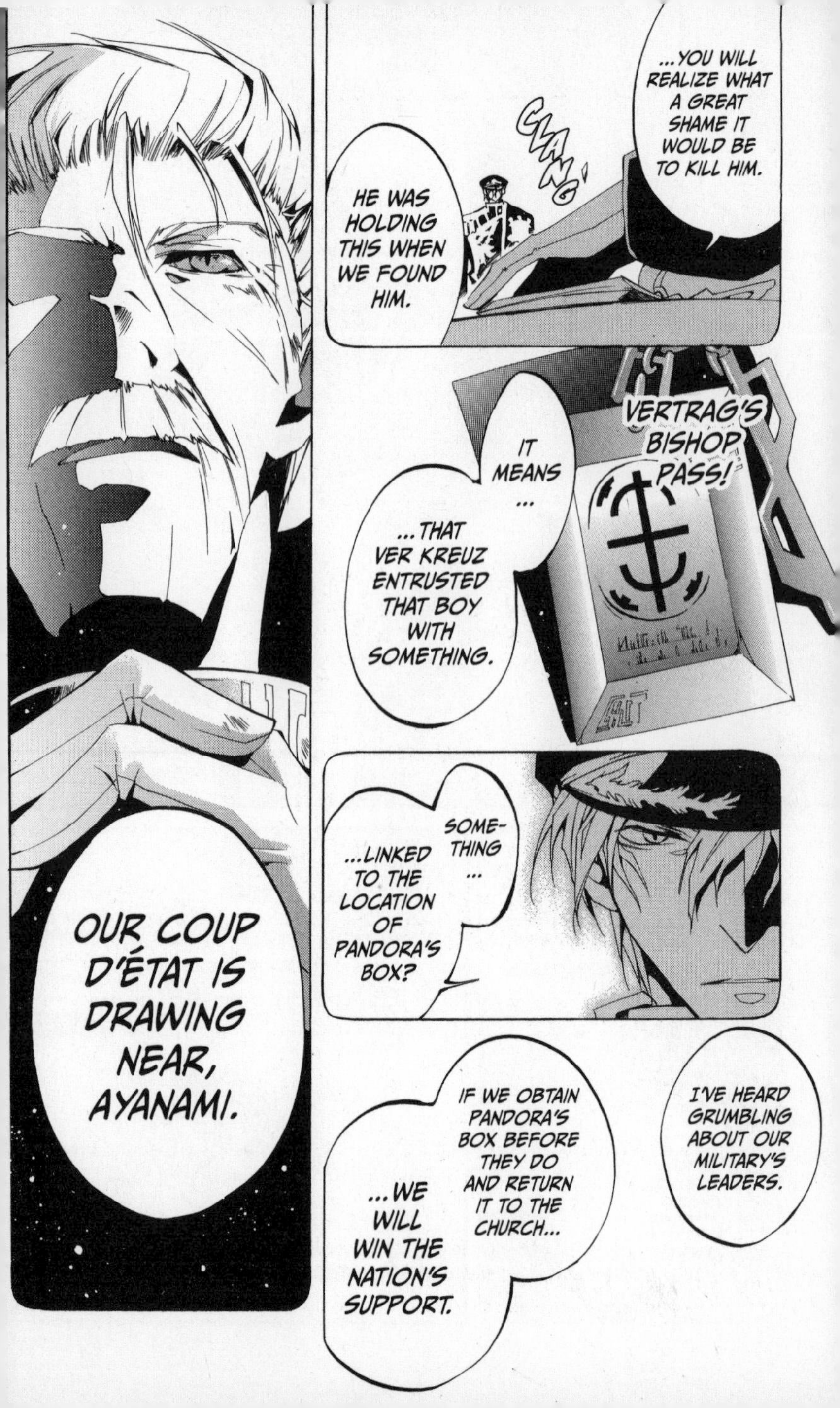
...YOU WILL REALIZE WHAT A GREAT SHAME IT WOULD BE TO KILL HIM.
CLANG!
HE WAS HOLDING THIS WHEN WE FOUND HIM.
VERTRAG'S BISHOP PASS!
IT MEANS...
...THAT VER KREUZ ENTRUSTED THAT BOY WITH SOMETHING.
SOMETHING...
...LINKED TO THE LOCATION OF PANDORA'S BOX?
I'VE HEARD GRUMBLING ABOUT OUR MILITARY'S LEADERS.
IF WE OBTAIN PANDORA'S BOX BEFORE THEY DO AND RETURN IT TO THE CHURCH...
...WE WILL WIN THE NATION'S SUPPORT.
OUR COUP D'ÉTAT IS DRAWING NEAR, AYANAMI.

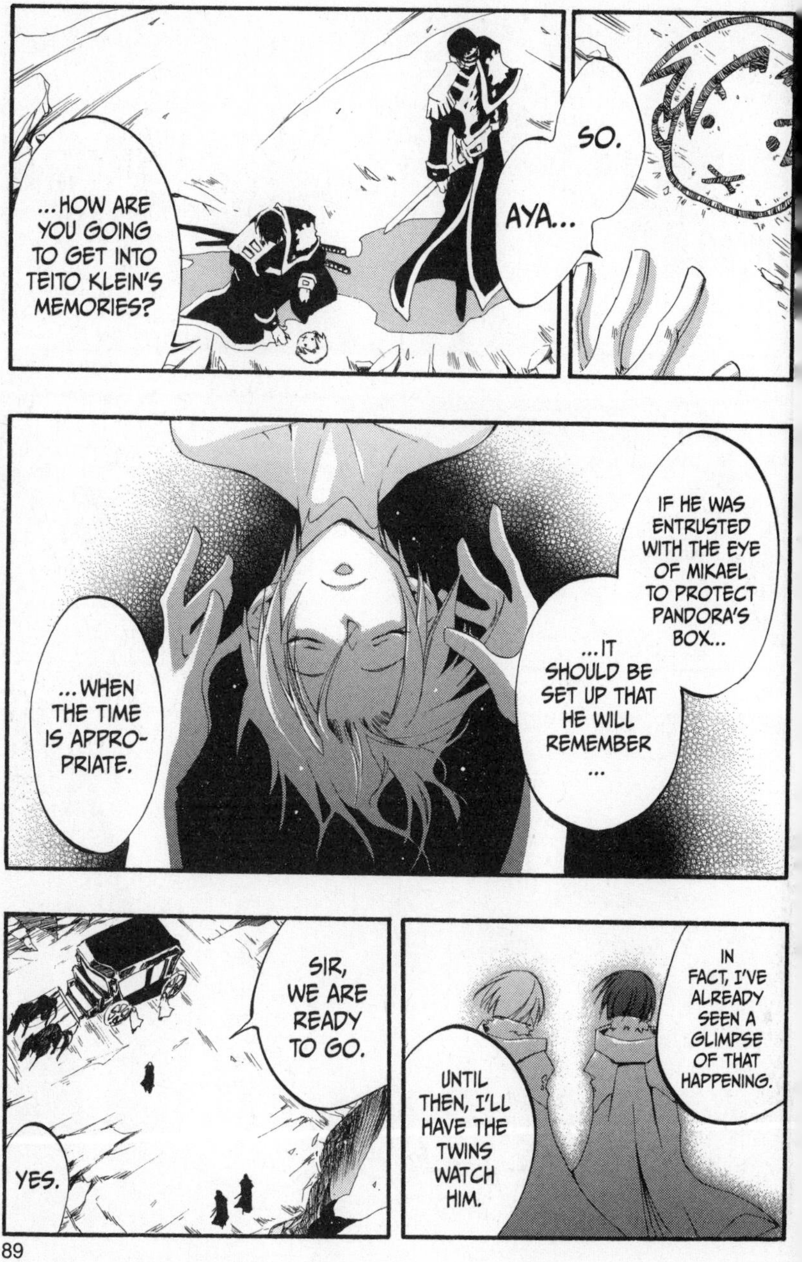
SO.
AYA...
...HOW ARE YOU GOING TO GET INTO TEITO KLEIN'S MEMORIES?
IF HE WAS ENTRUSTED WITH THE EYE OF MIKAEL TO PROTECT PANDORA'S BOX...
...IT SHOULD BE SET UP THAT HE WILL REMEMBER ...
...WHEN THE TIME IS APPRO-PRIATE.
IN FACT, I'VE ALREADY SEEN A GLIMPSE OF THAT HAPPENING.
UNTIL THEN, I'LL HAVE THE TWINS WATCH HIM.
SIR, WE ARE READY TO GO.
YES.

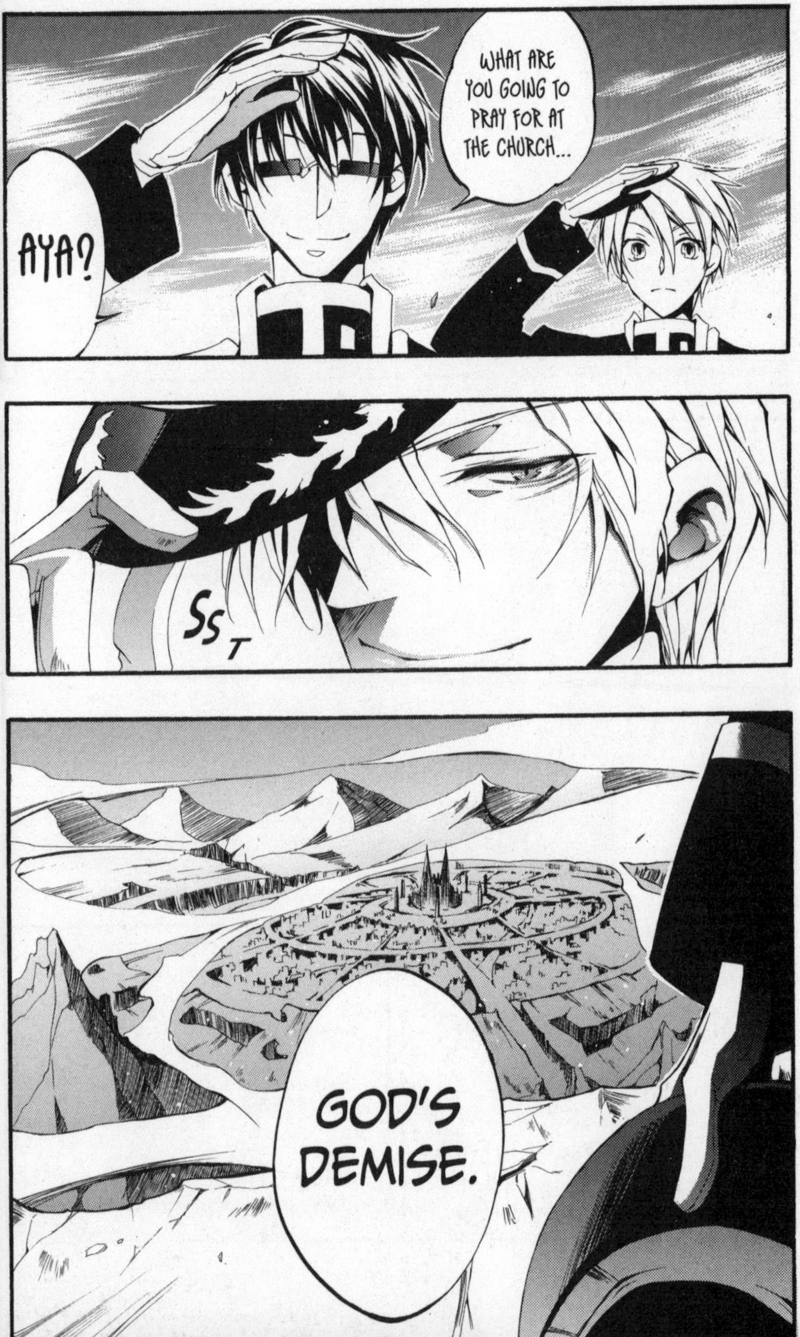
WHAT ARE YOU GOING TO PRAY FOR AT THE CHURCH...
AYA?
SSST
GOD'S DEMISE.

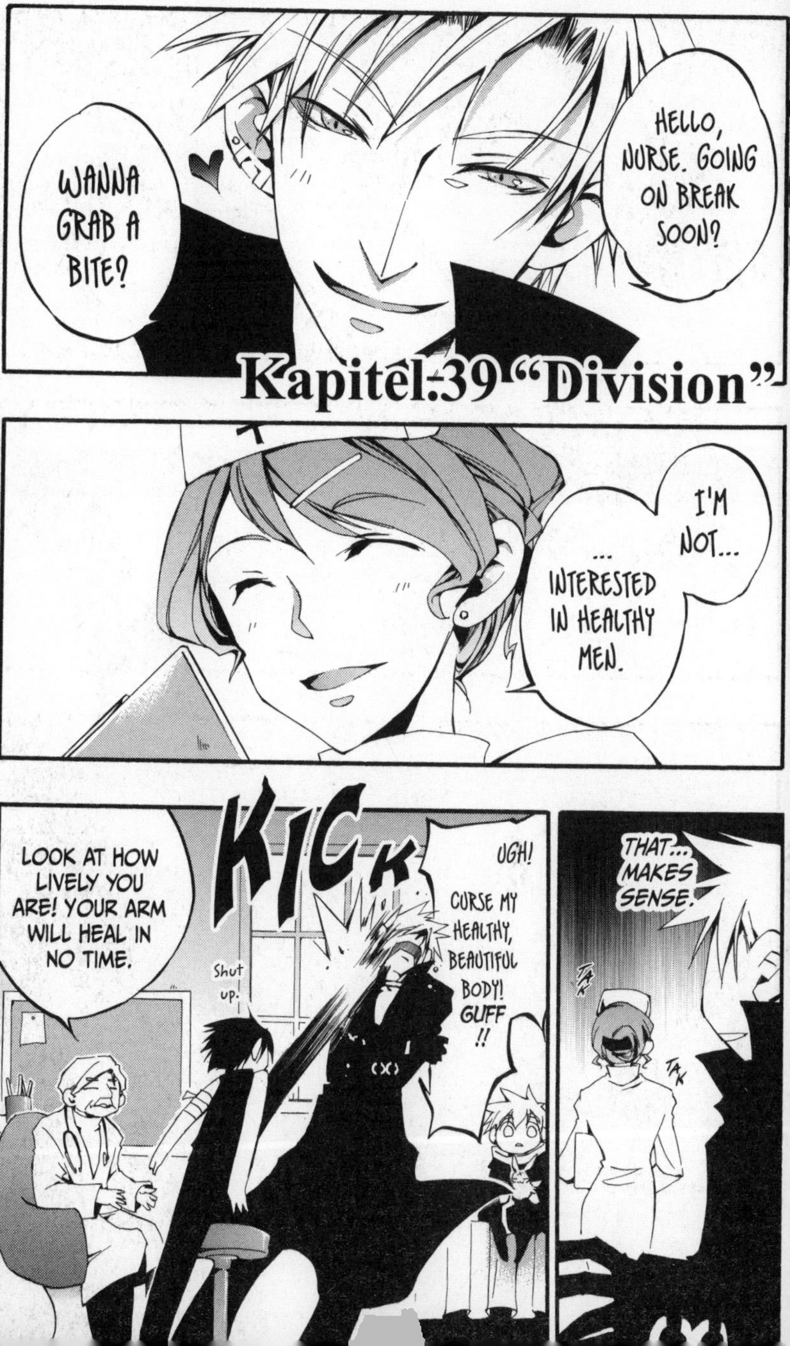
HELLO, NURSE. GOING ON BREAK SOON?
WANNA GRAB A BITE?
Kapitel:39 "Division"
I'M NOT...
... INTERESTED IN HEALTHY MEN.
THAT... MAKES SENSE.
TAK
TAK
UGH!
CURSE MY HEALTHY, BEAUTIFUL BODY! GUFF !!
KICK
LOOK AT HOW LIVELY YOU ARE! YOUR ARM WILL HEAL IN NO TIME.
Shut up.

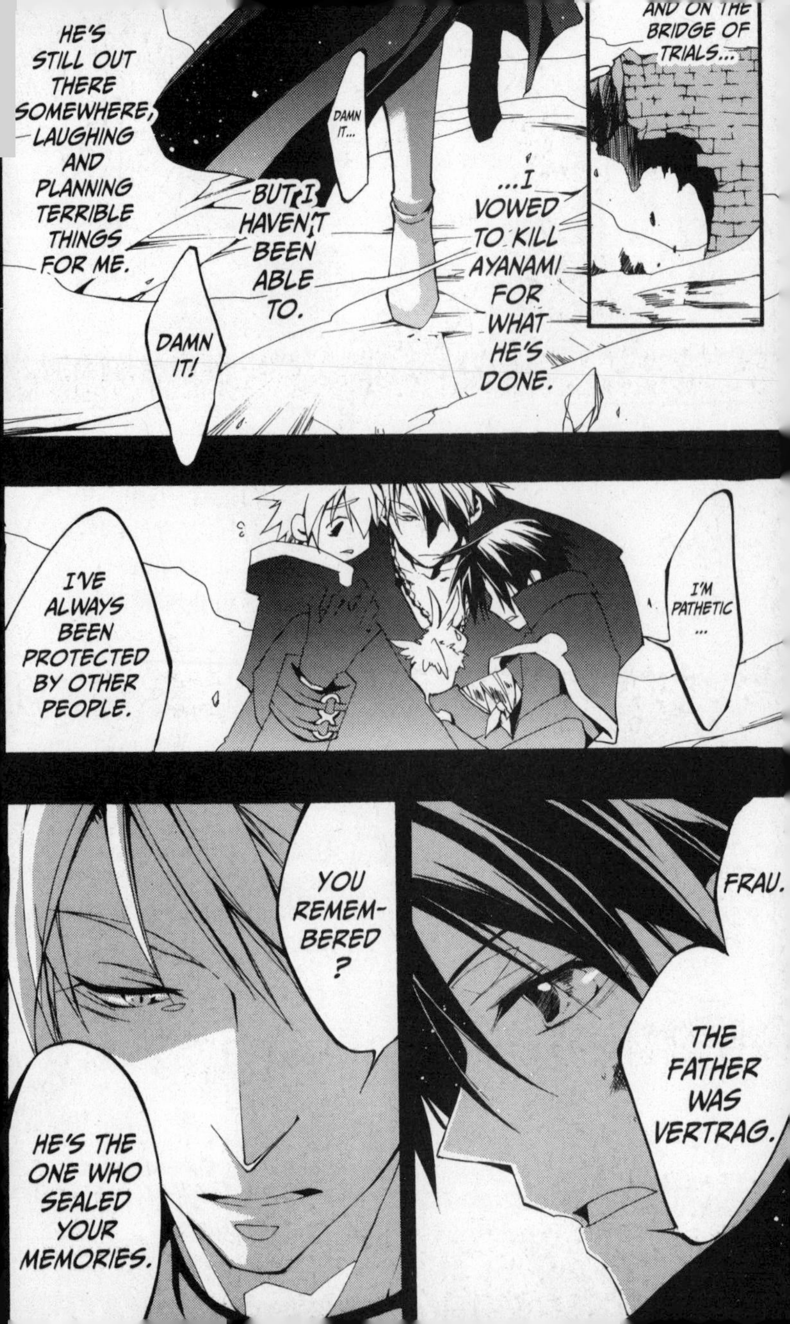
AND ON THE BRIDGE OF TRIALS...
...I VOWED TO KILL AYANAMI FOR WHAT HE'S DONE.
DAMN IT...
BUT I HAVEN'T BEEN ABLE TO.
HE'S STILL OUT THERE SOMEWHERE, LAUGHING AND PLANNING TERRIBLE THINGS FOR ME.
DAMN IT!
I'M PATHETIC...
I'VE ALWAYS BEEN PROTECTED BY OTHER PEOPLE.
FRAU.
THE FATHER WAS VERTRAG.
YOU REMEMBERED?
HE'S THE ONE WHO SEALED YOUR MEMORIES.

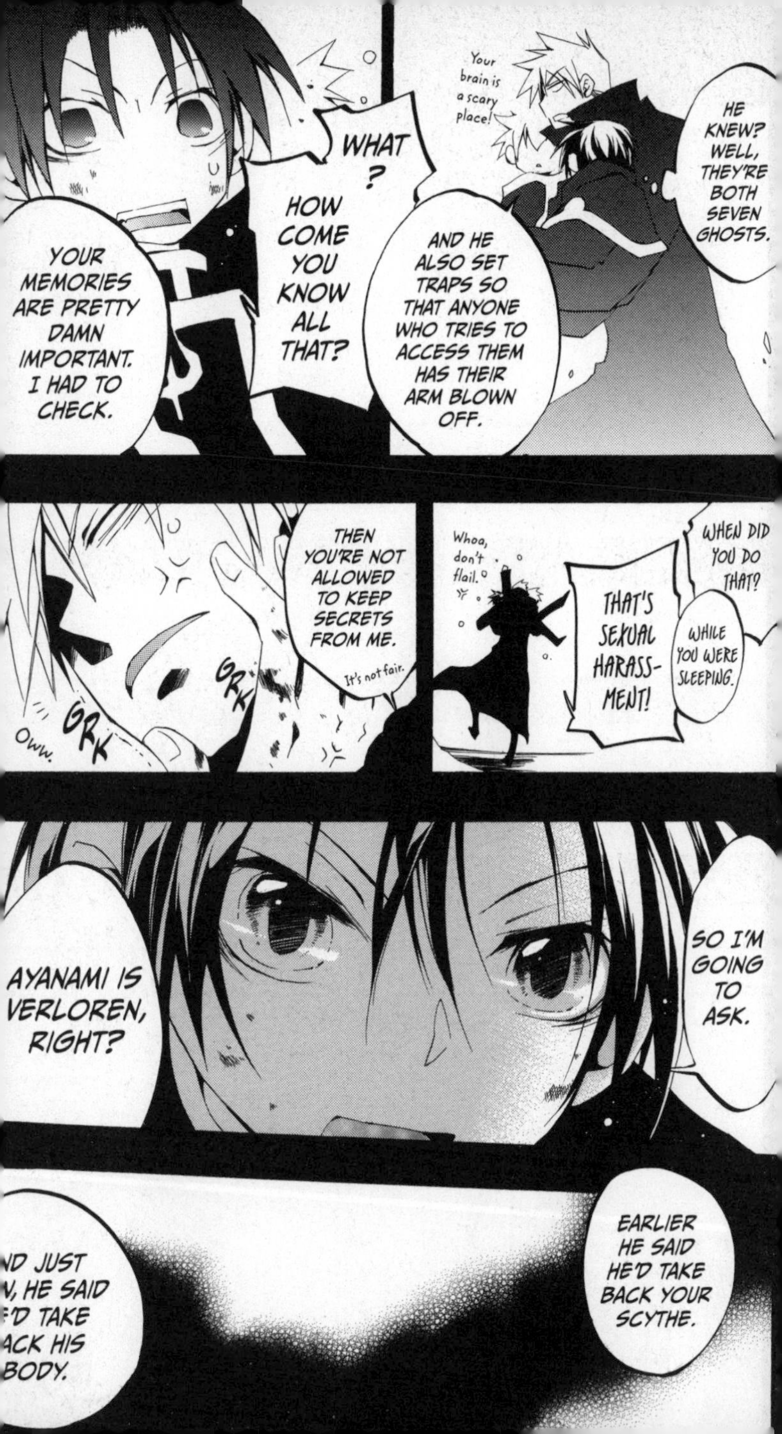
HE KNEW? WELL, THEY'RE BOTH SEVEN GHOSTS.
Your brain is a scary place!
AND HE ALSO SET TRAPS SO THAT ANYONE WHO TRIES TO ACCESS THEM HAS THEIR ARM BLOWN OFF.
WHAT? HOW COME YOU KNOW ALL THAT?
YOUR MEMORIES ARE PRETTY DAMN IMPORTANT. I HAD TO CHECK.
WHEN DID YOU DO THAT?
WHILE YOU WERE SLEEPING.
THAT'S SEXUAL HARASS-MENT!
Whoa, don't flail.
THEN YOU'RE NOT ALLOWED TO KEEP SECRETS FROM ME.
It's not fair.
GRK
GRK
Oww.
SO I'M GOING TO ASK.
AYANAMI IS VERLOREN, RIGHT?
EARLIER HE SAID HE'D TAKE BACK YOUR SCYTHE.
ND JUST
V, HE SAID
'D TAKE
ACK HIS
BODY.

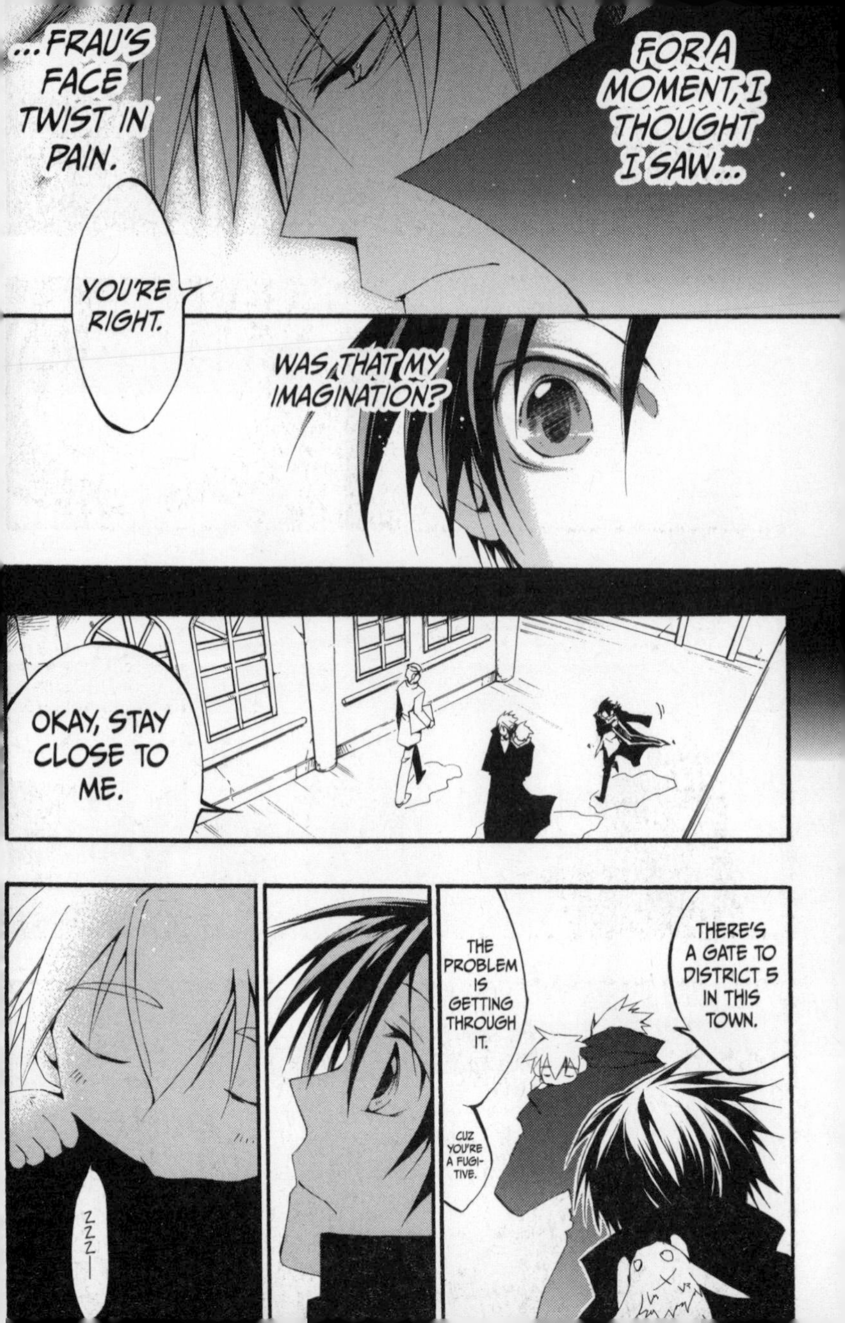
FOR A MOMENT, I THOUGHT I SAW...
...FRAU'S FACE TWIST IN PAIN.
YOU'RE RIGHT.
WAS THAT MY IMAGINATION?
OKAY, STAY CLOSE TO ME.
THERE'S A GATE TO DISTRICT 5 IN THIS TOWN.
THE PROBLEM IS GETTING THROUGH IT.
CUZ YOU'RE A FUGI-TIVE.
ZZZ—

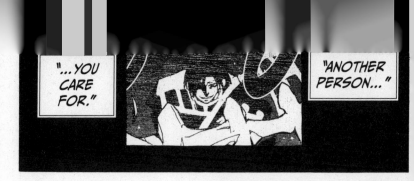

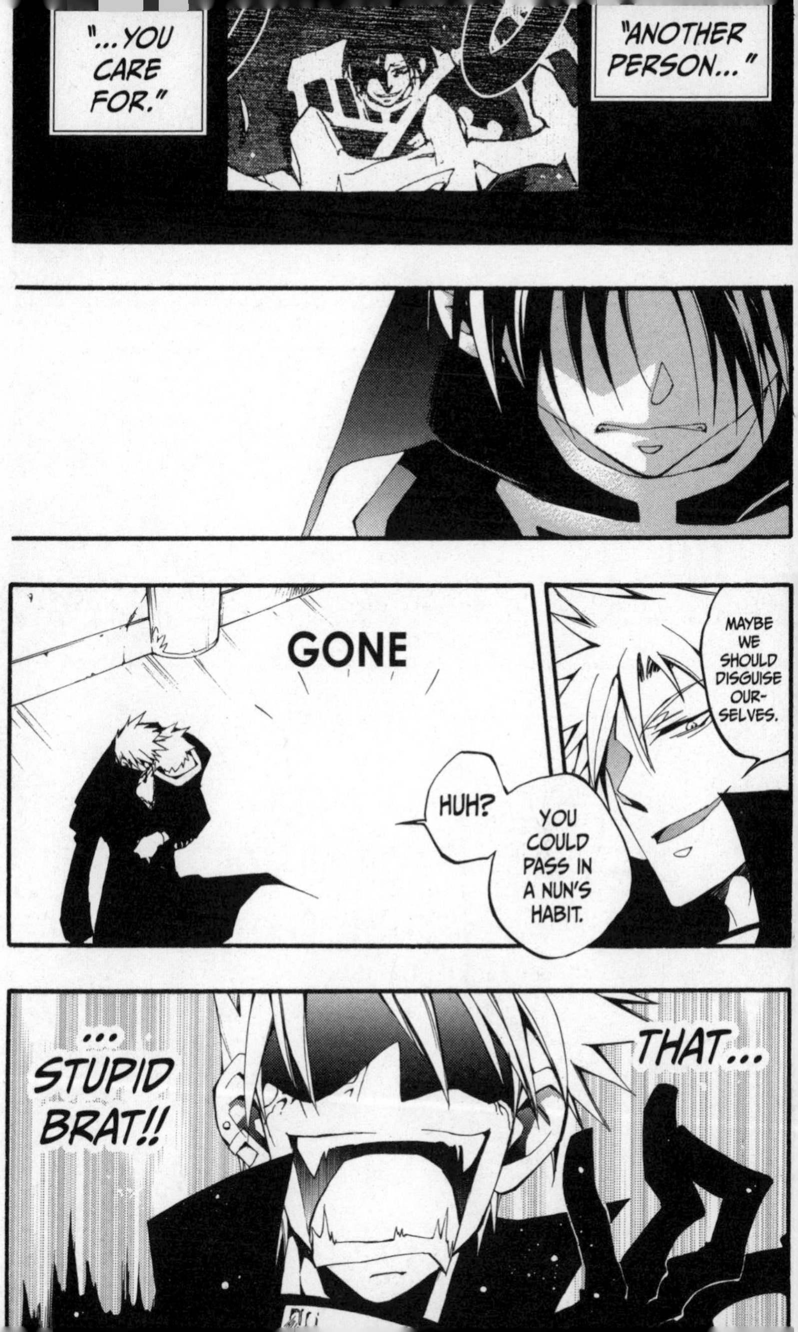
"ANOTHER PERSON..."
"...YOU CARE FOR."
MAYBE WE SHOULD DISGUISE OUR-SELVES.
HUH?
YOU COULD PASS IN A NUN'S HABIT.
GONE
THAT...
...STUPID BRAT!!

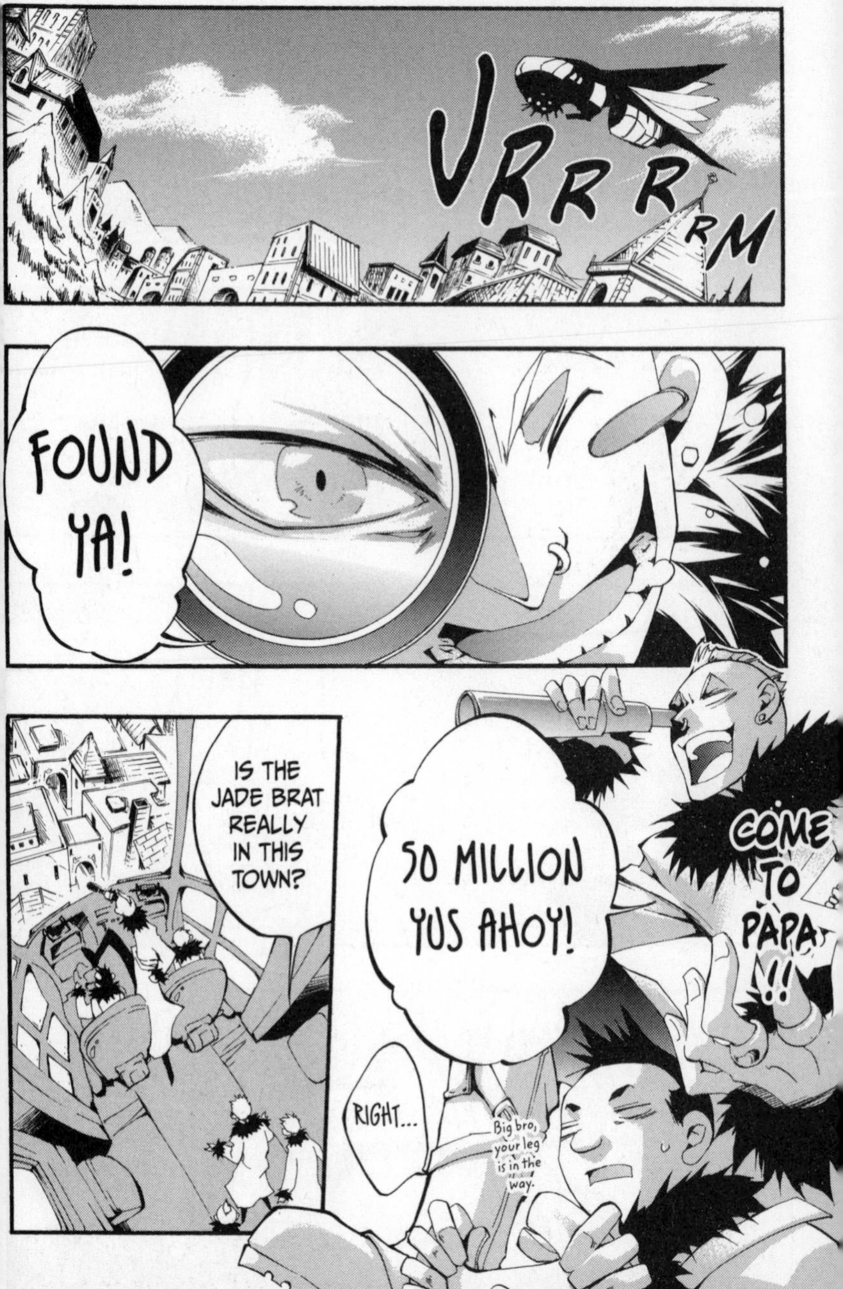
VRRRRRM
FOUND YA!
COME TO PAPA!!
50 MILLION YUS AHOY!
Big bro, your leg is in the way.
RIGHT...
IS THE JADE BRAT REALLY IN THIS TOWN?

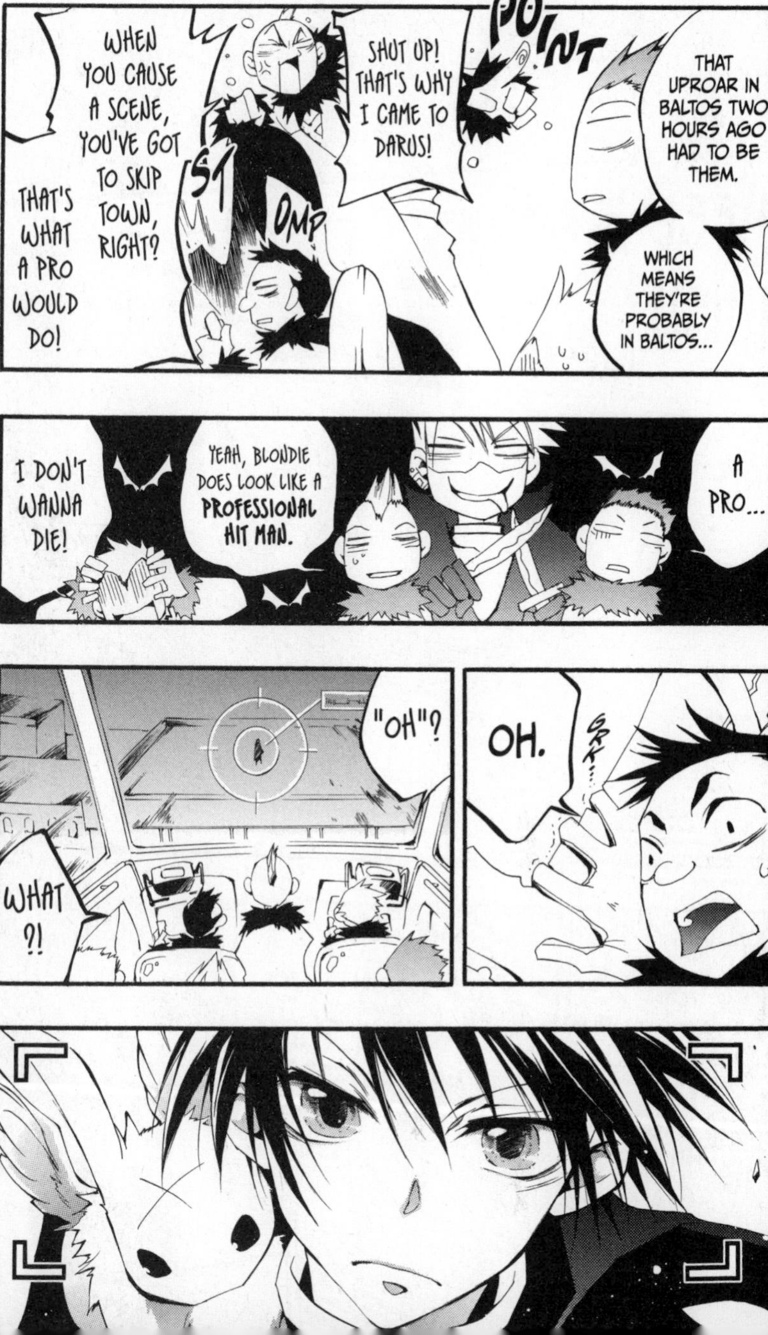
THAT UPROAR IN BALTOS TWO HOURS AGO HAD TO BE THEM.
WHICH MEANS THEY'RE PROBABLY IN BALTOS...
POINT
SHUT UP! THAT'S WHY I CAME TO DARUS!
STOMP
WHEN YOU CAUSE A SCENE, YOU'VE GOT TO SKIP TOWN, RIGHT?
THAT'S WHAT A PRO WOULD DO!
A PRO...
YEAH, BLONDIE DOES LOOK LIKE A PROFESSIONAL HIT MAN.
I DON'T WANNA DIE!
GRK...
OH.
"OH"?
WHAT?!

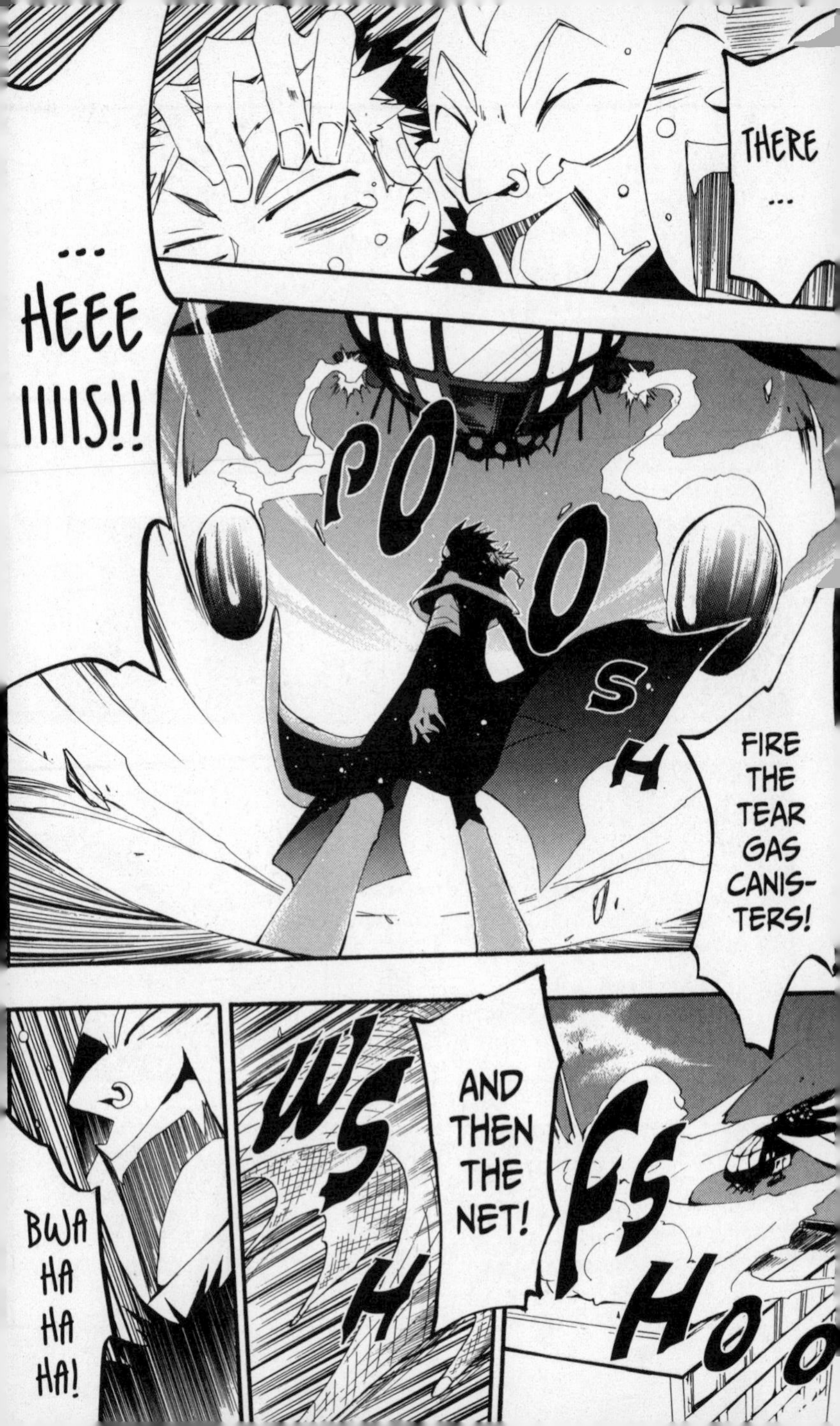

THERE ...
... HEEE IIIIS!!
POOSH
FIRE THE TEAR GAS CANIS-TERS!
PSHOO
AND THEN THE NET!
WSH
BWA HA HA HA!

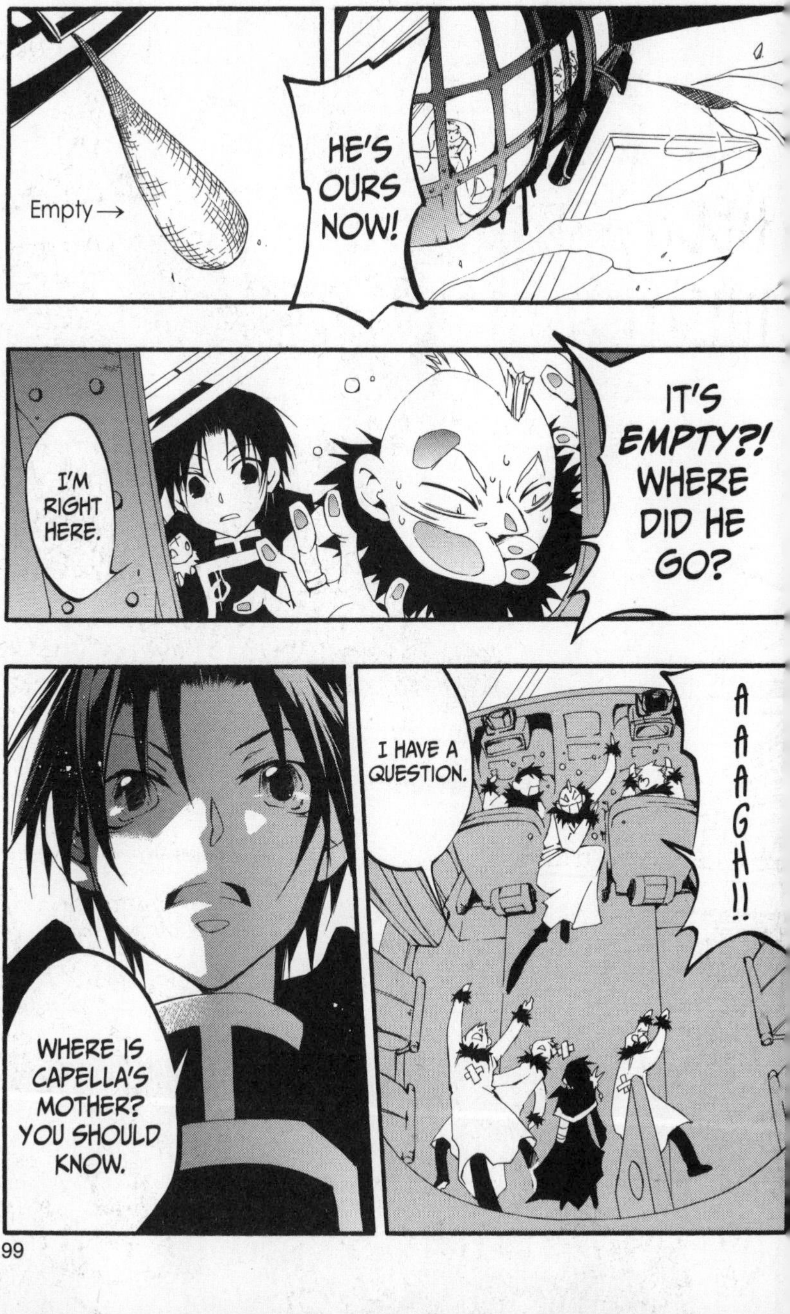
HE'S OURS NOW!
Empty →
IT'S *EMPTY?!* WHERE DID HE GO?
I'M RIGHT HERE.
AAAAGH!!
I HAVE A QUESTION.
WHERE IS CAPELLA'S MOTHER? YOU SHOULD KNOW.

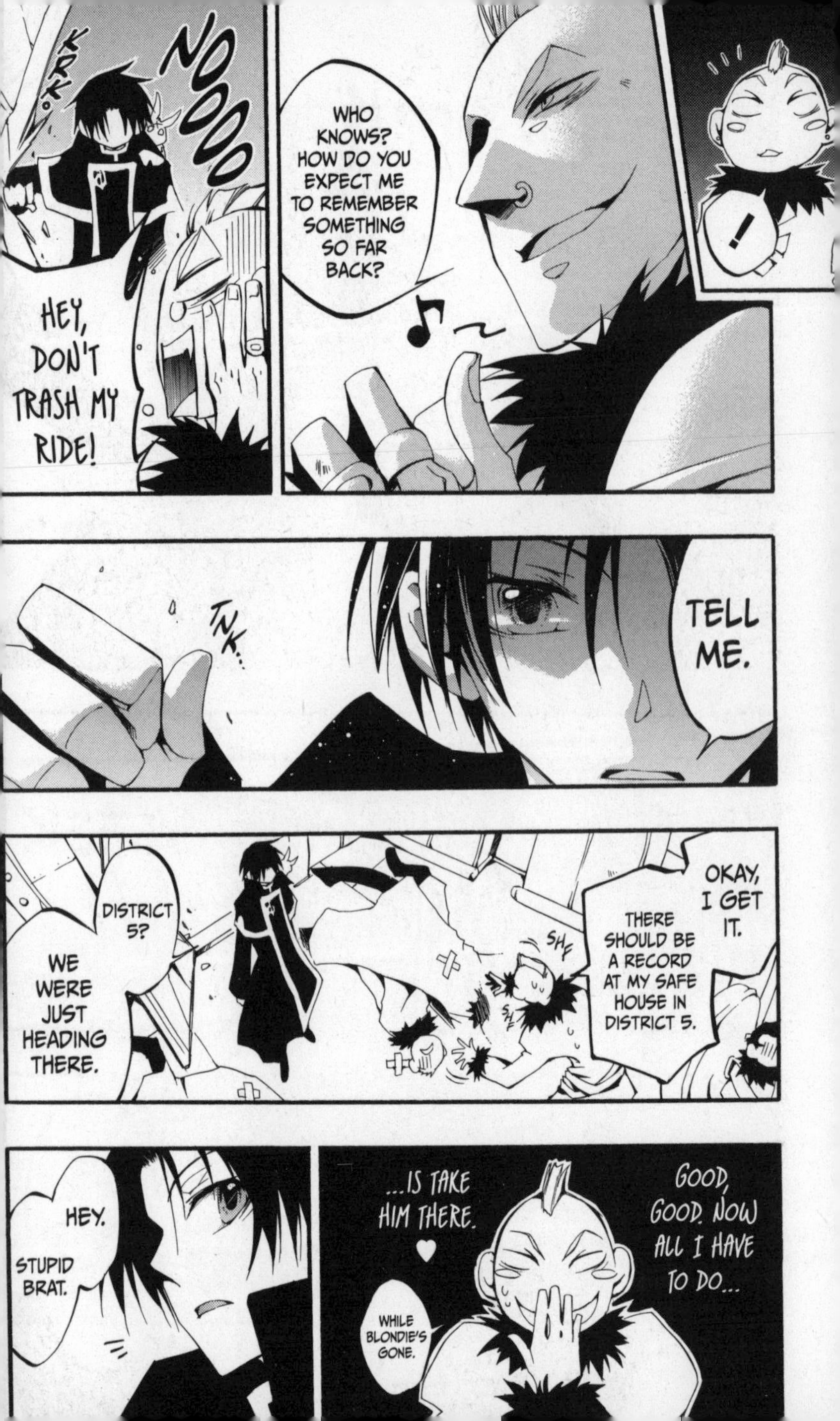
!
WHO KNOWS? HOW DO YOU EXPECT ME TO REMEMBER SOMETHING SO FAR BACK?
♪~
NOOOO
KRK
HEY, DON'T TRASH MY RIDE!
TELL ME.
TNK...
OKAY, I GET IT.
THERE SHOULD BE A RECORD AT MY SAFE HOUSE IN DISTRICT 5.
SHF
SHF
DISTRICT 5?
WE WERE JUST HEADING THERE.
GOOD, GOOD. NOW ALL I HAVE TO DO...
...IS TAKE HIM THERE. ♥
WHILE BLONDIE'S GONE.
HEY.
STUPID BRAT.

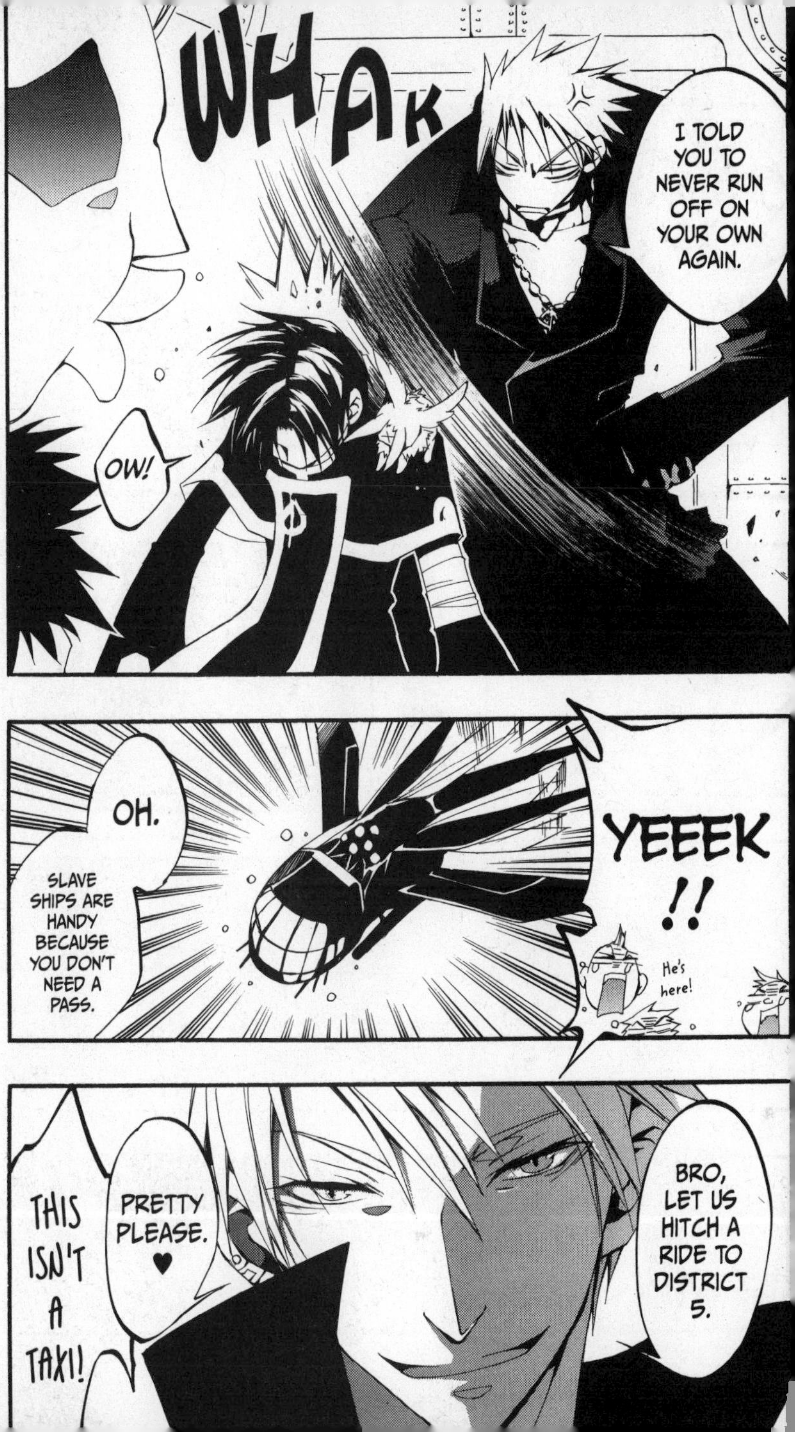
I TOLD YOU TO NEVER RUN OFF ON YOUR OWN AGAIN.
WHAK
OW!
YEEEK!!
He's here!
OH.
SLAVE SHIPS ARE HANDY BECAUSE YOU DON'T NEED A PASS.
BRO, LET US HITCH A RIDE TO DISTRICT 5.
PRETTY PLEASE. ♥
THIS ISN'T A TAXI!

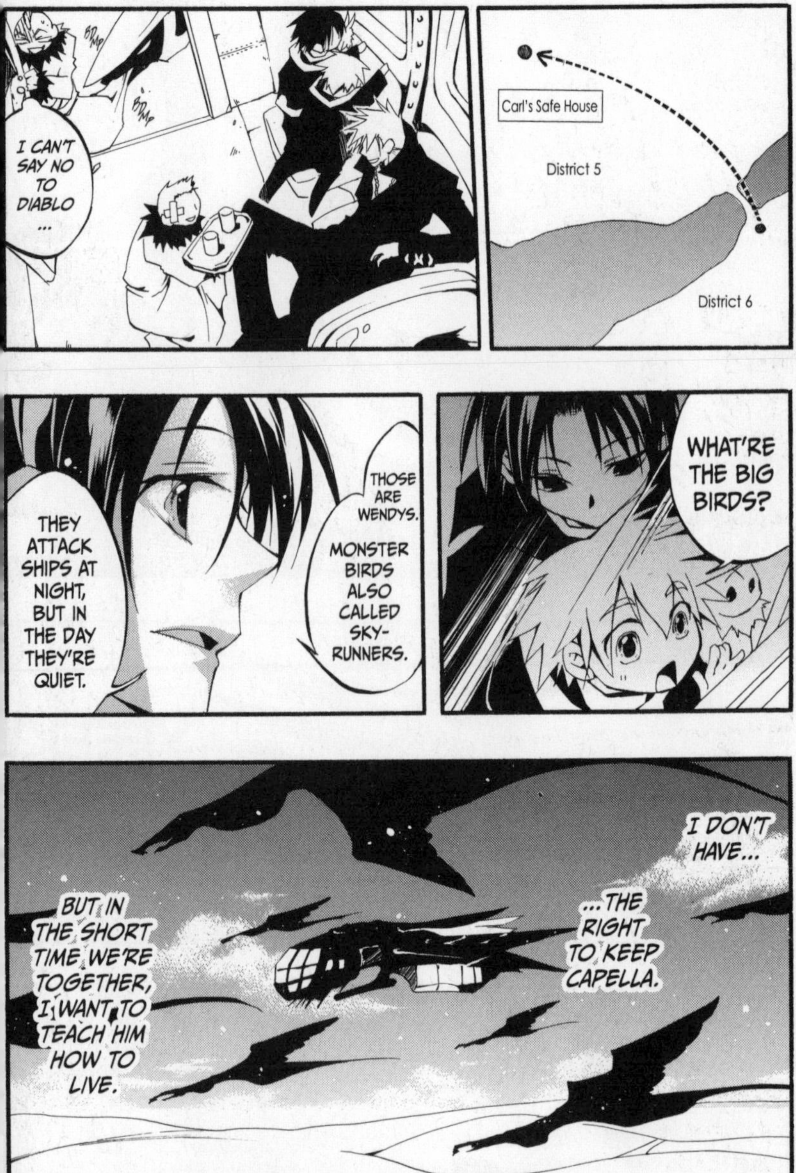
Carl's Safe House
District 5
District 6
BDMP
BDMP
I CAN'T SAY NO TO DIABLO...
WHAT'RE THE BIG BIRDS?
THOSE ARE WENDYS.
MONSTER BIRDS ALSO CALLED SKY-RUNNERS.
THEY ATTACK SHIPS AT NIGHT, BUT IN THE DAY THEY'RE QUIET.
I DON'T HAVE...
...THE RIGHT TO KEEP CAPELLA.
BUT IN THE SHORT TIME WE'RE TOGETHER, I WANT TO TEACH HIM HOW TO LIVE.

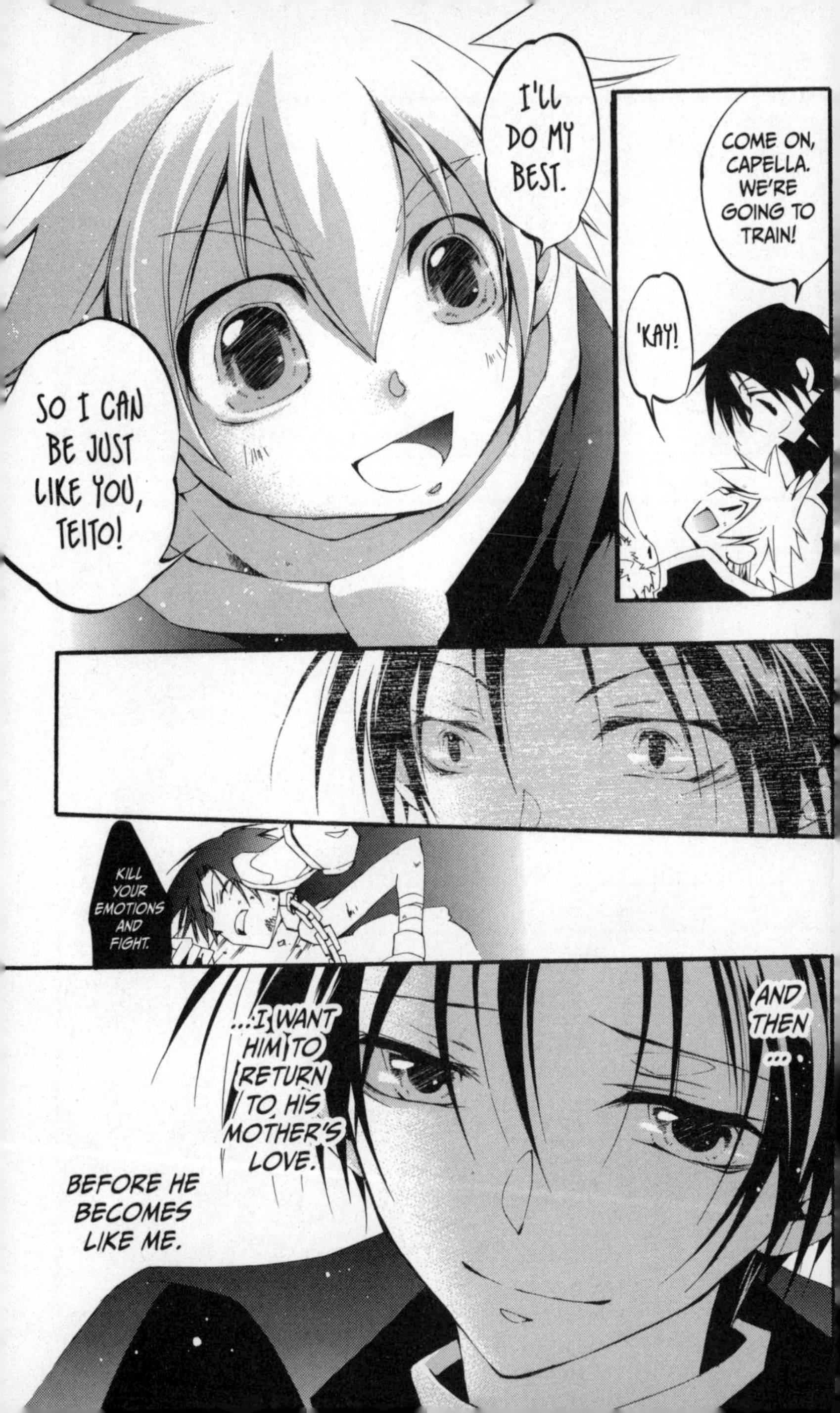
COME ON, CAPELLA. WE'RE GOING TO TRAIN!
'KAY!
I'LL DO MY BEST.
SO I CAN BE JUST LIKE YOU, TEITO!
KILL YOUR EMOTIONS AND FIGHT.
AND THEN...
...I WANT HIM TO RETURN TO HIS MOTHER'S LOVE.
BEFORE HE BECOMES LIKE ME.

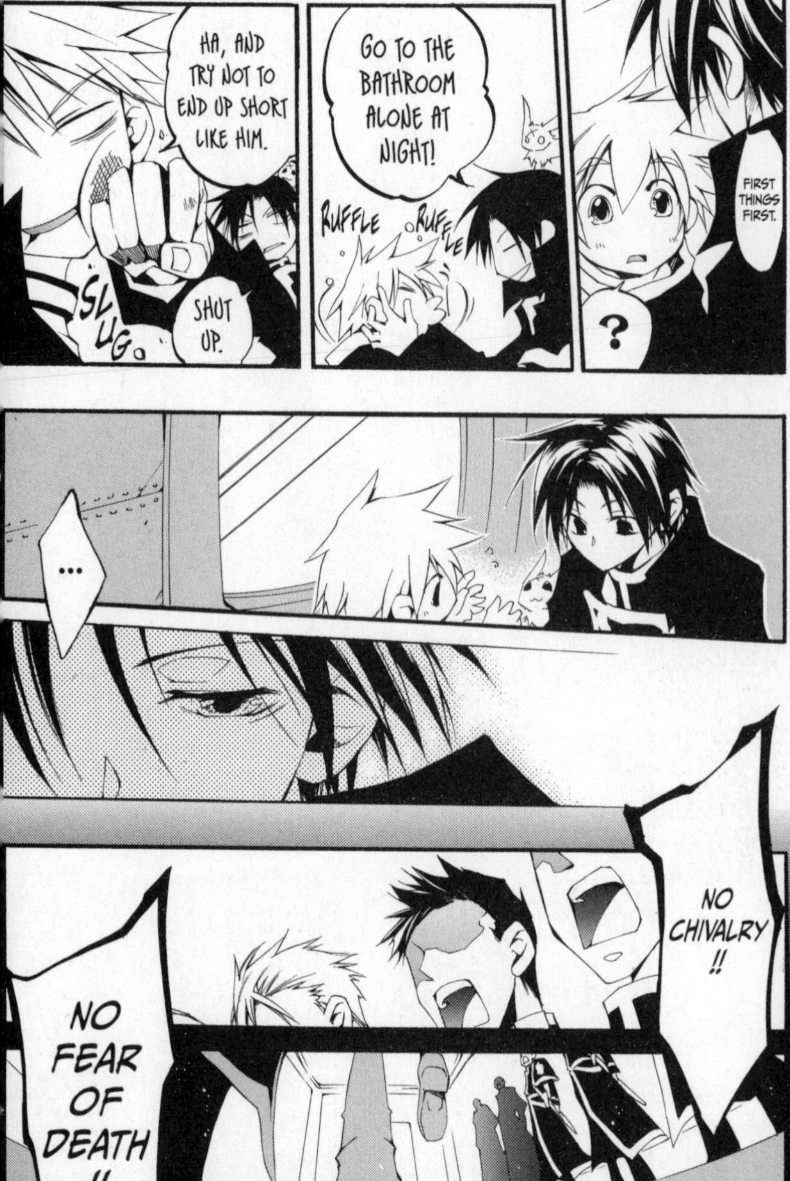
FIRST THINGS FIRST.
?
GO TO THE BATHROOM ALONE AT NIGHT!
RUFFLE
RUFFLE
HA, AND TRY NOT TO END UP SHORT LIKE HIM.
SLUG
SHUT UP.
...
NO CHIVALRY!!
NO FEAR OF DEATH!!

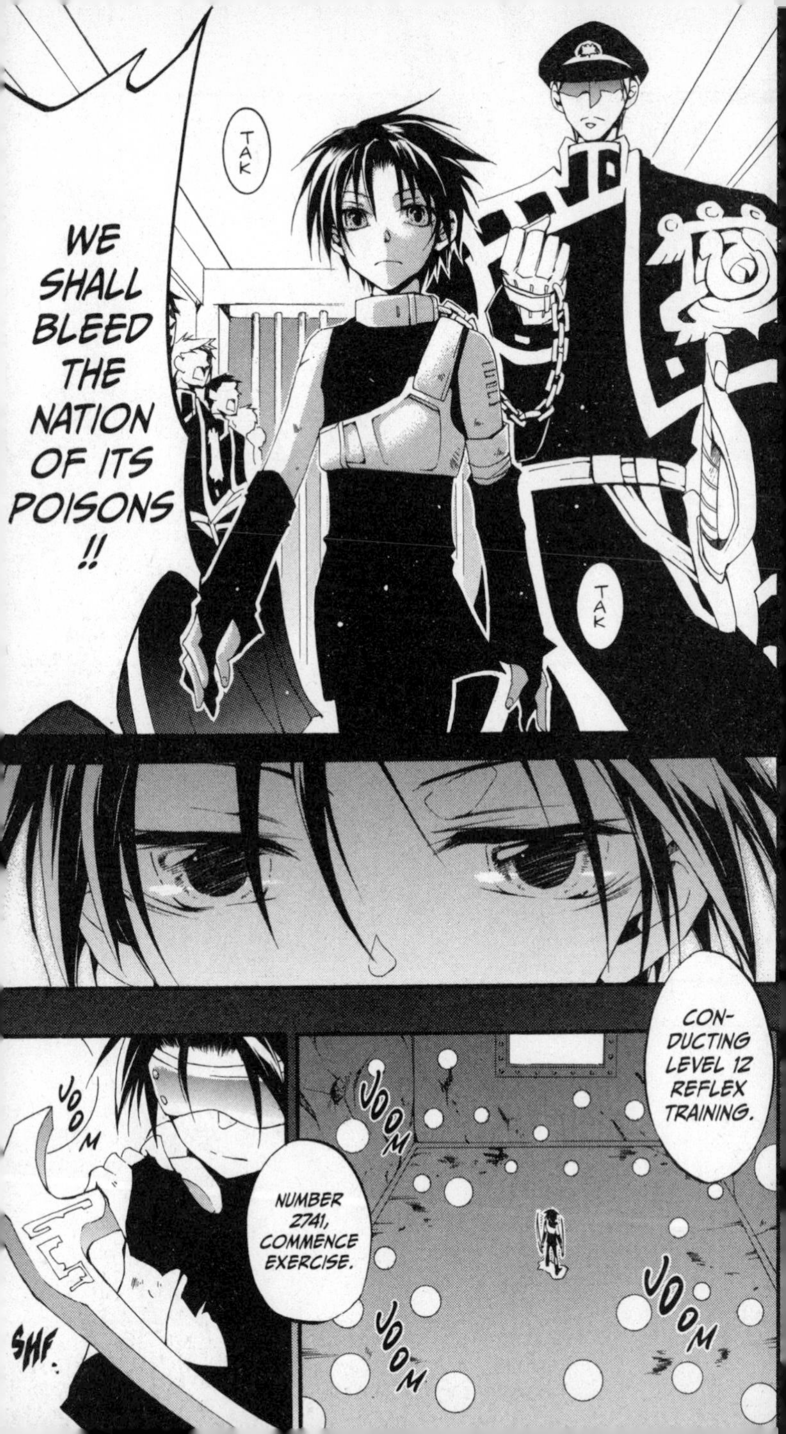
TAK
WE SHALL BLEED THE NATION OF ITS POISONS!!
TAK
CON-DUCTING LEVEL 12 REFLEX TRAINING.
JOOOM
NUMBER 2741, COMMENCE EXERCISE.
JOOOM
JOOOM
JOOOM
SHF

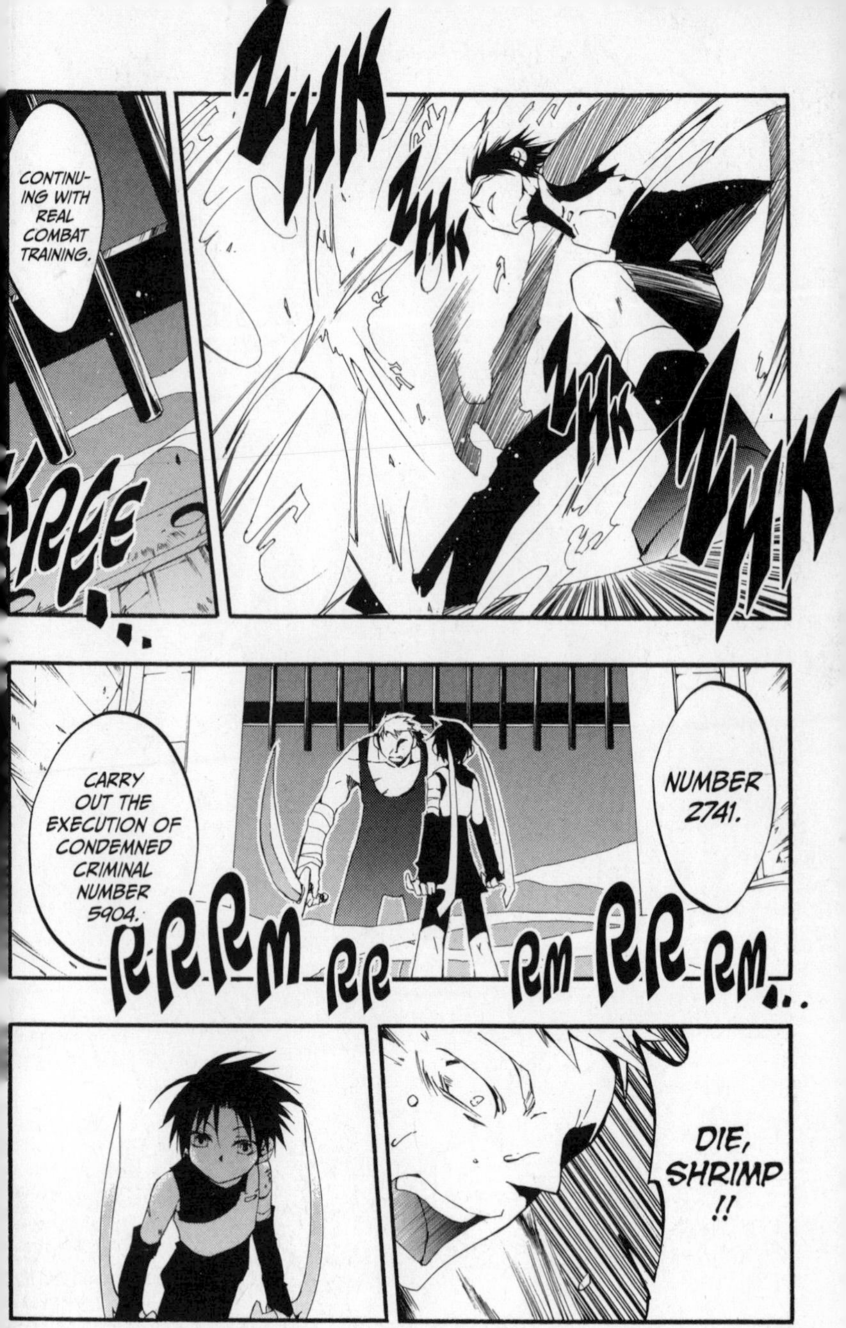
CONTINUING WITH REAL COMBAT TRAINING.
KREEE...
NUMBER 2741.
CARRY OUT THE EXECUTION OF CONDEMNED CRIMINAL NUMBER 5904.
RRRM RR RM RR RM...
DIE, SHRIMP !!

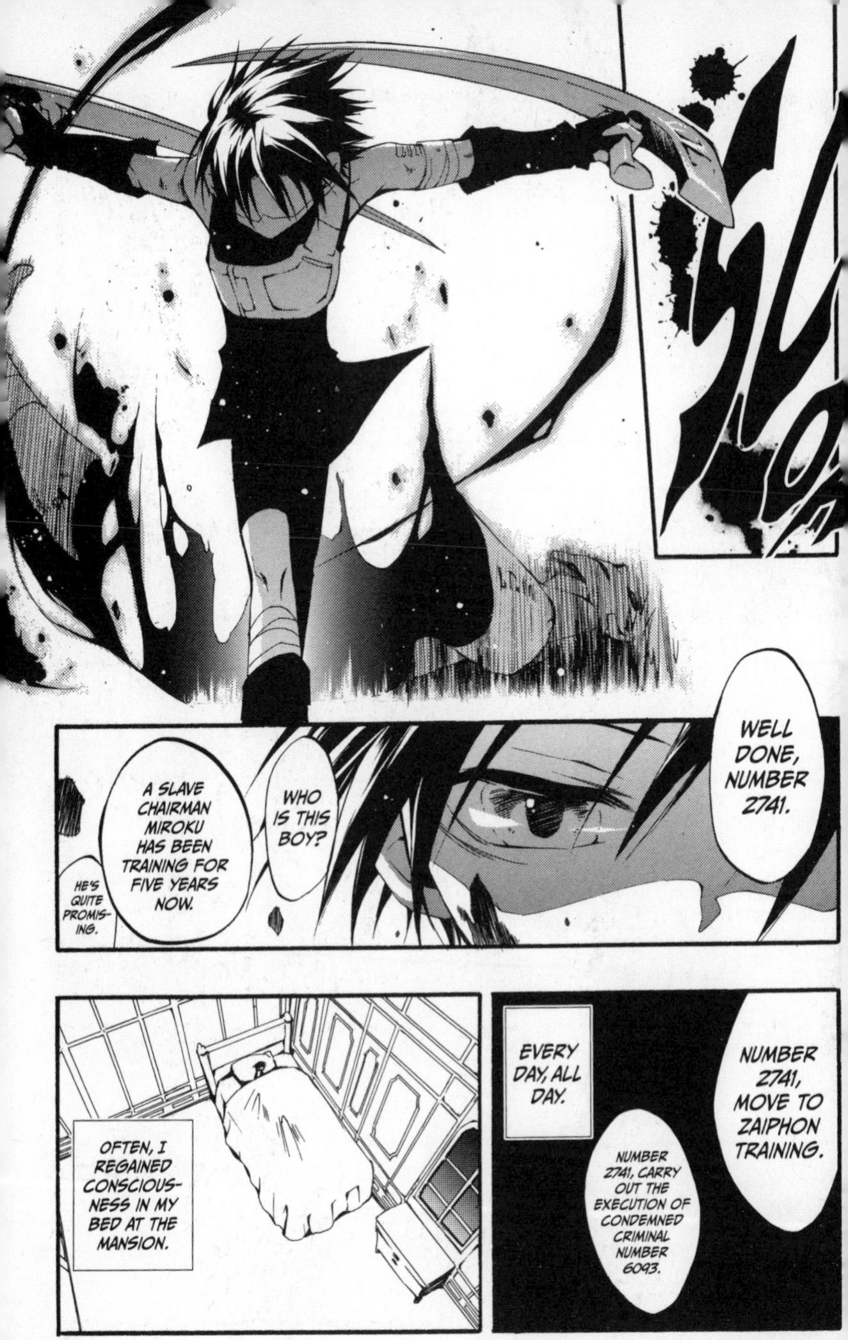
WELL DONE, NUMBER 2741.
WHO IS THIS BOY?
A SLAVE CHAIRMAN MIROKU HAS BEEN TRAINING FOR FIVE YEARS NOW.
HE'S QUITE PROMISING.
NUMBER 2741, MOVE TO ZAIPHON TRAINING.
EVERY DAY, ALL DAY.
NUMBER 2741, CARRY OUT THE EXECUTION OF CONDEMNED CRIMINAL NUMBER 6093.
OFTEN, I REGAINED CONSCIOUSNESS IN MY BED AT THE MANSION.

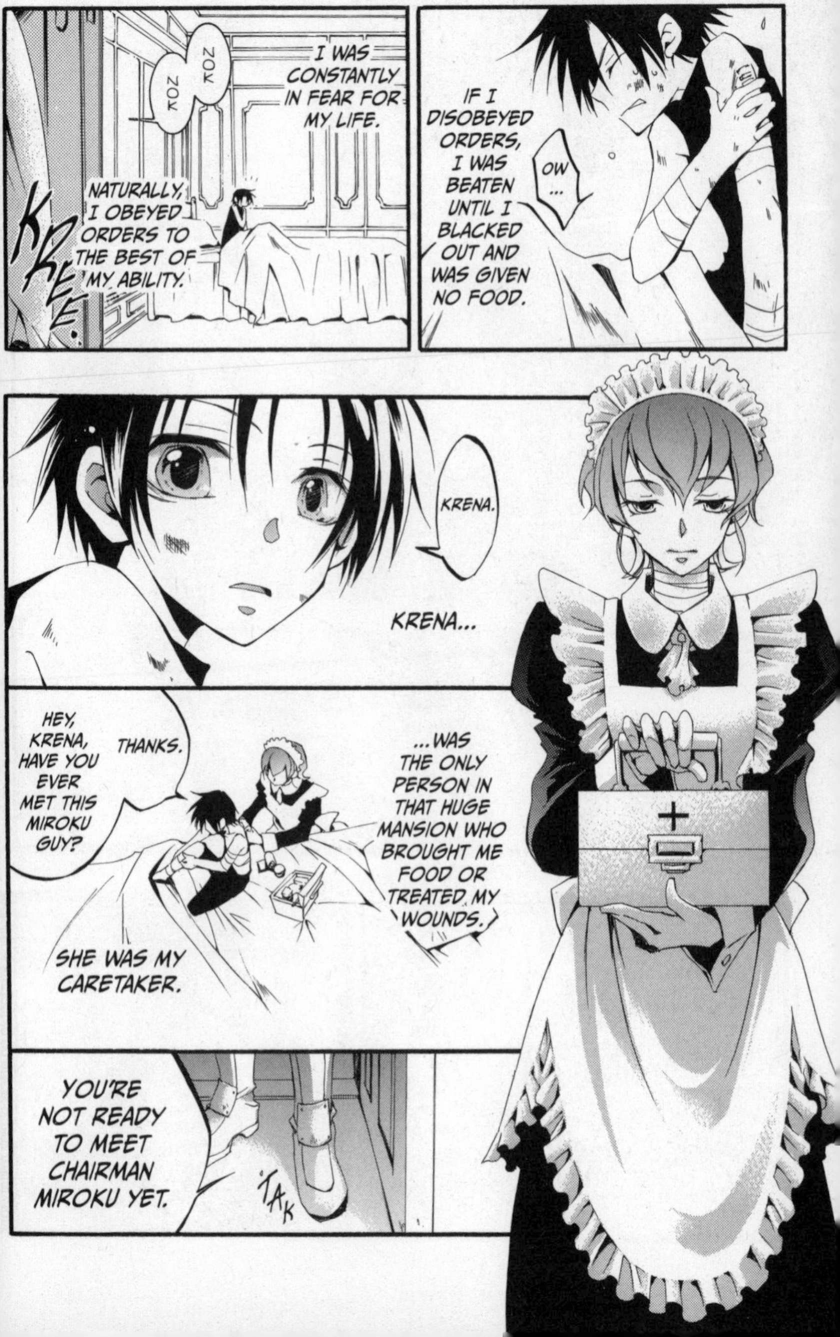
IF I DISOBEYED ORDERS, I WAS BEATEN UNTIL I BLACKED OUT AND WAS GIVEN NO FOOD.
OW ...
NOK NOK
I WAS CONSTANTLY IN FEAR FOR MY LIFE.
NATURALLY, I OBEYED ORDERS TO THE BEST OF MY ABILITY.
KREEE.
KRENA.
KRENA...
...WAS THE ONLY PERSON IN THAT HUGE MANSION WHO BROUGHT ME FOOD OR TREATED MY WOUNDS.
THANKS.
HEY, KRENA, HAVE YOU EVER MET THIS MIROKU GUY?
SHE WAS MY CARETAKER.
YOU'RE NOT READY TO MEET CHAIRMAN MIROKU YET.
TAK

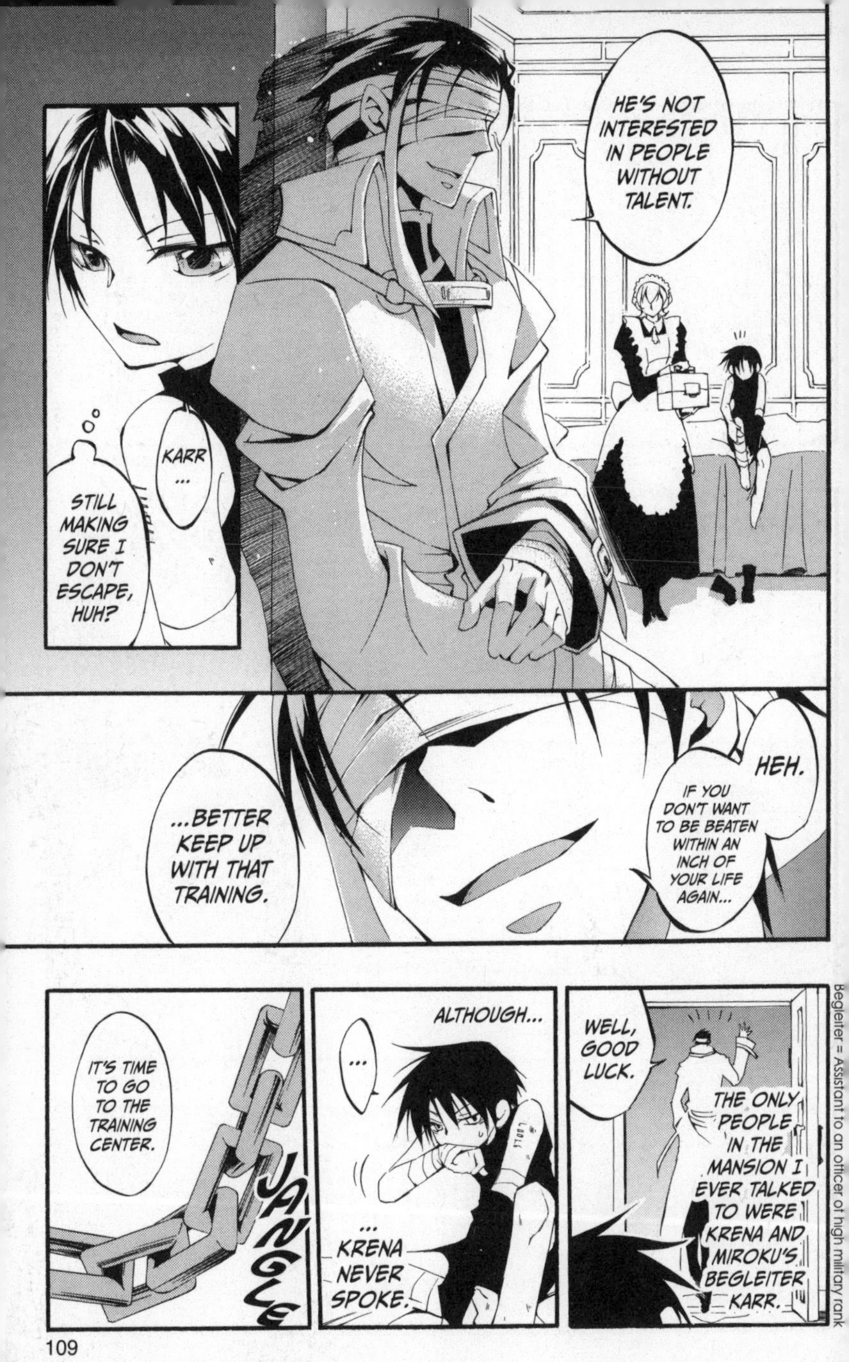
HE'S NOT INTERESTED IN PEOPLE WITHOUT TALENT.
KARR ...
STILL MAKING SURE I DON'T ESCAPE, HUH?
HEH.
IF YOU DON'T WANT TO BE BEATEN WITHIN AN INCH OF YOUR LIFE AGAIN...
...BETTER KEEP UP WITH THAT TRAINING.
WELL, GOOD LUCK.
THE ONLY PEOPLE IN THE MANSION I EVER TALKED TO WERE KRENA AND MIROKU'S BEGLEITER KARR.
ALTHOUGH...
...
... KRENA NEVER SPOKE.
IT'S TIME TO GO TO THE TRAINING CENTER.
JANGLE

Begleiter = Assistant to an officer of high military rank

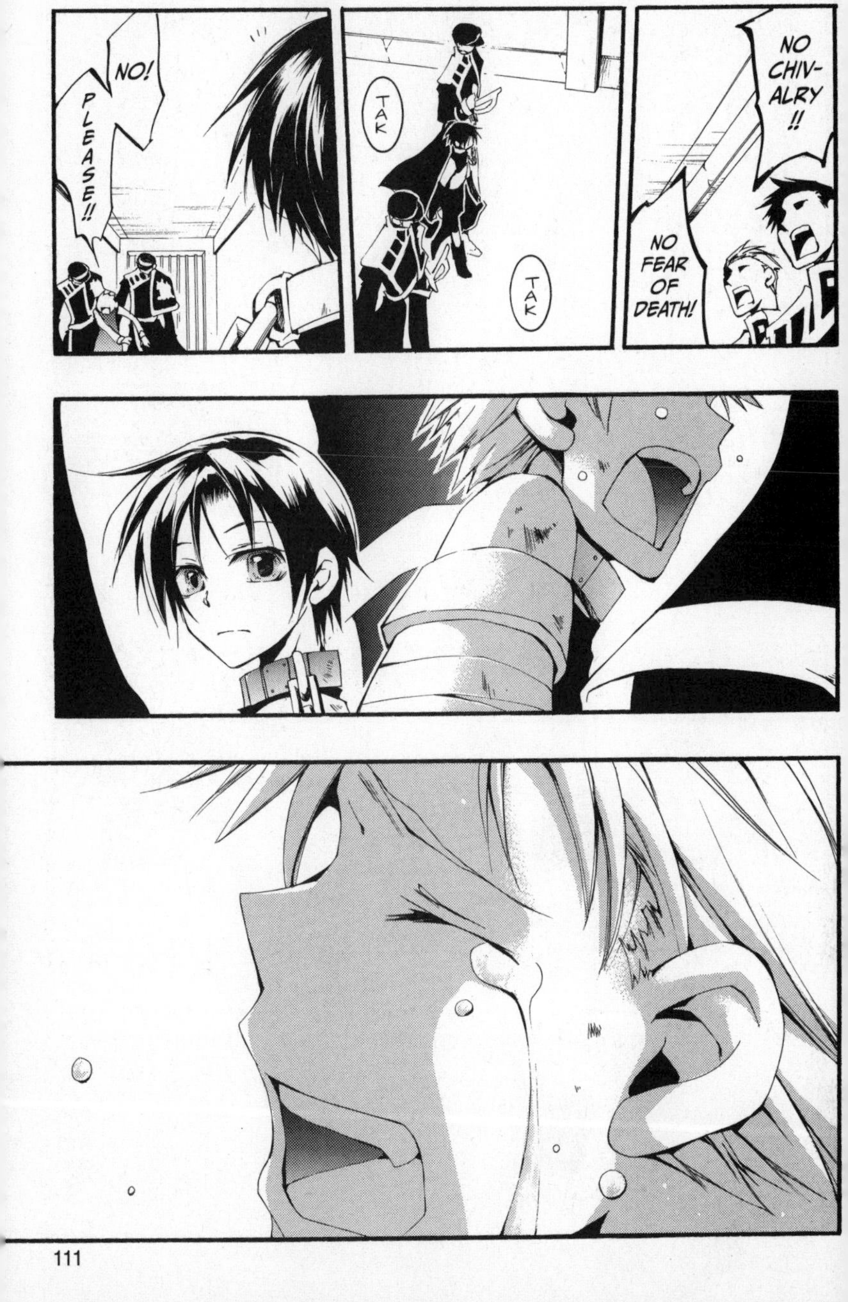
NO CHIVALRY!!
NO FEAR OF DEATH!
TAK
TAK
NO!
PLEASE!!

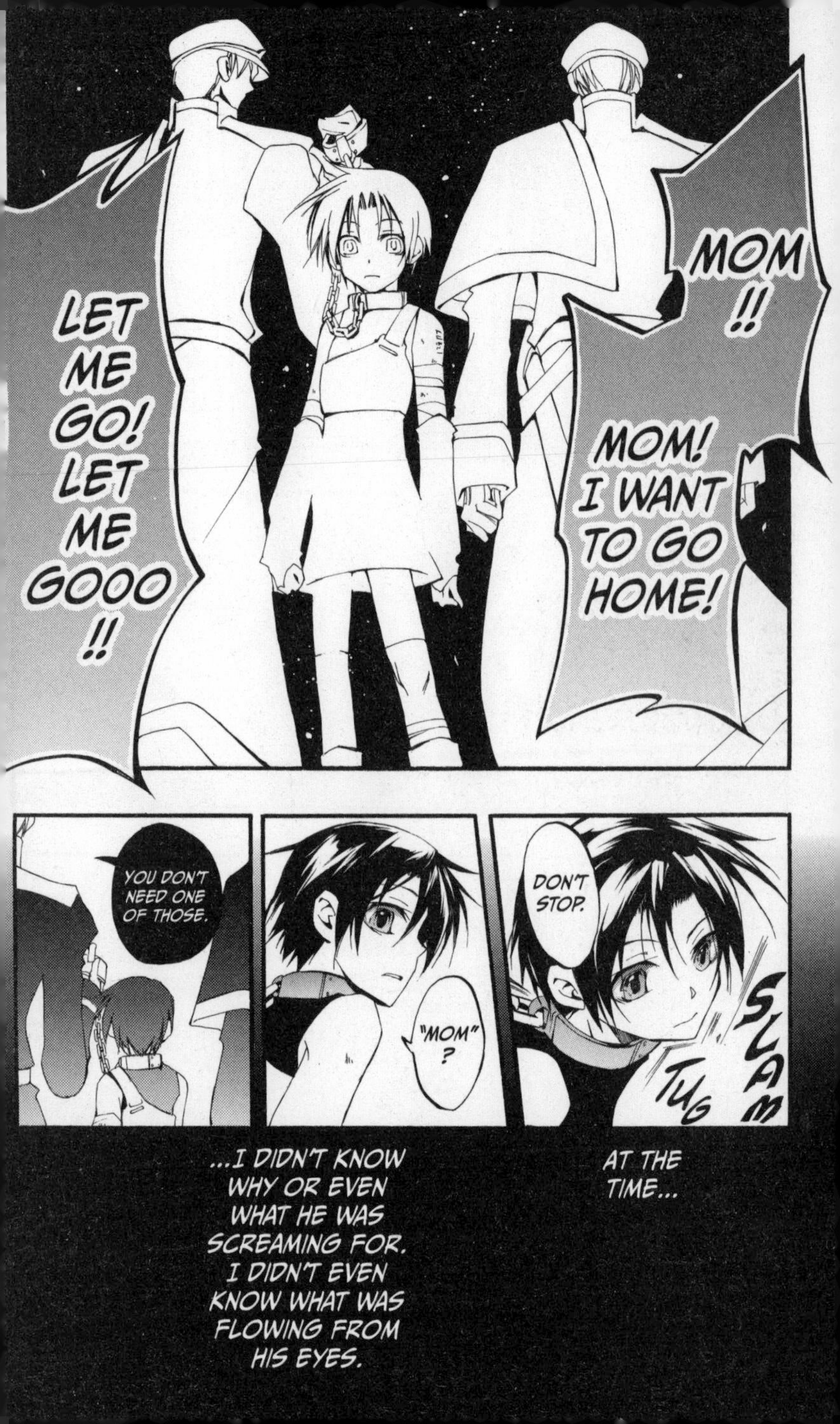
MOM!!
MOM! I WANT TO GO HOME!
LET ME GO! LET ME GOOO!!
DON'T STOP.
SLAM
TUG
"MOM"?
YOU DON'T NEED ONE OF THOSE.
AT THE TIME...
...I DIDN'T KNOW WHY OR EVEN WHAT HE WAS SCREAMING FOR. I DIDN'T EVEN KNOW WHAT WAS FLOWING FROM HIS EYES.

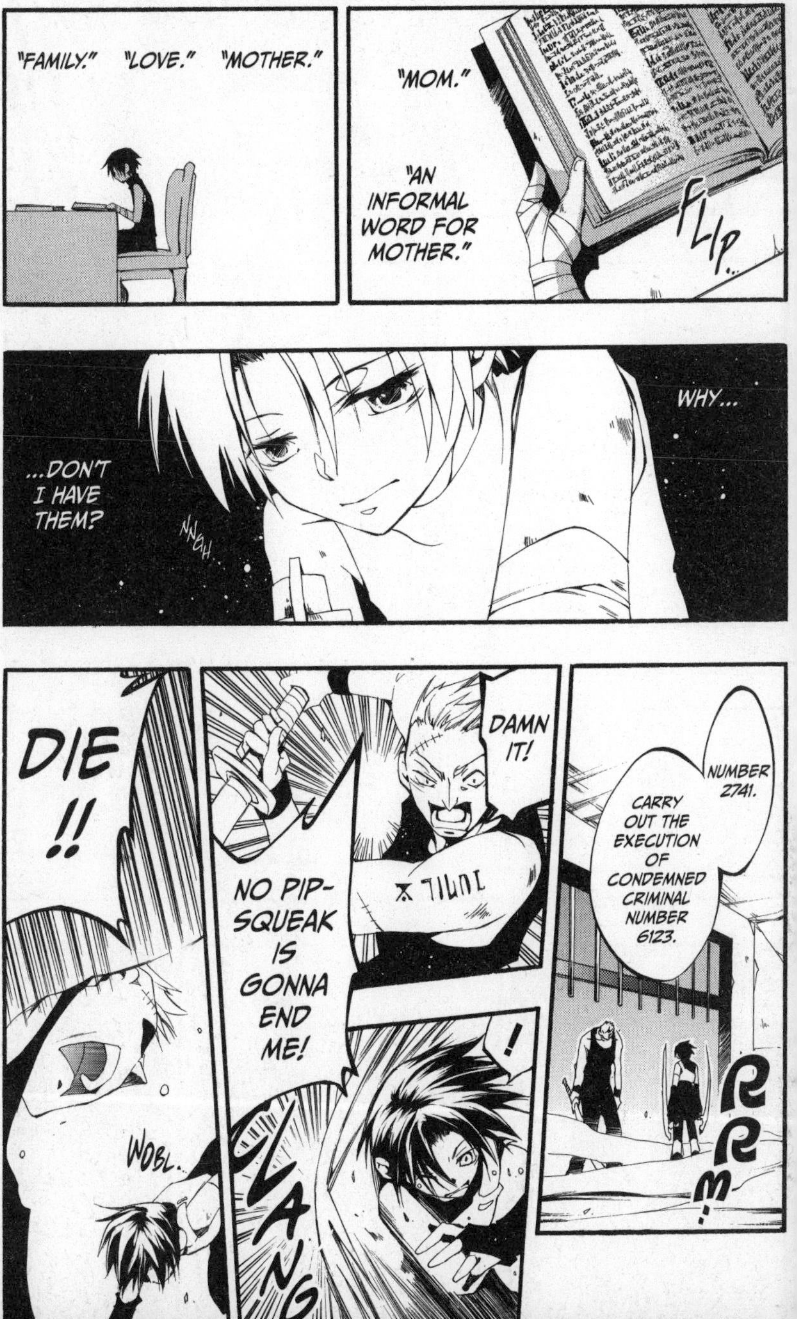
"MOM."
"AN INFORMAL WORD FOR MOTHER."
FLIP...
"FAMILY."
"LOVE."
"MOTHER."
WHY...
...DON'T I HAVE THEM?
NNGH
NUMBER 2741.
CARRY OUT THE EXECUTION OF CONDEMNED CRIMINAL NUMBER 6123.
RRRM...
DAMN IT!
NO PIP-SQUEAK IS GONNA END ME!
!
CLANG
DIE!!
WOBL...

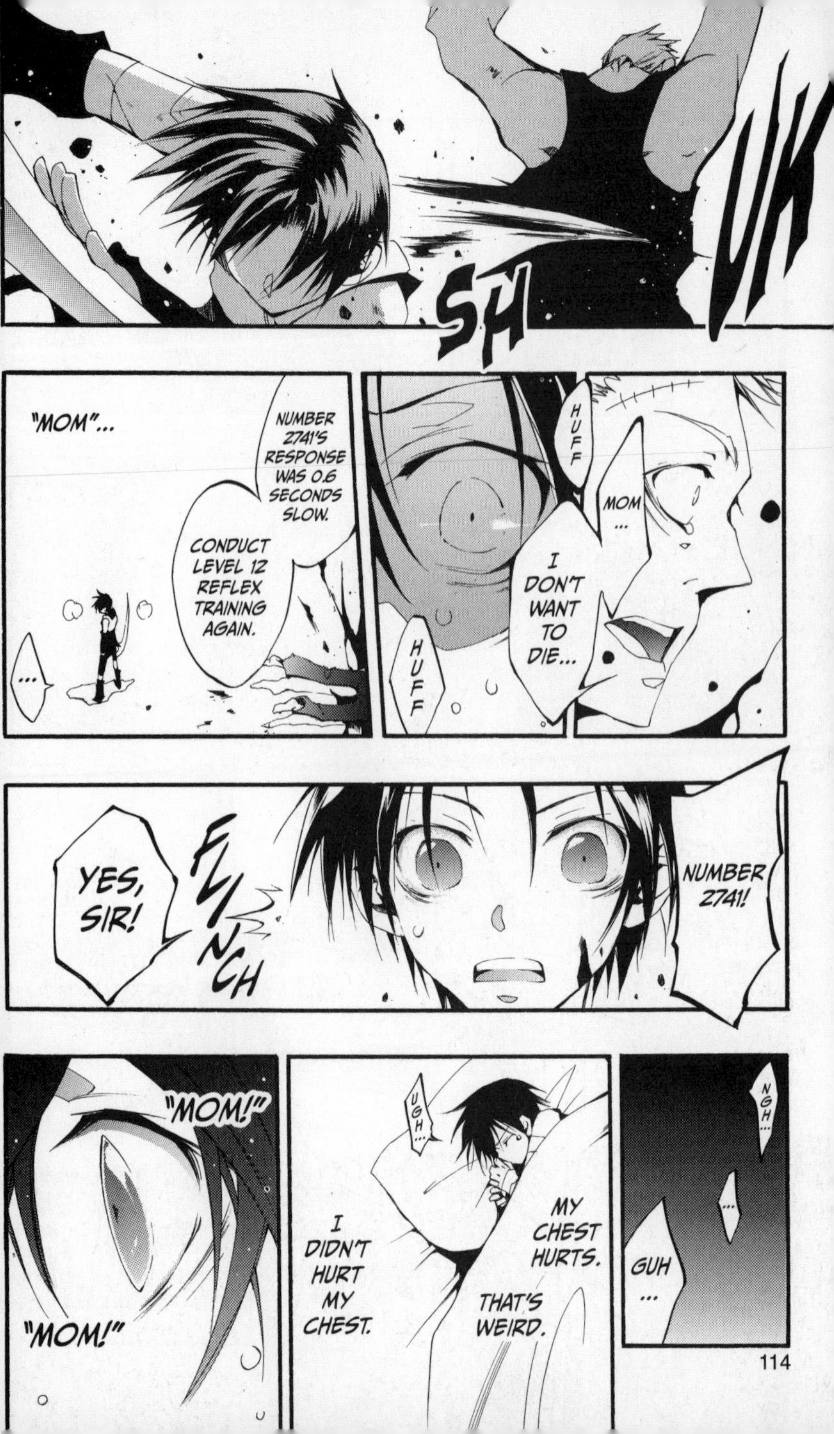
SH
UK
HUFF
MOM...
I DON'T WANT TO DIE...
HUFF
NUMBER 2741'S RESPONSE WAS 0.6 SECONDS SLOW.
CONDUCT LEVEL 12 REFLEX TRAINING AGAIN.
"MOM"...
...
NUMBER 2741!
FLINCH
YES, SIR!
NGH...
...
GUH...
UGH...
MY CHEST HURTS.
THAT'S WEIRD.
I DIDN'T HURT MY CHEST.
"MOM!"
"MOM!"

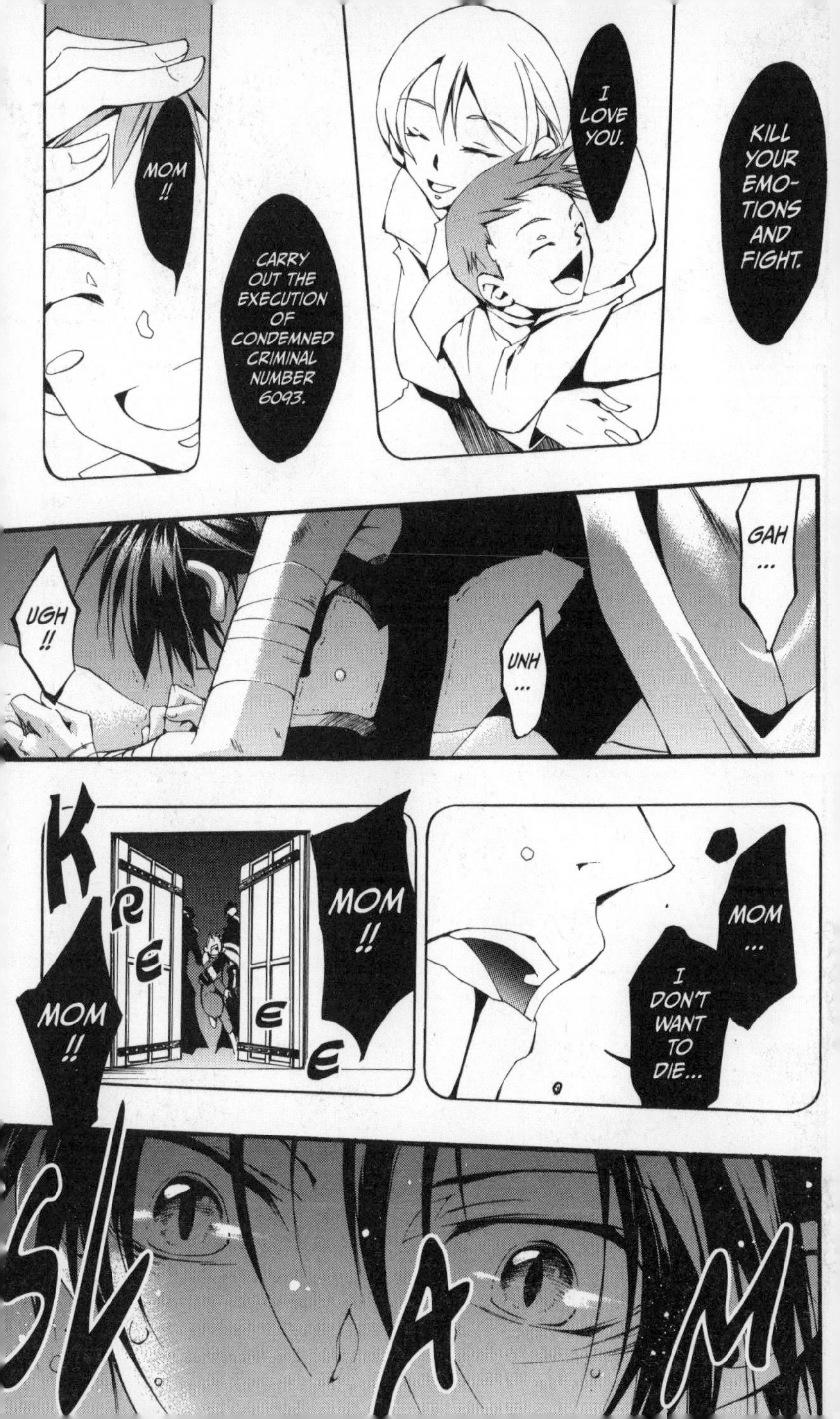
KILL YOUR EMOTIONS AND FIGHT.
I LOVE YOU.
CARRY OUT THE EXECUTION OF CONDEMNED CRIMINAL NUMBER 6093.
MOM!!
GAH...
UNH...
UGH!!
MOM...
I DON'T WANT TO DIE...
MOM!!
KREEEE
MOM!!
SLAM

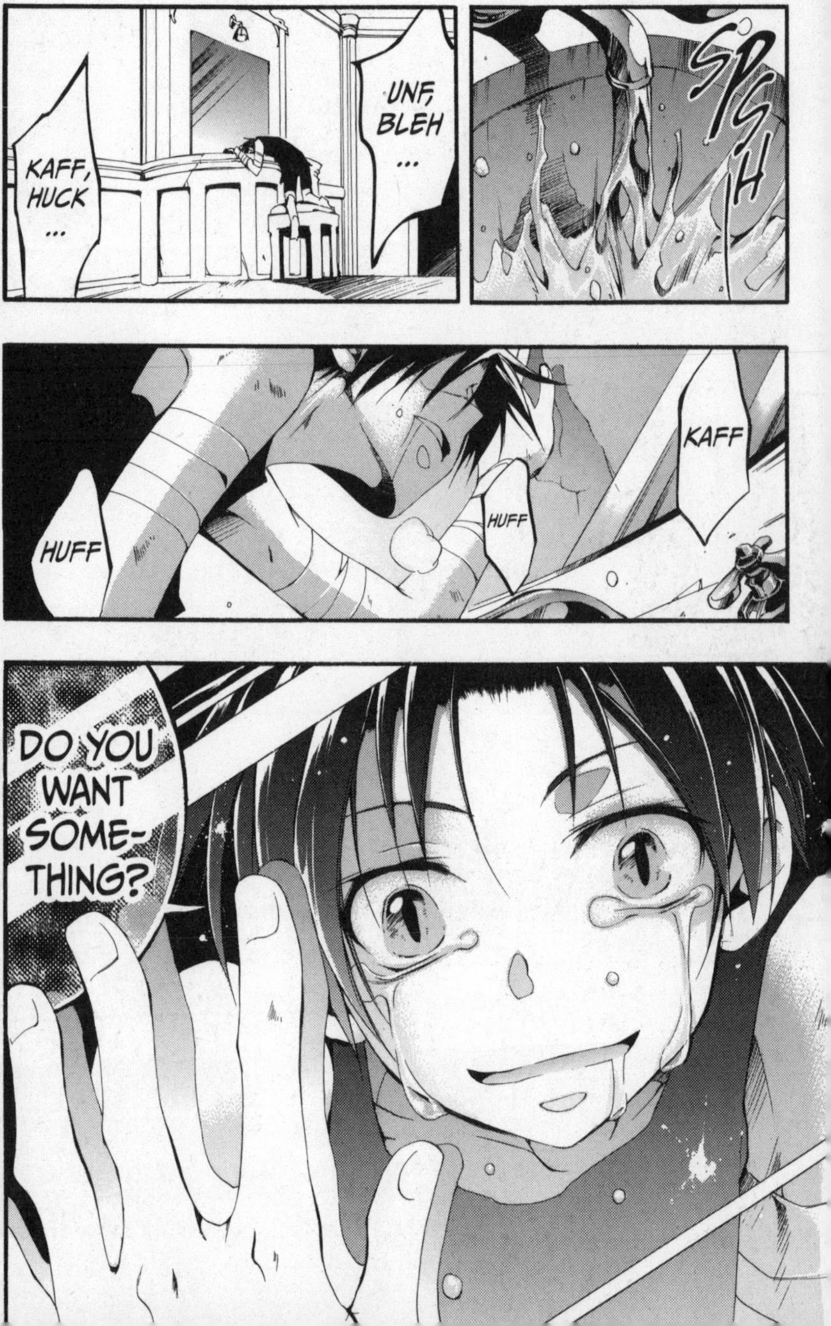
SPSH
UNF, BLEH ...
KAFF, HUCK ...
KAFF
HUFF
HUFF
DO YOU WANT SOME-THING?

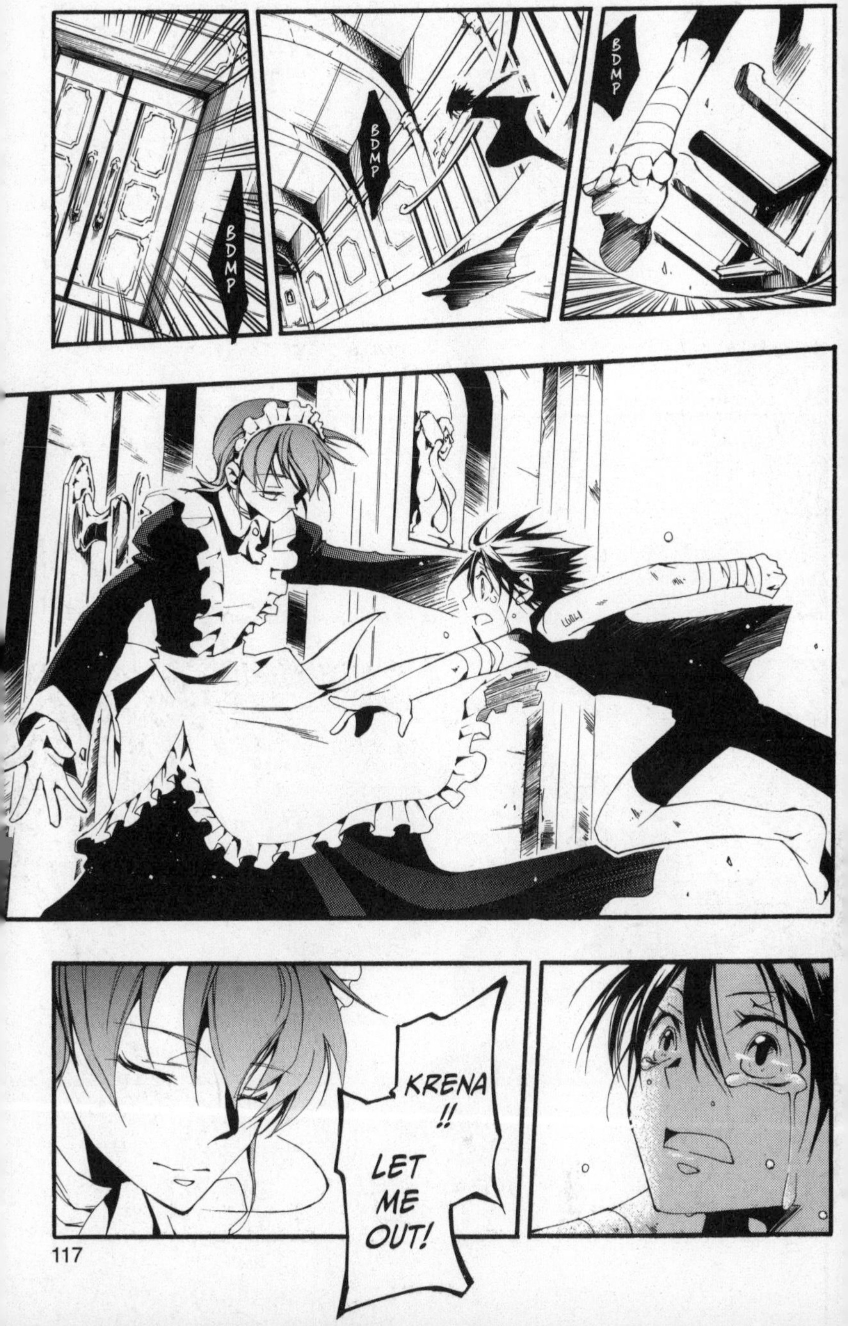
BDMP
BDMP
BDMP
KRENA !!
LET ME OUT!

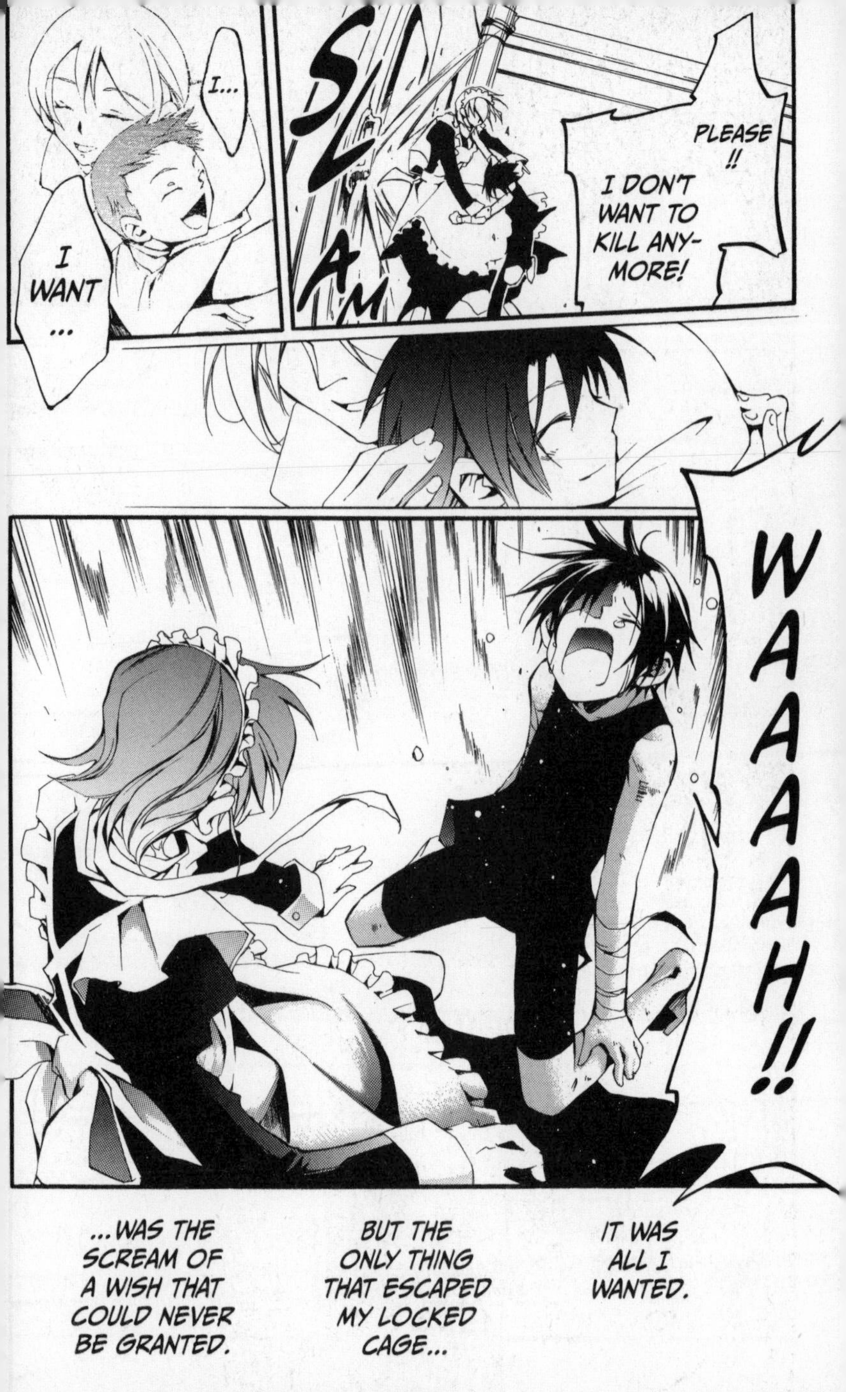
PLEASE!!
I DON'T WANT TO KILL ANY-MORE!
SLAM
I...
I WANT...
WAAAAH!!
IT WAS ALL I WANTED.
BUT THE ONLY THING THAT ESCAPED MY LOCKED CAGE...
...WAS THE SCREAM OF A WISH THAT COULD NEVER BE GRANTED.

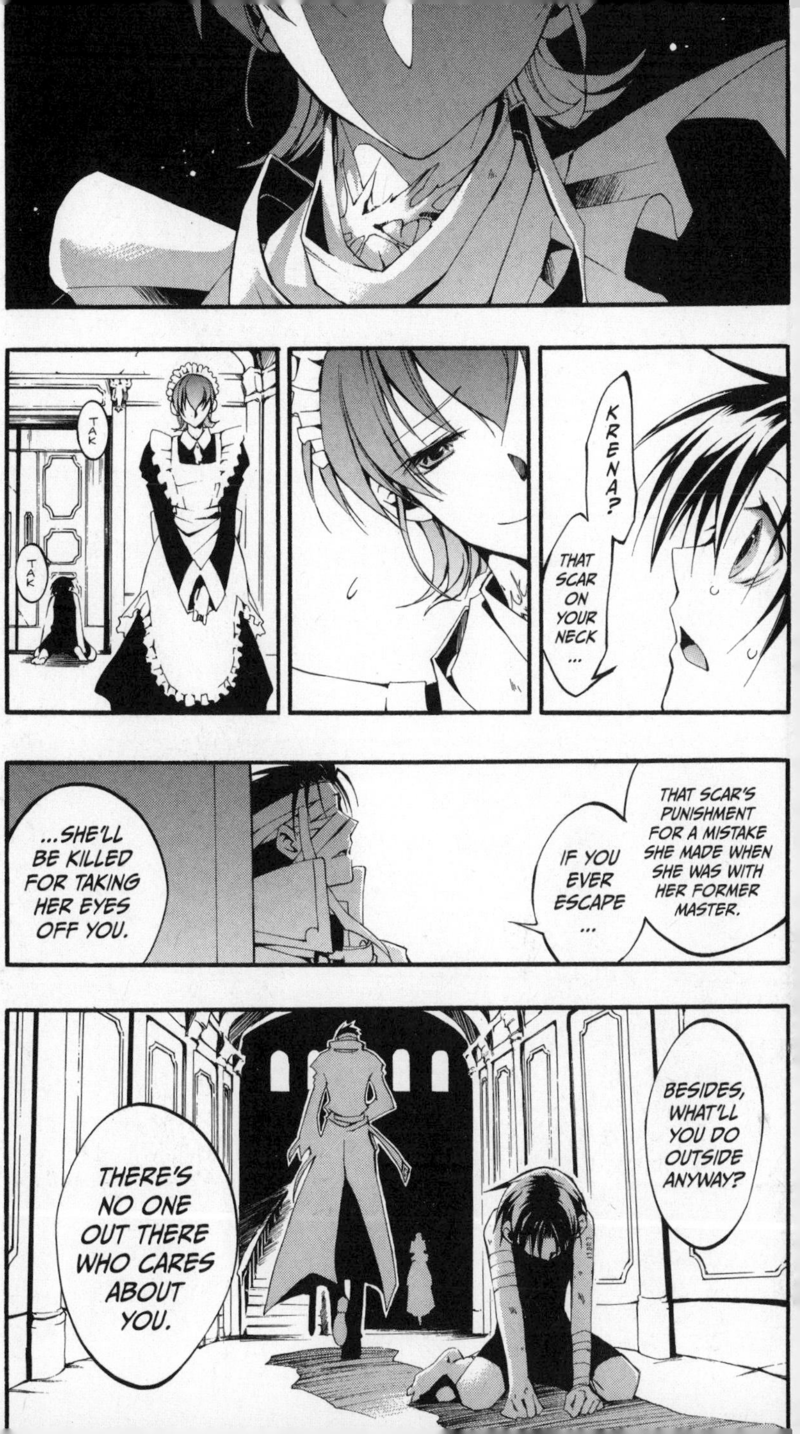
KRENA?
THAT SCAR ON YOUR NECK ...
TAK
TAK
THAT SCAR'S PUNISHMENT FOR A MISTAKE SHE MADE WHEN SHE WAS WITH HER FORMER MASTER.
IF YOU EVER ESCAPE ...
...SHE'LL BE KILLED FOR TAKING HER EYES OFF YOU.
BESIDES, WHAT'LL YOU DO OUTSIDE ANYWAY?
THERE'S NO ONE OUT THERE WHO CARES ABOUT YOU.

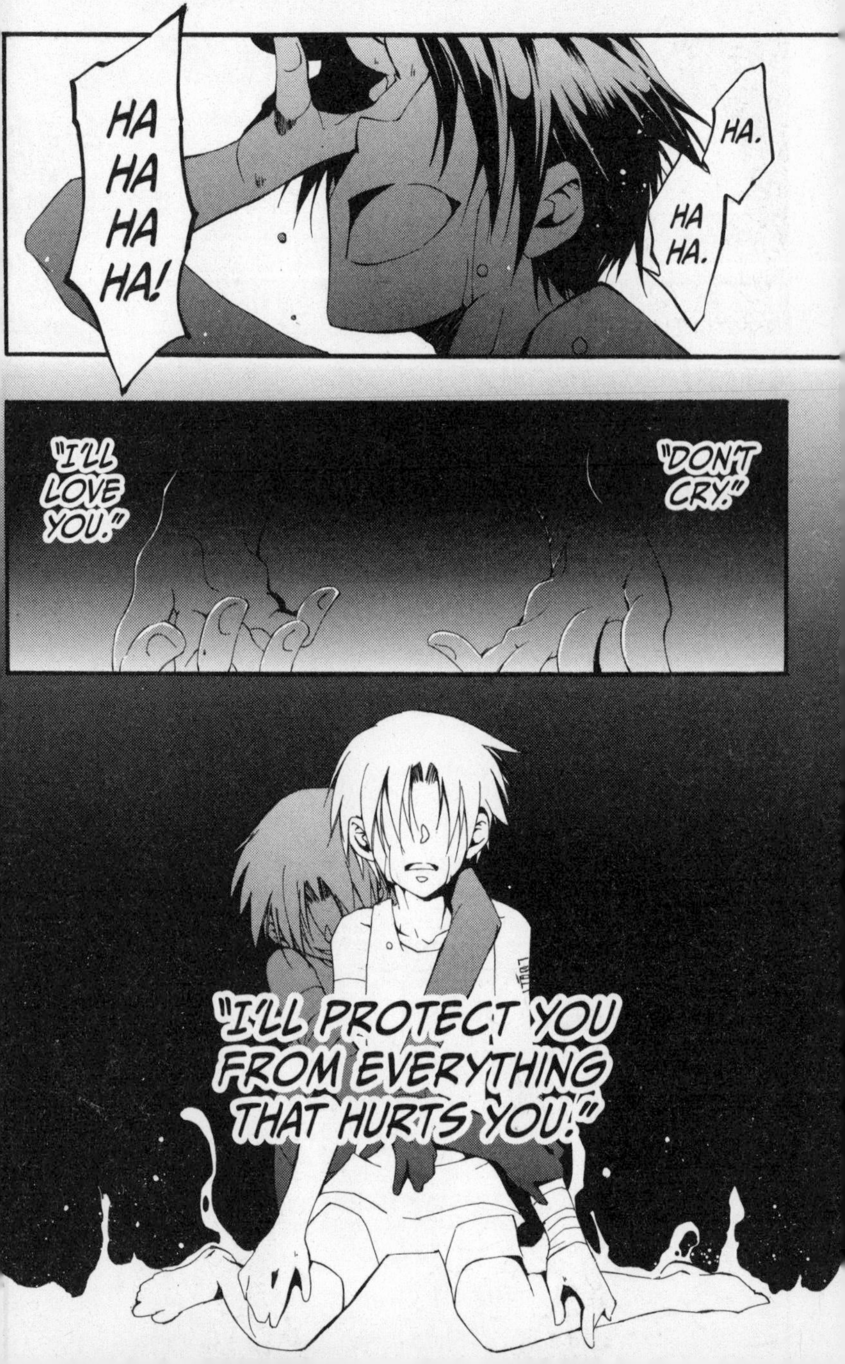
HA.
HA HA.
HA HA HA HA!
"DON'T CRY."
"I'LL LOVE YOU."
"I'LL PROTECT YOU FROM EVERYTHING THAT HURTS YOU."

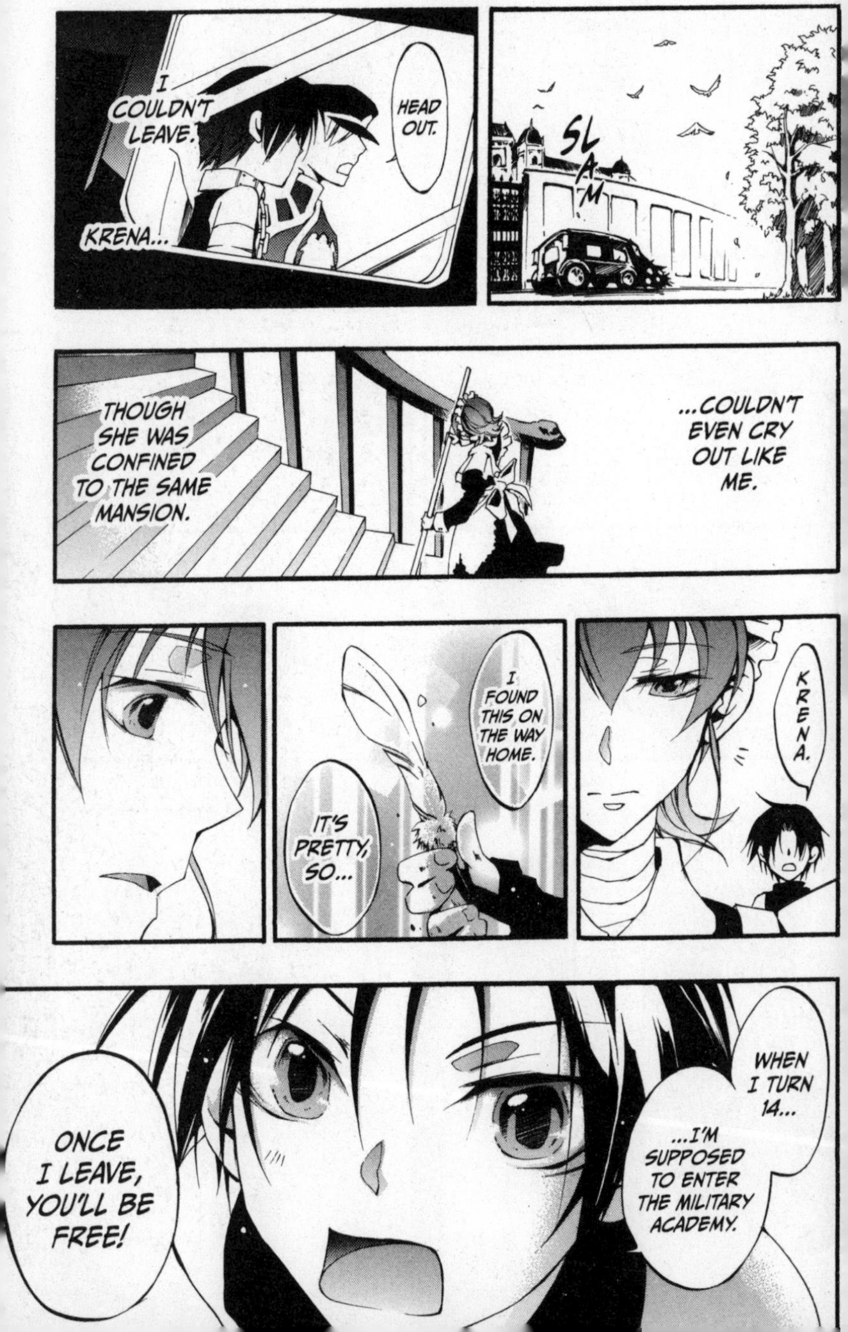
SLAM
HEAD OUT.
I COULDN'T LEAVE.
KRENA...
...COULDN'T EVEN CRY OUT LIKE ME.
THOUGH SHE WAS CONFINED TO THE SAME MANSION.
KRENA.
I FOUND THIS ON THE WAY HOME.
IT'S PRETTY, SO...
WHEN I TURN 14...
...I'M SUPPOSED TO ENTER THE MILITARY ACADEMY.
ONCE I LEAVE, YOU'LL BE FREE!

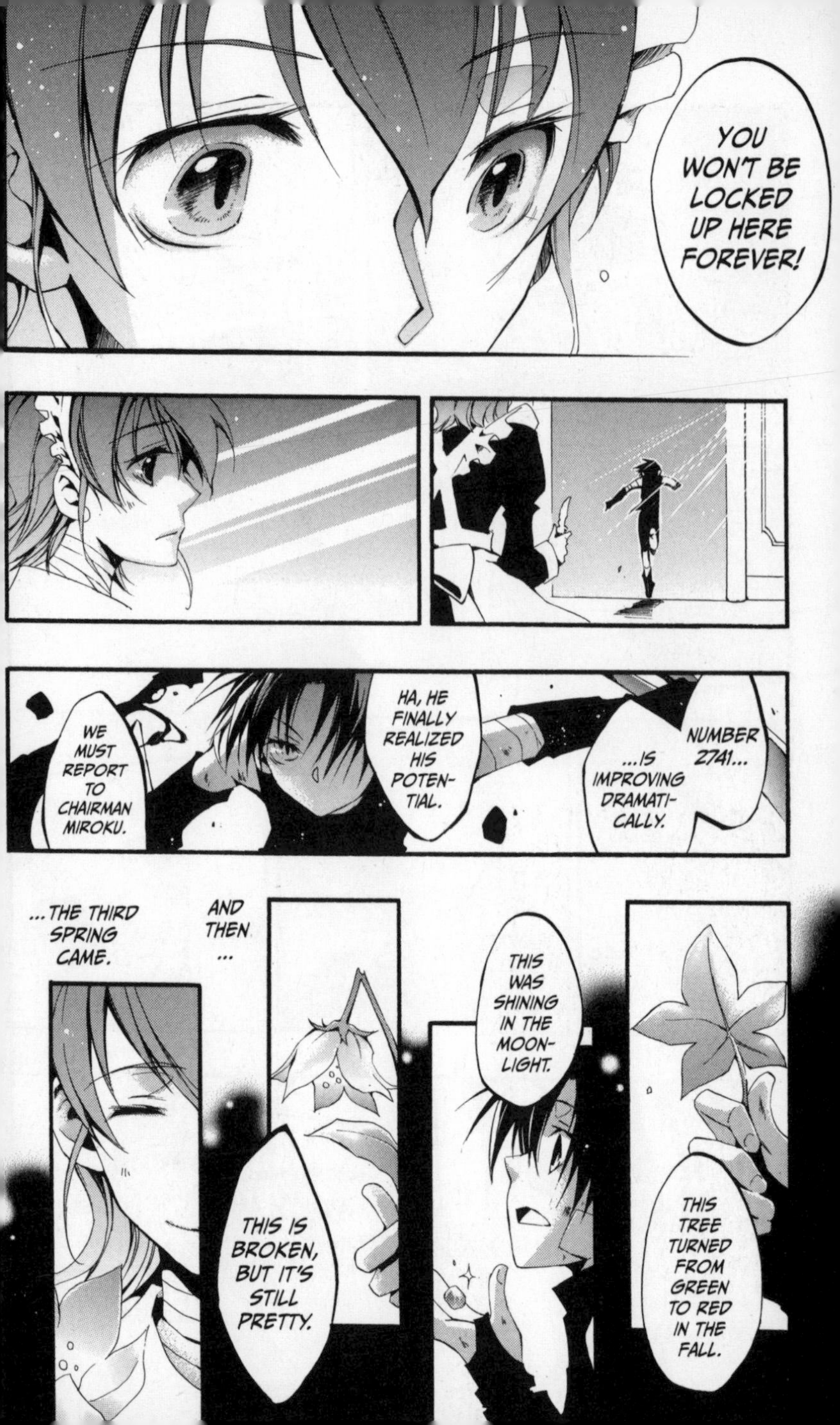
YOU WON'T BE LOCKED UP HERE FOREVER!
NUMBER 2741...
...IS IMPROVING DRAMATICALLY.
HA, HE FINALLY REALIZED HIS POTENTIAL.
WE MUST REPORT TO CHAIRMAN MIROKU.
AND THEN ...
...THE THIRD SPRING CAME.
THIS TREE TURNED FROM GREEN TO RED IN THE FALL.
THIS WAS SHINING IN THE MOONLIGHT.
THIS IS BROKEN, BUT IT'S STILL PRETTY.

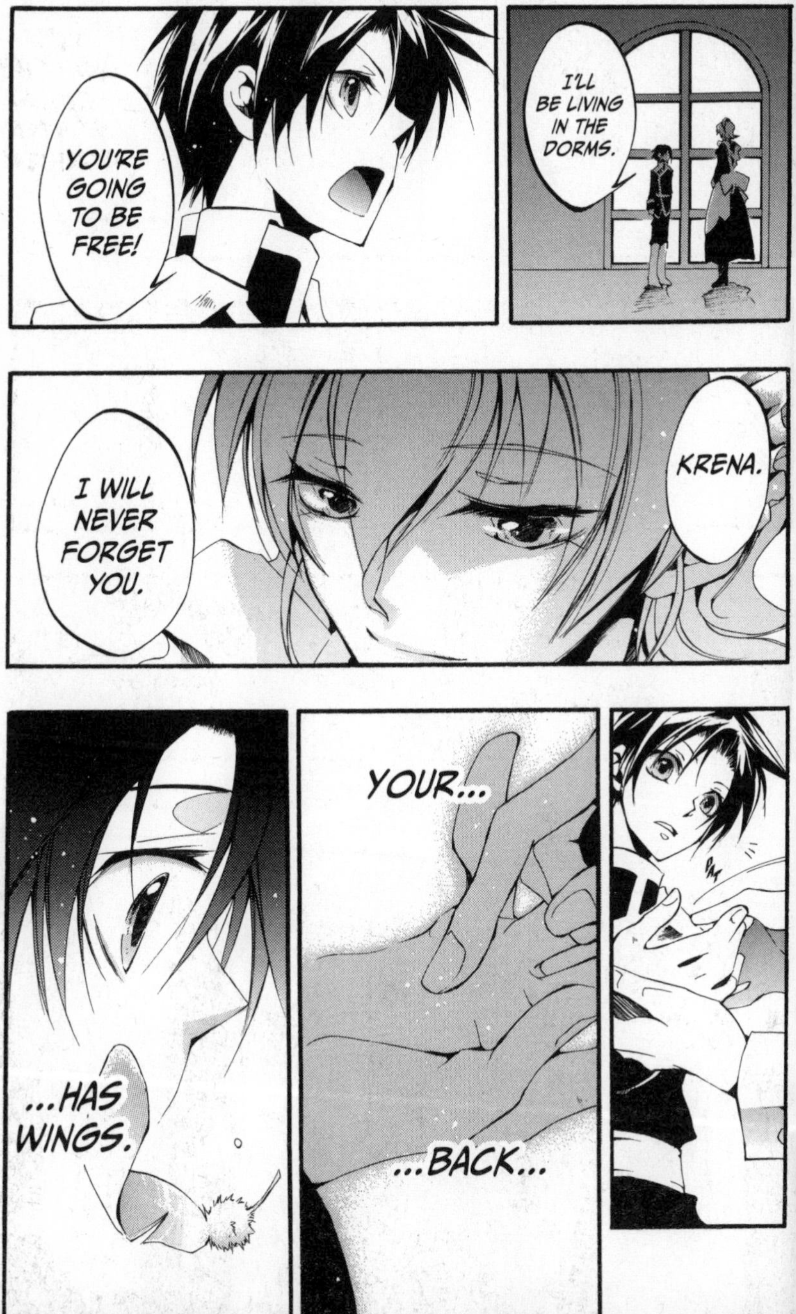
I'LL BE LIVING IN THE DORMS.
YOU'RE GOING TO BE FREE!
KRENA.
I WILL NEVER FORGET YOU.
YOUR...
...BACK...
...HAS WINGS.

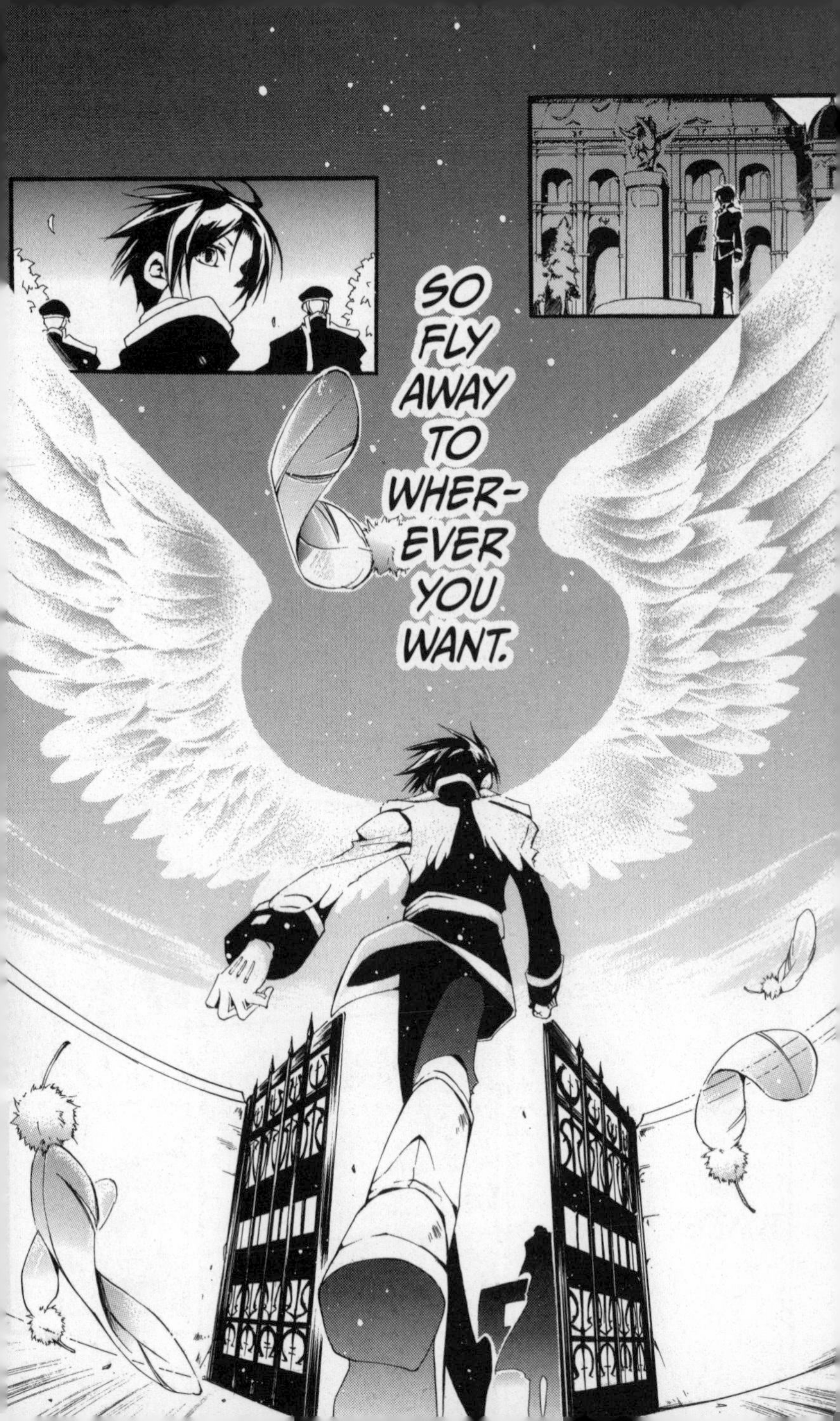
SO FLY AWAY TO WHER-EVER YOU WANT.

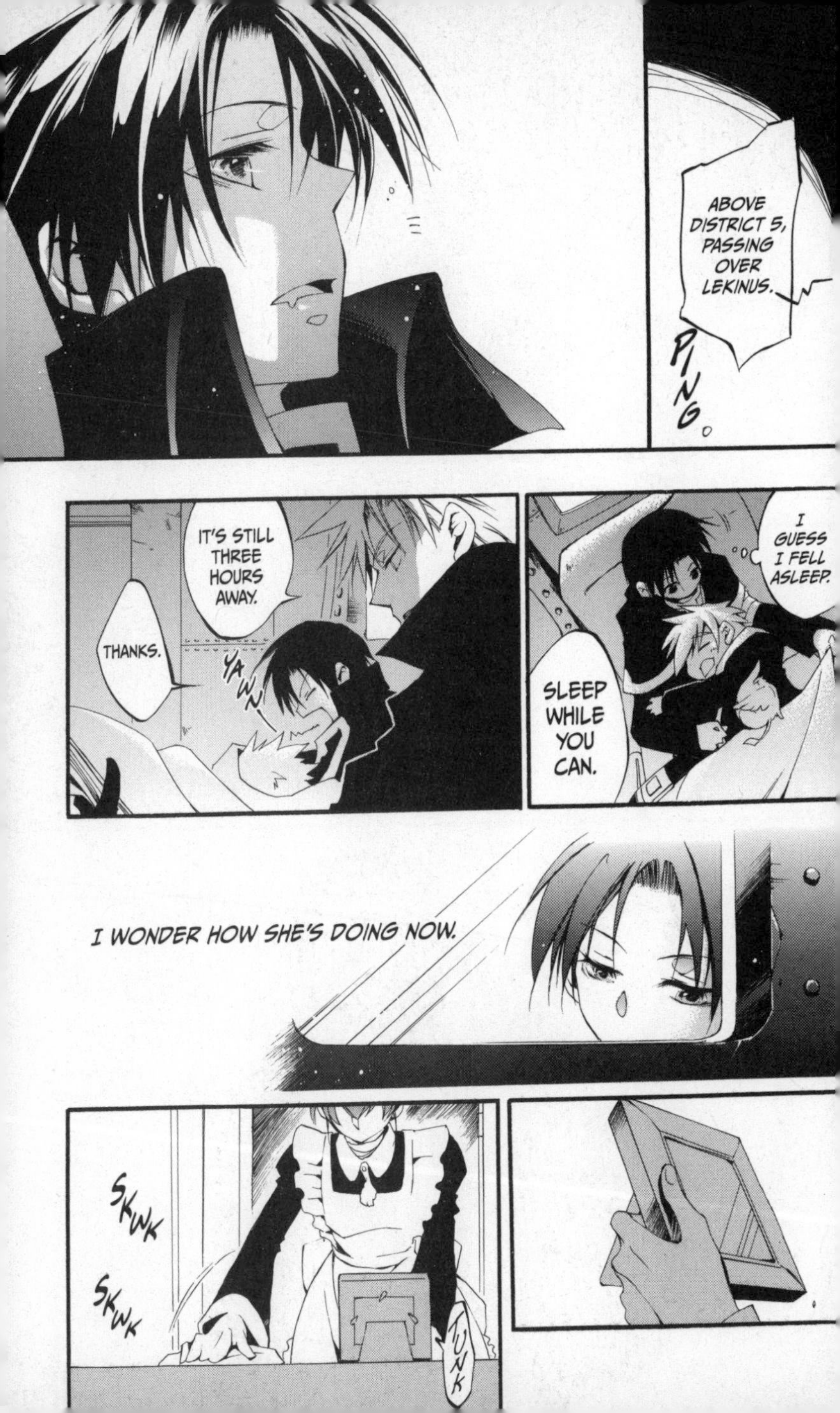
ABOVE DISTRICT 5, PASSING OVER LEKINUS.
PING
I GUESS I FELL ASLEEP.
SLEEP WHILE YOU CAN.
IT'S STILL THREE HOURS AWAY.
YAWN
THANKS.
I WONDER HOW SHE'S DOING NOW.
SKWK
SKWK
TUNK

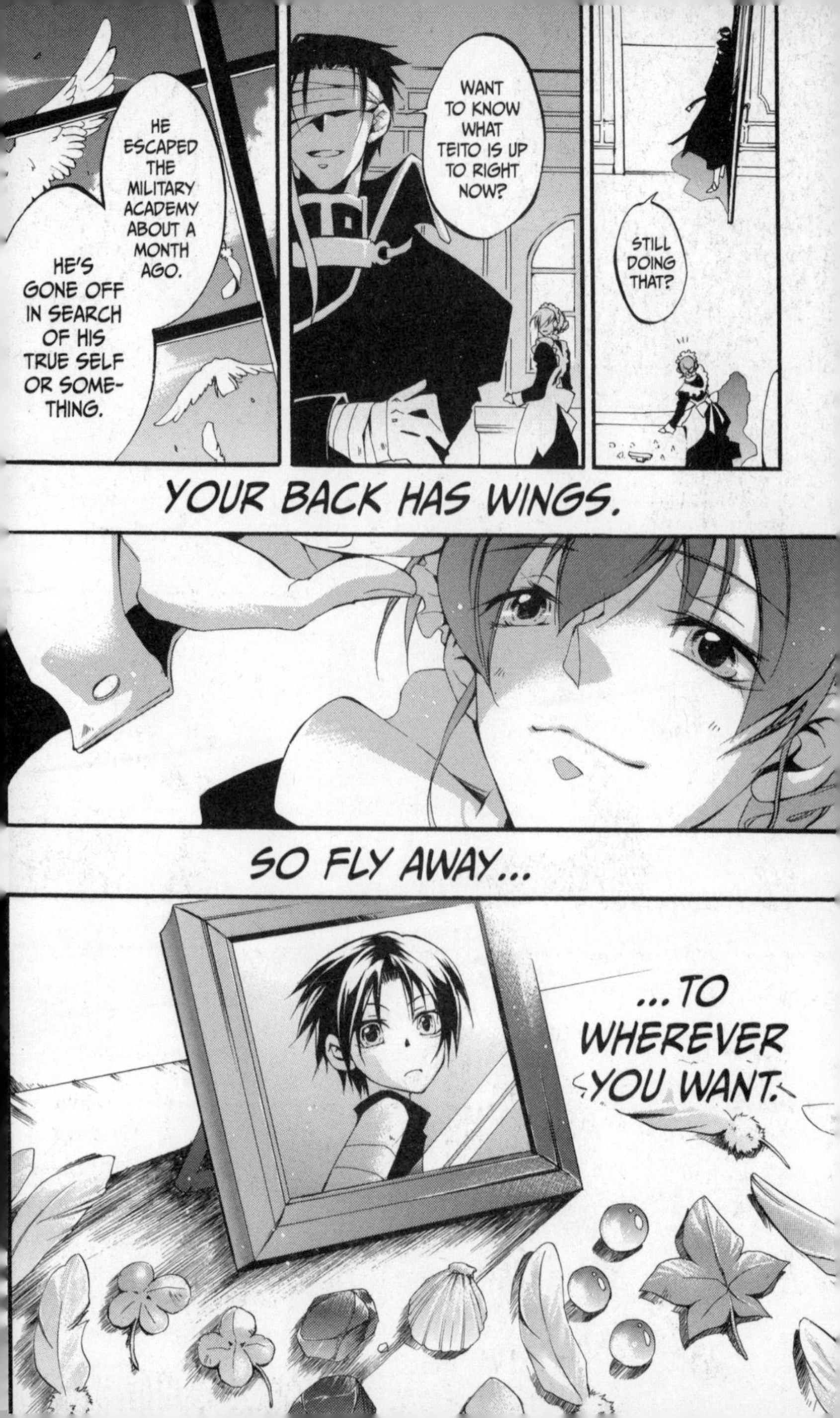
STILL DOING THAT?
WANT TO KNOW WHAT TEITO IS UP TO RIGHT NOW?
HE ESCAPED THE MILITARY ACADEMY ABOUT A MONTH AGO.
HE'S GONE OFF IN SEARCH OF HIS TRUE SELF OR SOME-THING.
YOUR BACK HAS WINGS.
SO FLY AWAY...
...TO WHEREVER YOU WANT.

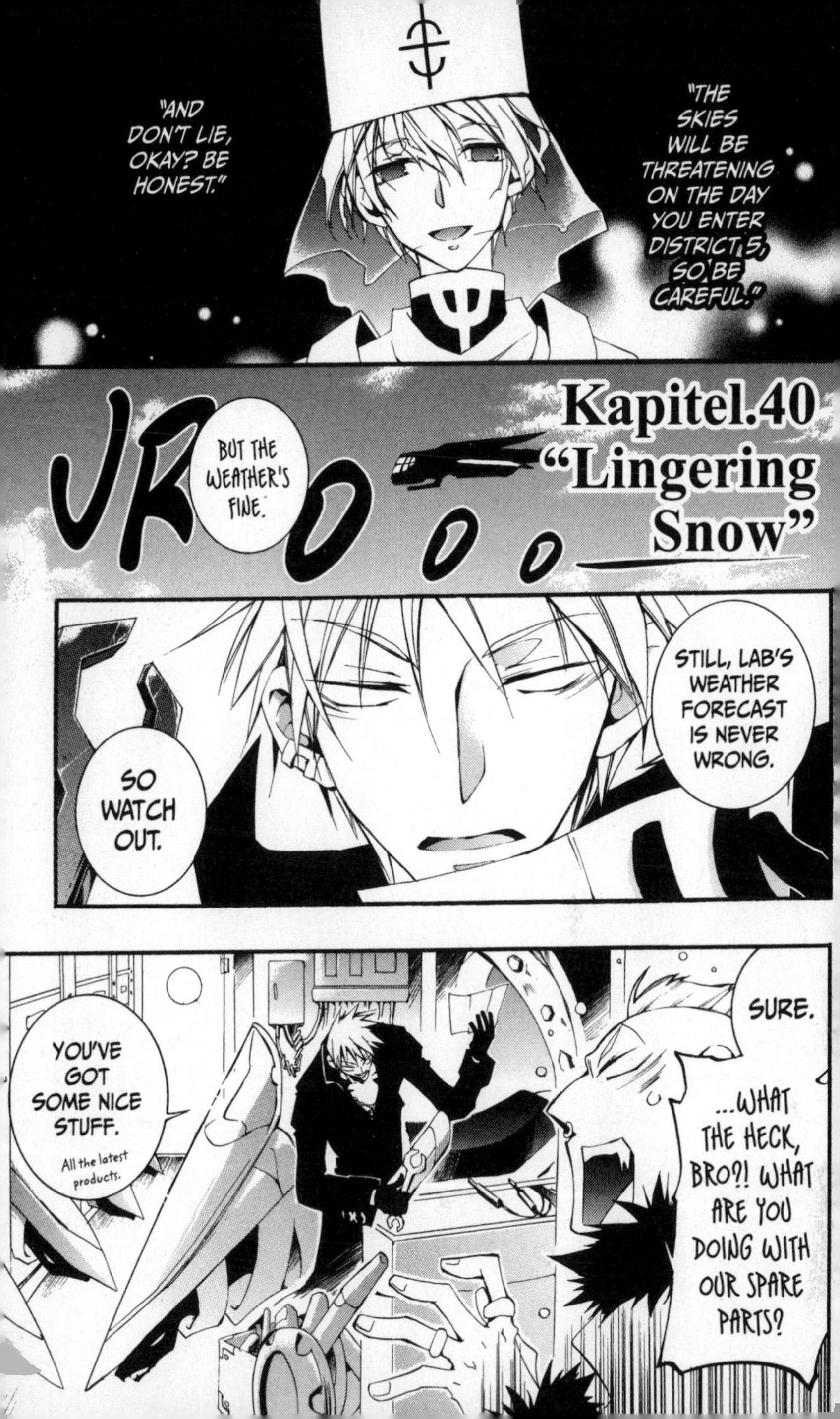
"THE SKIES WILL BE THREATENING ON THE DAY YOU ENTER DISTRICT 5, SO BE CAREFUL."
"AND DON'T LIE, OKAY? BE HONEST."
Kapitel.40 "Lingering Snow"
VROOOO
BUT THE WEATHER'S FINE.
STILL, LAB'S WEATHER FORECAST IS NEVER WRONG.
SO WATCH OUT.
SURE.
...WHAT THE HECK, BRO?! WHAT ARE YOU DOING WITH OUR SPARE PARTS?
YOU'VE GOT SOME NICE STUFF.
All the latest products.

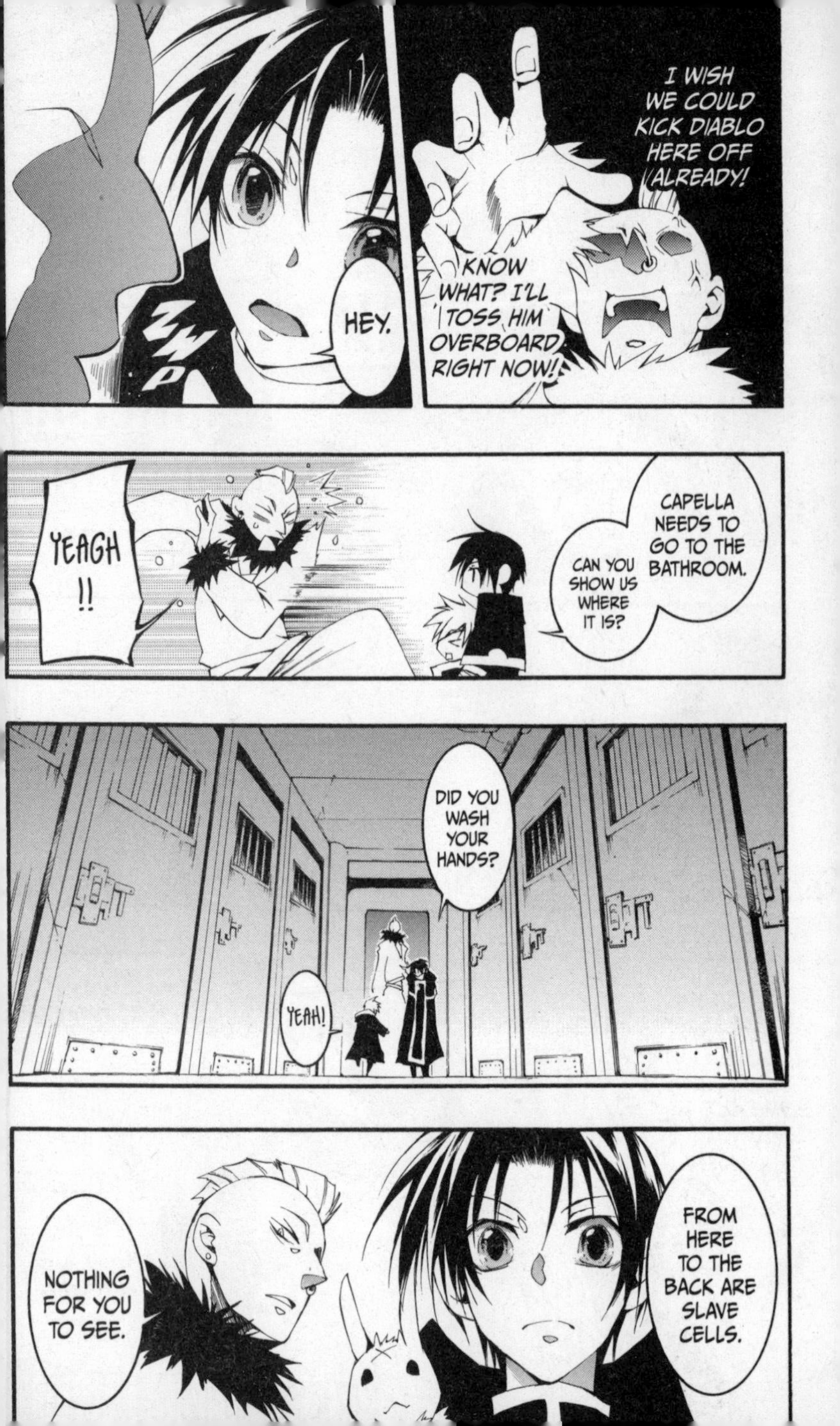
I WISH WE COULD KICK DIABLO HERE OFF ALREADY!
KNOW WHAT? I'LL TOSS HIM OVERBOARD RIGHT NOW!
HEY.
CAPELLA NEEDS TO GO TO THE BATHROOM.
CAN YOU SHOW US WHERE IT IS?
YEAGH !!
DID YOU WASH YOUR HANDS?
YEAH!
FROM HERE TO THE BACK ARE SLAVE CELLS.
NOTHING FOR YOU TO SEE.

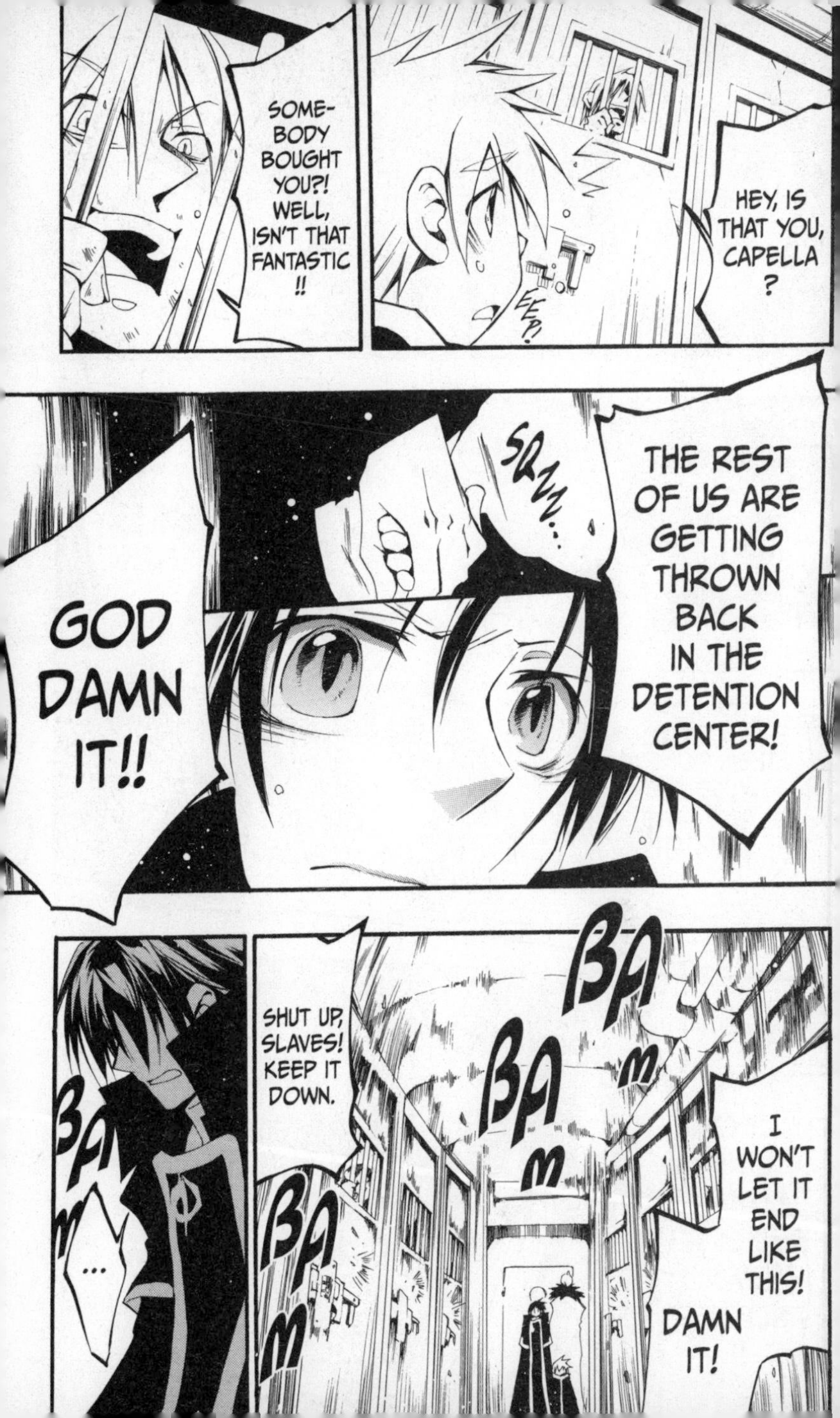
HEY, IS THAT YOU, CAPELLA?
EEP!
SOME-BODY BOUGHT YOU?! WELL, ISN'T THAT FANTASTIC!!
THE REST OF US ARE GETTING THROWN BACK IN THE DETENTION CENTER!
GOD DAMN IT!!
BAM
SHUT UP, SLAVES! KEEP IT DOWN.
BAM
I WON'T LET IT END LIKE THIS!
DAMN IT!
BAM
BAM
...

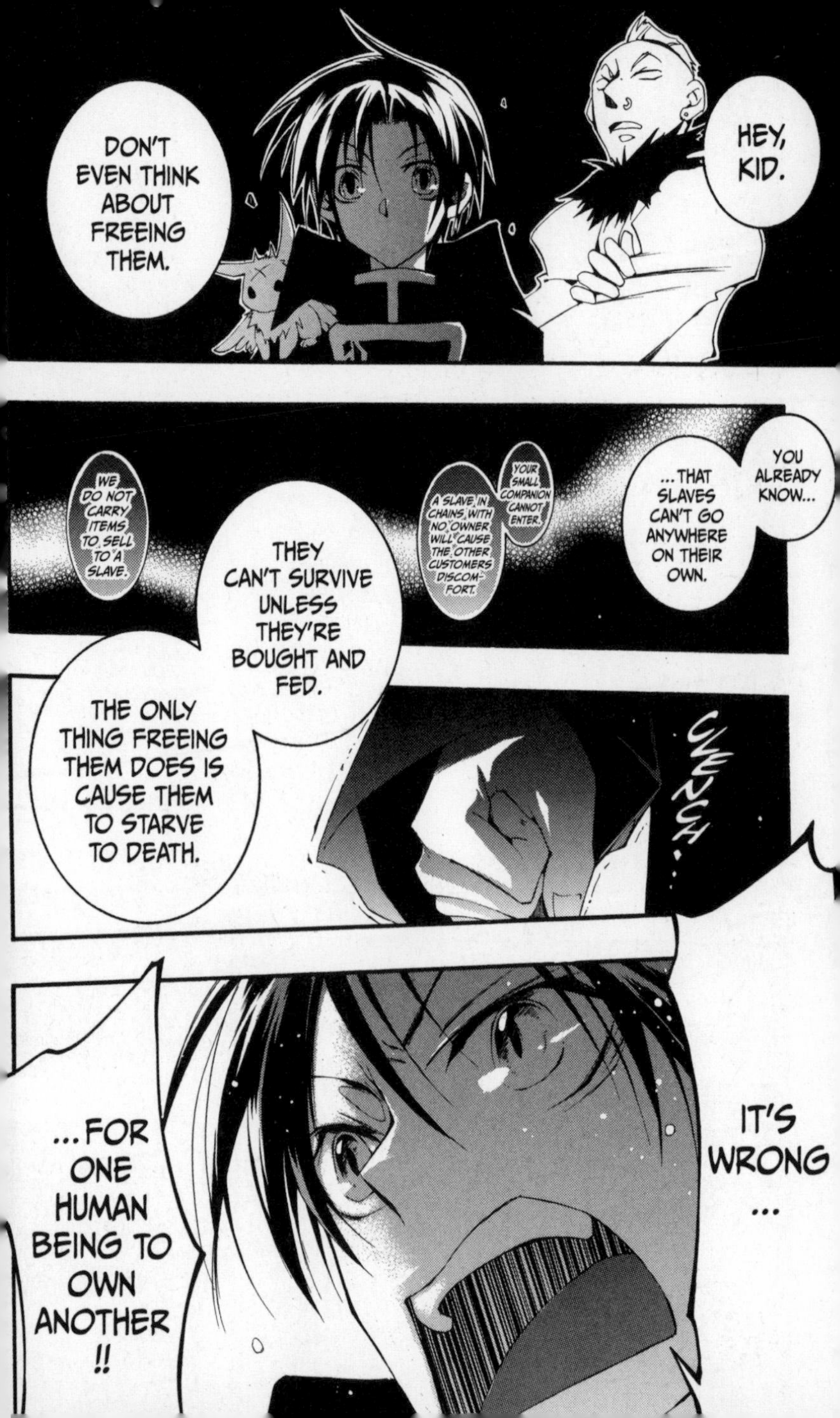
HEY, KID.
DON'T EVEN THINK ABOUT FREEING THEM.
YOU ALREADY KNOW...
...THAT SLAVES CAN'T GO ANYWHERE ON THEIR OWN.
YOUR SMALL COMPANION CANNOT ENTER.
A SLAVE IN CHAINS WITH NO OWNER WILL CAUSE THE OTHER CUSTOMERS DISCOMFORT.
WE DO NOT CARRY ITEMS TO SELL TO A SLAVE.
THEY CAN'T SURVIVE UNLESS THEY'RE BOUGHT AND FED.
THE ONLY THING FREEING THEM DOES IS CAUSE THEM TO STARVE TO DEATH.
CLENCH...
IT'S WRONG...
...FOR ONE HUMAN BEING TO OWN ANOTHER!!

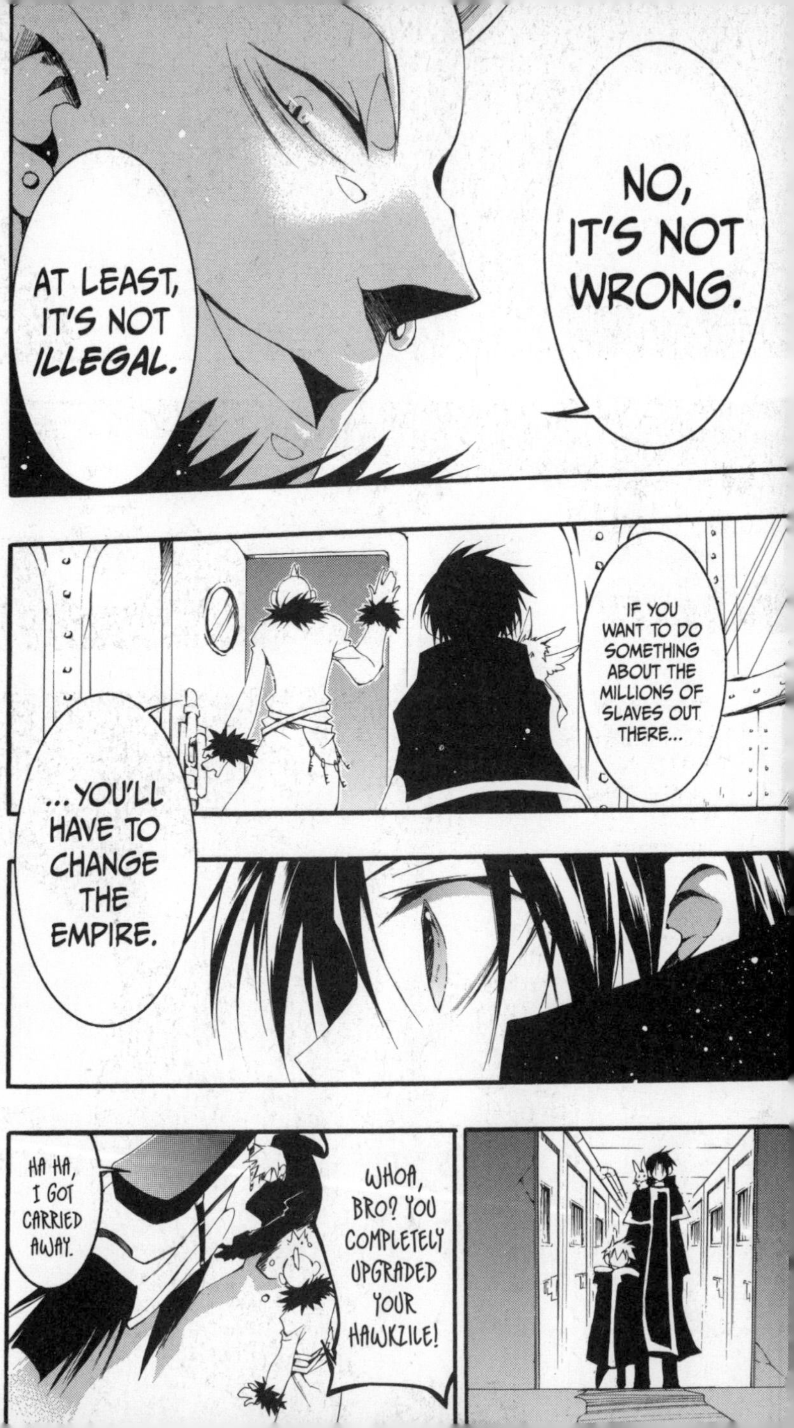
NO, IT'S NOT WRONG.
AT LEAST, IT'S NOT *ILLEGAL.*
IF YOU WANT TO DO SOMETHING ABOUT THE MILLIONS OF SLAVES OUT THERE...
...YOU'LL HAVE TO CHANGE THE EMPIRE.
WHOA, BRO? YOU COMPLETELY UPGRADED YOUR HAWKZILE!
HA HA, I GOT CARRIED AWAY.

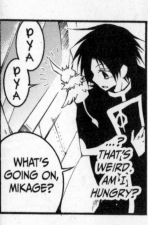

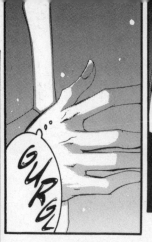

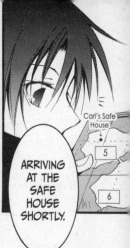

Carl's Safe House
5
6
ARRIVING AT THE SAFE HOUSE SHORTLY.
GURGL
...? THAT'S WEIRD. AM I HUNGRY?
PYA PYA
WHAT'S GOING ON, MIKAGE?
BIG BRO!!
THERE'S SOME-THING IN THE CLOUDS!
!
SWSH..
THERE ARE FOUR VESSELS RIGHT UNDER-NEATH US!
ARE THEY ARMY? MER-CHANT?
THEY'RE COMING!
!!
THEY'RE ...!!

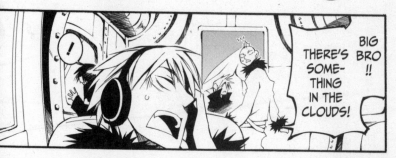

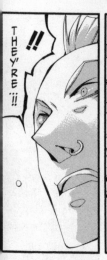

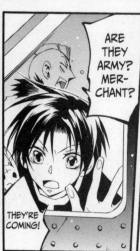

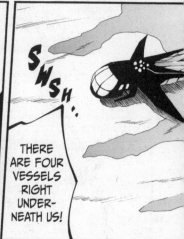

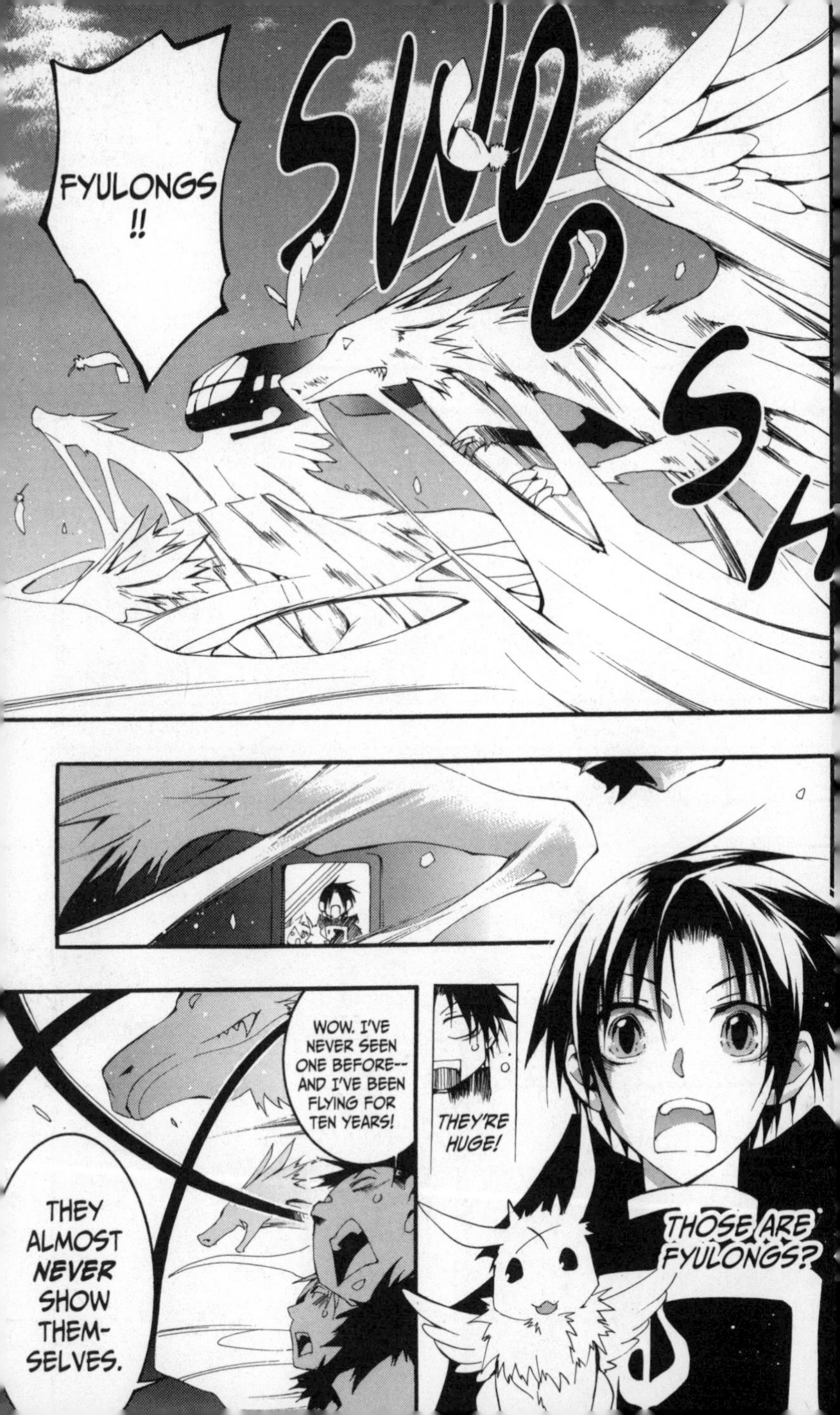
SWOOSH
FYULONGS!!
THOSE ARE FYULONGS?
THEY'RE HUGE!
WOW. I'VE NEVER SEEN ONE BEFORE--AND I'VE BEEN FLYING FOR TEN YEARS!
THEY ALMOST NEVER SHOW THEM-SELVES.

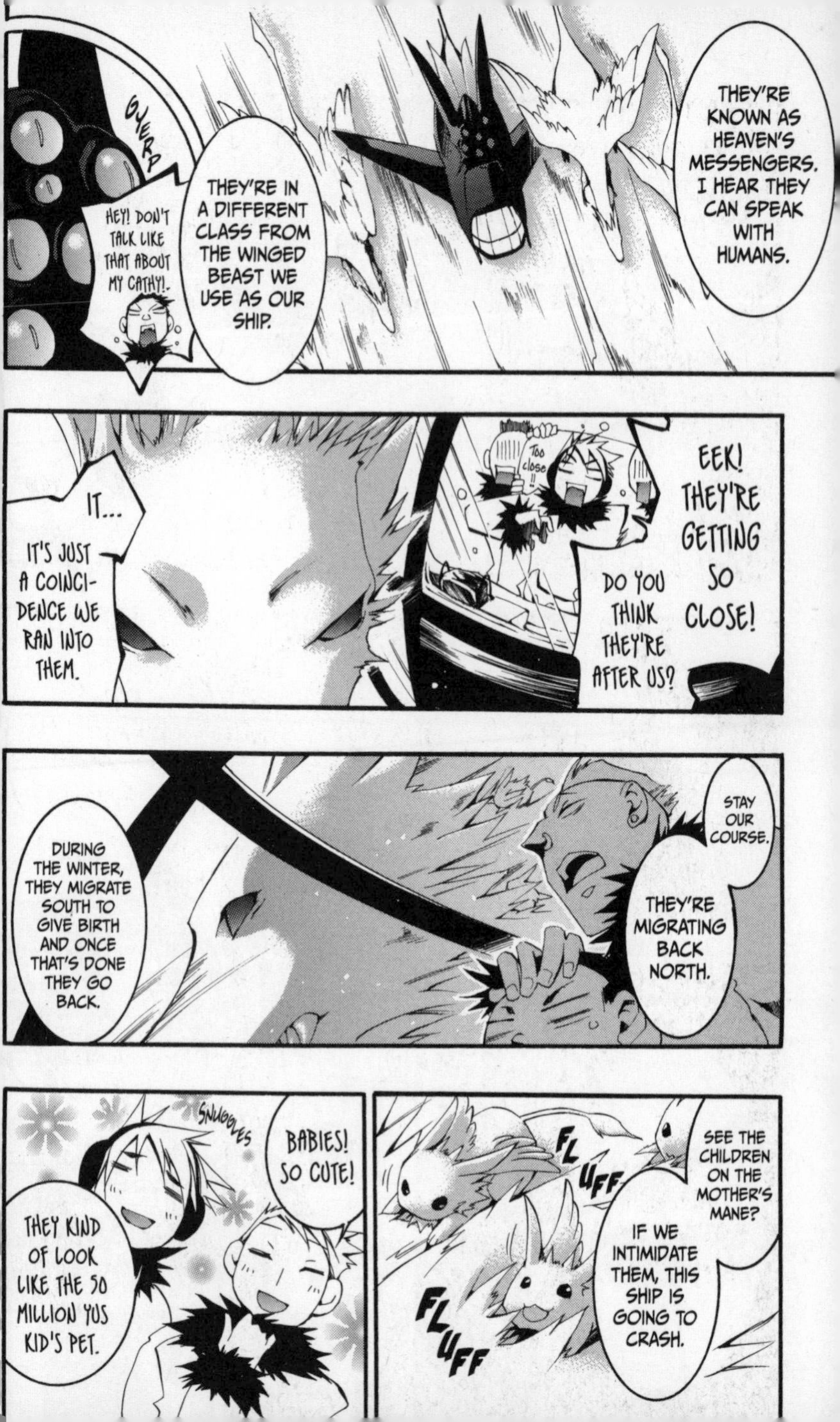
THEY'RE KNOWN AS HEAVEN'S MESSENGERS. I HEAR THEY CAN SPEAK WITH HUMANS.
THEY'RE IN A DIFFERENT CLASS FROM THE WINGED BEAST WE USE AS OUR SHIP.
GYERP
HEY! DON'T TALK LIKE THAT ABOUT MY CATHY!.
EEK! THEY'RE GETTING SO CLOSE!
Too close !!
DO YOU THINK THEY'RE AFTER US?
IT...
IT'S JUST A COINCI-DENCE WE RAN INTO THEM.
STAY OUR COURSE.
THEY'RE MIGRATING BACK NORTH.
DURING THE WINTER, THEY MIGRATE SOUTH TO GIVE BIRTH AND ONCE THAT'S DONE THEY GO BACK.
SEE THE CHILDREN ON THE MOTHER'S MANE?
FLUFF
FLUFF
IF WE INTIMIDATE THEM, THIS SHIP IS GOING TO CRASH.
BABIES! SO CUTE!
SNUGGLES
THEY KIND OF LOOK LIKE THE 50 MILLION YUS KID'S PET.

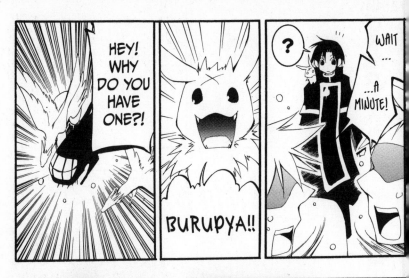

HEY! WHY DO YOU HAVE ONE?!

BURUPYA!!

?

WAIT ...A MINUTE!

Ah.

CRAP!

WHY? MIKAGE IS MY BEST FRIEND.

I STOLE MIKAGE FROM THAT FYULONG.

...? FRAU?

WHAT'S WRONG?

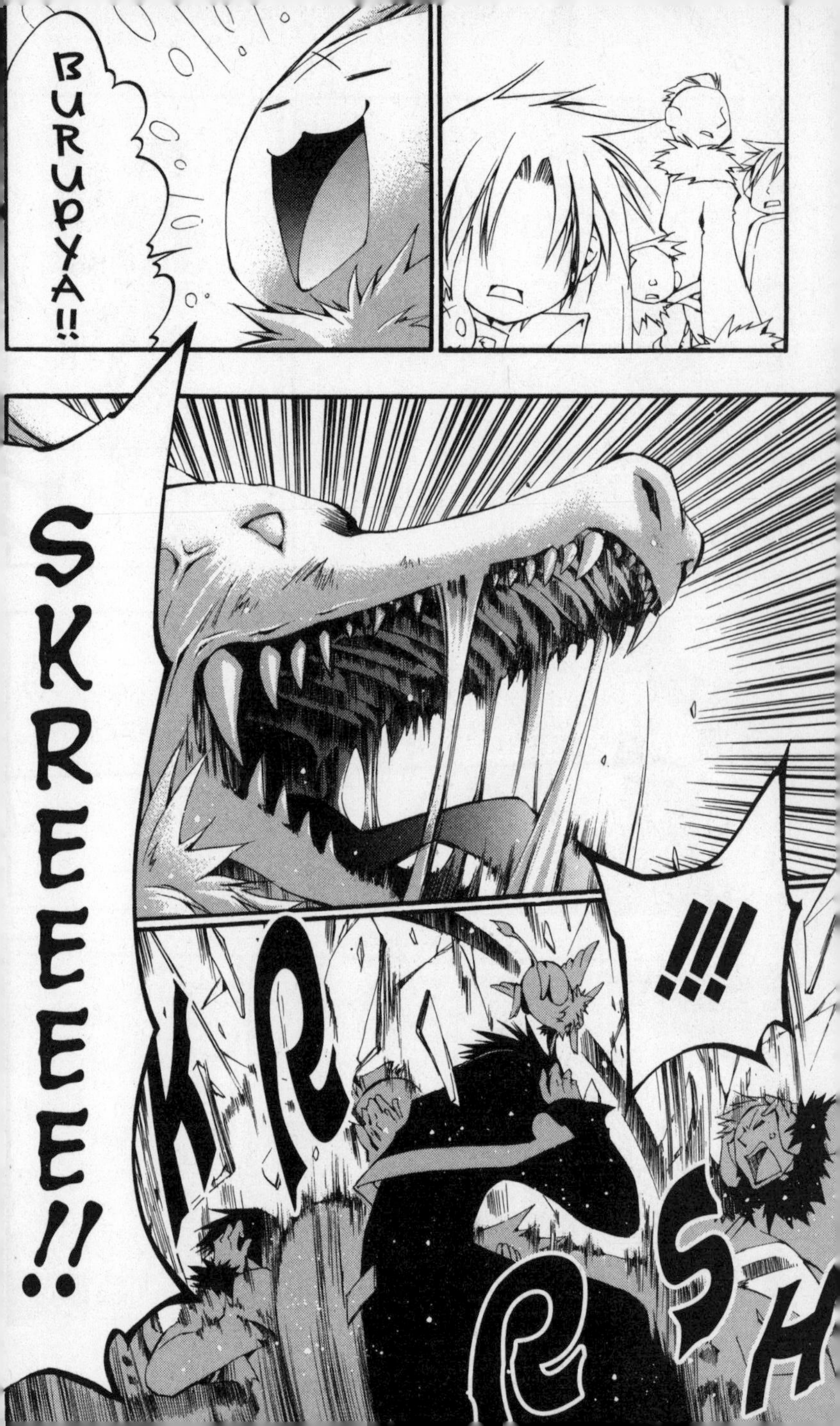
BURUPYA!!
SKREEEE!!
!!!

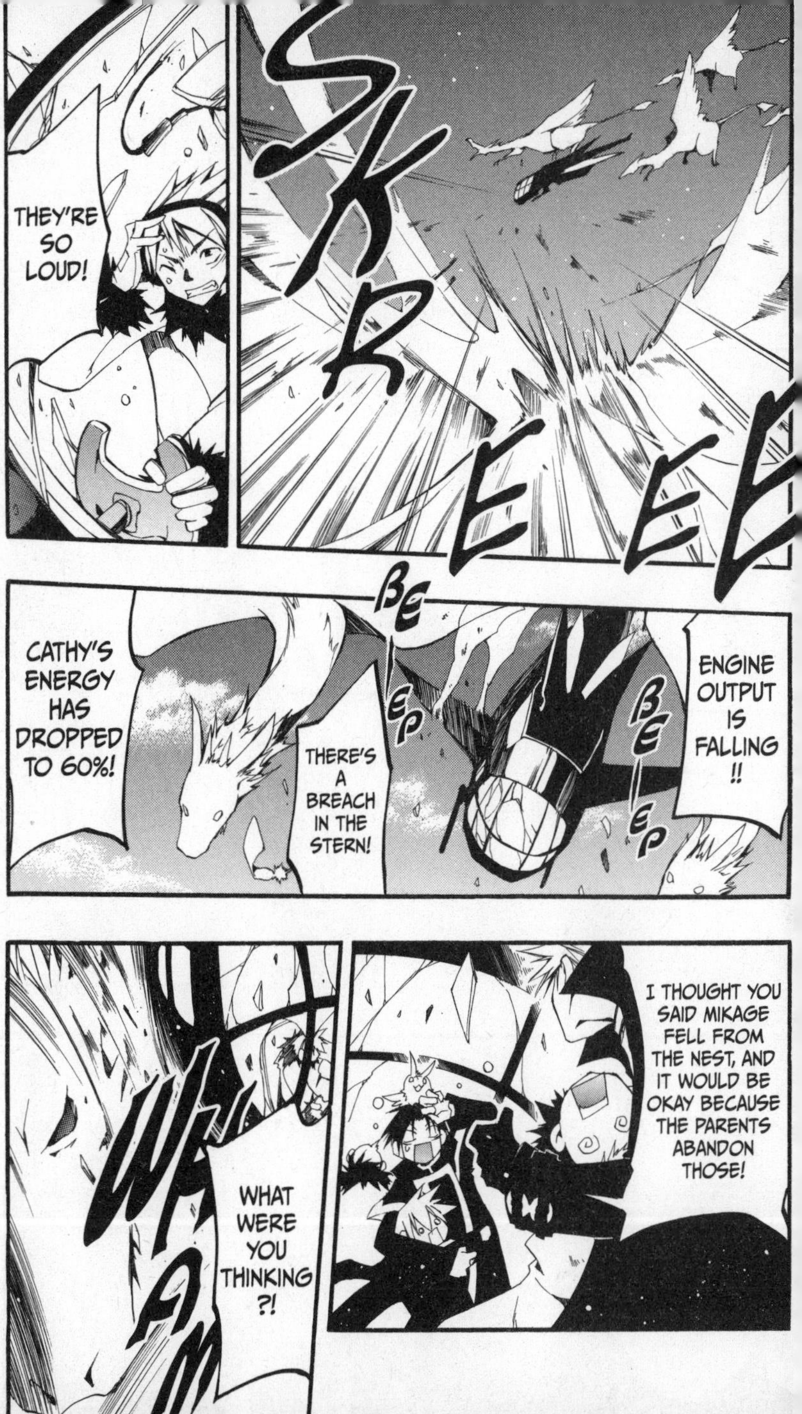
SKREEEE
THEY'RE SO LOUD!
ENGINE OUTPUT IS FALLING!!
BEEP
BEEP
THERE'S A BREACH IN THE STERN!
CATHY'S ENERGY HAS DROPPED TO 60%!
I THOUGHT YOU SAID MIKAGE FELL FROM THE NEST, AND IT WOULD BE OKAY BECAUSE THE PARENTS ABANDON THOSE!
WHAT WERE YOU THINKING?!

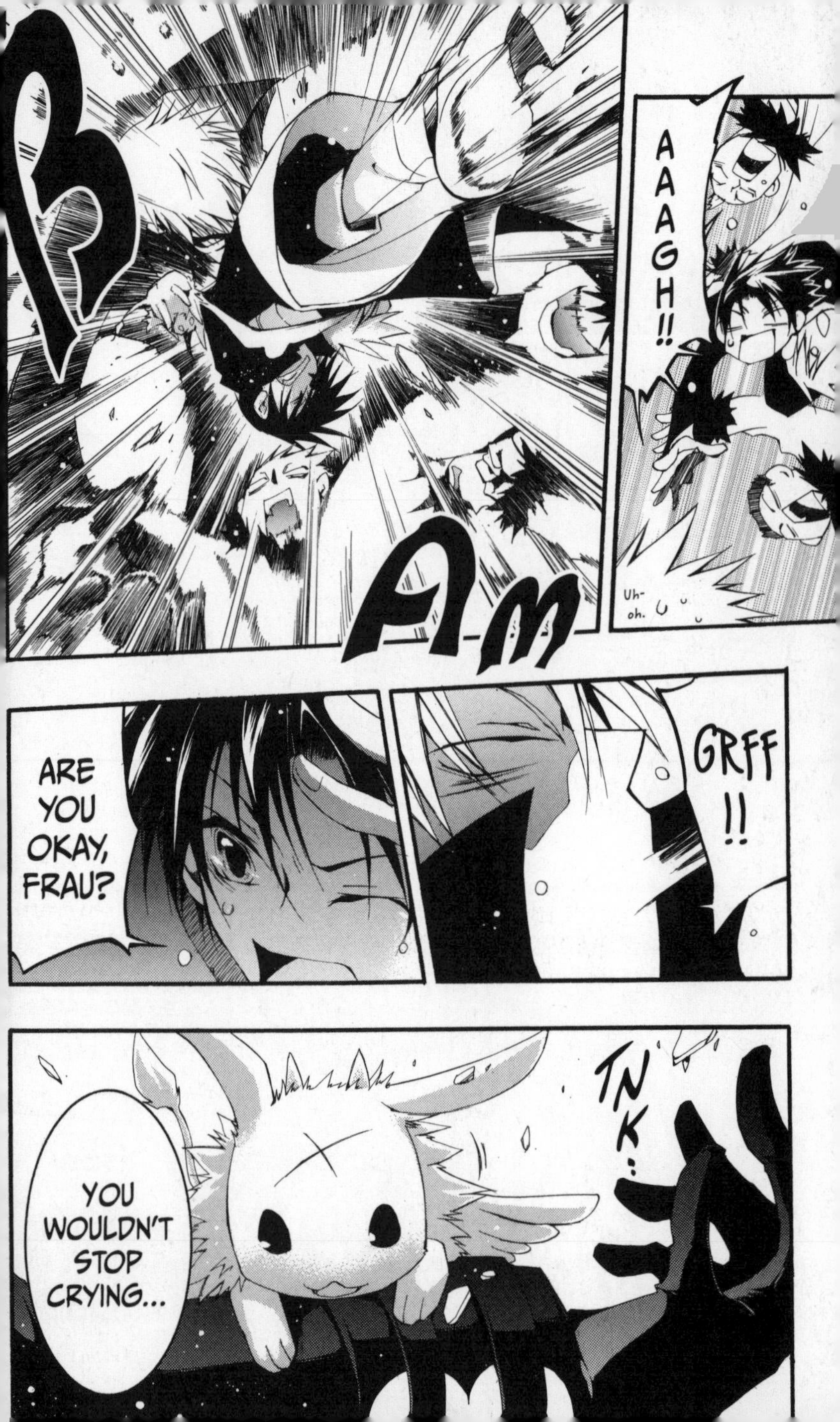
AAAAGH!!
Uh-oh.
BAM
GRFF!!
ARE YOU OKAY, FRAU?
TNK..
YOU WOULDN'T STOP CRYING...

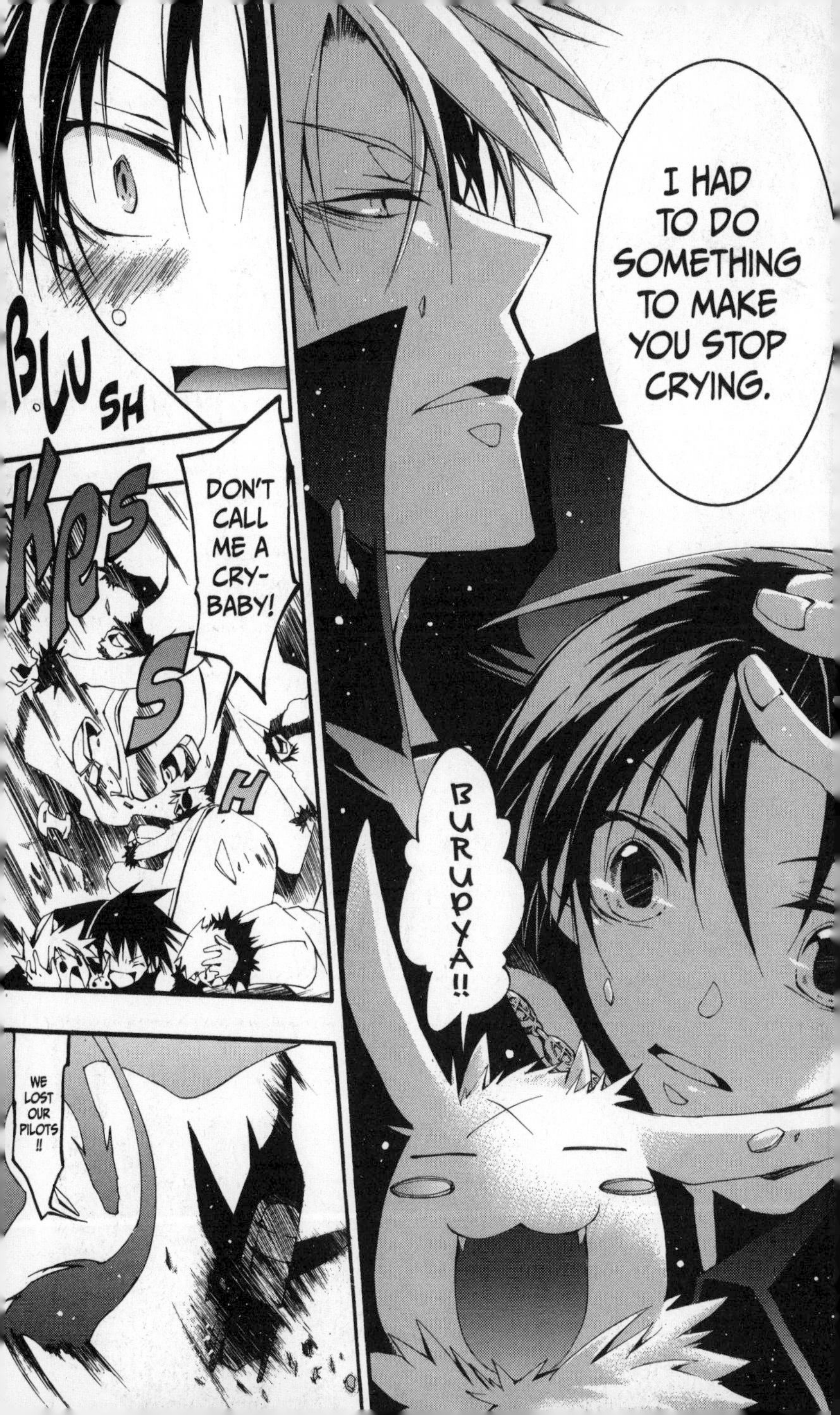
I HAD TO DO SOMETHING TO MAKE YOU STOP CRYING.
BURUPYA!!
BLUSH
DON'T CALL ME A CRY-BABY!
KESSH
WE LOST OUR PILOTS!!

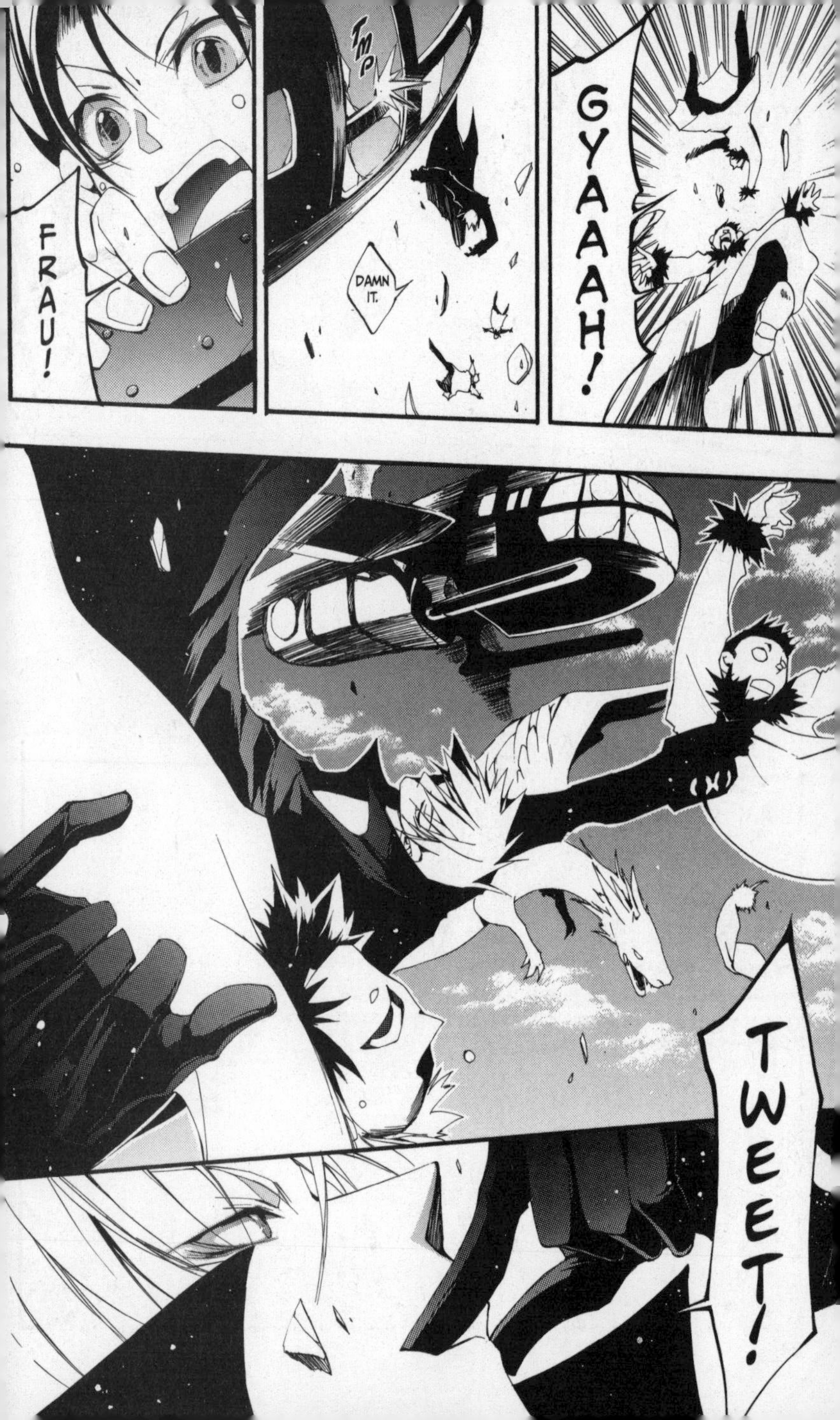
GYAAAH!
TMP
DAMN IT.
FRAU!
TWEET!

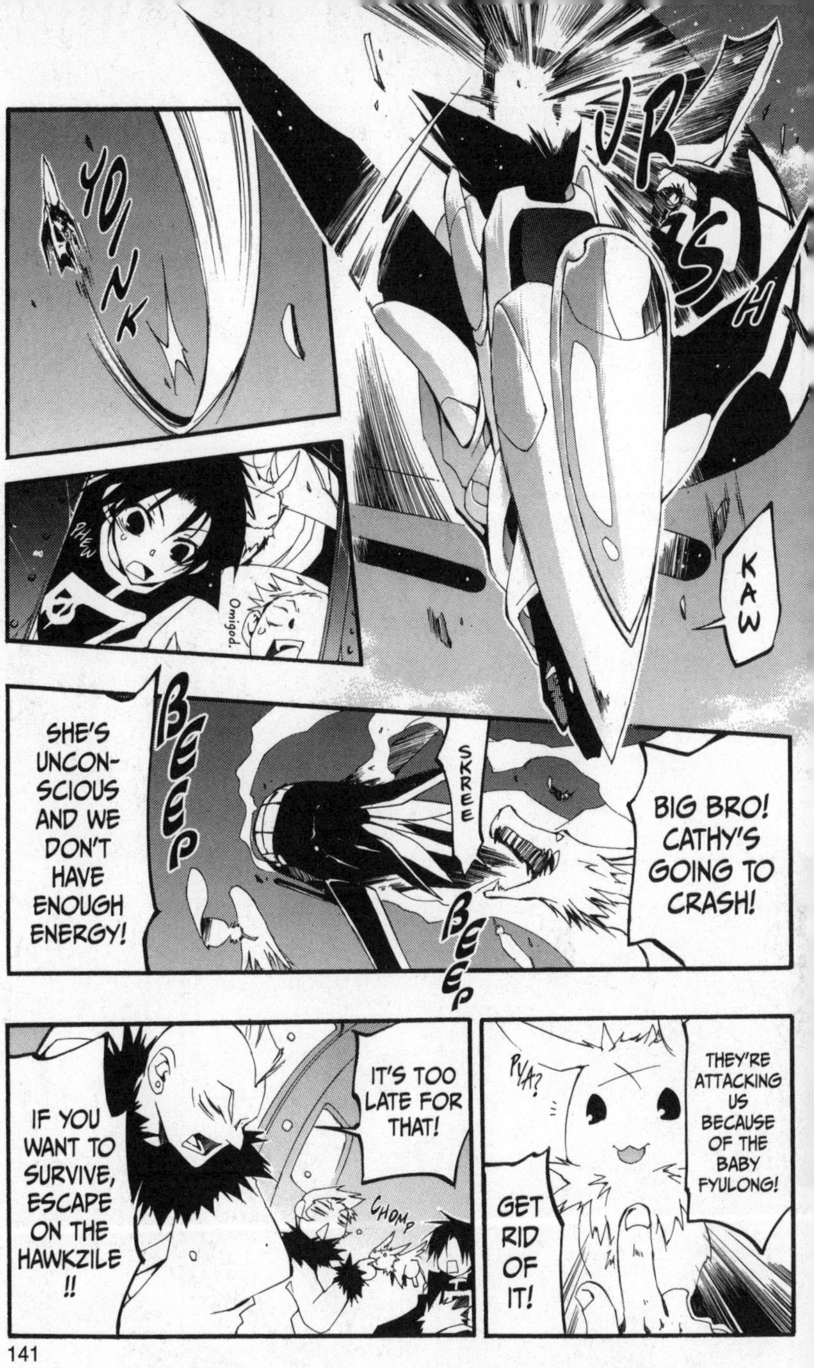
JRSH
KAW
YOINK
PHEW
Omigod.
BIG BRO! CATHY'S GOING TO CRASH!
SKREE
BEEP
BEEP
SHE'S UNCON-SCIOUS AND WE DON'T HAVE ENOUGH ENERGY!
THEY'RE ATTACKING US BECAUSE OF THE BABY FYULONG!
PYA?
GET RID OF IT!
IT'S TOO LATE FOR THAT!
CHOMP
IF YOU WANT TO SURVIVE, ESCAPE ON THE HAWKZILE !!

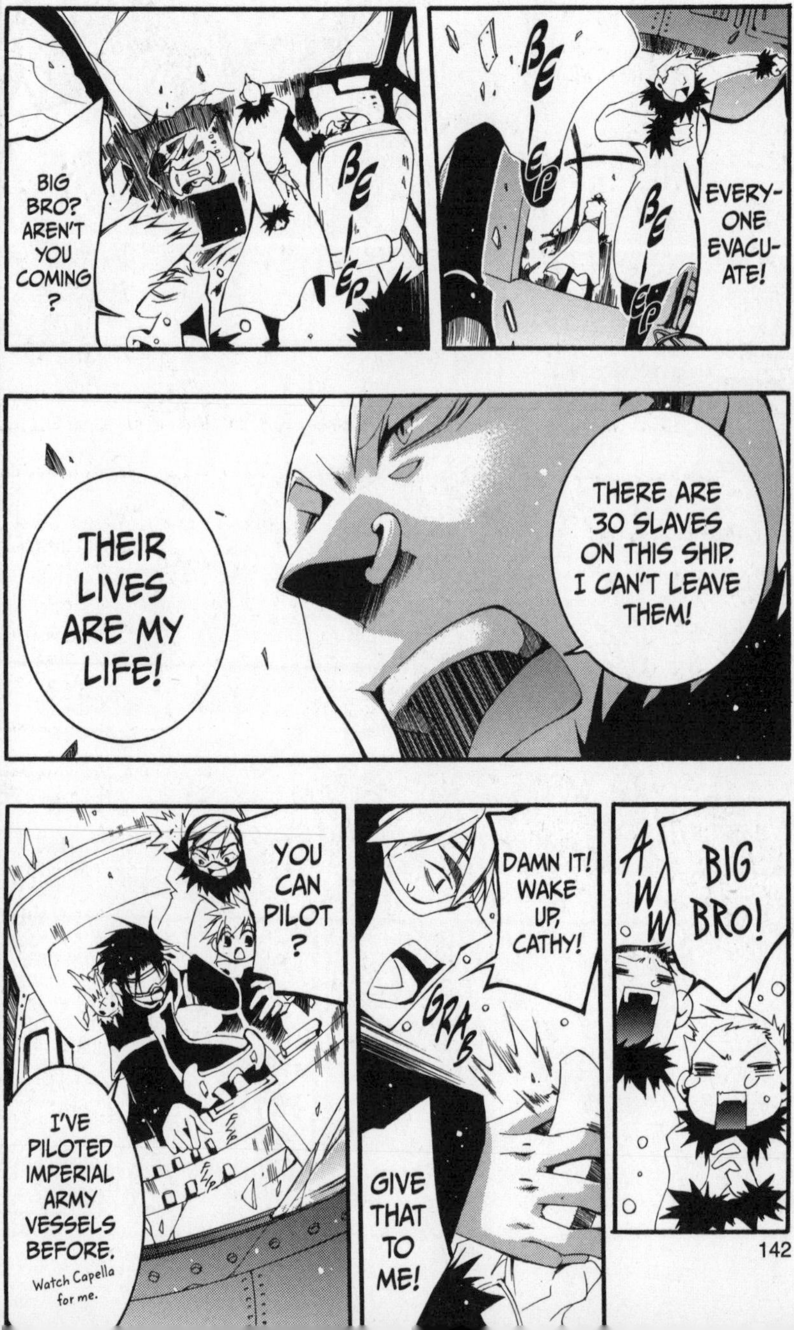
BEEP
BEEP
EVERY-ONE EVACU-ATE!
BEEP
BIG BRO? AREN'T YOU COMING?
THERE ARE 30 SLAVES ON THIS SHIP. I CAN'T LEAVE THEM!
THEIR LIVES ARE MY LIFE!
AWW
BIG BRO!
DAMN IT! WAKE UP, CATHY!
GRAB
GIVE THAT TO ME!
YOU CAN PILOT?
FLIP
FLIP
I'VE PILOTED IMPERIAL ARMY VESSELS BEFORE.
Watch Capella for me.

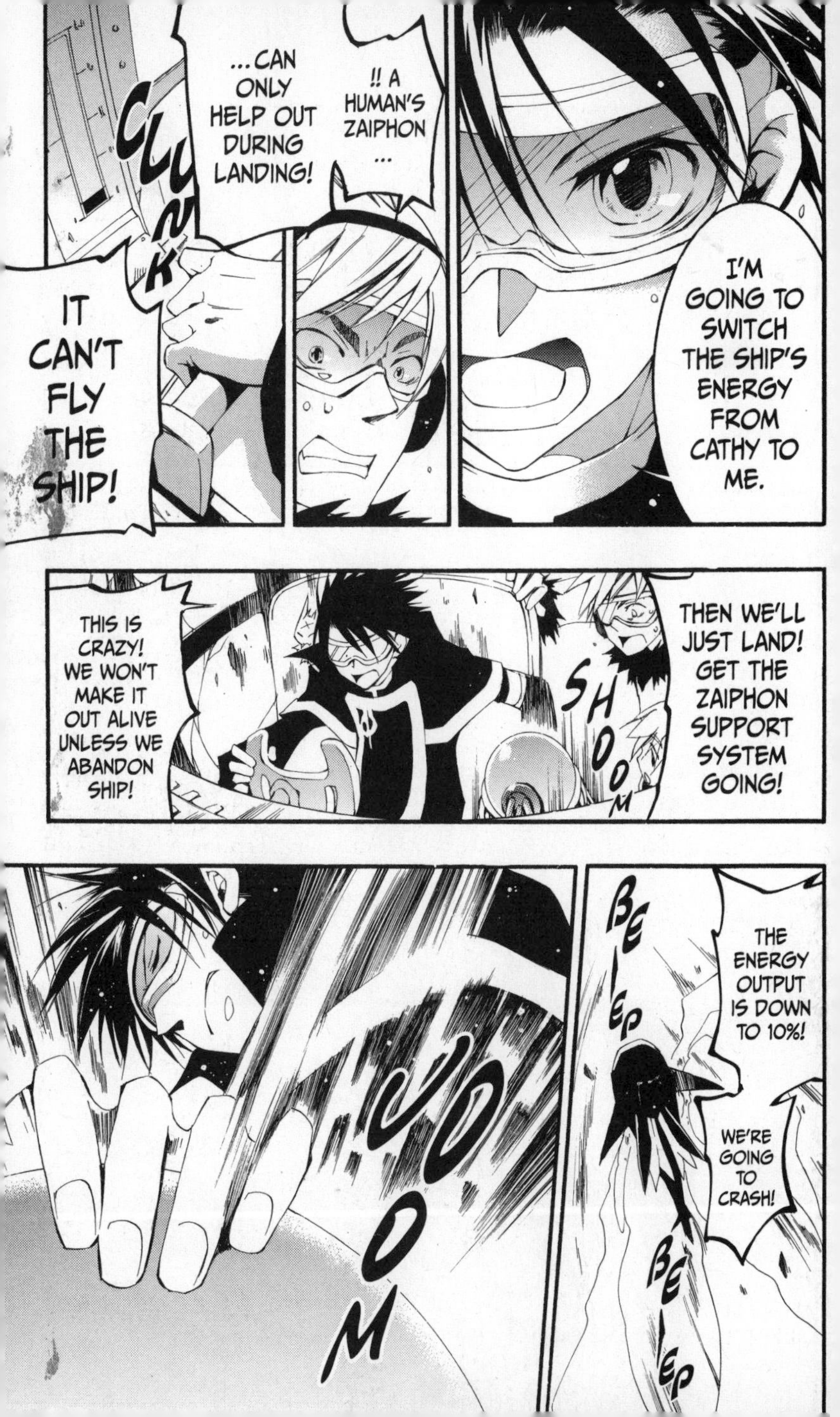
I'M GOING TO SWITCH THE SHIP'S ENERGY FROM CATHY TO ME.
!! A HUMAN'S ZAIPHON ...
...CAN ONLY HELP OUT DURING LANDING!
CLUNK
IT CAN'T FLY THE SHIP!
THEN WE'LL JUST LAND! GET THE ZAIPHON SUPPORT SYSTEM GOING!
SHOOOM
THIS IS CRAZY! WE WON'T MAKE IT OUT ALIVE UNLESS WE ABANDON SHIP!
BEEP
THE ENERGY OUTPUT IS DOWN TO 10%!
WE'RE GOING TO CRASH!
BEEP

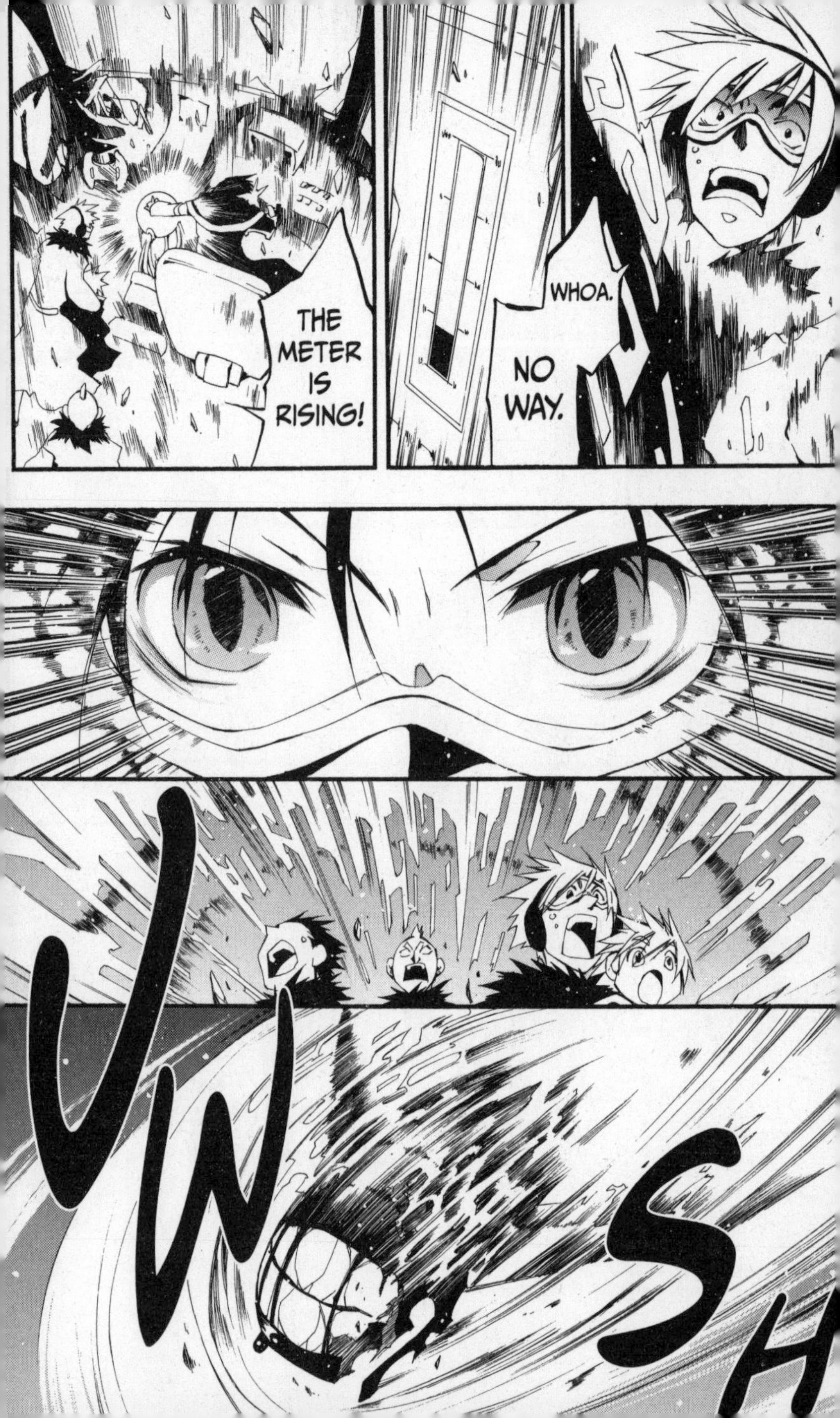
WHOA.
NO WAY.
THE METER IS RISING!
VWSH

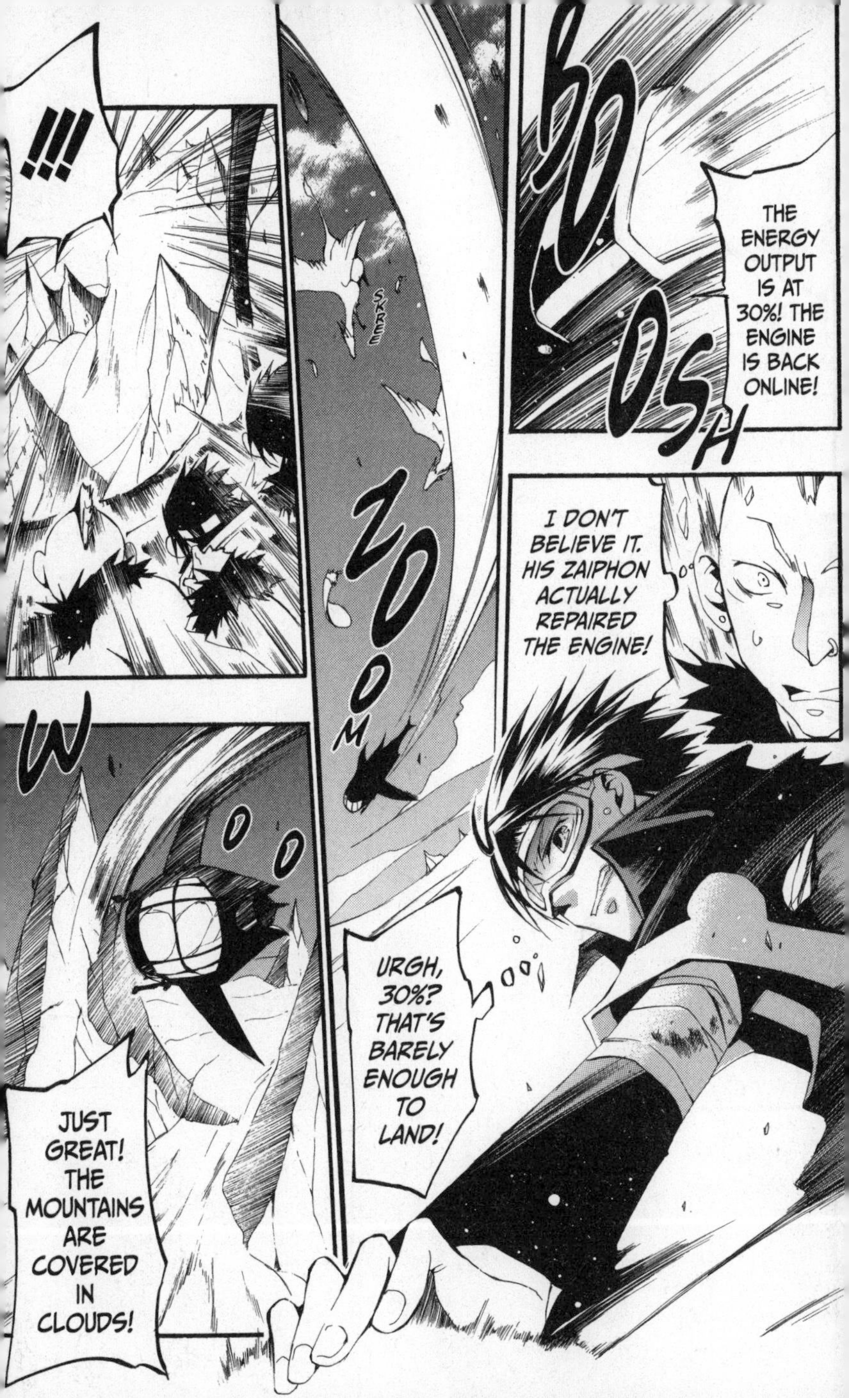
WHOOSH
THE ENERGY OUTPUT IS AT 30%! THE ENGINE IS BACK ONLINE!
I DON'T BELIEVE IT. HIS ZAIPHON ACTUALLY REPAIRED THE ENGINE!
URGH, 30%? THAT'S BARELY ENOUGH TO LAND!
SKREE
ZOOOM
!!!!
WOO
JUST GREAT! THE MOUNTAINS ARE COVERED IN CLOUDS!

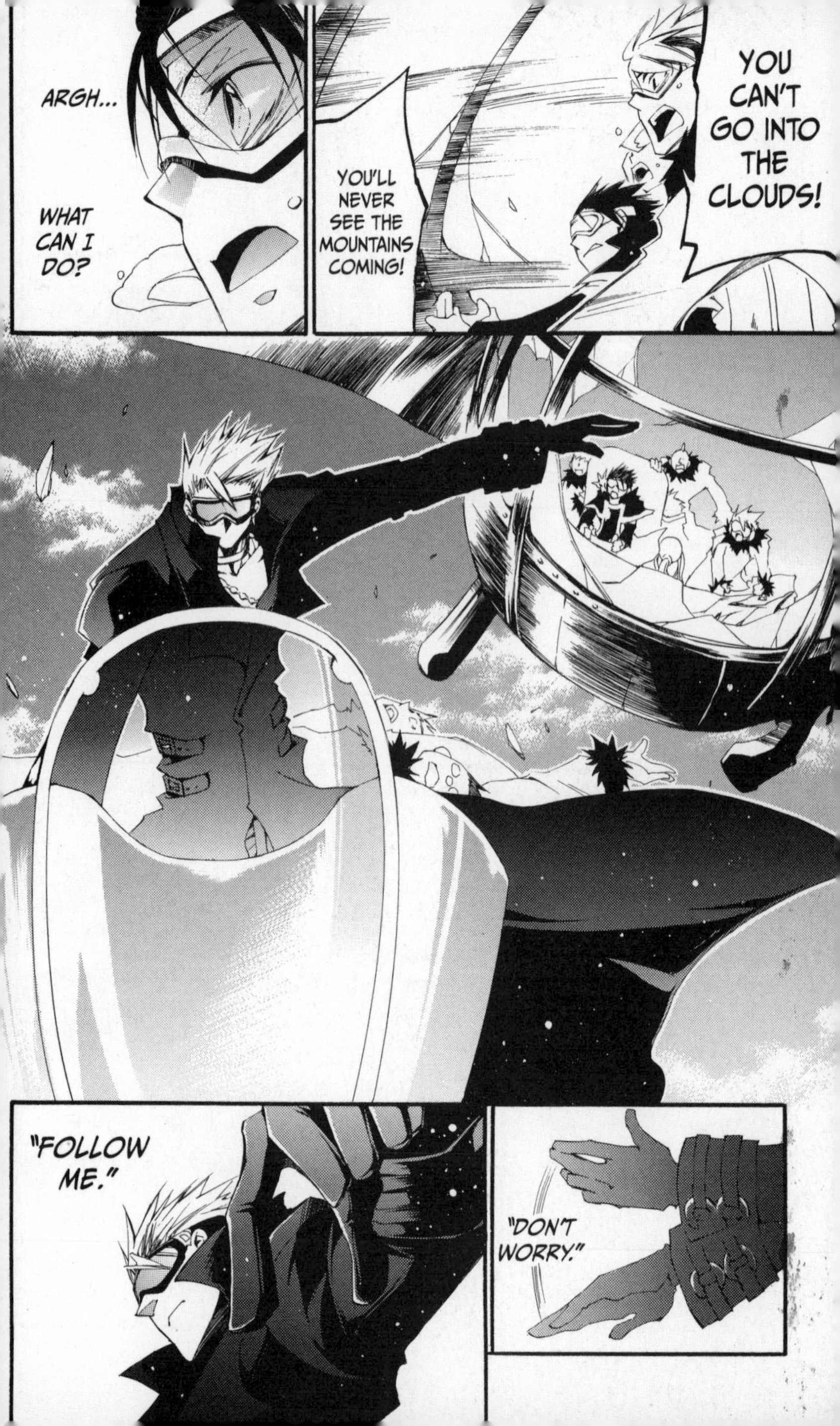
YOU CAN'T GO INTO THE CLOUDS!
YOU'LL NEVER SEE THE MOUNTAINS COMING!
ARGH...
WHAT CAN I DO?
"DON'T WORRY."
"FOLLOW ME."

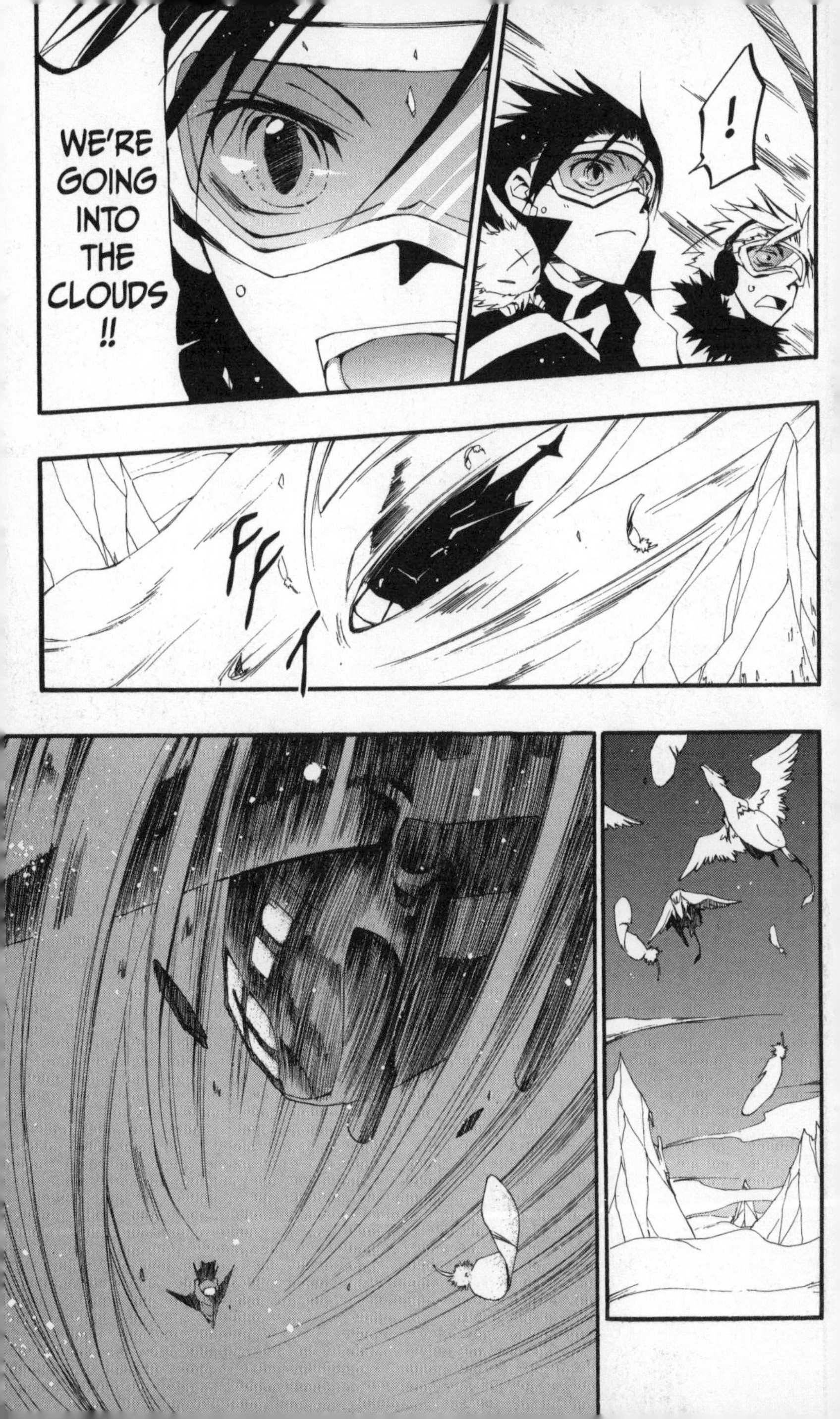
!
WE'RE GOING INTO THE CLOUDS !!
FFT

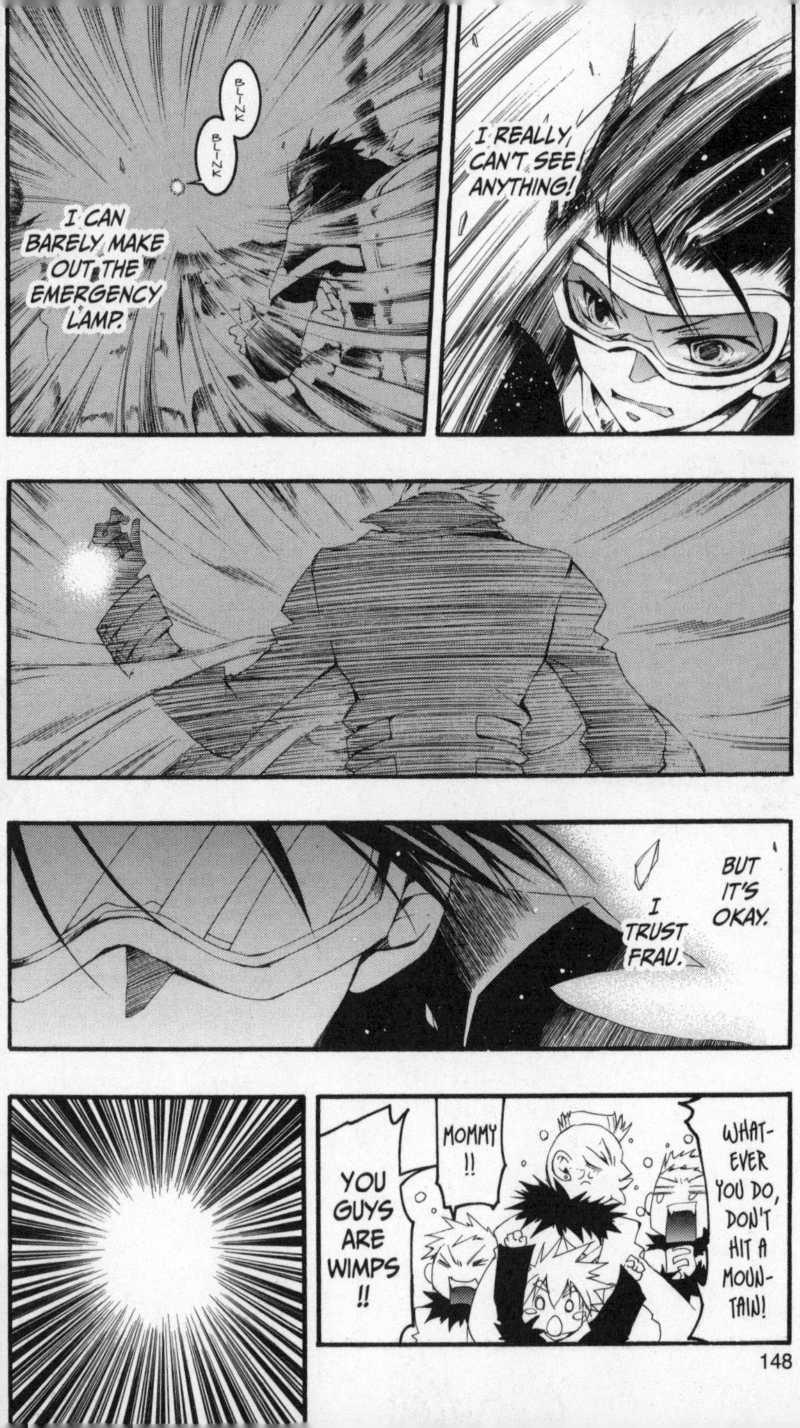
I REALLY CAN'T SEE ANYTHING!
BLINK BLINK
I CAN BARELY MAKE OUT THE EMERGENCY LAMP.
BUT IT'S OKAY.
I TRUST FRAU.
WHAT-EVER YOU DO, DON'T HIT A MOUN-TAIN!
MOMMY !!
YOU GUYS ARE WIMPS !!

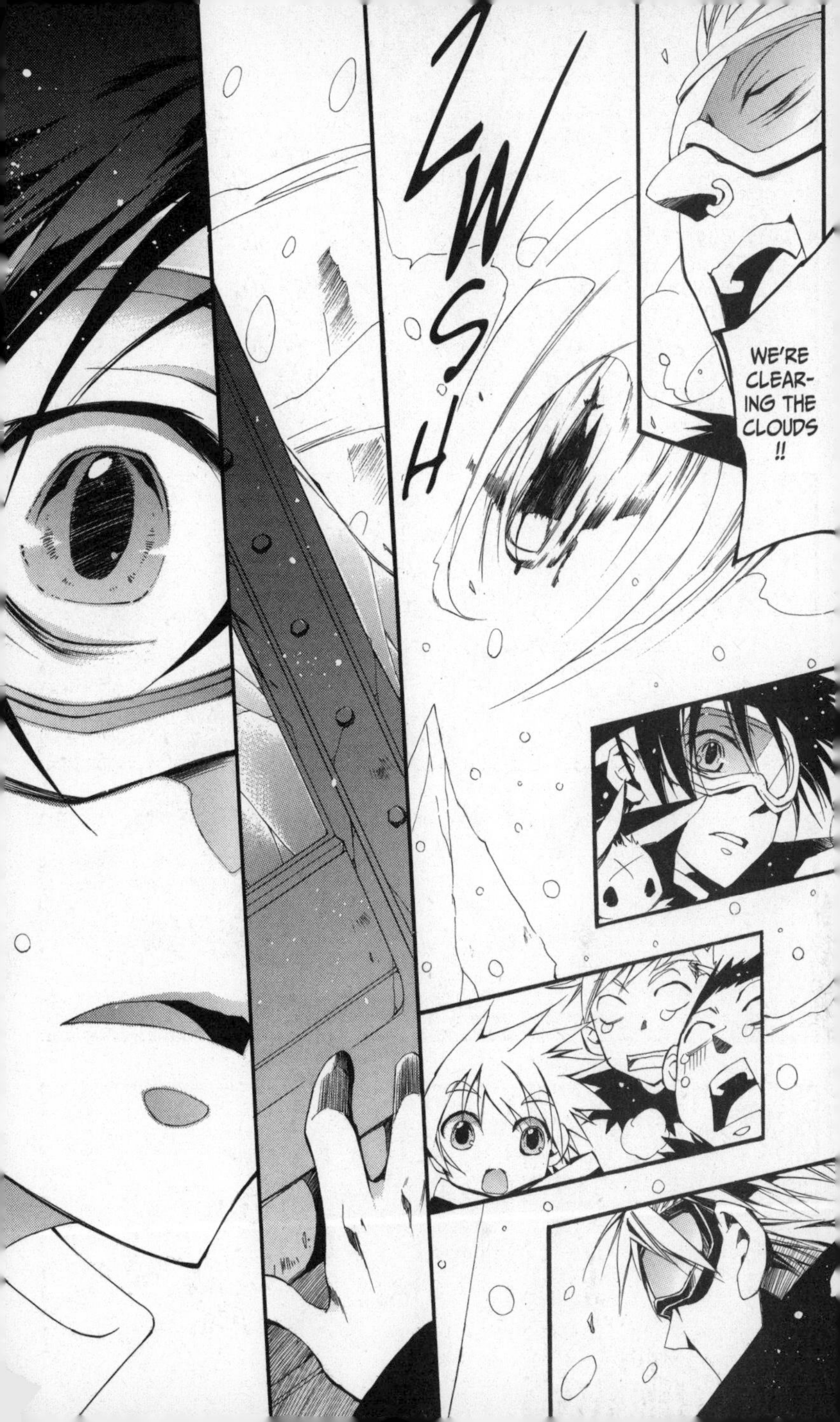
FWSSH
WE'RE CLEARING THE CLOUDS !!

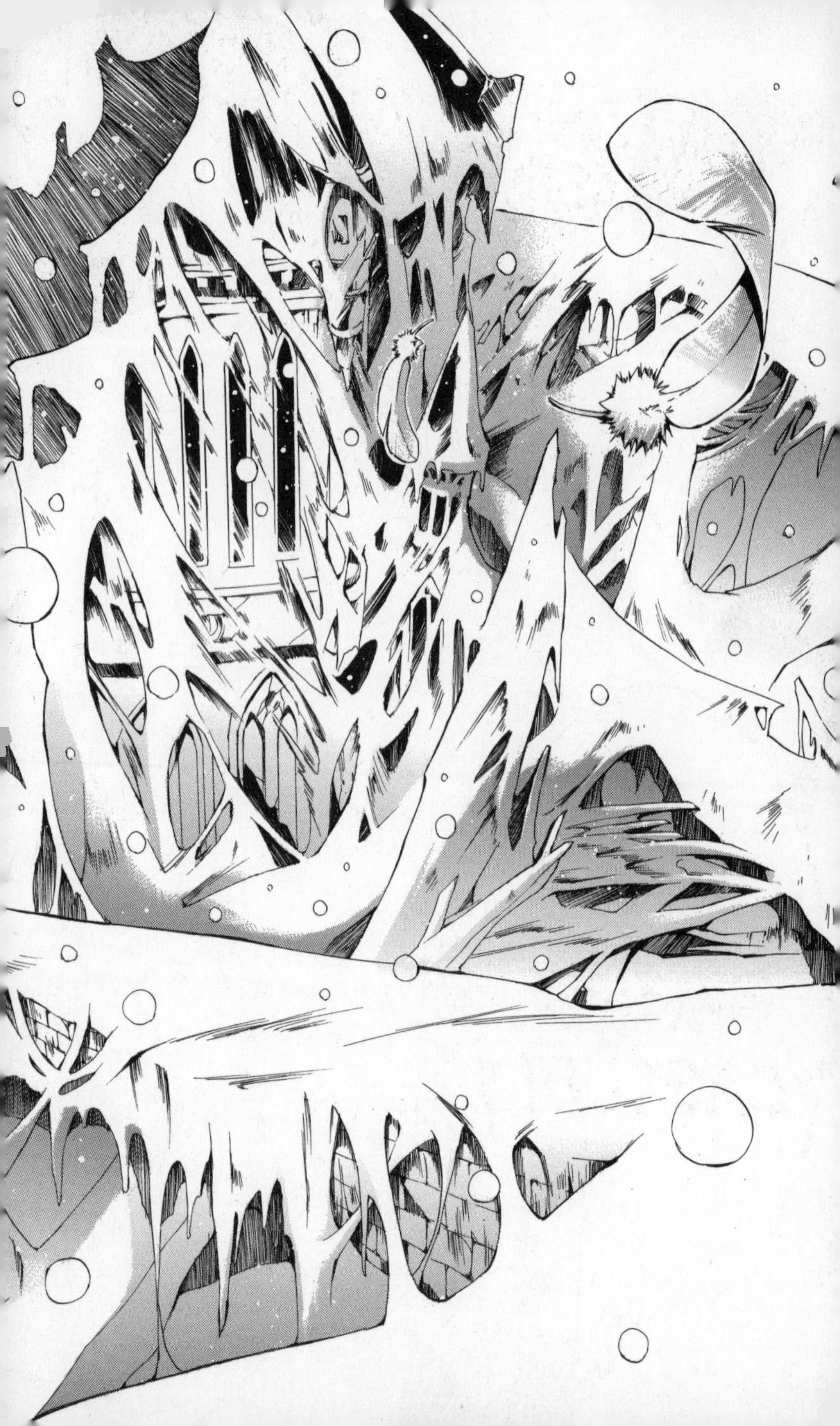

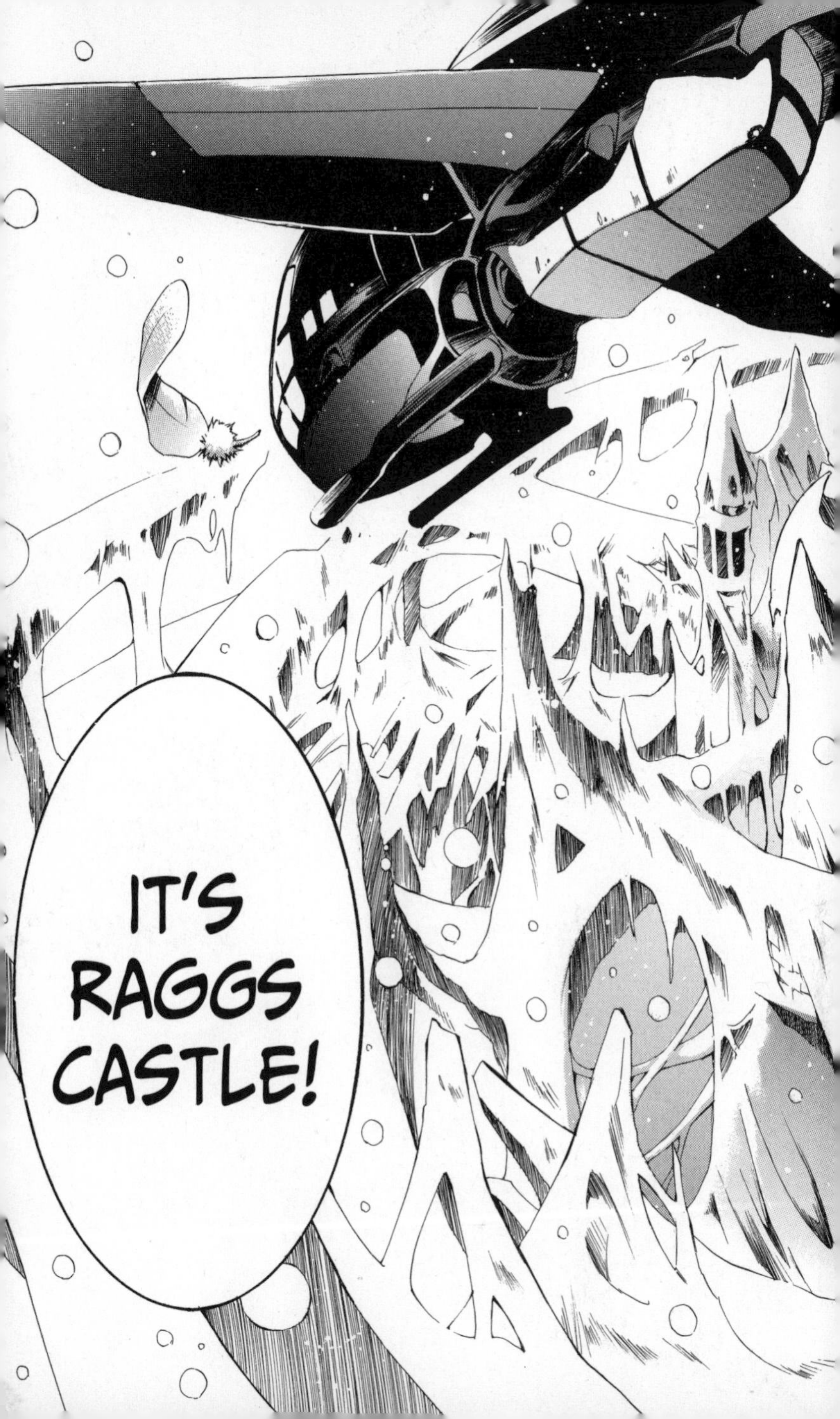
IT'S RAGGS CASTLE!

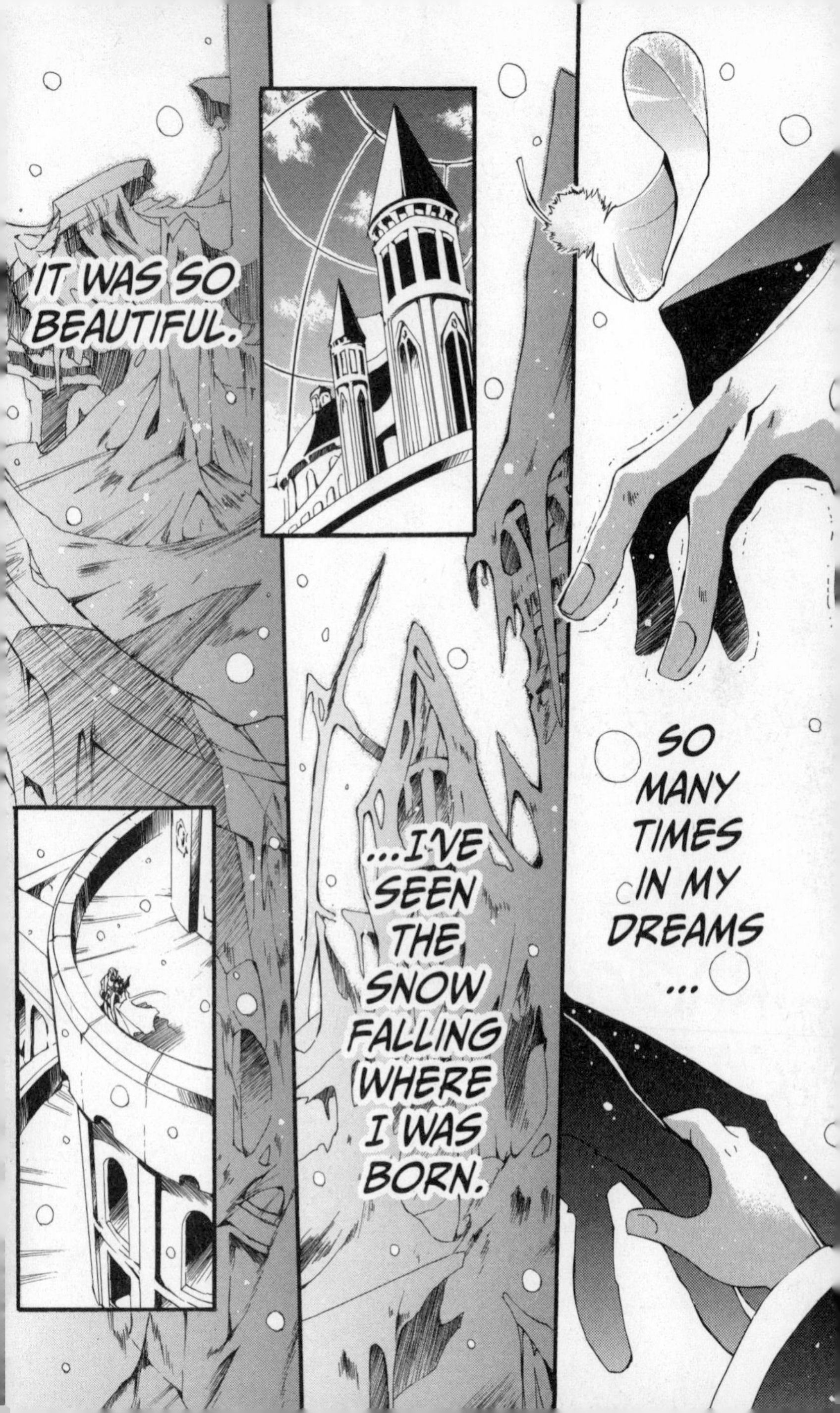
SO MANY TIMES IN MY DREAMS ...
...I'VE SEEN THE SNOW FALLING WHERE I WAS BORN.
IT WAS SO BEAUTIFUL.

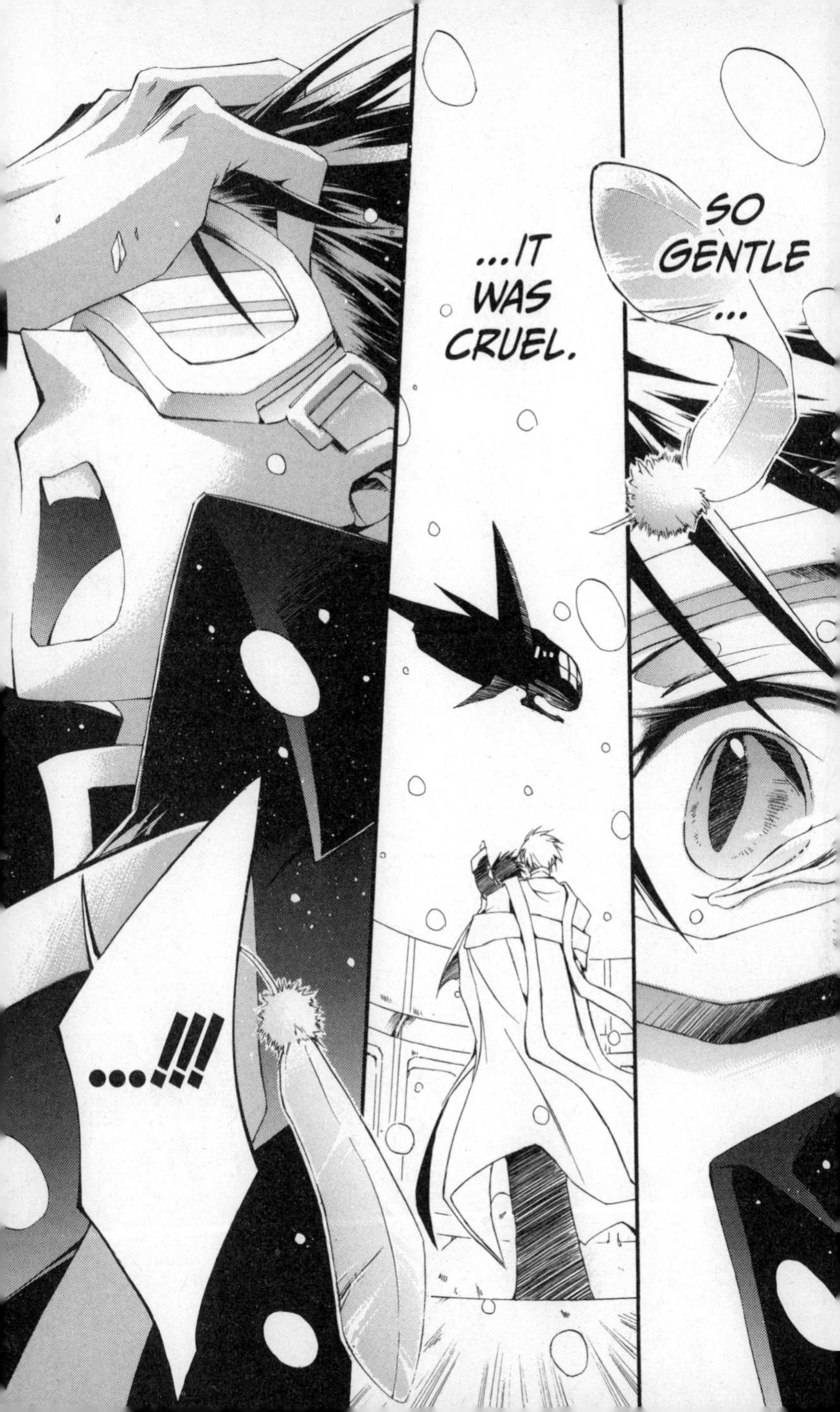
SO GENTLE ...
...IT WAS CRUEL.
...!!!

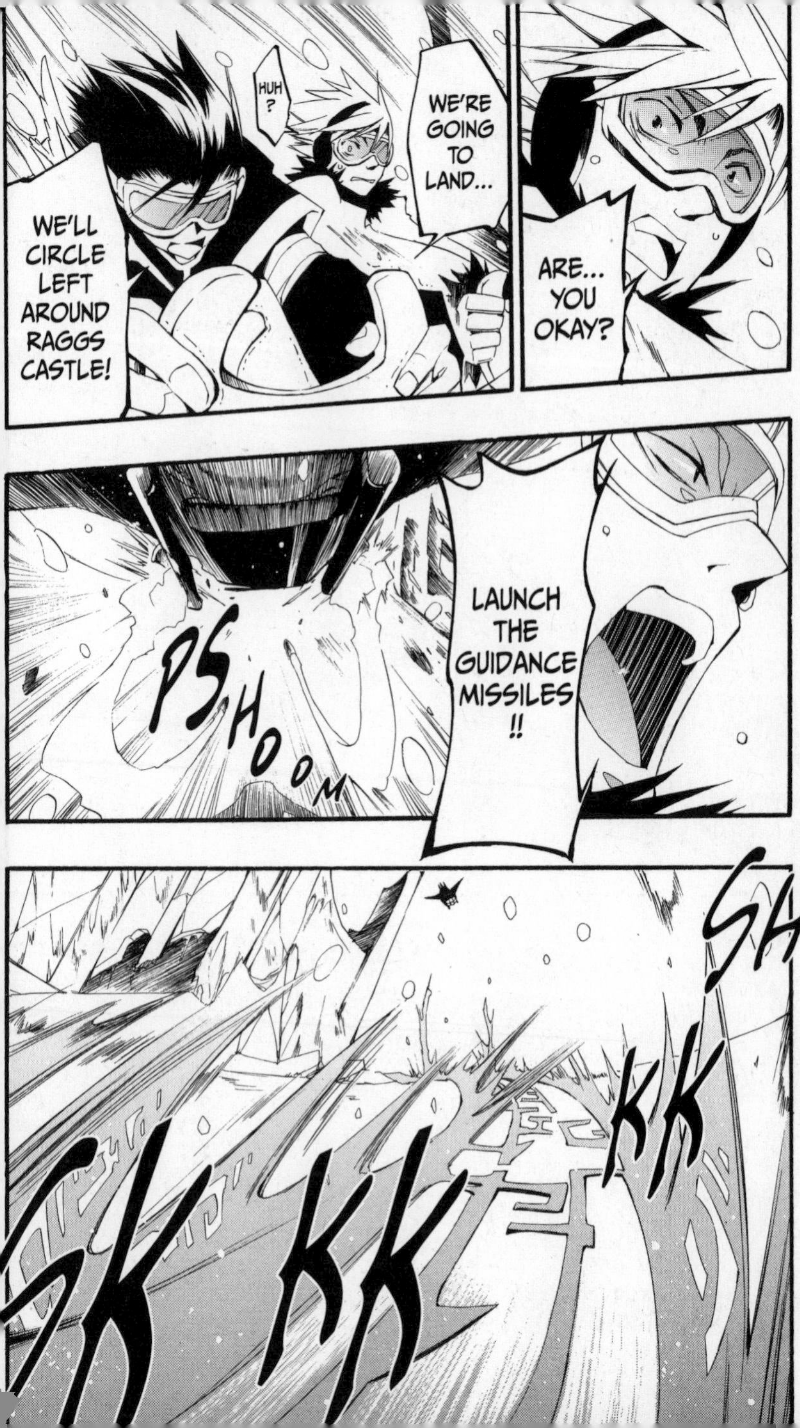
ARE... YOU OKAY?
WE'RE GOING TO LAND...
HUH ?
WE'LL CIRCLE LEFT AROUND RAGGS CASTLE!
LAUNCH THE GUIDANCE MISSILES !!
PSHOOOM
SH
KK
SK KK

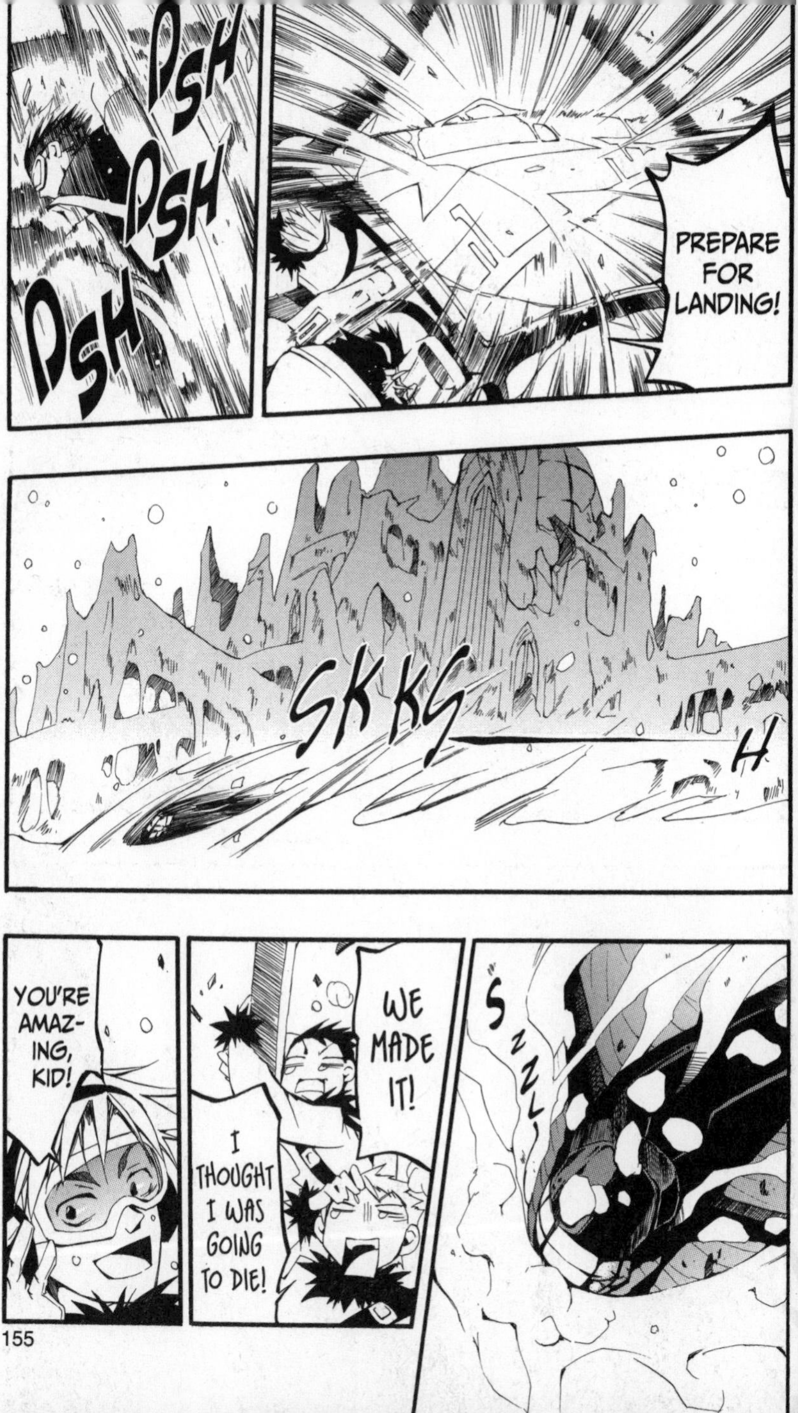
PREPARE FOR LANDING!
PSH
PSH
PSH
SKKS
H
SZZL
WE MADE IT!
I THOUGHT I WAS GOING TO DIE!
YOU'RE AMAZ-ING, KID!

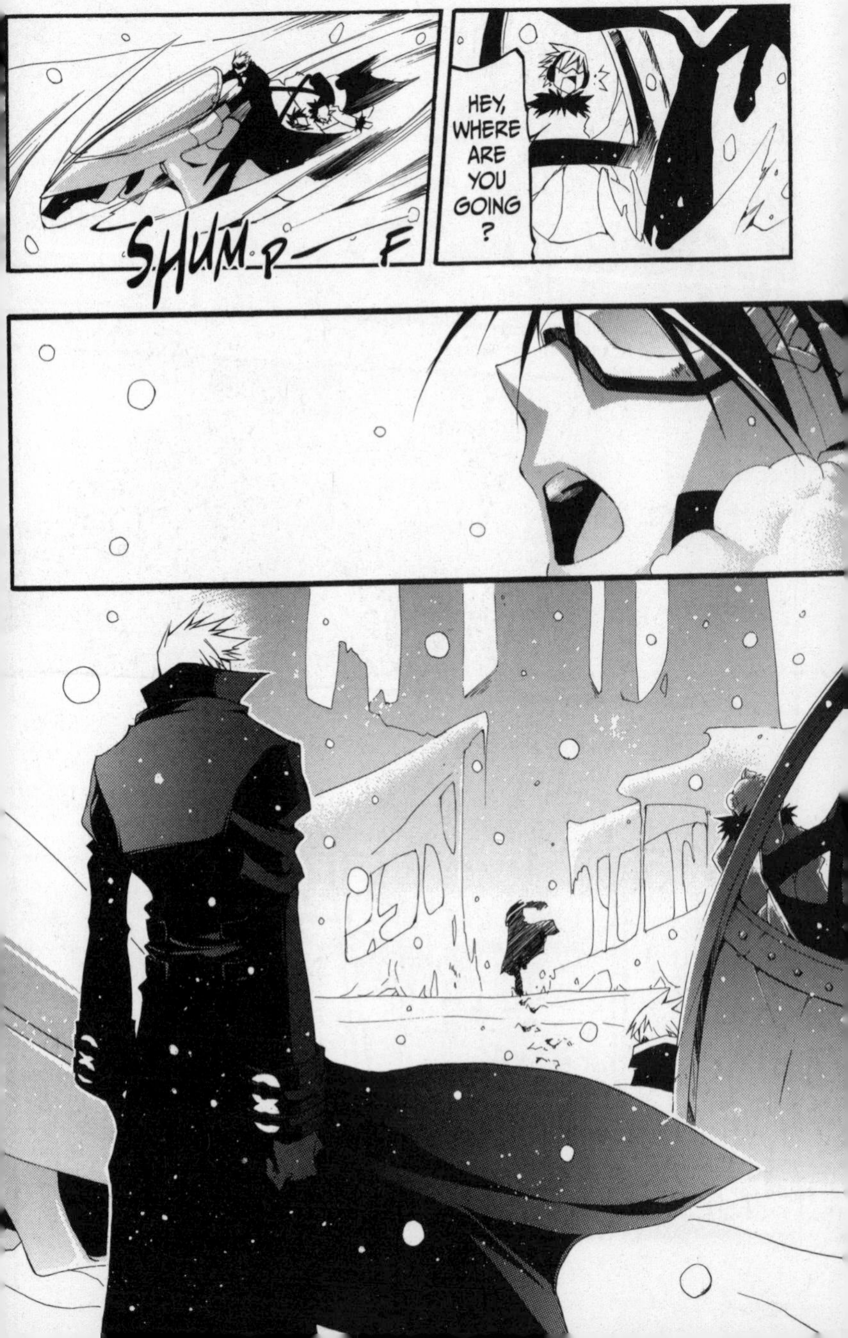
HEY, WHERE ARE YOU GOING ?
SHUMP F

Kapitel. 41 "Omen"

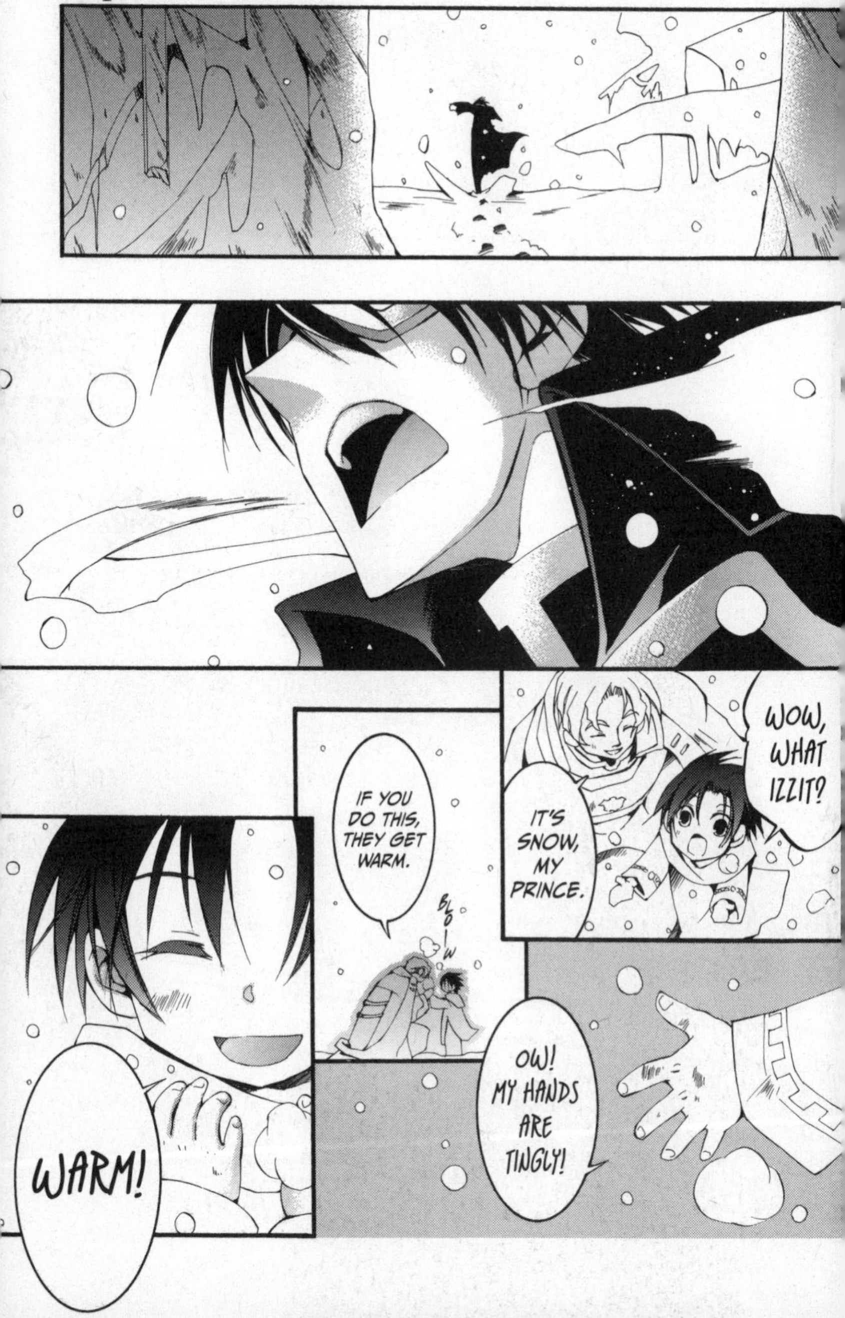
WOW, WHAT IZZIT?
IT'S SNOW, MY PRINCE.
OW! MY HANDS ARE TINGLY!
IF YOU DO THIS, THEY GET WARM.
BLOW
WARM!

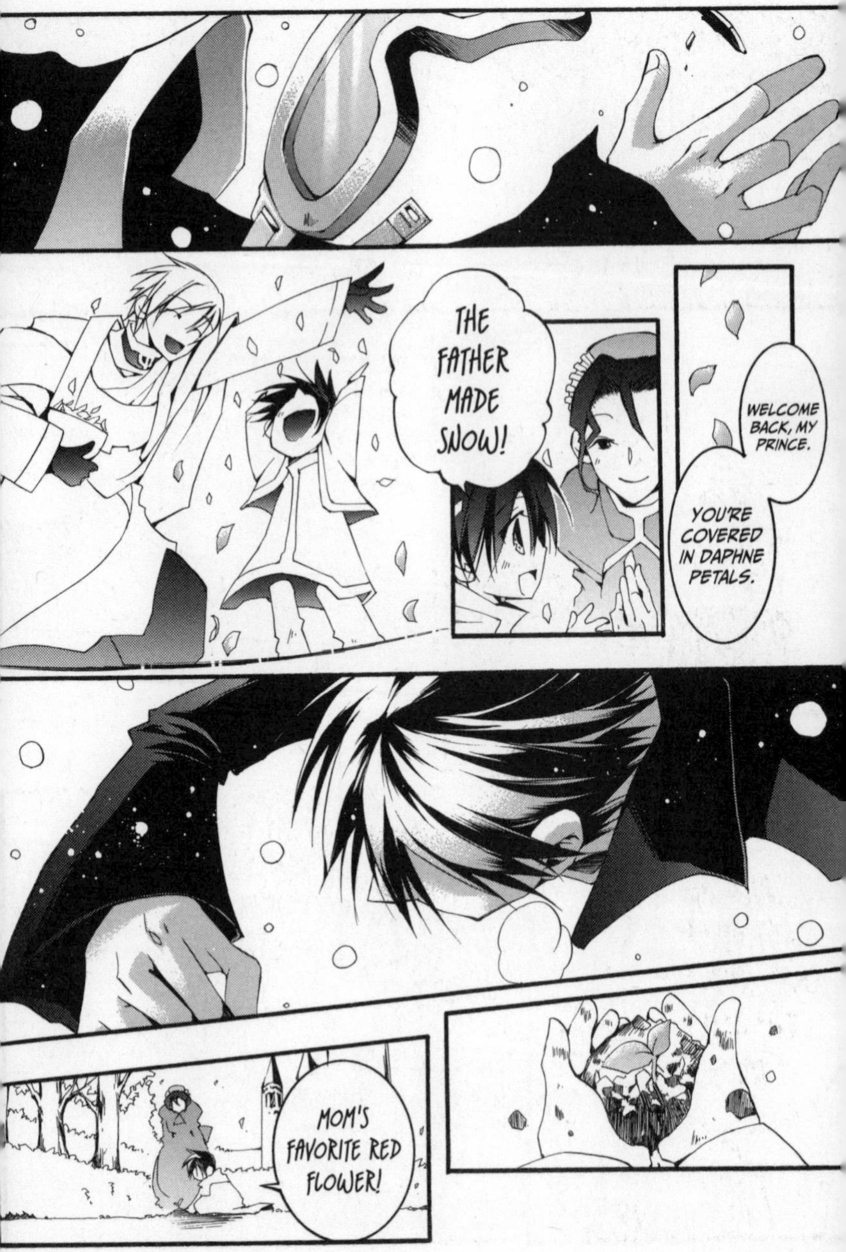
WELCOME BACK, MY PRINCE.
YOU'RE COVERED IN DAPHNE PETALS.
THE FATHER MADE SNOW!
MOM'S FAVORITE RED FLOWER!

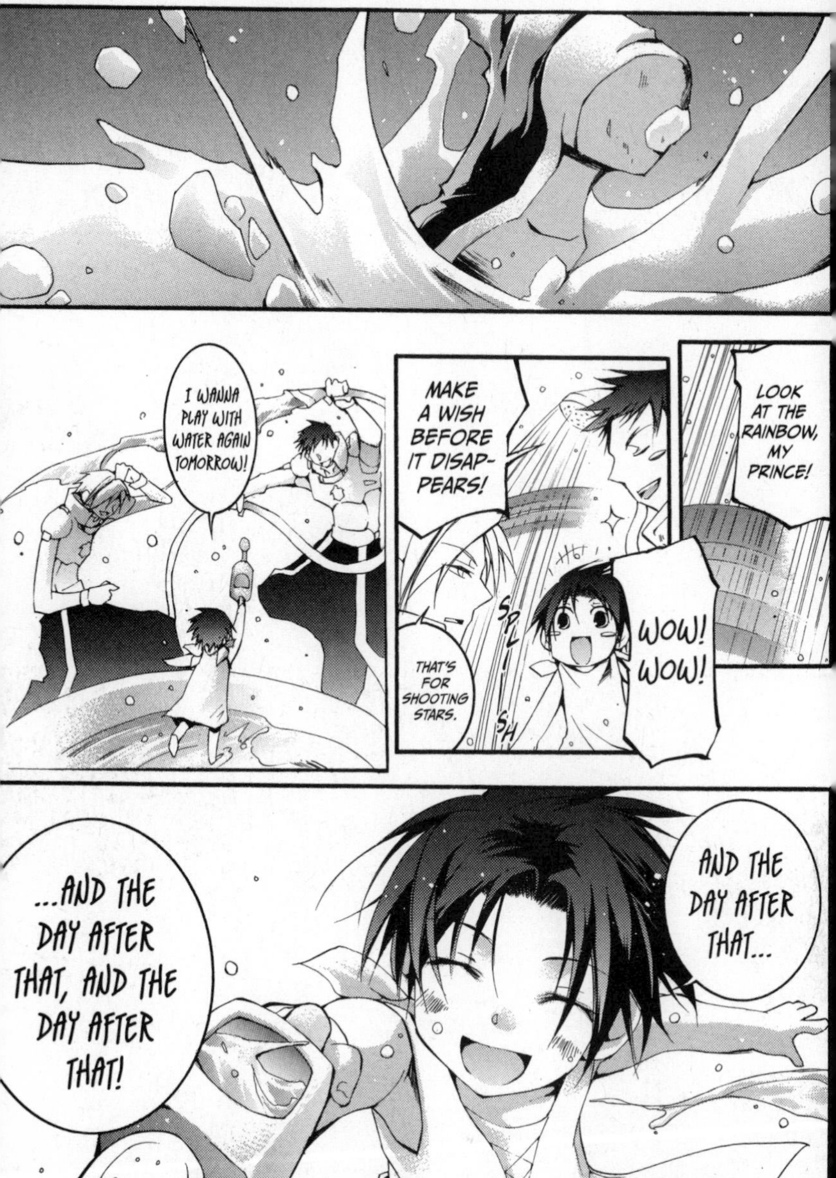
LOOK AT THE RAINBOW, MY PRINCE!
MAKE A WISH BEFORE IT DISAPPEARS!
WOW! WOW!
SPLISH
THAT'S FOR SHOOTING STARS.
I WANNA PLAY WITH WATER AGAIN TOMORROW!
AND THE DAY AFTER THAT...
...AND THE DAY AFTER THAT, AND THE DAY AFTER THAT!

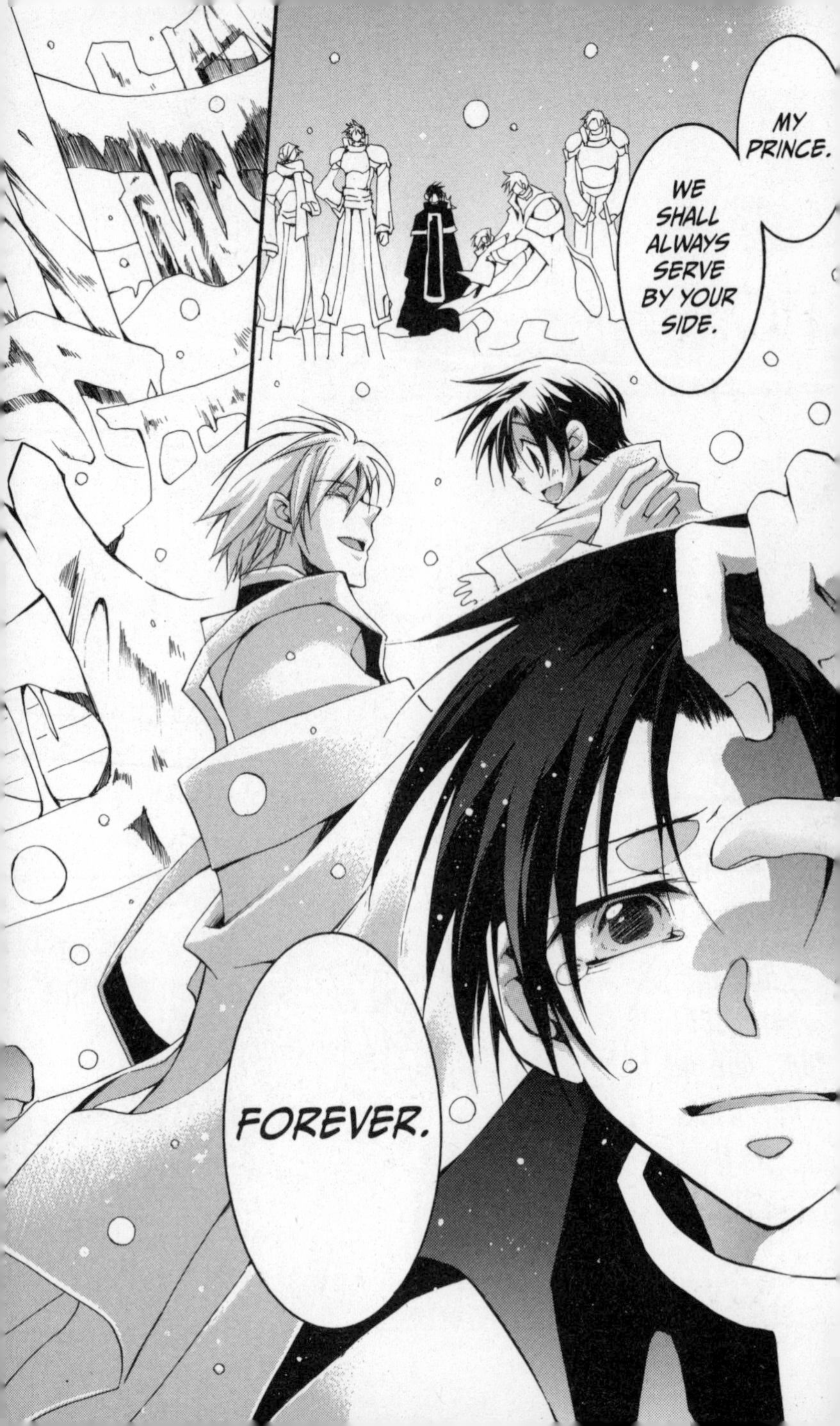
MY PRINCE.
WE SHALL ALWAYS SERVE BY YOUR SIDE.
FOREVER.

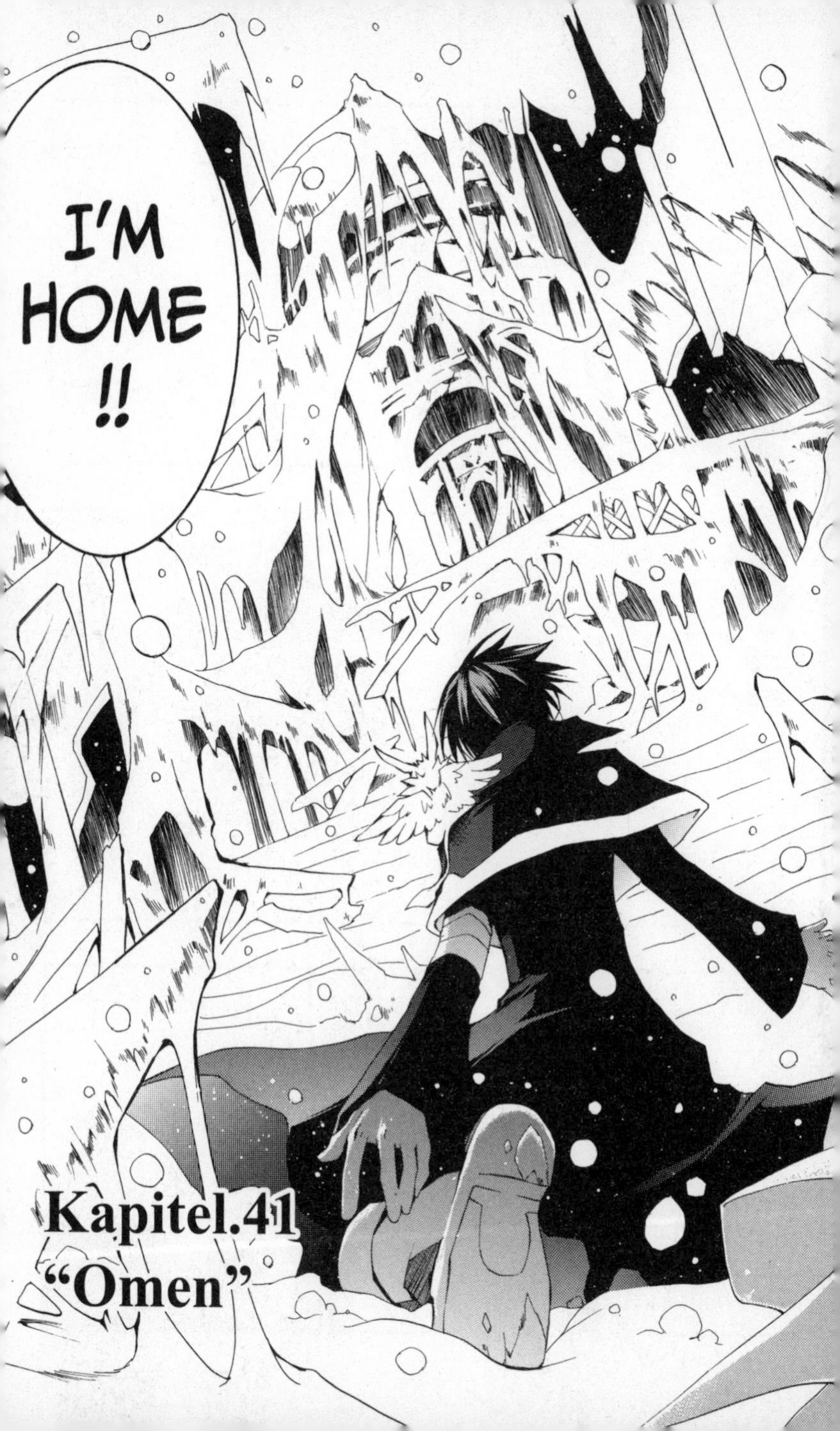
I'M HOME !!
Kapitel.41
"Omen"

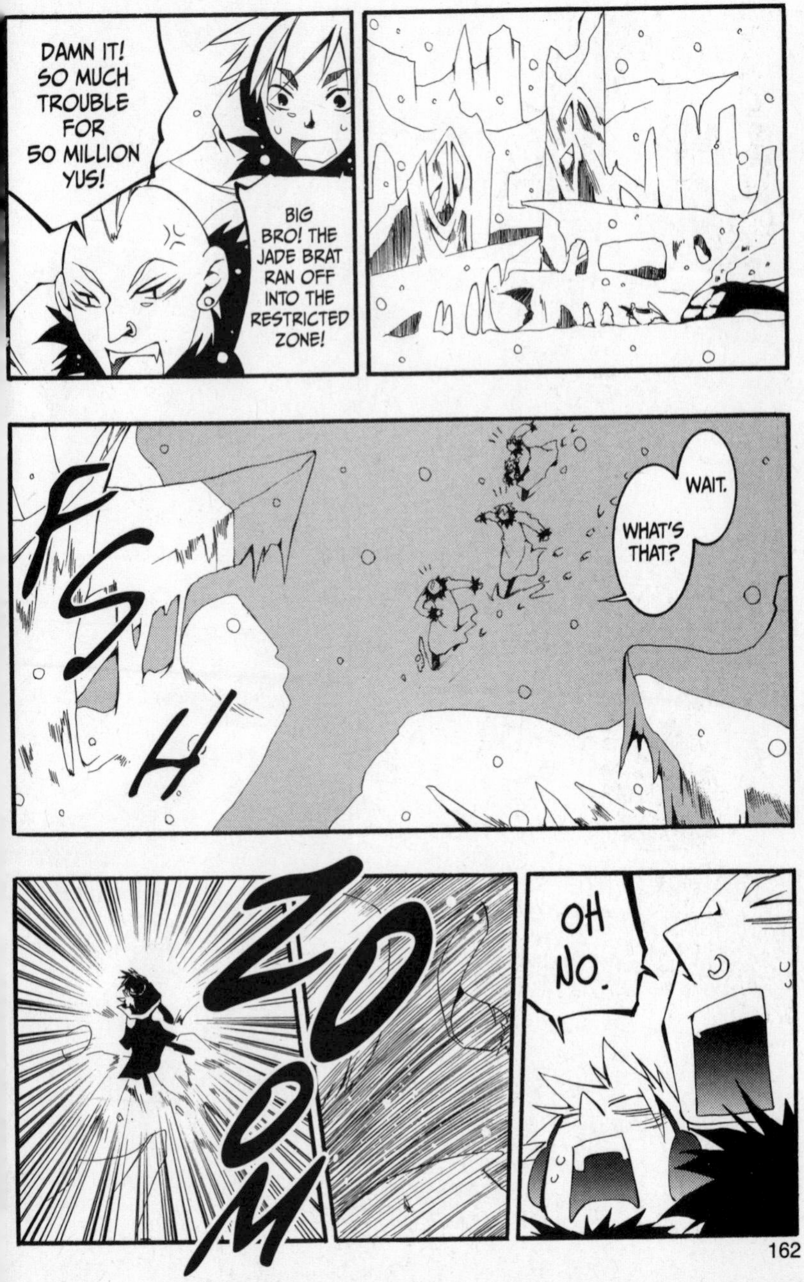
BIG BRO! THE JADE BRAT RAN OFF INTO THE RESTRICTED ZONE!
DAMN IT! SO MUCH TROUBLE FOR 50 MILLION YUS!
WAIT.
WHAT'S THAT?
FSH
OH NO.
ZOOM

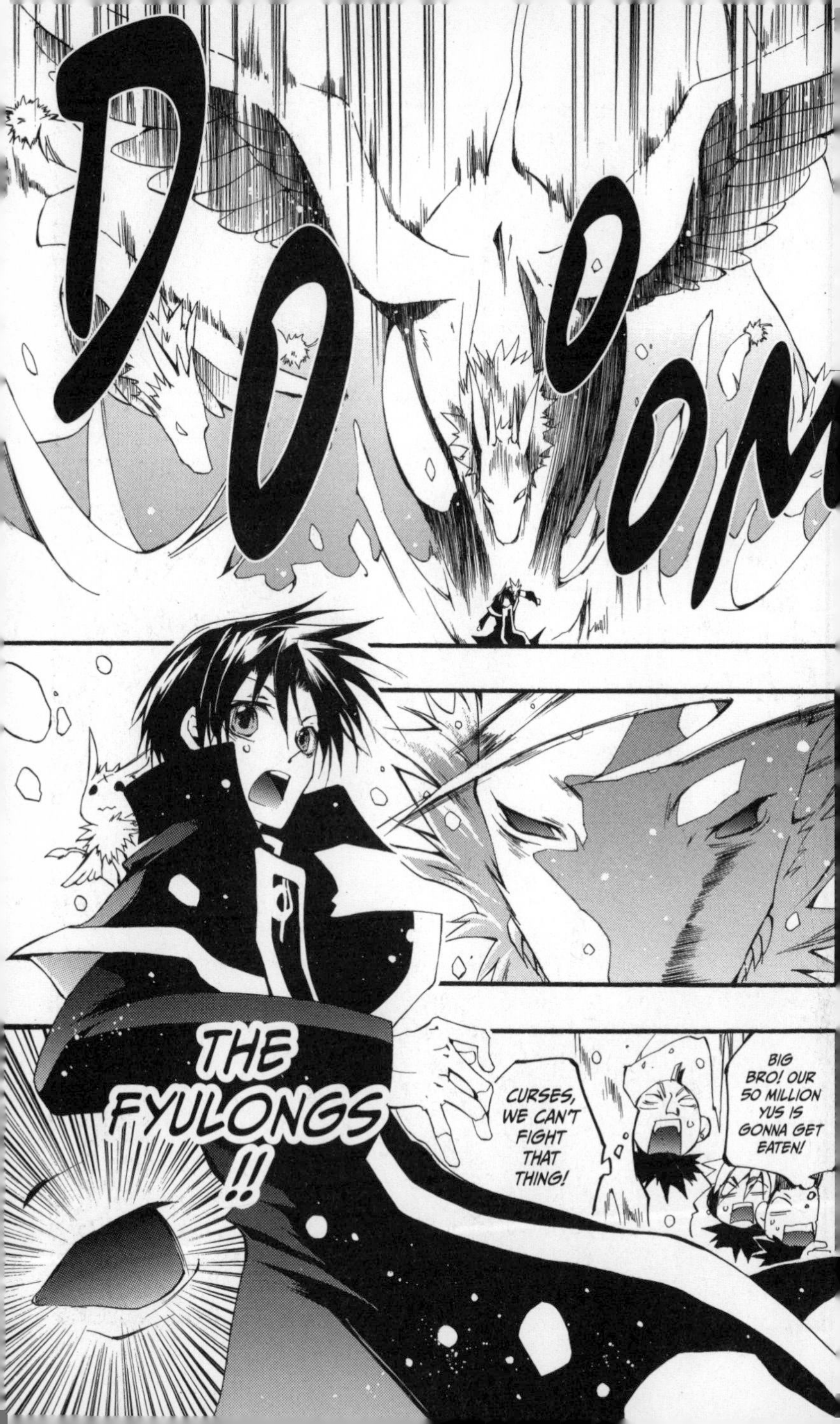
DOOOOM
BIG BRO! OUR 50 MILLION YUS IS GONNA GET EATEN!
CURSES, WE CAN'T FIGHT THAT THING!
THE FYULONGS!!

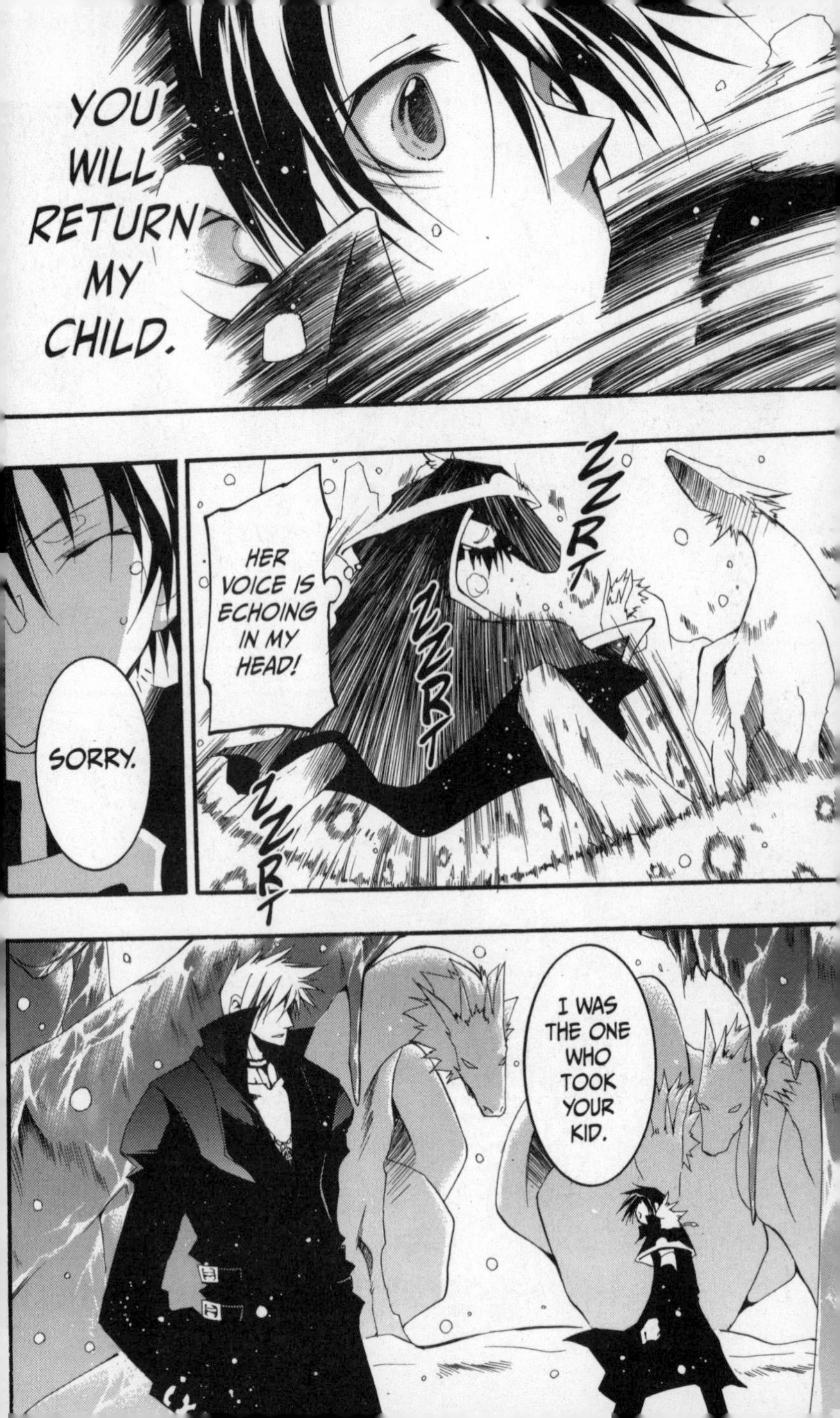
YOU WILL RETURN MY CHILD.
ZZRT
HER VOICE IS ECHOING IN MY HEAD!
ZZZRT
ZZZRT
SORRY.
I WAS THE ONE WHO TOOK YOUR KID.

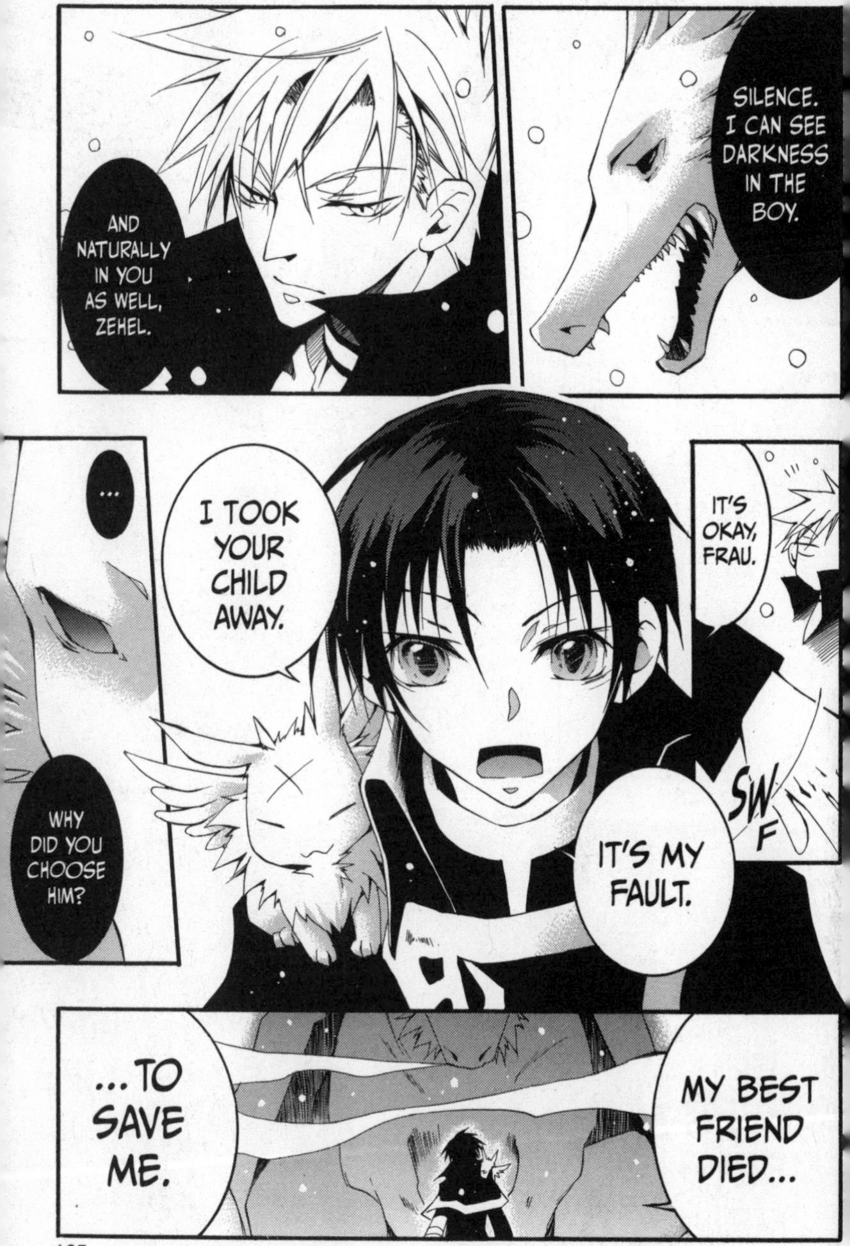

SILENCE. I CAN SEE DARKNESS IN THE BOY.
AND NATURALLY IN YOU AS WELL, ZEHEL.
IT'S OKAY, FRAU.
SWF
IT'S MY FAULT.
I TOOK YOUR CHILD AWAY.
...
WHY DID YOU CHOOSE HIM?
MY BEST FRIEND DIED...
...TO SAVE ME.

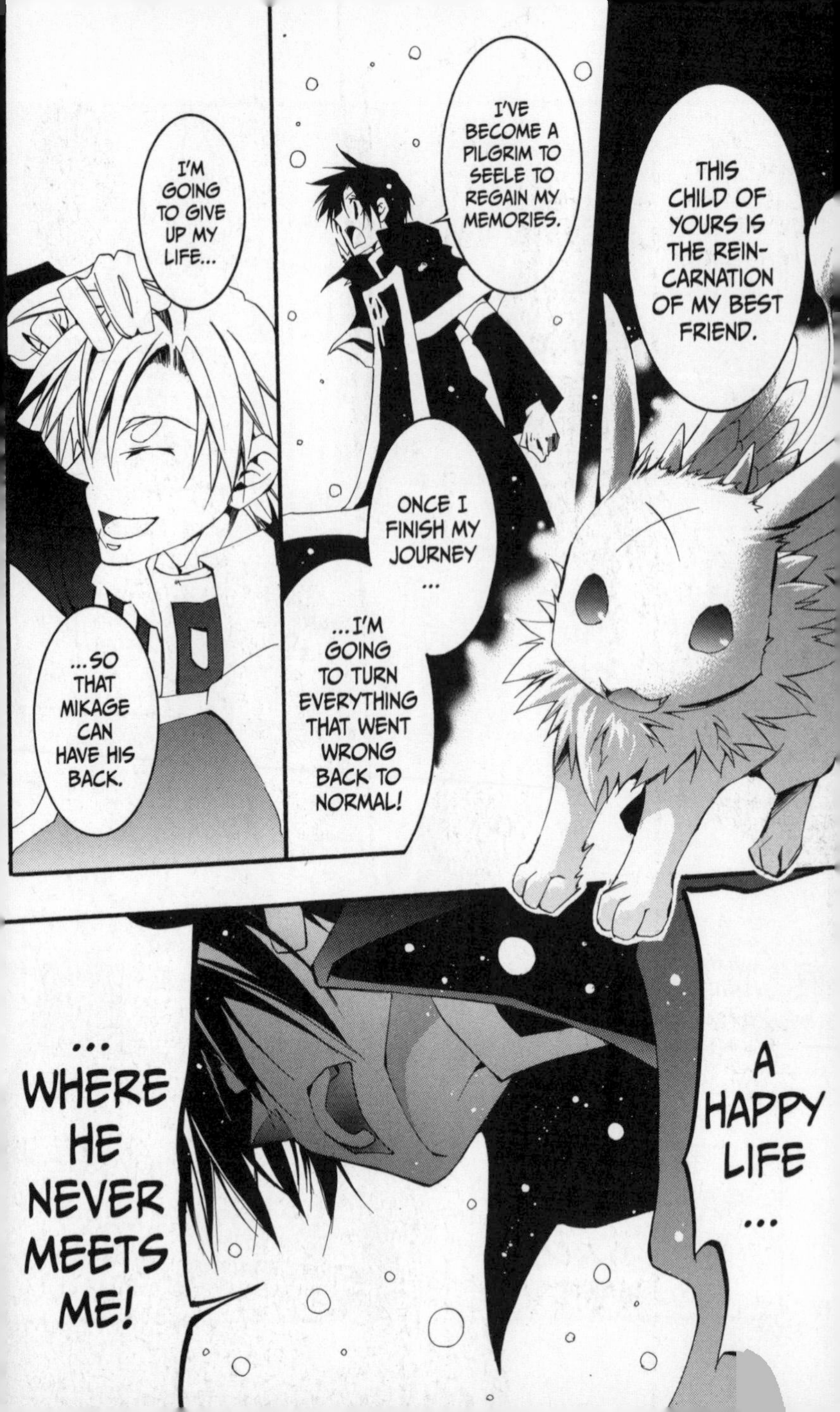
THIS CHILD OF YOURS IS THE REIN-CARNATION OF MY BEST FRIEND.
I'VE BECOME A PILGRIM TO SEELE TO REGAIN MY MEMORIES.
ONCE I FINISH MY JOURNEY...
...I'M GOING TO TURN EVERYTHING THAT WENT WRONG BACK TO NORMAL!
I'M GOING TO GIVE UP MY LIFE...
...SO THAT MIKAGE CAN HAVE HIS BACK.
A HAPPY LIFE...
...WHERE HE NEVER MEETS ME!

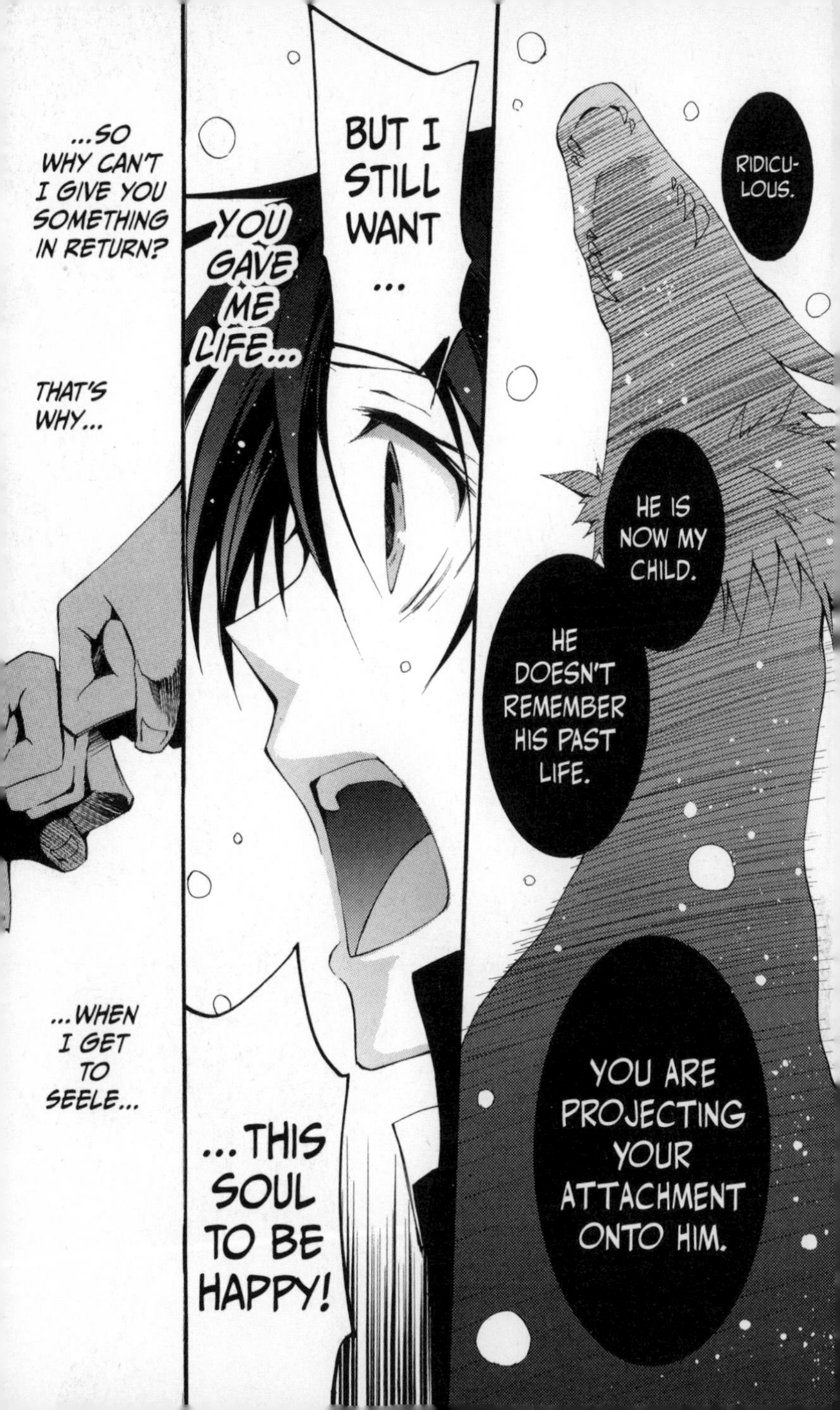
RIDICULOUS.
HE IS NOW MY CHILD.
HE DOESN'T REMEMBER HIS PAST LIFE.
YOU ARE PROJECTING YOUR ATTACHMENT ONTO HIM.
BUT I STILL WANT ...
YOU GAVE ME LIFE...
... THIS SOUL TO BE HAPPY!
...SO WHY CAN'T I GIVE YOU SOMETHING IN RETURN?
THAT'S WHY...
...WHEN I GET TO SEELE...

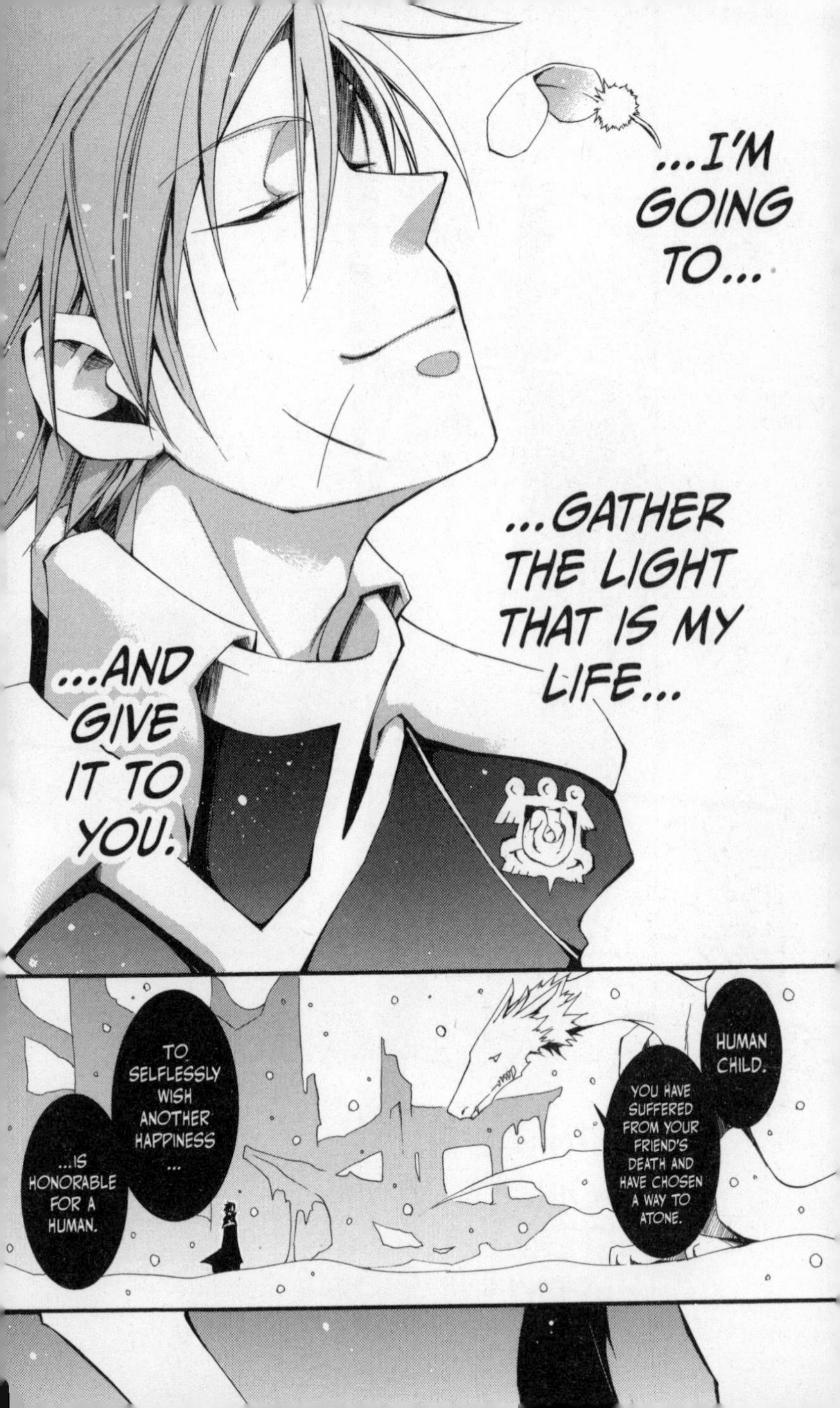
...I'M GOING TO...
...GATHER THE LIGHT THAT IS MY LIFE...
...AND GIVE IT TO YOU.
HUMAN CHILD.
YOU HAVE SUFFERED FROM YOUR FRIEND'S DEATH AND HAVE CHOSEN A WAY TO ATONE.
TO SELFLESSLY WISH ANOTHER HAPPINESS ...
...IS HONORABLE FOR A HUMAN.

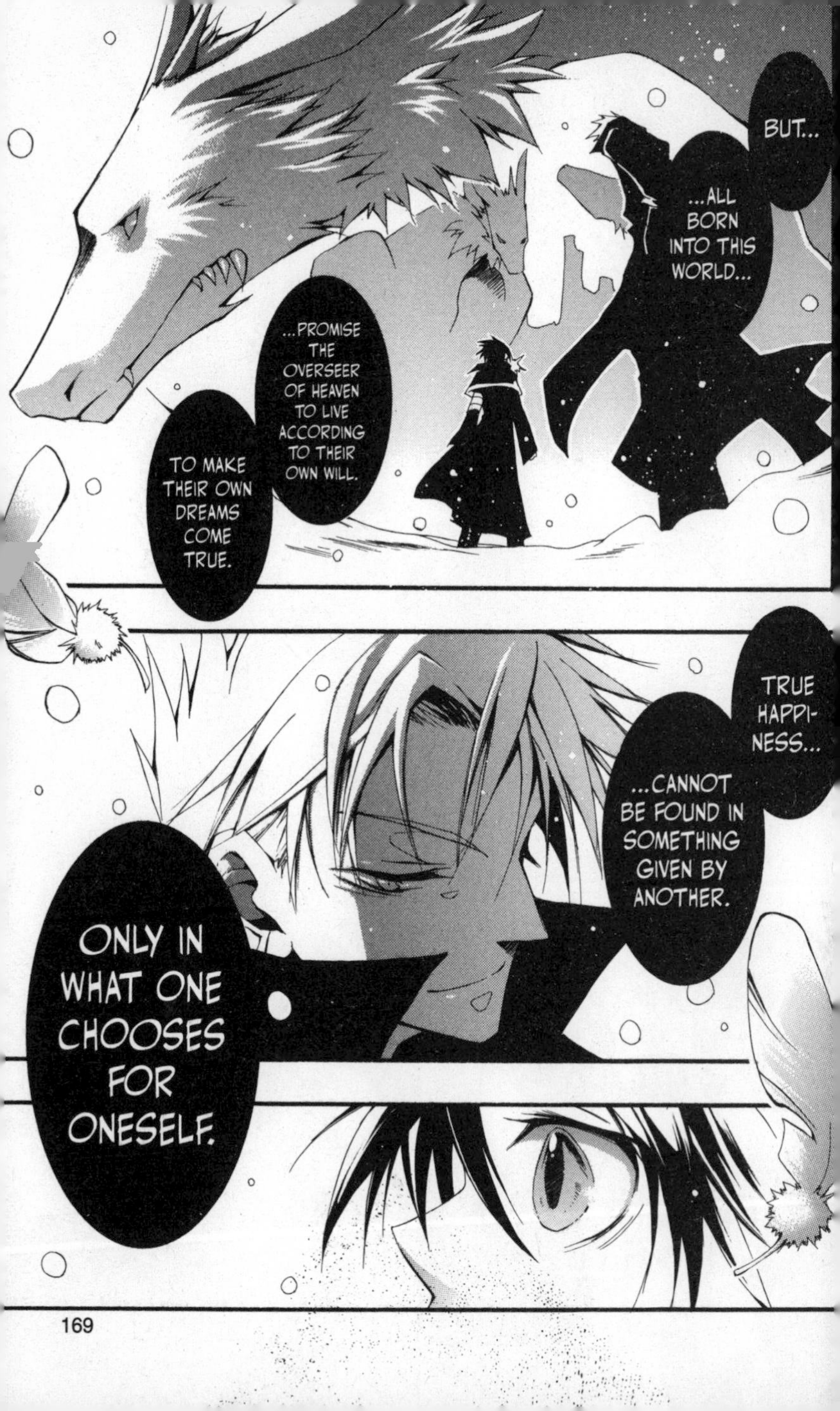
BUT...
...ALL BORN INTO THIS WORLD...
...PROMISE THE OVERSEER OF HEAVEN TO LIVE ACCORDING TO THEIR OWN WILL.
TO MAKE THEIR OWN DREAMS COME TRUE.
TRUE HAPPINESS...
...CANNOT BE FOUND IN SOMETHING GIVEN BY ANOTHER.
ONLY IN WHAT ONE CHOOSES FOR ONESELF.

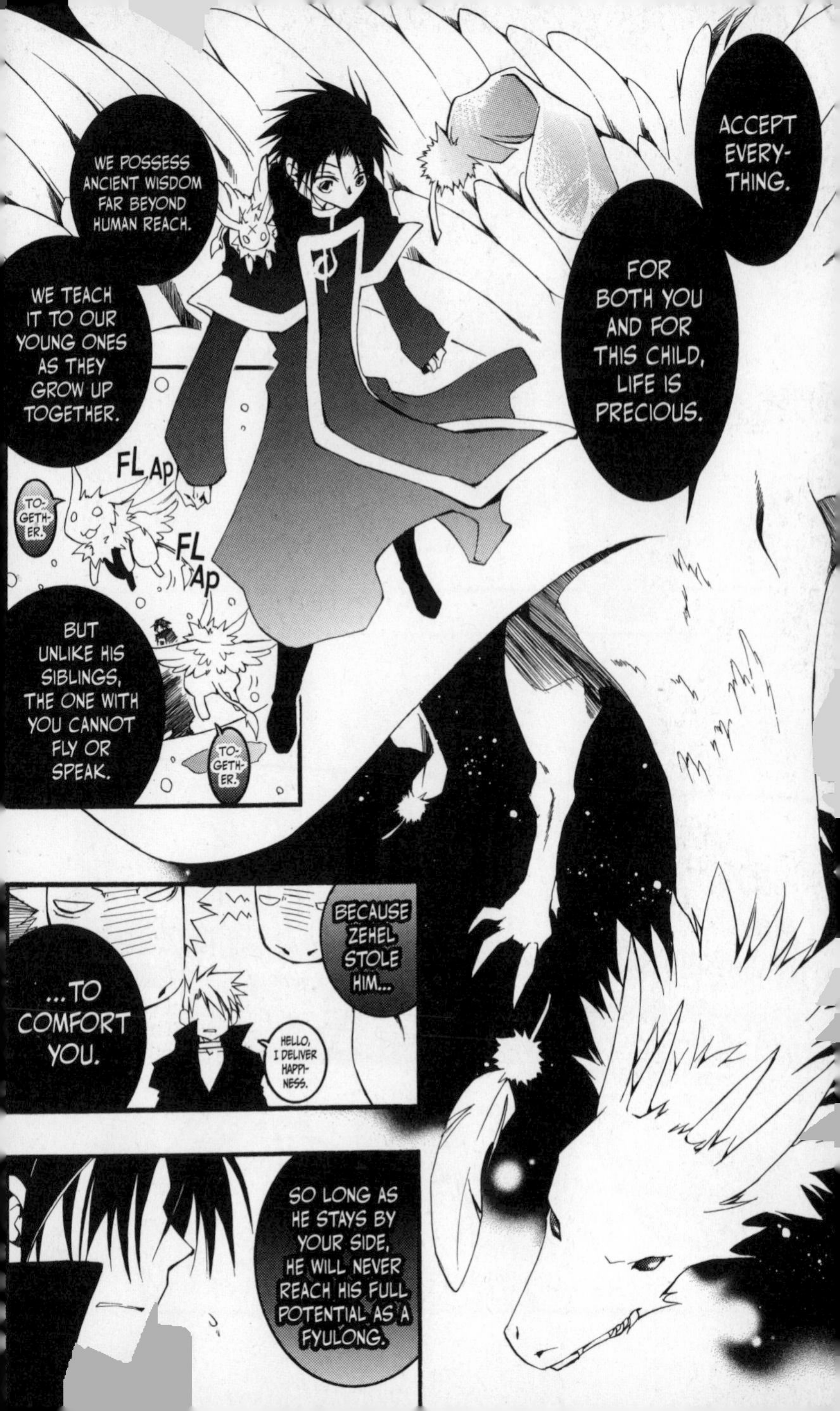
ACCEPT EVERYTHING.
FOR BOTH YOU AND FOR THIS CHILD, LIFE IS PRECIOUS.
WE POSSESS ANCIENT WISDOM FAR BEYOND HUMAN REACH.
WE TEACH IT TO OUR YOUNG ONES AS THEY GROW UP TOGETHER.
FLAP
TOGETHER.
FLAP
BUT UNLIKE HIS SIBLINGS, THE ONE WITH YOU CANNOT FLY OR SPEAK.
TOGETHER.
BECAUSE ZEHEL STOLE HIM...
HELLO, I DELIVER HAPPINESS.
...TO COMFORT YOU.
SO LONG AS HE STAYS BY YOUR SIDE, HE WILL NEVER REACH HIS FULL POTENTIAL AS A FYULONG.

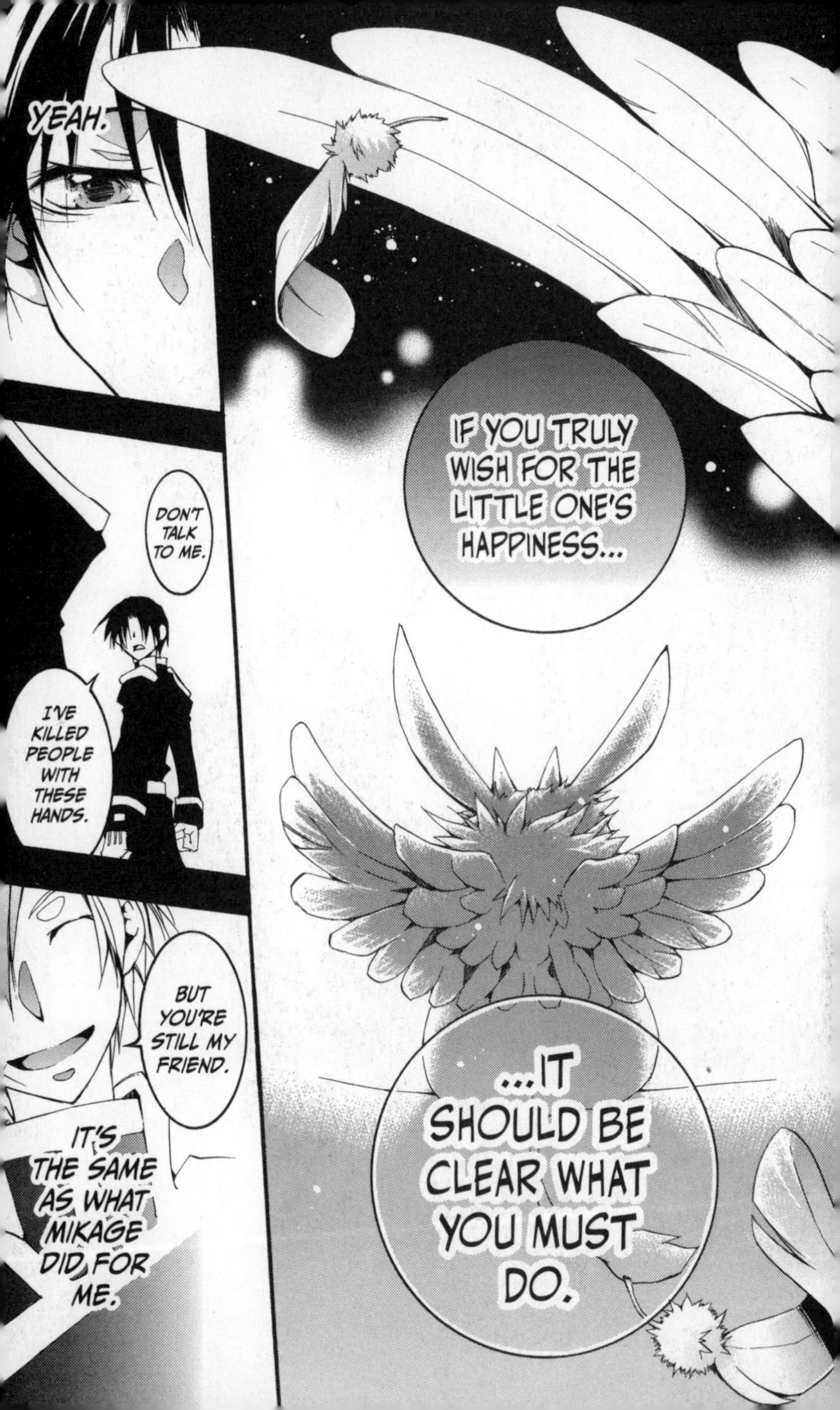
IF YOU TRULY WISH FOR THE LITTLE ONE'S HAPPINESS...
...IT SHOULD BE CLEAR WHAT YOU MUST DO.
YEAH.
DON'T TALK TO ME.
I'VE KILLED PEOPLE WITH THESE HANDS.
BUT YOU'RE STILL MY FRIEND.
IT'S THE SAME AS WHAT MIKAGE DID FOR ME.

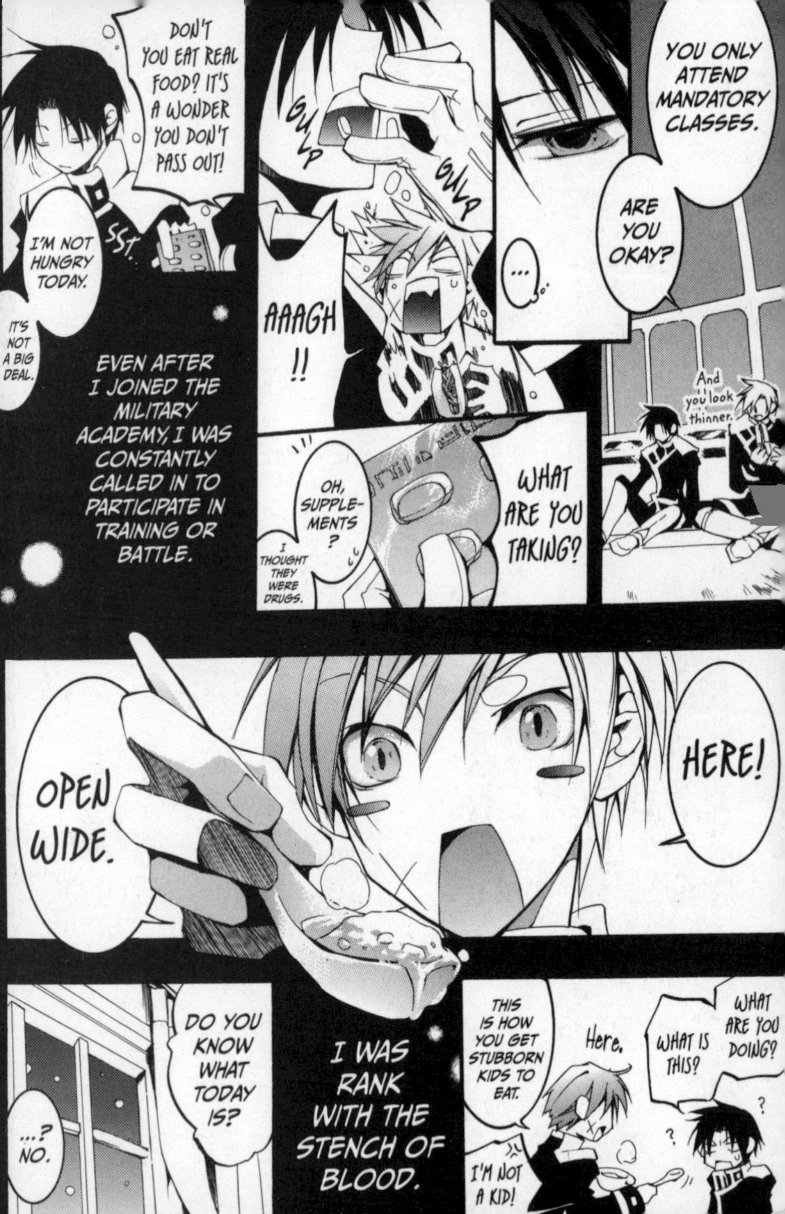
YOU ONLY ATTEND MANDATORY CLASSES.
ARE YOU OKAY?
And you look thinner.
...
GULP
GULP
AAAGH!!
WHAT ARE YOU TAKING?
OH, SUPPLEMENTS?
I THOUGHT THEY WERE DRUGS.
DON'T YOU EAT REAL FOOD? IT'S A WONDER YOU DON'T PASS OUT!
SST
I'M NOT HUNGRY TODAY.
IT'S NOT A BIG DEAL.
EVEN AFTER I JOINED THE MILITARY ACADEMY, I WAS CONSTANTLY CALLED IN TO PARTICIPATE IN TRAINING OR BATTLE.
HERE!
OPEN WIDE.
WHAT ARE YOU DOING?
WHAT IS THIS?
Here.
THIS IS HOW YOU GET STUBBORN KIDS TO EAT.
I'M NOT A KID!
I WAS RANK WITH THE STENCH OF BLOOD.
DO YOU KNOW WHAT TODAY IS?
...? NO.

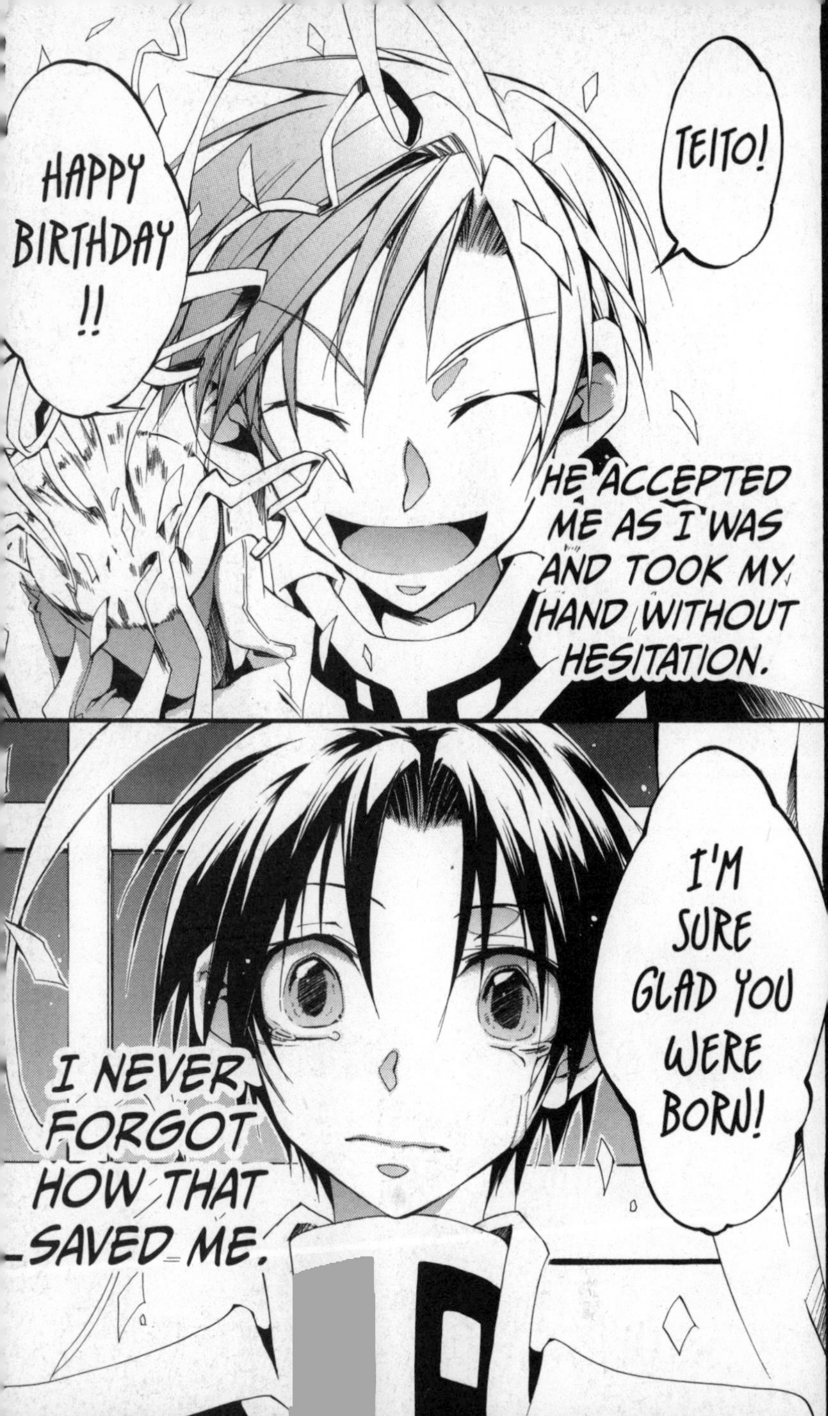
TEITO!
HAPPY BIRTHDAY!!
HE ACCEPTED ME AS I WAS AND TOOK MY HAND WITHOUT HESITATION.
I'M SURE GLAD YOU WERE BORN!
I NEVER FORGOT HOW THAT SAVED ME.

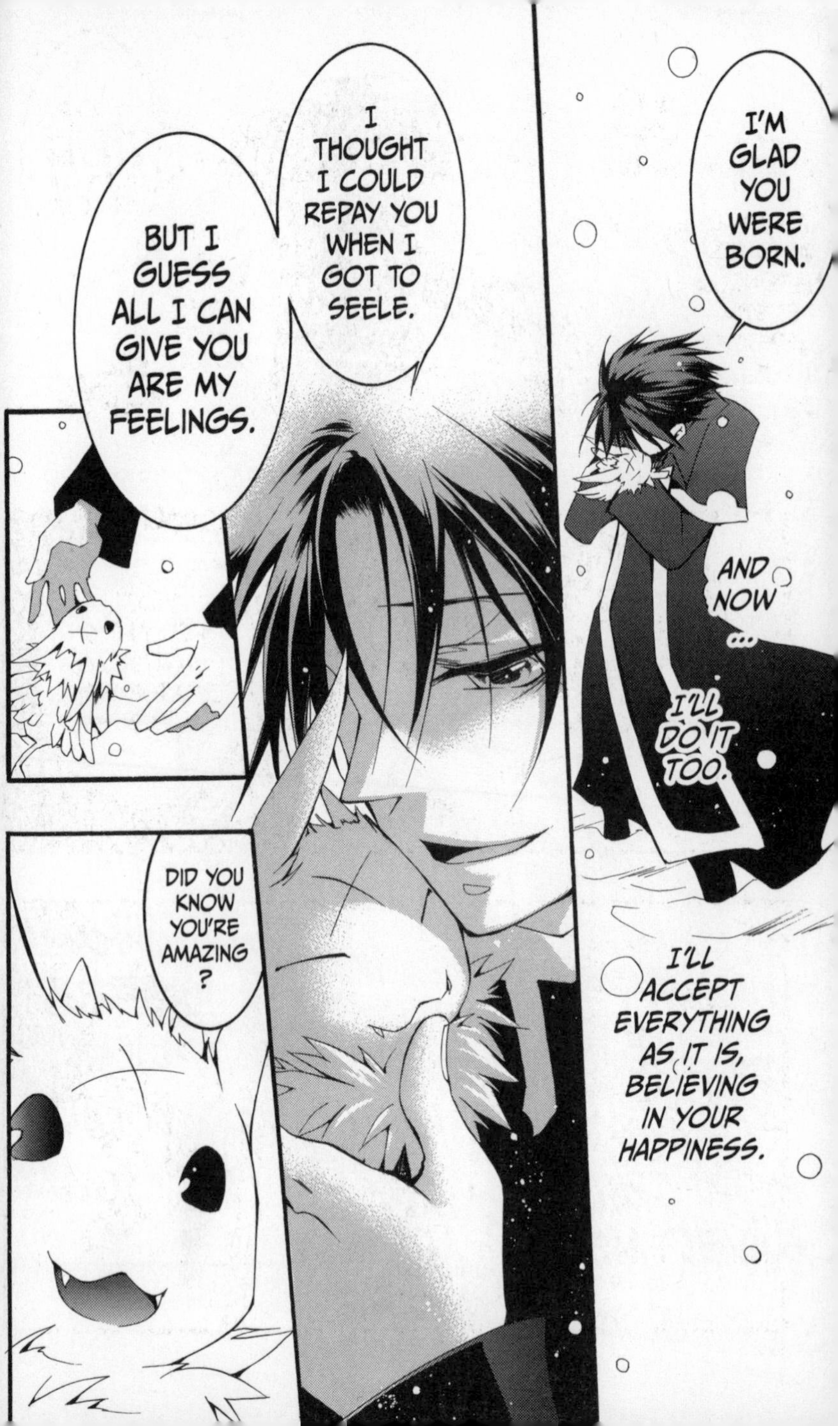
I'M GLAD YOU WERE BORN.
AND NOW...
I'LL DO IT TOO.
I'LL ACCEPT EVERYTHING AS IT IS, BELIEVING IN YOUR HAPPINESS.
I THOUGHT I COULD REPAY YOU WHEN I GOT TO SEELE.
BUT I GUESS ALL I CAN GIVE YOU ARE MY FEELINGS.
DID YOU KNOW YOU'RE AMAZING?

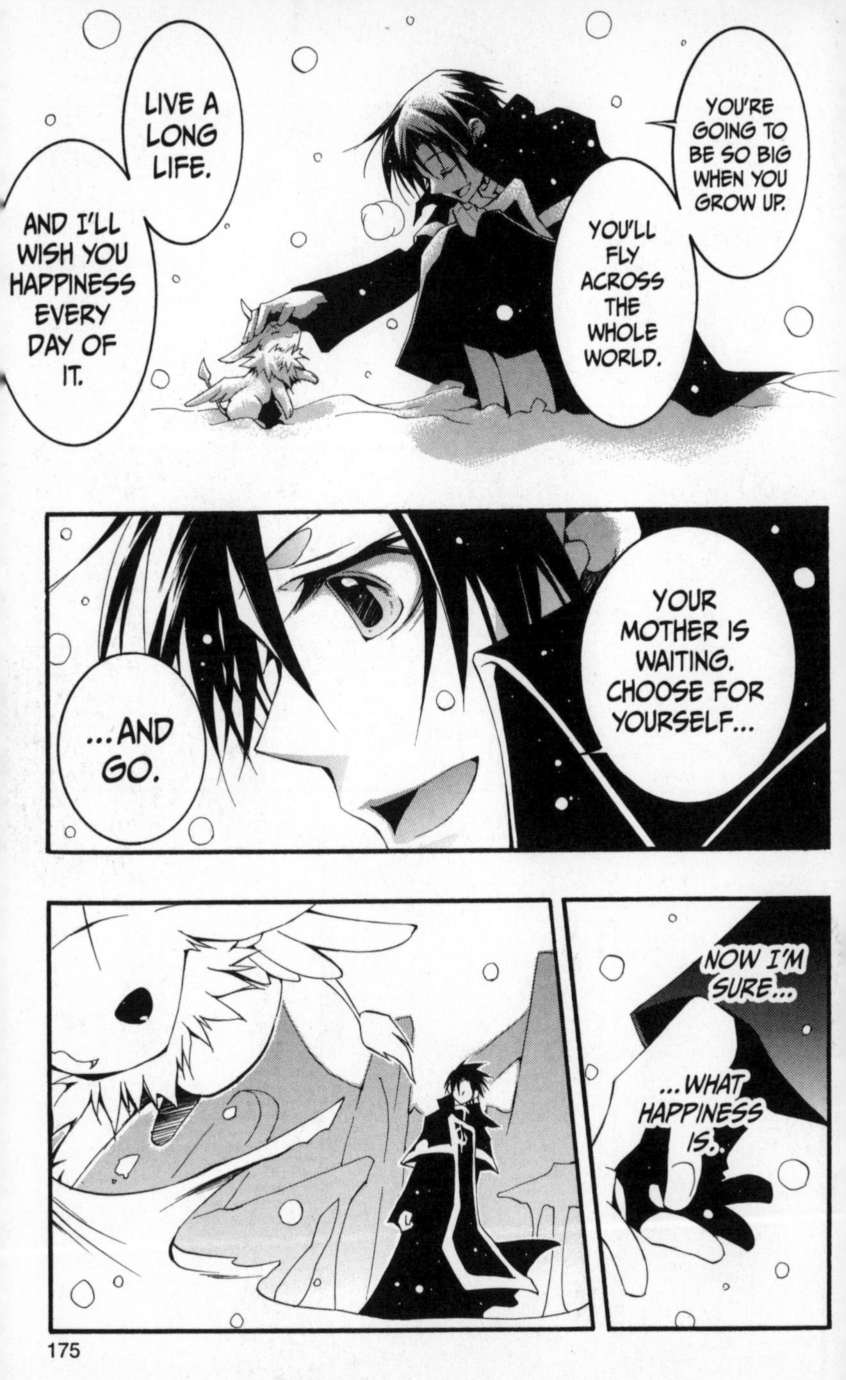
YOU'RE GOING TO BE SO BIG WHEN YOU GROW UP.
YOU'LL FLY ACROSS THE WHOLE WORLD.
LIVE A LONG LIFE.
AND I'LL WISH YOU HAPPINESS EVERY DAY OF IT.
YOUR MOTHER IS WAITING. CHOOSE FOR YOURSELF...
...AND GO.
NOW I'M SURE...
...WHAT HAPPINESS IS.

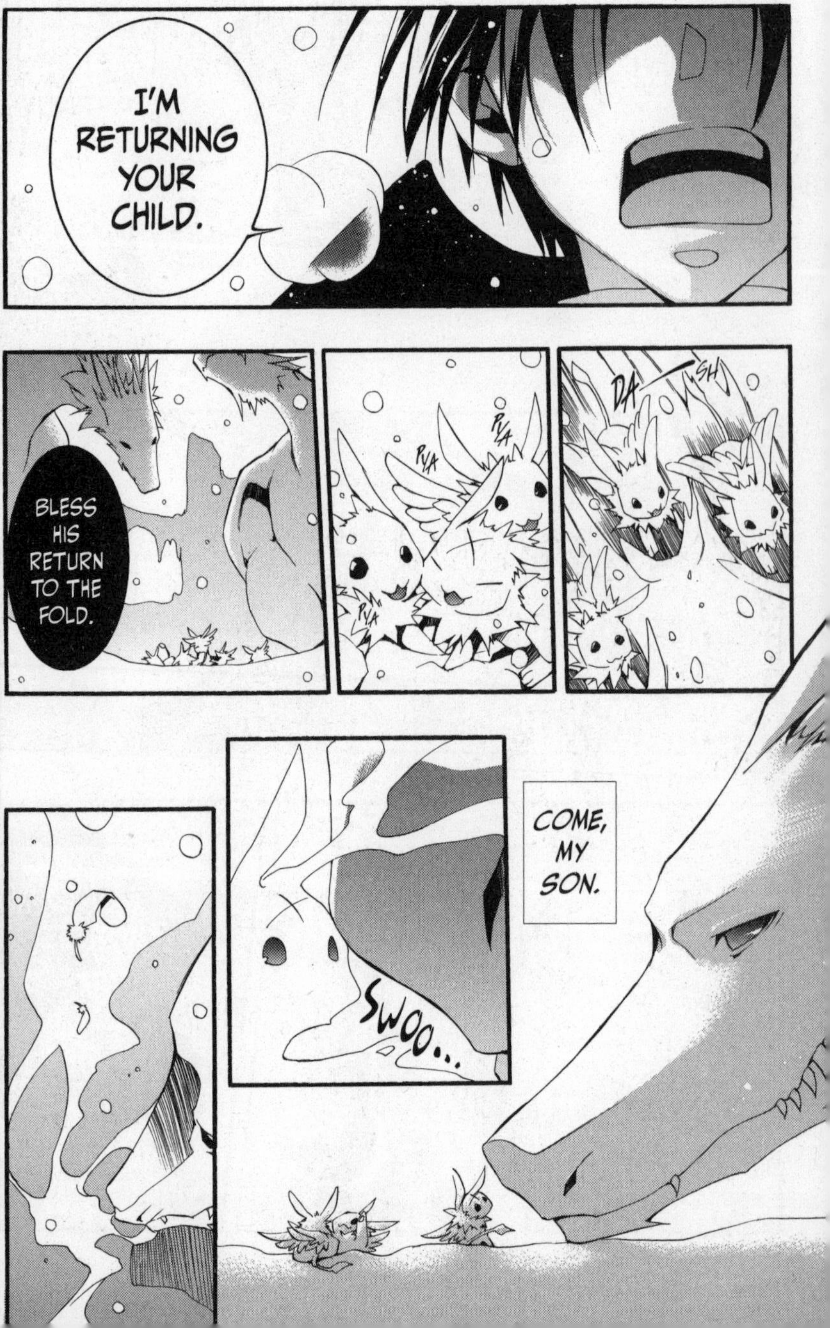
I'M RETURNING YOUR CHILD.
DA—SH
PYA
PYA
PYA
BLESS HIS RETURN TO THE FOLD.
COME, MY SON.
SWOO...

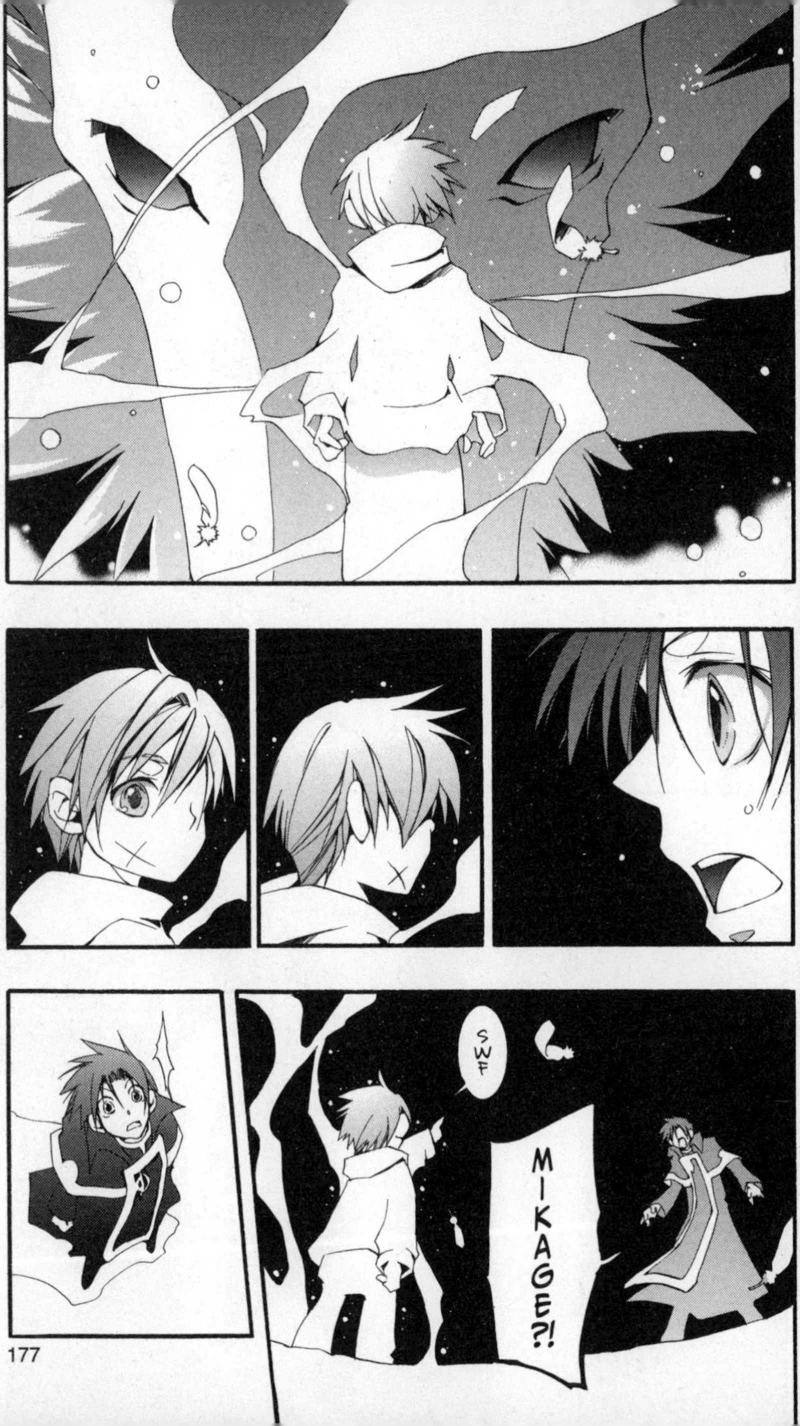
SWF
MIKAGE?!

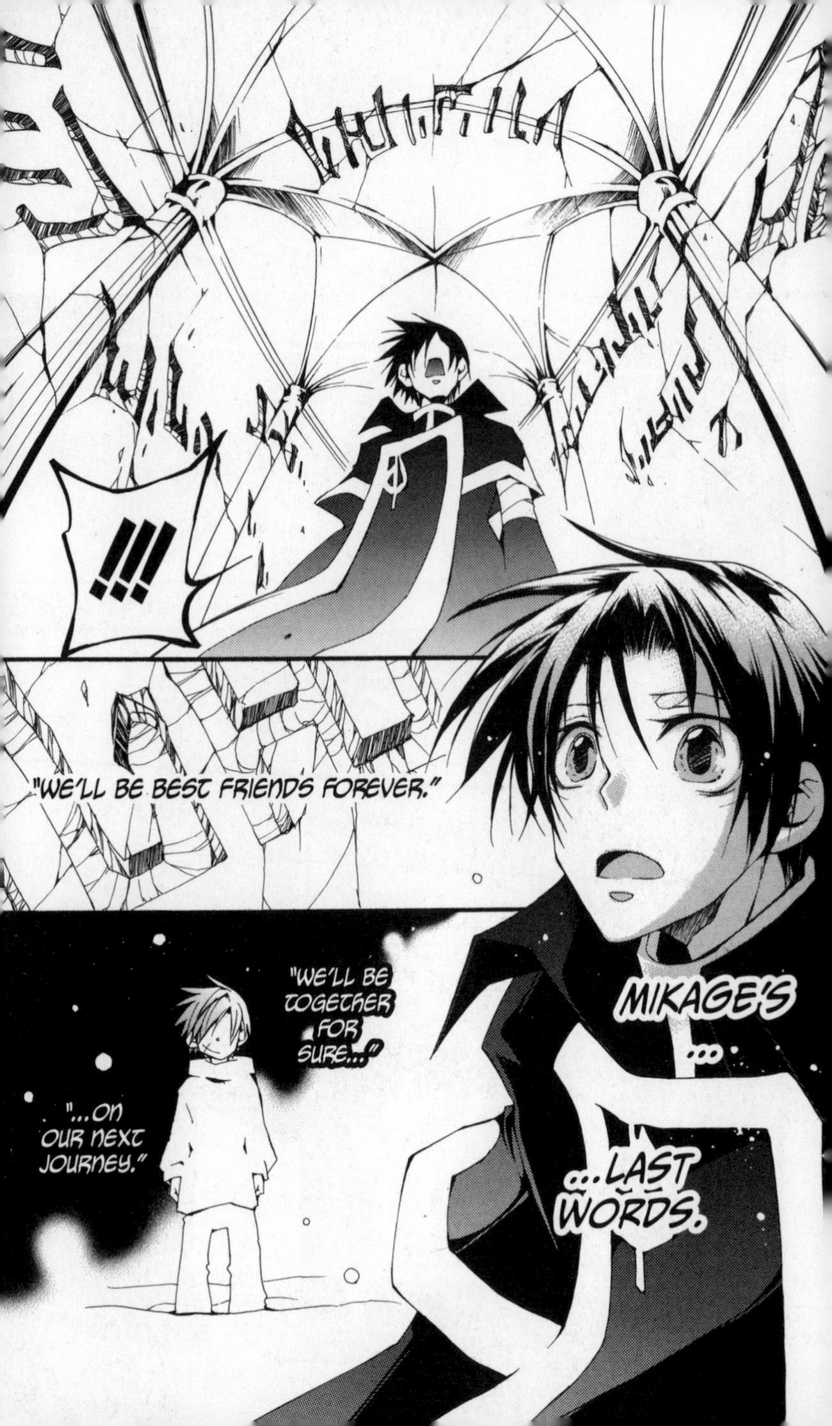
!!!
MIKAGE'S ...
...LAST WORDS.
"WE'LL BE BEST FRIENDS FOREVER."
"WE'LL BE TOGETHER FOR SURE..."
"...ON OUR NEXT JOURNEY."

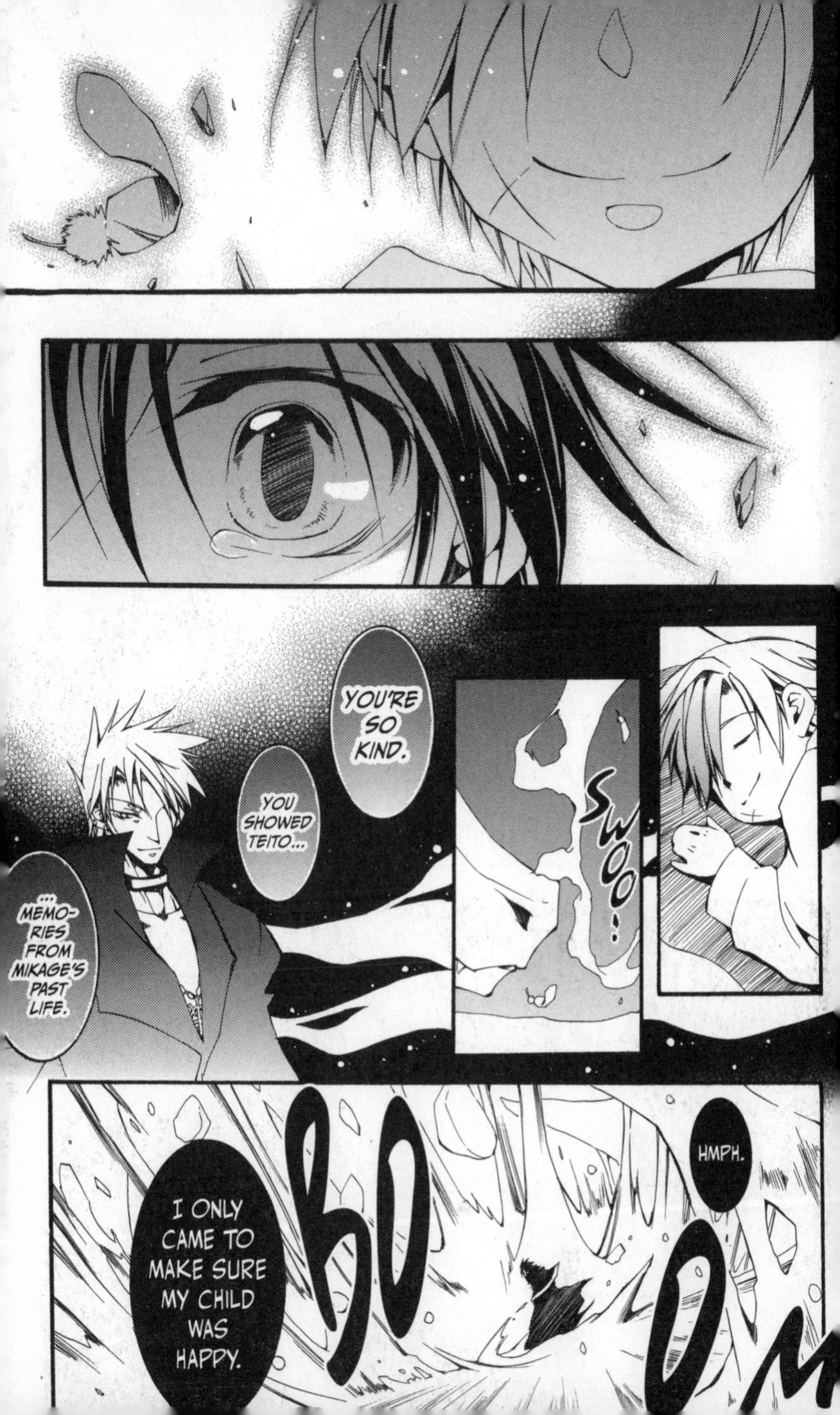
SWOO...
YOU'RE SO KIND.
YOU SHOWED TEITO...
...MEMO-RIES FROM MIKAGE'S PAST LIFE.
HMPH.
BOOOM
I ONLY CAME TO MAKE SURE MY CHILD WAS HAPPY.

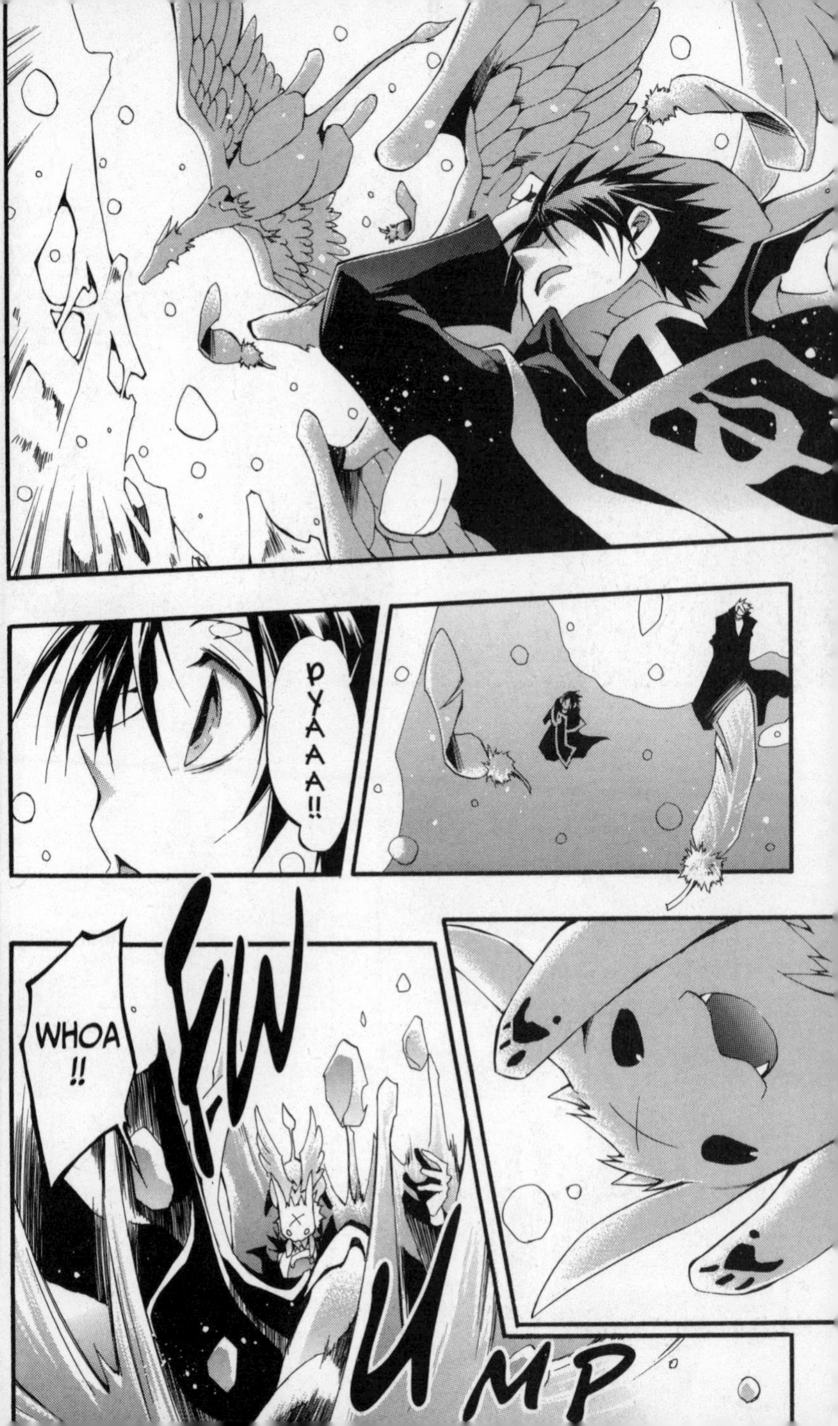
PYAAAA!!
WHOA!!

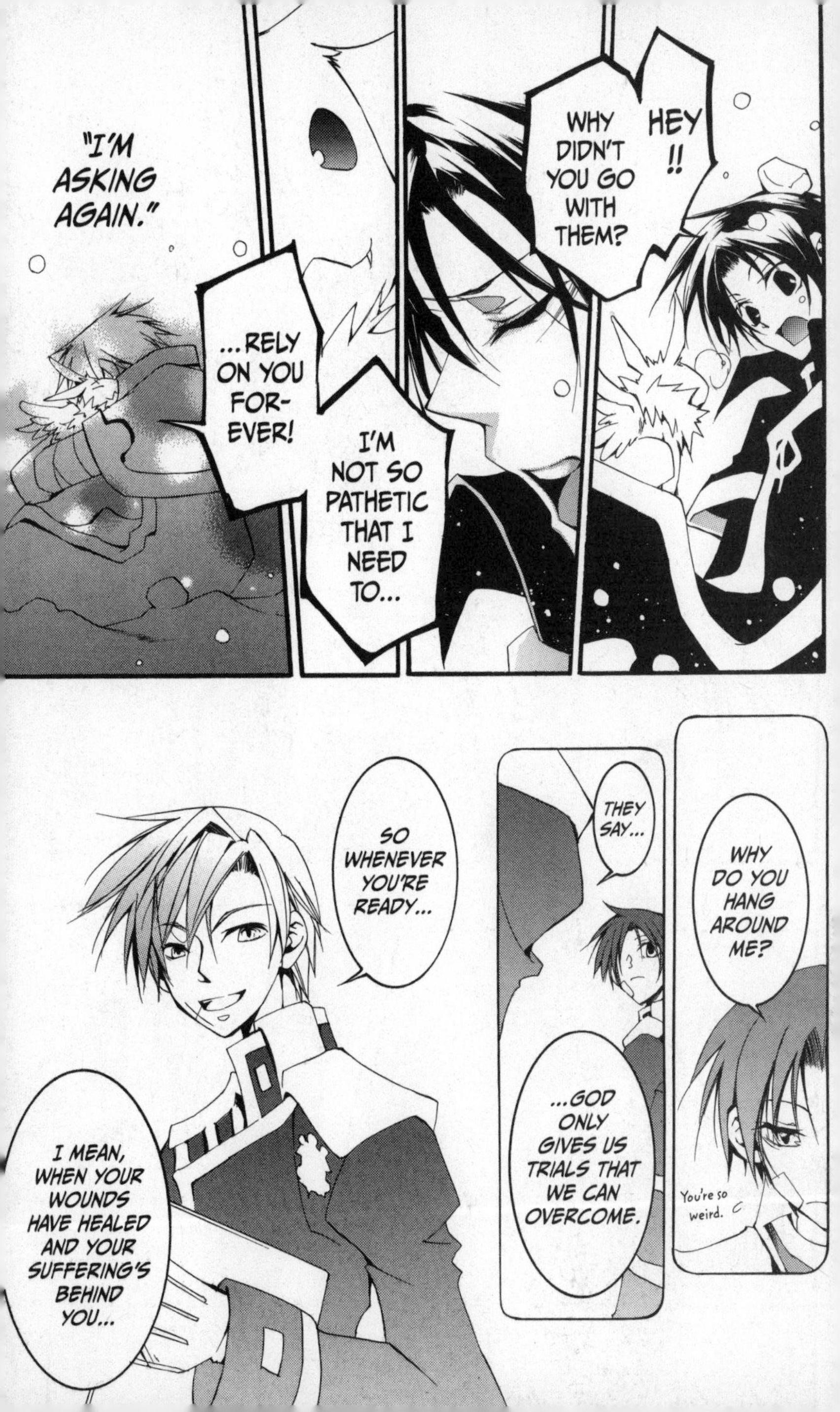
HEY !!
WHY DIDN'T YOU GO WITH THEM?
I'M NOT SO PATHETIC THAT I NEED TO...
...RELY ON YOU FOR-EVER!
"I'M ASKING AGAIN."
WHY DO YOU HANG AROUND ME?
You're so weird.
THEY SAY...
...GOD ONLY GIVES US TRIALS THAT WE CAN OVERCOME.
SO WHENEVER YOU'RE READY...
I MEAN, WHEN YOUR WOUNDS HAVE HEALED AND YOUR SUFFERING'S BEHIND YOU...

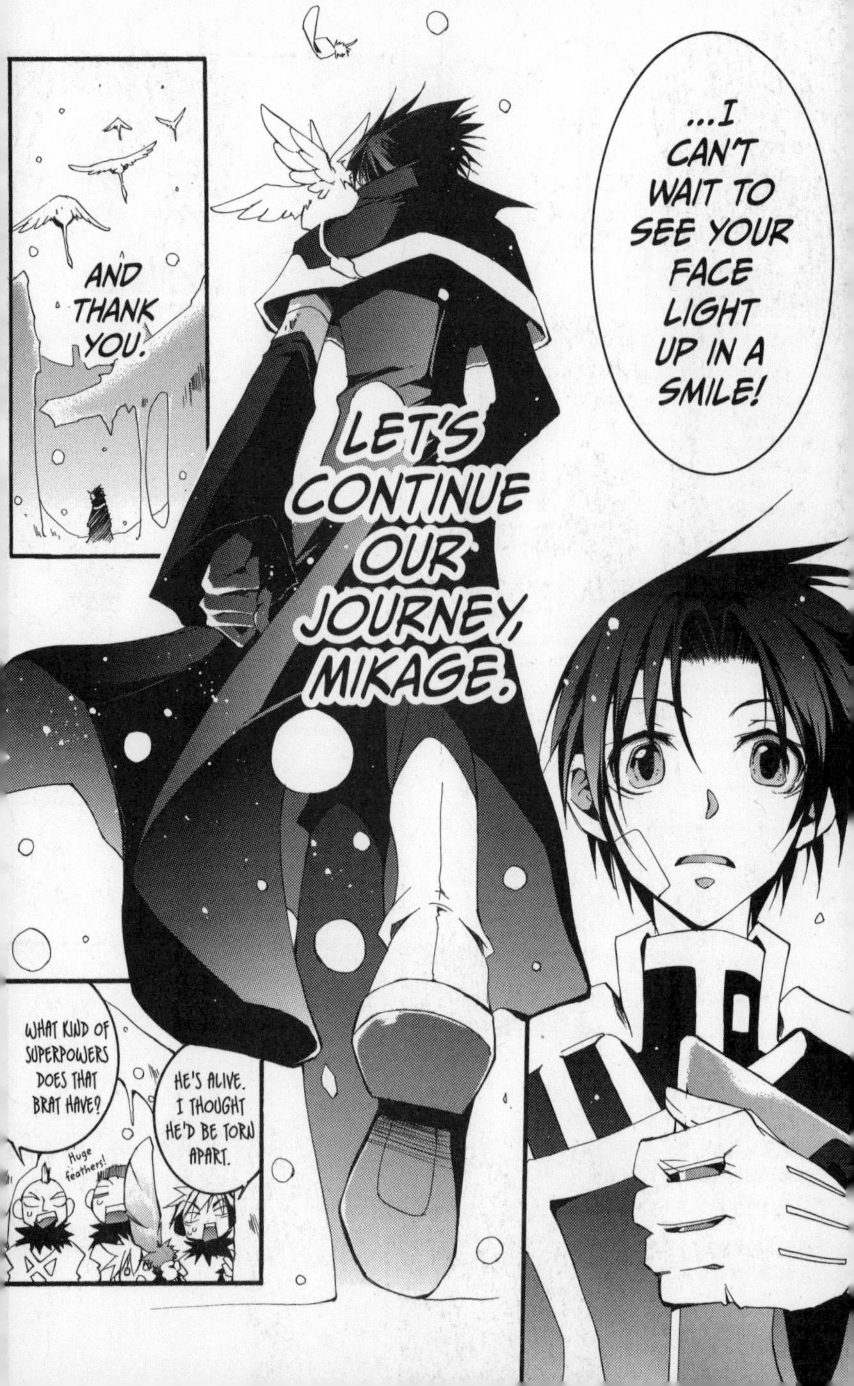
...I CAN'T WAIT TO SEE YOUR FACE LIGHT UP IN A SMILE!
AND THANK YOU.
LET'S CONTINUE OUR JOURNEY, MIKAGE.
HE'S ALIVE. I THOUGHT HE'D BE TORN APART.
WHAT KIND OF SUPERPOWERS DOES THAT BRAT HAVE?
Huge feathers!

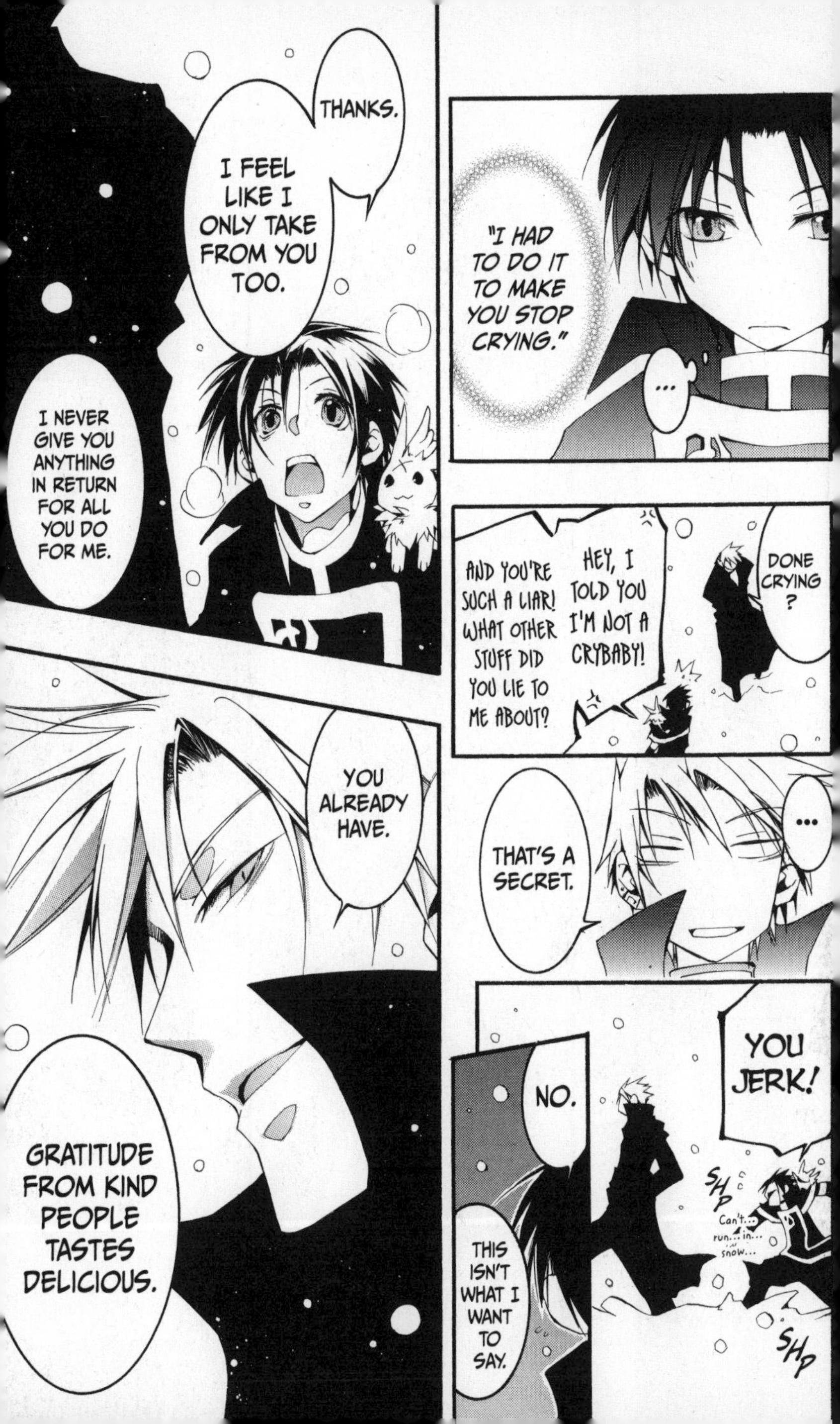
"I HAD TO DO IT TO MAKE YOU STOP CRYING."
...
DONE CRYING?
HEY, I TOLD YOU I'M NOT A CRYBABY!
AND YOU'RE SUCH A LIAR! WHAT OTHER STUFF DID YOU LIE TO ME ABOUT?
...
THAT'S A SECRET.
YOU JERK!
SHP
Can't... run... in... snow...
SHP
NO.
THIS ISN'T WHAT I WANT TO SAY.
THANKS.
I FEEL LIKE I ONLY TAKE FROM YOU TOO.
I NEVER GIVE YOU ANYTHING IN RETURN FOR ALL YOU DO FOR ME.
YOU ALREADY HAVE.
GRATITUDE FROM KIND PEOPLE TASTES DELICIOUS.

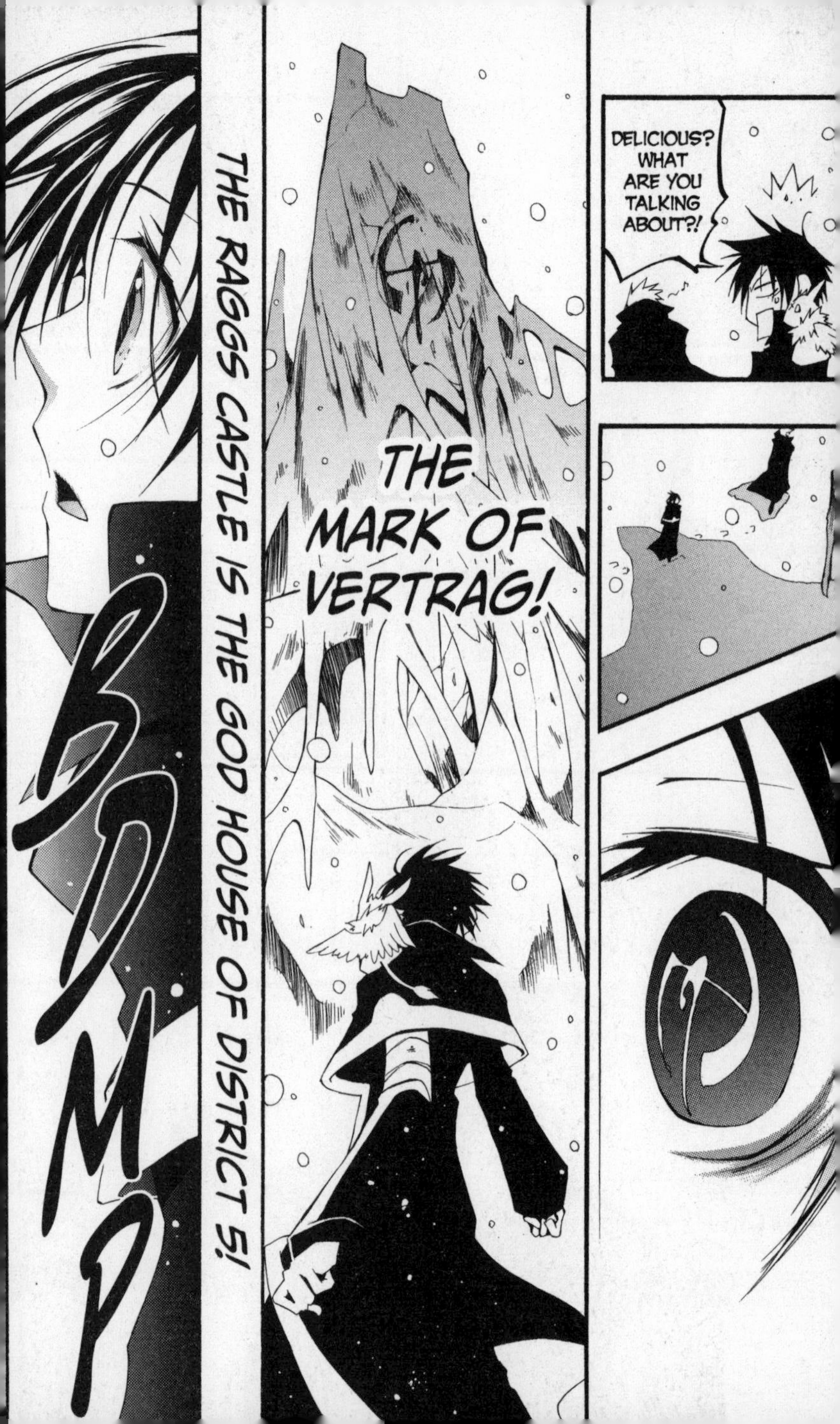
DELICIOUS? WHAT ARE YOU TALKING ABOUT?!
THE MARK OF VERTRAG!
THE RAGGS CASTLE IS THE GOD HOUSE OF DISTRICT 5!

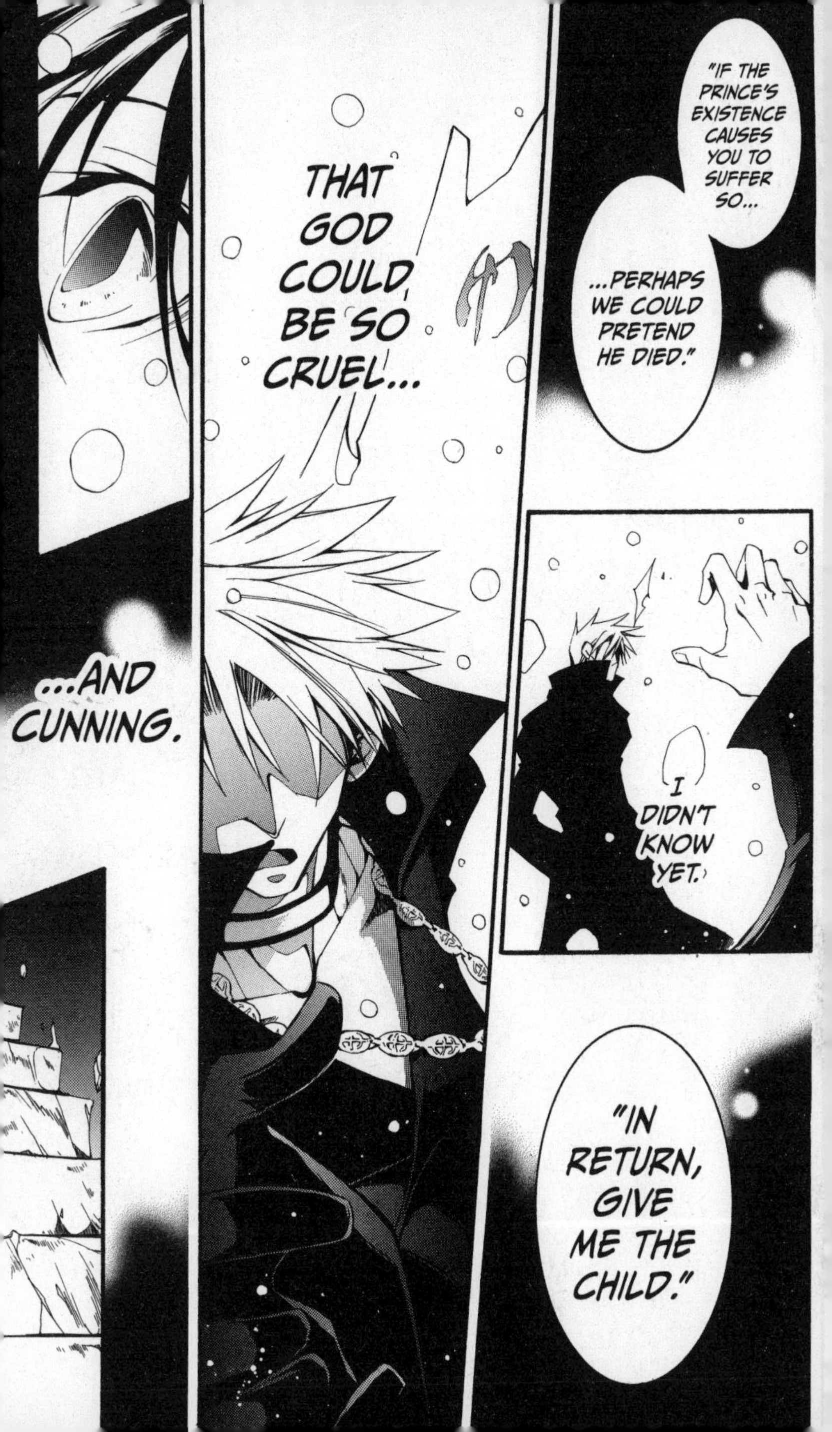
"IF THE PRINCE'S EXISTENCE CAUSES YOU TO SUFFER SO...
...PERHAPS WE COULD PRETEND HE DIED."
I DIDN'T KNOW YET.
"IN RETURN, GIVE ME THE CHILD."
THAT GOD COULD BE SO CRUEL...
...AND CUNNING.

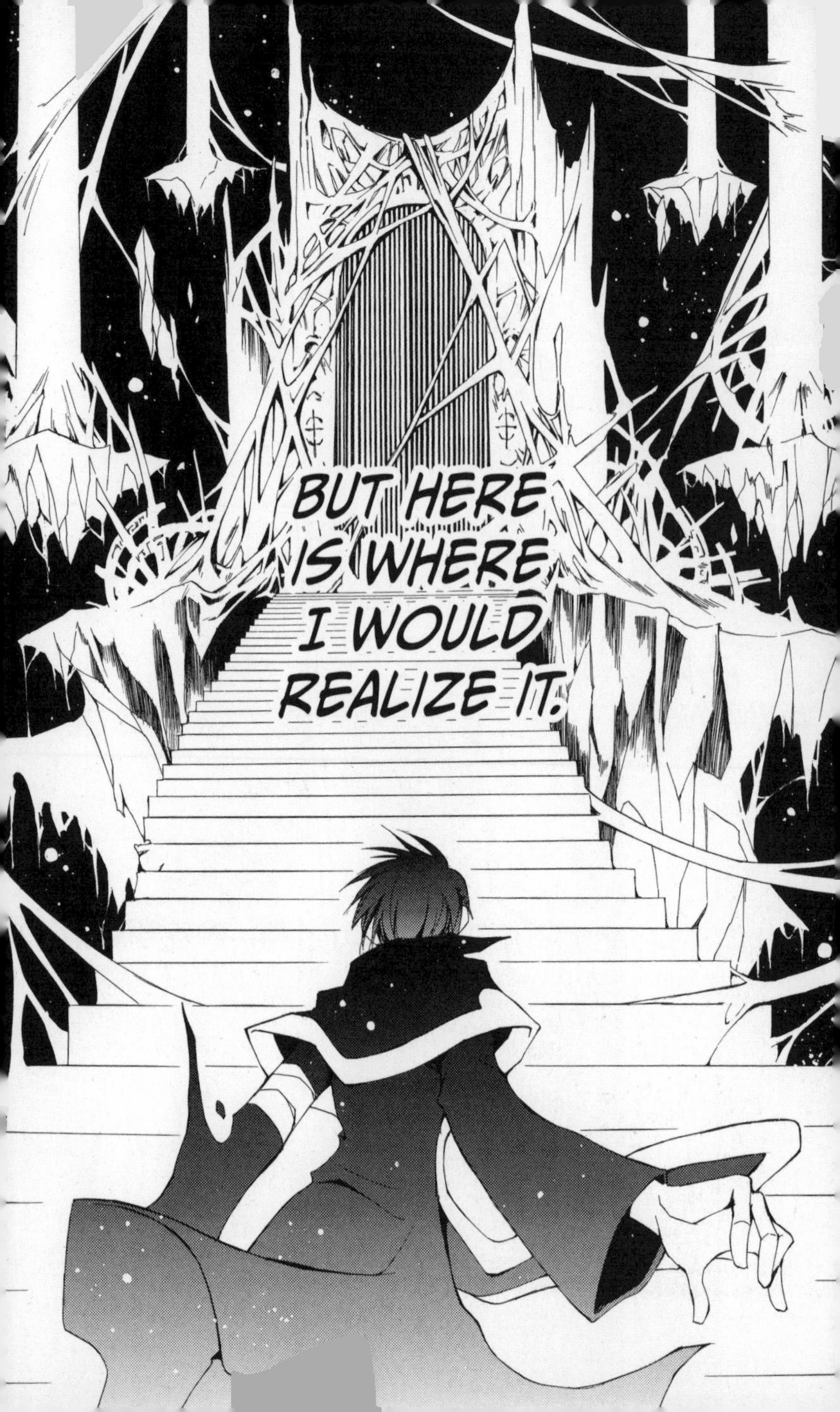
BUT HERE IS WHERE I WOULD REALIZE IT.

A Test of Maturity: Part 1

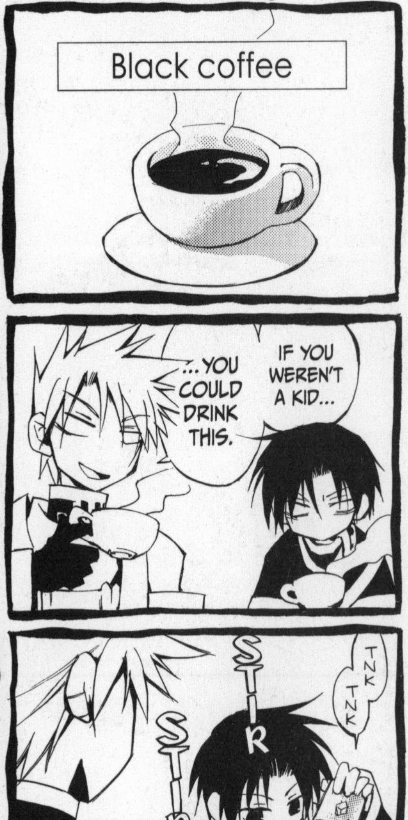
Black coffee
IF YOU WEREN'T A KID...
...YOU COULD DRINK THIS.
STIR
TNK TNK
STIR
WANT SOME COFFEE WITH THAT SUGAR?
GLORP!!

A Test of Maturity: Part 2

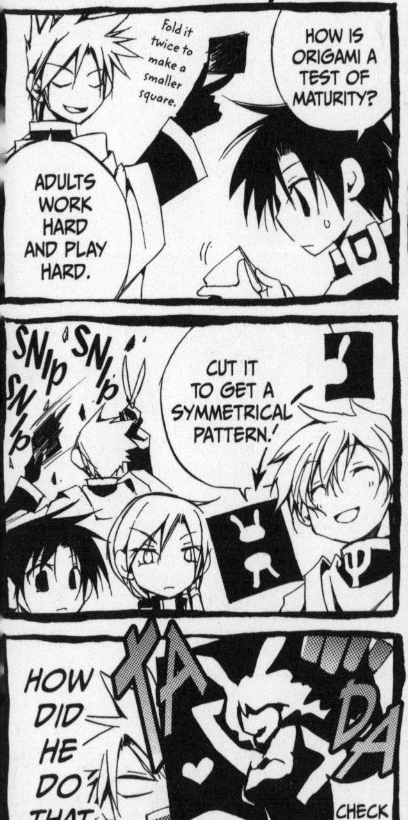
HOW IS ORIGAMI A TEST OF MATURITY?
Fold it twice to make a smaller square.
ADULTS WORK HARD AND PLAY HARD.
CUT IT TO GET A SYMMETRICAL PATTERN!
SNIP SNIP SNIP
TA DA
CHECK OUT MY BUNNY!!
HOW DID HE DO THAT?!
For the advanced.
DO YOU FOLD THE PAPER A CERTAIN WAY?
MMBL
DON'T THINK.
FEEL.
Heh...
It's not even symmetrical...
MMBL
...

A Test of Maturity: Part 3

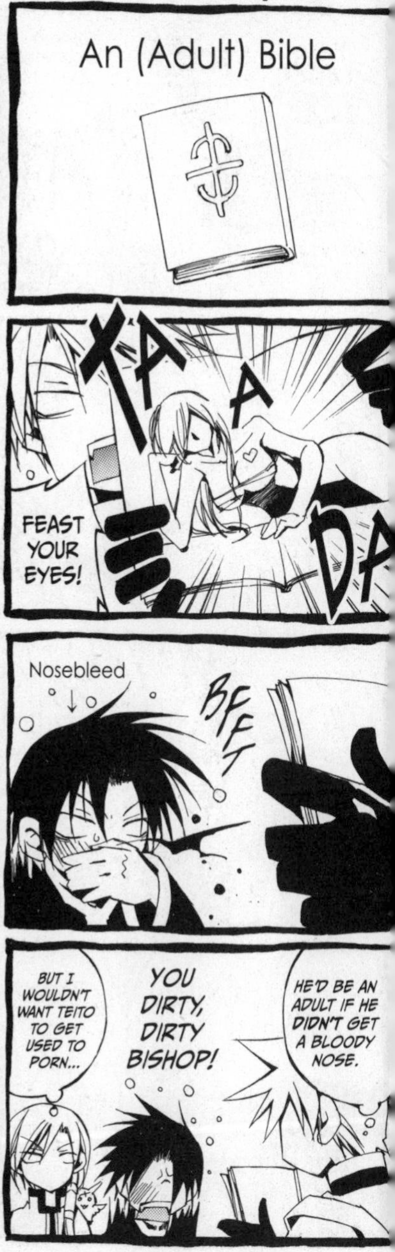
An (Adult) Bible
FEAST YOUR EYES!
Nosebleed
HE'D BE AN ADULT IF HE DIDN'T GET A BLOODY NOSE.
YOU DIRTY, DIRTY BISHOP!
BUT I WOULDN'T WANT TEITO TO GET USED TO PORN...

A Test of Maturity: Part 4

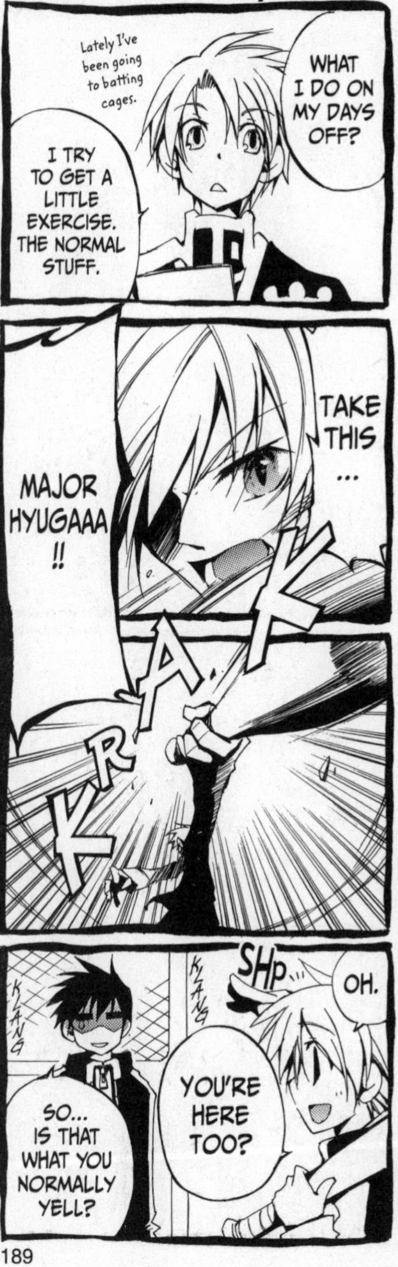
WHAT I DO ON MY DAYS OFF?
Lately I've been going to batting cages.
I TRY TO GET A LITTLE EXERCISE. THE NORMAL STUFF.
TAKE THIS...
MAJOR HYUGAAA!!
KRAK
SHp...
OH.
KLANG
KLANG
YOU'RE HERE TOO?
SO... IS THAT WHAT YOU NORMALLY YELL?

Thanks for Your Letters: Part 1

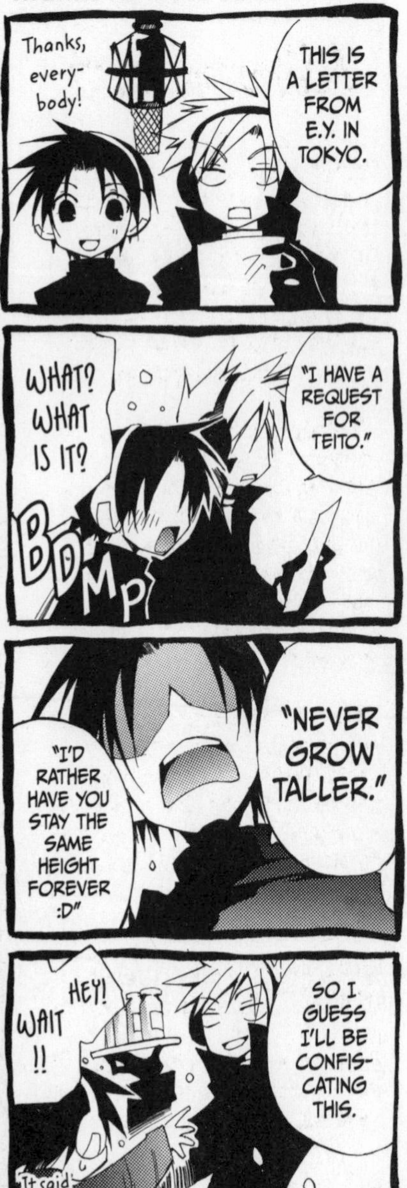
THIS IS A LETTER FROM E.Y. IN TOKYO.
Thanks, everybody!
"I HAVE A REQUEST FOR TEITO."
WHAT? WHAT IS IT?
BDMP
"NEVER GROW TALLER."
"I'D RATHER HAVE YOU STAY THE SAME HEIGHT FOREVER :D"
SO I GUESS I'LL BE CONFISCATING THIS.
HEY!
WAIT !!
It said ":D"!

Thanks for Your Letters: Part 2

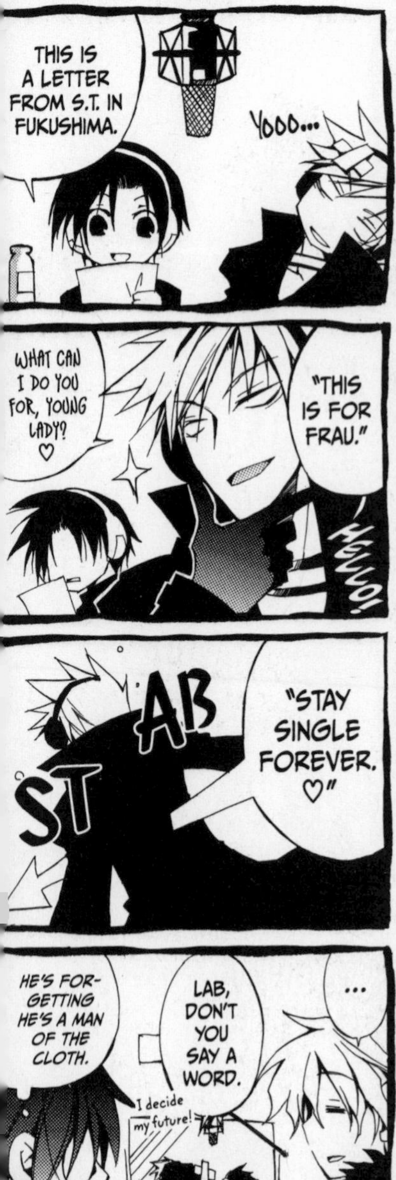
THIS IS A LETTER FROM S.T. IN FUKUSHIMA.
YOOO...
"THIS IS FOR FRAU."
WHAT CAN I DO YOU FOR, YOUNG LADY? ♡
HELLO!
"STAY SINGLE FOREVER. ♡"
STAB
...
LAB, DON'T YOU SAY A WORD.
HE'S FORGETTING HE'S A MAN OF THE CLOTH.
I decide my future!

Afterword

Thanks to everyone for helping us reach volume 7. We've worked hard with our editor to get this far. Since the title of the series has a "7" in it, we were really hoping to reach volume 7, and yay, it looks like we'll also be continuing on past that.

It's really thanks to all of you readers that we can keep drawing *07-Ghost*. Thank you so much. We hope this series touches your heart. We don't know how many of you already feel that way, but we will certainly endeavor to enchant the rest of you.

And we're very grateful for the anime series. This wonderful opportunity feels like nothing short of a miracle. There's simply not enough thanks in the world to express our gratitude to everyone involved in the production of the anime.

07-Ghost is a very lucky series that we're elated to be a part of.

Thank you for reading this far. We hope to see you again in the next volume.

Amemiya & Ichihara October 2008

Thank you very much.

FAQ

THIS IS MAJOR HYUGA AND KONATSU.
WE'RE HERE TO ANSWER A FREQUENTLY ASKED QUESTION. ☆
I guess.
Sorry, this is part of my job.
PLEASE TELL US YOUR GENDER, LT. COLONEL KUROYURI.
IT'S A SECRET. ♡
COME ON, KUROYURI.
Hey, Major!
JUST TELL US.
DO YOU WANT TO DIE?

The end.

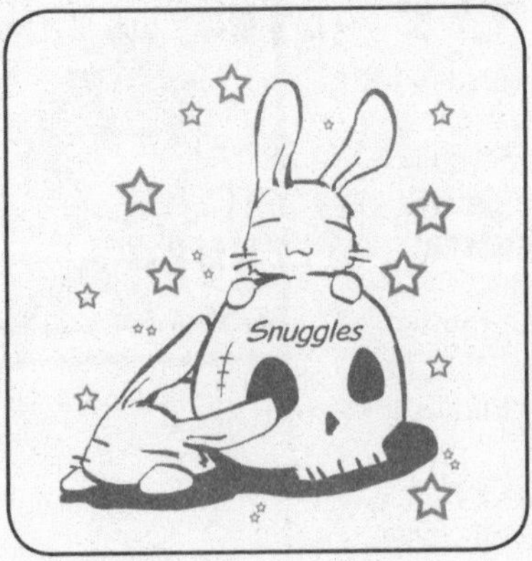
Snuggles

We've been cooking our rice in an earthenware pot. Food just tastes better when you work harder for it. ♥ Thank you, farmers.

—Yuki Amemiya & Yukino Ichihara, 2008

Yuki Amemiya was born in Miyagi, Japan, on March 25. Yukino Ichihara was born in Fukushima, Japan, on November 24. Together they write and illustrate *07-Ghost*, the duo's first series. Since its debut in 2005, *07-Ghost* has been translated into a dozen languages, and in 2009 it was adapted into a TV anime series.

07-GHOST

Volume 7

STORY AND ART BY
YUKI AMEMIYA and
YUKINO ICHIHARA

Translation/Satsuki Yamashita
Touch-up Art & Lettering/Vanessa Satone
Design/Yukiko Whitley
Editor/Hope Donovan

07-GHOST © 2008
by Yuki Amemiya/Yukino Ichihara
All rights reserved.
Original Japanese edition published by
ICHIJINSHA, INC., Tokyo.
English translation rights arranged with
ICHIJINSHA, INC.

Printed in Canada

Published by VIZ Media, LLC
P.O. Box 77010
San Francisco, CA 94107

10 9 8 7 6 5 4 3 2 1
First printing, November 2013

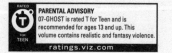

VIZ
MEDIA
www.viz.com

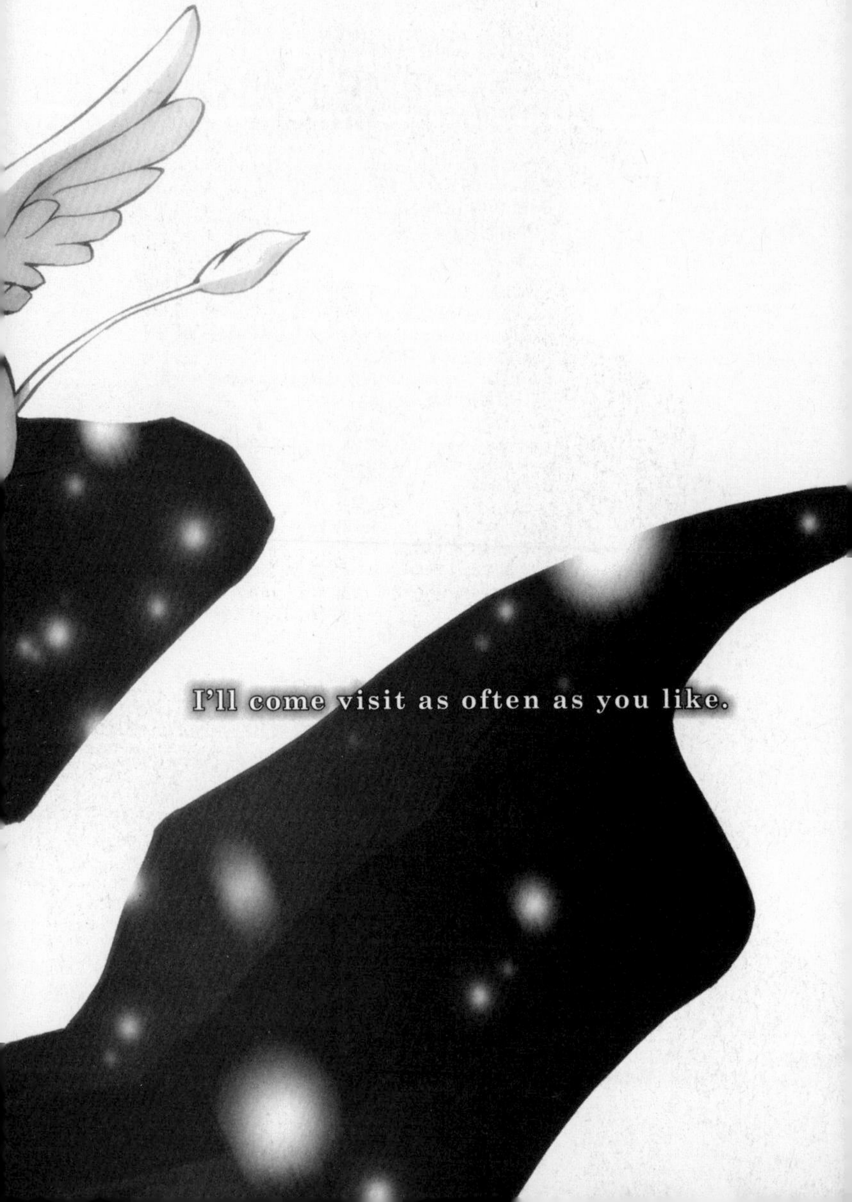
I'll come visit as often as you like.

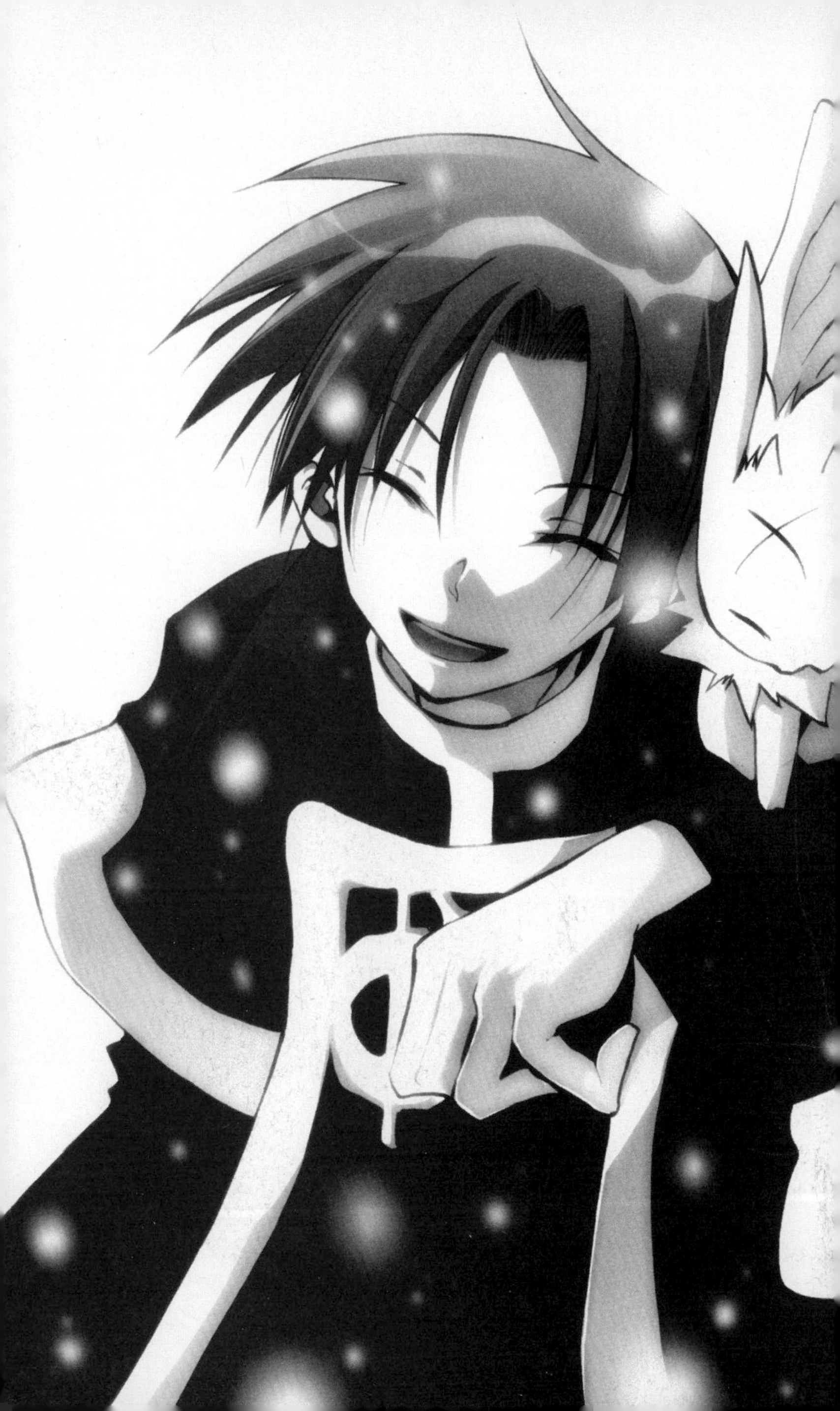

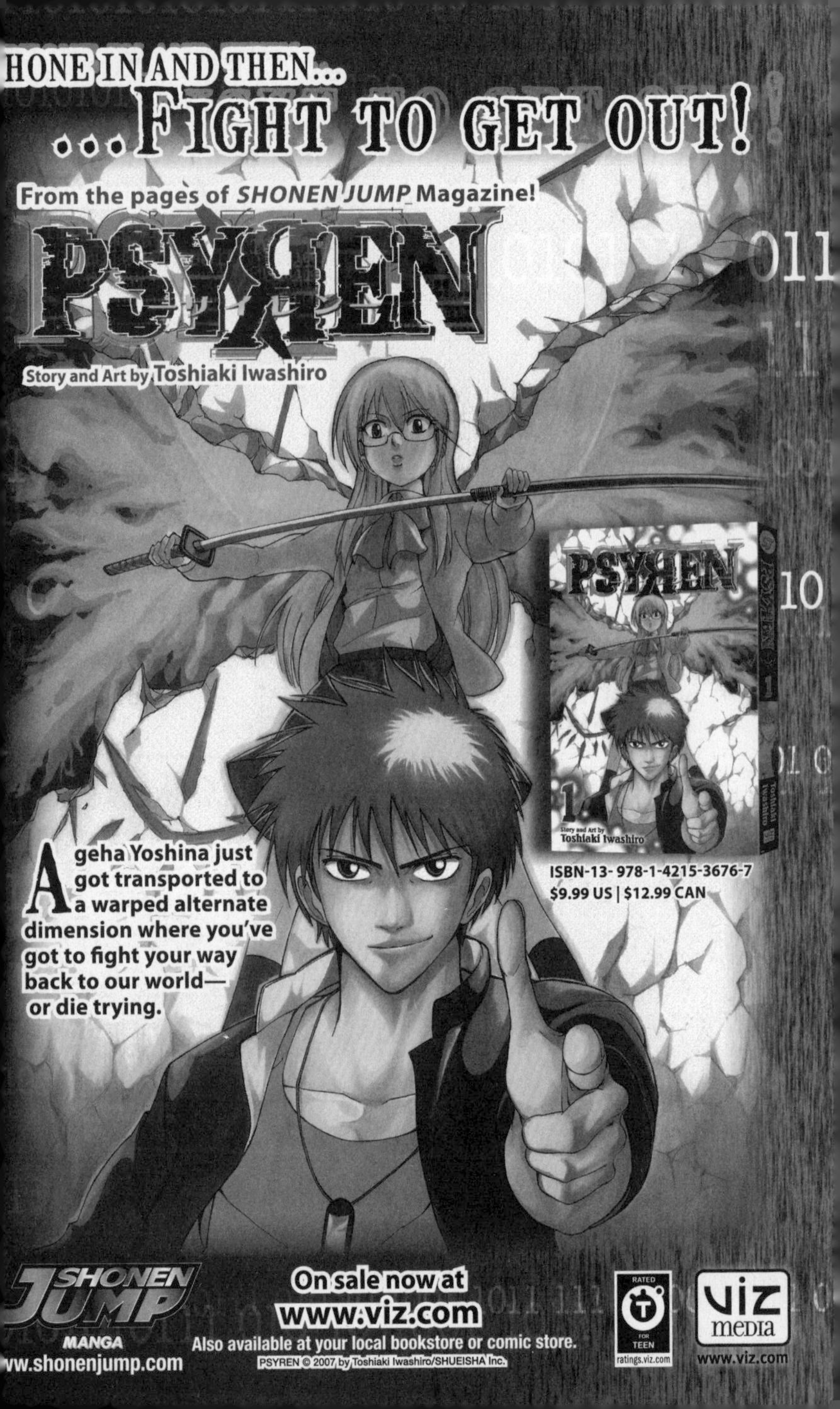
HONE IN AND THEN...
...FIGHT TO GET OUT!
From the pages of SHONEN JUMP Magazine!
PSYREN
Story and Art by Toshiaki Iwashiro
Ageha Yoshina just got transported to a warped alternate dimension where you've got to fight your way back to our world—or die trying.
ISBN-13- 978-1-4215-3676-7
$9.99 US | $12.99 CAN
SHONEN JUMP
MANGA
www.shonenjump.com
On sale now at
www.viz.com
Also available at your local bookstore or comic store.
PSYREN © 2007 by Toshiaki Iwashiro/SHUEISHA Inc.
RATED T FOR TEEN
ratings.viz.com
VIZ media
www.viz.com

VIZMANGA
Read manga anytime, anywhere!

...om our newest hit series to the classics you know ...d love, the best manga in the world is now available ...gitally. **Buy a volume*** of digital manga for your:

- ...OS device (**iPad®**, **iPhone®**, **iPod®** touch) ...through the **VIZ Manga** app

- ...Android-powered device (**phone or tablet**) ...with a browser by visiting **VIZManga.com**

- **Mac or PC computer** by visiting **VIZManga.com**

VIZ Digital has loads to offer:

- 500+ ready-to-read volumes
- New volumes each week
- FREE previews
- Access on multiple devices! Create a log-in through the app
  so you buy a book once, and read it on your device of choice!*

To learn more, visit www.viz.com/apps

* Some series may not be available for multiple devices.
  Check the app on your device to find out what's available.

DEATH NOTE © 2003 by Tsugumi Ohba, Takeshi Obata/SHUEISHA Inc.
NURARIHYON NO MAGO © 2008 by Hiroshi Shiibashi/SHUEISHA Inc.
ONE PIECE © 1997 by Eiichiro Oda/SHUEISHA Inc.

viz.com/apps

Hey! You're Reading in the Wrong Direction!

This is the end of this graphic novel!

To properly enjoy this VIZ graphic novel, please turn it around and begin reading from right to left. Unlike English, Japanese is read right to left, so Japanese comics are read in reverse order from the way English comics are typically read.

This book has been printed in the original Japanese format in order to preserve the orientation of the original artwork. Have fun with it!

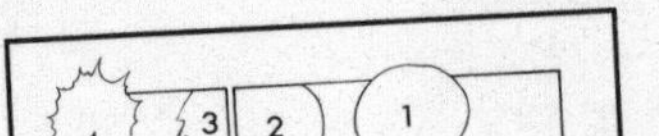
1
2
3
4
1
2
5
6
7
8
3
4
9
5
142

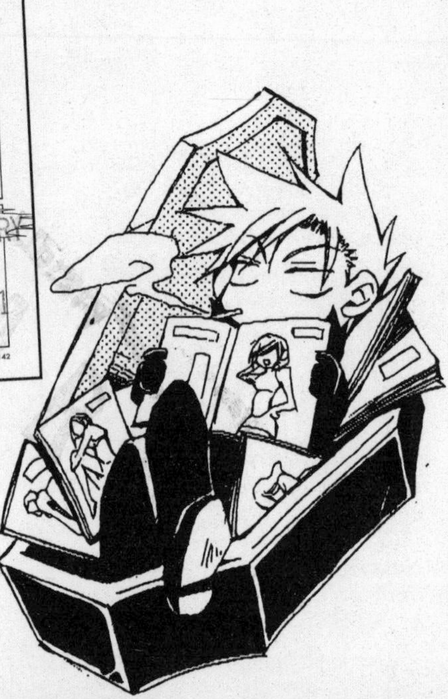